FROM THE TABLE OF PLENTY

Food For The Body, Manna For The Soul

By Marion O. Celenza

Acknowledgments

Editor	Marion O. Celenza
Advisor to Editor	Chip Celenza
Interior Text/Graphic Design	Irene Lang
Cover Art	Paula Shea Barbarotto
Cover Graphics	Irene Lang
Photography	Marion O. Celenza, Chip Celenza (or as noted)
Editorial Assistant	Annemarie Mascolo
Published by	Marion O. Celenza

Cherry Lane Litho, Printer

Cataloging-in-Publication Data
    Celenza, Marion O.
FROM THE TABLE OF PLENTY: Food For the Body, Manna For The Soul
    1. Cookbook
    2. Inspirational

ISBN: 9780979195327

LCCN: 2008907386

Dedication

FROM THE TABLE OF PLENTY *is dedicated to the hand who
fed me, my Mother, Josephine Capriglione Orlando;
and to my angel, my Dad, Dominick Orlando.
This book is filled with love and inspiration
and is written in grateful memory
of the hundreds of Orlandos and Caprigliones,
present, past, to come.
Share and Enjoy the Lord's Bounty.
Ó fame. Vorréi mangiare.
Salute e buon appetito!*

Preface

Selecting the Title

MENU LOG: A Collection of Recipes as Coordinated Menus
LUNCH IS IN THE BAG! A Celebration of the Midday Meal

FROM THE TABLE OF PLENTY: Food for the Body, Manna for the Soul,
*my third menu cookbook, differs from the others, in as much as
FROM THE TABLE OF PLENTY includes recipe contributions from
family members and friends, in addition to my own menu creations.
Some of these recipes, including several contributed by my Mother,
are collectors' recipes, an inheritance from my family's archives.*

*I envision my family and my family of friends, sitting around my table of plenty,
sharing their delicious gifts of food and conversation with all of us. After all,
the true meaning of "breaking bread" infers that we share our "bread" with
others at a meal.*

*I believe that our generous gathering of Menus and Reflections
provides a bounty of food for the body and manna for the soul
FROM THE TABLE OF PLENTY.*

Marion O. Celenza

Cathy, Chip, Jet
and Teller.

Contents From The Table of Plenty

Acknowledgments..ii

Dedication iii

Preface iv

Table of Contents v

One Reflection at a Time (Fall/Winter) vi

One Reflection at a Time (Spring/Summer) vii

One Reflection at a Time (Summer/Fall) viii

One Reflection at a Time (Pasta) ix

Fall-Winter Menus 2

Spring-Summer Menus...85

Summer-Fall Menus..185

Pasta Menus..289

Dressings, Sauces and Gravies..384

Bibliography and Credits...404

Food for the Body, Nourishment for the Soul..405

Index 406

About the Author (Kiss the Cook)..426

One Reflection at a Time

One does not live by bread alone,
but by every word that comes from the mouth of God.
——Matthew: 4,4

Acknowledgments ii

Dedication iii

Preface- Selecting the Title iv

Fall – Winter

Sharing the Gifts...1

Friendship Is the First Course 5

Recipes of Our Ancestors (2 parts) 8, 13

From Mama's Recipe Box or "How to Treat a Girl-Child" 18

Ah! The Romance of the Colorful Italian Language 22

Cooking Is a Prayer and Special Blessings 26

"Mama I Don't Feel So Good."-For a Sick Day 31

"Give Her Something to Eat." 35

Zie Prevete Goes A-Hunting 39

Secrets of a Fridge 43

Cooking for a Snow Storm 47

Healthy Cooking 51

And Then, the Cake Fell 55

"We Don't Hire Skinny Cooks at This Restaurant." 59

A Husband's Advice 63

"Good News" 68

Dinner Parties to Remember 76

Cooking for Your Mother-In-Law..80

One Reflection at a Time
Spring – Summer

Bless the Cook, O Lord; I Need It! 84

When Is It Ripe?_And Other Helpful Hints 88

Our Hostess with the Mostest...92

Green, White and Red 99

"Yes! I Do Care a Fig." 103

From My Mother's Box of Kitchen Secrets 108

"I Knew You When You Drank Manischewitz." 112

Cookin' with Ludwig, Pete and Freddie 117

Patron Saints of Cooks 122

His First Word Was_"Cheese". 126

Grandpas Are Good Teachers 130

Moses and the Exodus from Egypt 135

2000 Years in the Making _

   (A Suggested Script for Food Network TV) 140

Washing Dishes May Be Beneficial to Your Health.

   (Not to Mention What Scrubbing Pots and Pans Can Do.) 146

Planting and Growing a Vegetable Garden 150

Not Everyone Eats Cheerios for Breakfast 154

The Doggie Bag or "2 for the Price of 1" 158

Shake Vigorously, and Other Cooking Instructions 162

Food for Thought 166

It May Not Be the Slightest Gourmet; But It's Totally Ergonomic.........170

The Science of the Art of Cooking

   Or Is It? "The Art of the Science of Cooking" 175

Notes on Preparing and Processing Vegetables 180

One Reflection at a Time

Summer – Fall

What Kids Prefer 184

A Backyard Buffet 189

"I'm going away for the weekend;

    __ would you mind feeding my husband and kids while I'm gone?" 194

A Sit-Down Dinner 198

"Let's Eat!" 203

My Favorite Prayer 207

What Does My Gardener Eat for Lunch? 210

Guess Who Just Stopped By 214

Wine and Dine 219

Before You Write a Cookbook, Hire an Attorney. 223

Grasses and Grains 228

"Honey, I've Just Bought 3000 Shares, Each,

    of Alcoa & Kimberly-Clark." 233

Garlic 236

Statti Zitto e Mangia! 240

At what age did you discover there are *at least* 2 Other Ways

    to Make a Peanut Butter Sandwich? 245

Olive Oil 249

M(N)IX the Butter with the Eggs 253

Set a Place for Your Dog 258

Wine (2 parts) 262, 266

"This is the Table with Two Desserts." 269

Bite Your Tongue! Use Your Brain! 273

Thanksgiving Day with Linda and Alan 279

One Reflection at a Time

Pasta

Food for the Gods 288

Salt 295

Everyone Has An Angel 308

Great Stuff ! - Tomatoes 324

The Hand Who Fed Me 347

A Delicious Remembrance from Filomena Ramaglia,
   Our "Kitchen Bouquet" 363

Food for the Body, Nourishment for the Soul 405

KISS THE COOK (About The Author) 426

Fall -Winter

Sharing the Gifts

Think of this – if you don't feed your body, you may not be around to enjoy the wonders in our world – people, places, things. That's putting it very simply. When you supply nutrition to your body (or to others) you are caring for the priceless gift of life. You're a caretaker, blending, mixing, combining nourishment for the body. You take nature's gifts and transform them into life supports. And our civilized world enables a cook to tie a big satin ribbon around their culinary creations (a far cry from caveman roasting wild boar). Be a cook: care for the gift of your body, and the bodies of others – a sharing of gifts.

Teller with a "catch".
Photo by: Donna Kelliher

Fall -Winter

PROSCIUTTO AND CECI
BALSAMIC-OLIVE OIL DRESSING
ROULADE OF PORK WITH APRICOTS
VEGETABLE CROQUETTES
COMPOTE OF PINEAPPLE IN RUM

PROSCIUTTO AND CECI

3 cups baby romaine lettuce, rinsed, drained

1 tbsp. olive oil

1 small yellow onion, thinly sliced

3 garlic cloves, chopped

$\frac{1}{2}$ tsp. salt, freshly ground black pepper - to taste

1 red pepper, seeded, sliced into thin strips

6-8 slices prosciutto

1 lg. can (20 oz.) ceci

3-4 basil leaves, torn into strips

Balsamic-Olive Oil Dressing (see page 384)

Prepare Balsamic-Olive Oil Dressing in a jar. Store in refrigerator until 1 hour before using. Prepare a thick layer of baby romaine on the bottom of a large ceramic salad bowl. In a 2-quart saucepan, heat oil and lightly brown onion and garlic; add pepper strips and soften (about 2 minutes). Cut the prosciutto into ribbons with a pair of kitchen shears and add to saucepan. Stir in chickpeas, salt and pepper. Cook on low heat for 1-2 minutes until heated through. Spoon over lettuce; drizzle dressing over the salad and toss to mix. Garnish with basil leaves. Serve warm. Serves 6.

ROULADE OF PORK WITH APRICOTS

a 4-pound boneless loin of pork
kitchen string

STUFFING:

2 garlic cloves, minced

$\frac{1}{4}$ cup chopped parsley

1 tbsp. dried thyme leaves

$\frac{1}{2}$ cup packaged corn bread crumbs

4 white mushrooms, cleaned, chopped

$\frac{1}{2}$ red bell pepper, seeded, chopped

$\frac{1}{4}$ cup slivered almonds

1 dozen dried apricot halves, coarsely chopped

$\frac{1}{4}$ cup hot water

1 tbsp. olive oil

salt, black pepper to taste

SAUCE:

2 tbsp. olive oil

1 small onion, chopped

2 garlic cloves, chopped

1 celery stalk, trimmed, chopped

$\frac{1}{4}$ cup flour

1 cup dry white wine

4 cups beef broth (low-salt variety)

1 tbsp. each: fresh chopped parsley, dried thyme

1 bay leaf

$\frac{1}{4}$ cup tomato paste

freshly ground black pepper

Preheat oven 350°.

With a sharp knife make a slit along the boned side of the pork several inches deep (to mid-section). In a bowl, combine all of the stuffing ingredients. Sprinkle $\frac{1}{4}$ cup hot water blended with 1 tablespoon olive oil over the stuffing and toss to mix thoroughly. Spread open the slit in the loin of pork and pack the stuffing into the opening. Re-form the loin of pork (enclosing the stuffing) and tie it at 1-inch intervals with kitchen string. Season the surface of the roast with salt and pepper to taste.

In a roasting pan, heat oil to moderate high; place the roast in the pan and brown it all over. Transfer the pork to a platter. To the roasting pan, add onion, garlic and celery and cook over moderate heat, stirring and scraping the bottom of pan, for 5-6 minutes. Onion will become golden. Stir in the flour, stirring for 1 minute; add wine, broth, tomato paste, herbs and spices. Stir to mix; bring to a boil, stirring; then return roast to pan. Roast the pork, covered with a sheet of foil, in the oven at 350° for $1\frac{1}{2}$ hours, until meat thermometer registers 180°. Transfer pork to cutting board. (Keep sauce very warm and stir it occasionally.) Cut the strings and discard. Discard bay leaf. Cut the roast into thick (1-inch) slices. Arrange slices on serving platter and spoon some of the sauce over the pork. Serve remaining sauce separately. Serves 6.

VEGETABLE CROQUETTES

4 all-purpose potatoes, pared, cut into
    small chunks
1 lg. carrot, pared, cut into chunks
1 small onion, finely chopped
4 small white mushrooms, finely chopped
$\frac{1}{2}$ cup frozen peas
1 tbsp. chopped parsley

$\frac{1}{4}$ tsp. black pepper
dash of salt
$\frac{1}{4}$ cup low-fat evaporated milk (fat-free available)
1 cup flour, sprinkling of black pepper to taste
canola oil for frying

Cook potatoes, carrot and onion in a 2-quart pot with $\frac{1}{2}$ cup water for 10 minutes. Drain and transfer vegetables to a large bowl. Add pepper and salt. Mash to blend. Stir in parsley, peas, mushrooms, milk, and $\frac{1}{4}$ cup flour (with a dash of black pepper). Spread the rest of the flour on a sheet of waxed paper. Heat oil in a large skillet to moderate high, about 300°-320°. With the aid of a large serving spoon, scoop potato-vegetable mix and with hands, form croquettes the size of small fat knockwurst. Pack croquettes firmly and roll them into flour to coat all over. Fry the croquettes in about $\frac{1}{4}$-inch canola oil, lightly browning them on all sides (I turn them twice more, a three-sided croquette). Drain them on paper towels and transfer the croquettes to an oven-proof serving dish. Serve warm. Serves 6.

COMPOTE OF PINEAPPLE IN RUM

1 ripe pineapple, cut off top shrub and base; slice into 1-inch rounds; pare rind
    and cut out core; cut pineapple into small chunks, place in a bowl
juice of 1 lemon
rind of 1 lemon
$\frac{1}{4}$ cup dark rum
$\frac{1}{4}$ cup mint leaves
several sprigs of mint for garnish

Place pineapple chunks in a large serving bowl. Sprinkle juice of 1 lemon and rum over pineapple. Sprinkle lemon rind over bowl of fruit. Add mint leaves and toss to mix. Refrigerate until serving, up to 1 hour. Toss again and garnish with mint sprigs. Serves 6.

Fall -Winter

Friendship Is the First Course

*F*amily gatherings. *The joyous weddings, baptisms, birthdays, cousins' club feasts. The final life's-end celebrations. My large family has extended its membership from east coast to west coast, probably 500 blood relatives and counting. I'm always hearing about the latest Cousins Club weekend__ around a campsite in the San Fernando valley or at a southern New Jersey amusement park. Our oldest members are blessed and grateful to embrace four generations of the Orlando and Capriglione blood lines. It's strangely exciting, thrilling, almost mind-boggling to contemplate the scores of my family coming together each year to celebrate life's beginnings, ends and in-betweens. Vicariously, I ponder the table settings, musical selections, table decorations, eulogies, the "menu". It's a given: family gatherings around a table; plenty of good food and wine to celebrate. Family friendship is unrivaled, unparalleled. A "two for the price of one" relationship.*

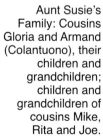

Aunt Susie's Family: Cousins Gloria and Armand (Colantuono), their children and grandchildren; children and grandchildren of cousins Mike, Rita and Joe.

Fall-Winter

PROVOLONE AND PEPPER SALAD WITH CROUTONS
A HOME-STYLE POT ROAST
FRUIT AND NUT BROWNIE ROLL

PROVOLONE AND PEPPER SALAD WITH CROUTONS

6 strips bacon, cooked crisp, drained, crumbled

3 yellow bell peppers, seeded, sliced thin

$\frac{1}{2}$ lb. extra sharp provolone, cubed

2 tbsp. olive oil

1 Vidalia onion, peeled, thinly shaved

6 plum tomatoes, washed, quartered

6 basil leaves, torn into pieces

$\frac{1}{2}$ cup packaged herbed croutons

In a 4-quart salad bowl, combine peppers, provolone, onion, tomatoes, basil, crumbled bacon and croutons. Drizzle olive oil over salad. Toss to coat thoroughly. Serves 6.

A HOME-STYLE POT ROAST

a 4-lb. beef rump roast

$\frac{1}{2}$ tsp. freshly ground black pepper

dash of salt

$\frac{1}{4}$ cup canola oil

2 green bell peppers, seeded, cut into chunks

4-6 celery stalks, cleaned,
    cut into small chunks

2-3 onions, sliced thin

5-6 medium-size carrots, pared,
    cut into thick chunks

4 cups beef broth (less-salt variety)

3 tbsp. cider vinegar

6 tbsp. mustard spread

1 bay leaf

$\frac{1}{4}$ cup fresh parsley, chopped

1 tsp. dried thyme

Rub meat with salt and pepper. Heat oil to moderate-high in a large, heavy pot and brown meat all over, turning roast frequently. Do not burn. Add onions and peppers to the pot and continue to cook, stirring occasionally, until onions are just golden brown. Add broth, vinegar, mustard and herbs to the pot and bring to a boil. Lower heat and simmer roast, partly covered, for 2 to $2\frac{1}{2}$ hours, until meat is tender. Add carrots and celery; cover and simmer for an additional 30-35 minutes until vegetables and meat are very tender. Remove bay leaf and discard. Transfer roast to cutting board and cut into $\frac{1}{2}$-inch slices. Arrange slices on serving platter; add vegetables around the roast and spoon juices over the meat. Serves 6.

FRUIT AND NUT BROWNIE ROLL
(Prepare in advance.)

6 oz. dark chocolate, broken into small pieces

1 cup water

$\frac{3}{4}$ cup sugar

5 eggs, separated

pinch of salt

2 tbsp. chopped white raisins

$\frac{1}{4}$ cup chopped walnuts

FILLING:

1 pt. heavy cream for whipping

$\frac{1}{4}$ cup tiny dark chocolate morsels

1 cup confectioners' sugar to dust cake

    (additional confectioners' sugar at serving)

(1 clean linen kitchen towel)

Grease an 8x12-inch jelly roll pan. Pour dark chocolate pieces into top-half of a 2-pint double boiler; fill bottom-half with 1 cup water. Bring water to a low simmer. Melt the chocolate over simmering water, occasionally stirring the chocolate, for about 5-6 minutes. Preheat oven 350°. In a medium-size bowl, beat sugar and egg yolks for 2-3 minutes until thick. Fold in slightly cooled chocolate, raisins and walnuts. Beat egg whites with a pinch of salt in a small bowl at high speed to form stiff peaks. Fold one-quarter of the beaten egg whites into the cooled chocolate mix; then carefully fold in rest of egg whites. Transfer this mixture to the prepared jelly roll pan and bake in preheated oven at 350° for 25 minutes, or until just firm to the touch. Remove pan from oven to cool.

In a medium-size clean bowl, beat the cream at high speed to form stiff peaks. Fold in chocolate morsels. Refrigerate until needed.

Lay a clean kitchen cloth on a wood board. Spread 1 cup sifted confectioners' sugar on a towel. Invert cake pan onto sugared towel and remove cake onto the towel. With a sharp knife cut off the edges of the cooled cake. Spread the whipped cream filling over the cake. Starting from the short end, roll the cake away from you, using the sugared towel to assist you. Form a cream-filled roll, coated with confectioners' sugar into a neat package. Lift towel-covered roll onto a cake plate; refrigerate cake for several hours. Just before serving, carefully remove towel from cake and transfer cake onto a clean serving plate. Dust with additional confectioners' sugar and serve. Serves 6.

Fall -Winter

Recipes of Our Ancestors

I've often given thought to how my ancestors may have lived, what foods they enjoyed, how these foods were prepared. The reference books of my heritage include the Old and New Testaments- THE BIBLE. The information I have gleaned just from years of reading and studying THE BIBLE is mind-boggling. Of course, their grocery list has always captured my interest.

Bread, basically, was leavened. Grain was crushed and ground into flour (wheat or barley). Yeast-filled dough, from the previous day's baking was used to start the bread of the day. (However, in the time of Moses, the Israelites had no time to leaven their bread when they fled Egypt and crossed the desert.) Their leavened bread was usually formed into large, round loaves, only one-half-inch thick. (Genesis 18:6) Bread was made not only at home but in "bakeries" who sold sourdough starters for baking at home, besides selling loaves of bakery-made bread.

In addition to bread, olive oil, olives and wine were standard fare. The climate and terrain of the Holy Land were conducive to grow grapes for wine. Milk and cheese from goats were also drunk and eaten. Lentils, chickpeas, cucumbers, garlic, onions, leeks, grapes and figs were available. A lentil stew satisfied the hungry Esau who had traded his birthright for the meal. (Genesis 25:29-34) Basically, the accepted diet was largely vegetarian.

Faith and food are inextricably linked in human experience and belief. Strict dietary laws were observed. "Clean" animals such as oxen, cattle, sheep and goats were suitable for sacrificial use and human consumption; the unclean animals documented pigs, camels, rabbits as well as birds who ate their prey. Generally, meat would be eaten with guests or at special occasions and was butchered under strict dietary laws.

Fish was divided into clean and unclean. Acceptable for human consumption were any fish with fins and scales: sardines, biny (carp family), musht (large fish). The unclean seafood included shrimp and clams and eels. Fish was a popular food, but only accessible from the Mediterranean and Sea of Galilee. You had to be near water. When the Israelites fled Egypt, and during their long and arduous desert journey, they longed for fish (the book of Exodus). In the New Testament, several apostles were fishermen: Simon, Peter, Andrew, James and John. (Continued on page 13)

Fall -Winter

MARINATED EEL (ANGUILLA) (heirloom)

BACCALA FRITTO (heirloom)

BACCALA IN SALSA PICCANTE (SPICY SAUCE) (heirloom)

CONIGLIO ALLA CACCIATORA (RABBIT STEW- HUNTER'S STYLE) (heirloom)

or

LAMB STEW

(Select a Salad and a Dessert from this book to accompany the Entrée)

MARINATED EEL (ANGUILLA)

$2\frac{1}{2}$-3 lbs. freshwater eel,
    cleaned, leave skin

1 cup red wine vinegar

1 cup water

6 garlic cloves, chopped

1 lg. onion, thinly sliced

1 tsp. salt

$\frac{1}{2}$ tsp. black pepper

2-3 bay leaves

1 tsp. each: dried marjoram and thyme

2 tsp. olive oil

(*NOTE: at end of recipe)

Preheat broiler 500° or set grill to broil.

Cut eel into rounds, about 2 inches thick. Grill or broil pieces for 3-4 minutes on both sides. Meanwhile in a 1-quart sauce pot with cover, boil vinegar, water, garlic, onion, salt, pepper, herbs and oil for 20 minutes. Pour this marinade over grilled eel in a large tray. Allow eel to marinate, covered, for 24 hours in refrigerator. Serve cold. Serves 6.

*NOTE: Anguilla (eels) were and still are an Italian menu tradition at Christmas. I was introduced to a "piece of the action" at five years of age. It was two days before Christmas and I was spending the afternoon at my Aunt Susie's large Victorian home (with a gorgeous wrap-around enclosed porch). Only one of my six Colantuono cousins was younger than I – Arthur. Although the home was a three-story dwelling, there was only one bathroom on the first floor. Nature called; I turned the knob on the bathroom door. It was a large, long room; it was a wintry sundown. I turned on the light switch and refocused my child's eyes to accommodate the semi-darkness. And then, I screamed. Courageous little soul I was (an only child is gifted with extraordinary emotional fiber). Even as the scream shook the solid mahogany rafters, I edged my way to the eight-foot white bath tub and forced myself to peer inside. The six-foot eel was swimming in a foot or so of water, in the bathtub. This is where my Aunt Susie, Uncle Frank and six cousins (not to forget Nonna Laurette and Grandpa Joe) bathed. Here, in this tub, where a six-foot eel was doing the breast stroke. In just one day, this creature would become part of the traditional Christmas Eve celebratory meal.

BACCALA FRITTO
(Commence preparation on the day before.)

2 lbs. baccala (salted cod)

1 cup flour

black pepper

olive oil for frying (enough oil to coat bottom
of skillet ⅛-inch)

juice of 2 lemons

The day before: *In a bowl, cover the baccala with cold water; place a plate directly on top of the fish in the bowl and rest a weight or mallet on the plate (to apply pressure). Refrigerate the fish to soften the dried cod, for 12 hours, changing the water several times.*

Drain the baccala; pat it dry with paper towels. Lay the fish on a cutting board. Pull off the skin with your fingers with the aid of a sharp knife. Bone the fish; place a sheet of waxed paper over the fish and briefly pound it with a mallet to soften it. Cut it into wide strips and dredge the pieces in flour which you've spread over the board. Sprinkle the eel with black pepper.

Over moderate high heat, sauté the pieces of fish for a few minutes on both sides, in olive oil until they are golden. Drain fried baccala on paper towels. Transfer to platter and serve baccala warm or at room temperature with a sprinkling of lemon juice. Serves 6.

BACCALA IN SALSA PICCANTE (Spicy Sauce)
(Start on the day before.)

2 lbs. baccala (salted cod)

1 lg. onion, chopped

2 Italian frying peppers, seeded, sliced thin

1 hot Italian pepper, seeded, sliced thin

2 tbsp. tomato paste and ½ cup hot water

½ cup dry white wine

¼ cup chopped, pitted black olives

1 tbsp. capers

¼ cup chopped parsley

2 bay leaves

¼ cup flour

salt, black pepper

¼ cup olive oil

1 cup hot water

The day before: *In a bowl, cover the baccala with cold water; place a plate directly on top of the fish and rest a weight (or mallet) on the plate to apply pressure (to soften the fish). Refrigerate the fish for 12 hours, changing the water several times.*

Drain the baccala. Lay the fish on a board and pull off the skin. Boil the fish for 15 minutes. Drain it; pat it dry; cut it into pieces. Flour the pieces of fish and sauté them in oil in a large skillet, a few pieces at a time, transferring them to a heat-resistant pan to keep warm in a low oven.

Preheat oven to 350º.

Sauté onion and peppers in the same oil until light brown. Stir tomato paste into hot water and add to onion mix in skillet. Cook to simmer for a couple of minutes. Stir in wine, olives, capers, parsley, bay leaves , a little salt and pepper. (Remember: baccala is a salted fish.) Pour sauce over baccala. Gradually, add 1 cup hot water over the pan; cover the pan tightly with a piece of foil and simmer for 30 minutes or so. Add more water if needed. Sauce should be thick, not dry. Remove and discard bay leaves before serving. Serves 6.

CONIGLIO ALLA CACCIATORA
(Rabbit Stew-Hunter's Style)
*(*NOTE: below)*

3-4 lbs. rabbits (about 2 rabbits, dressed),
    cut into pieces
      (You may be able to find frozen rabbits
      in gourmet supermarkets or through a
      butcher shop.)
$\frac{1}{4}$ cup olive oil
1 small can (6 oz.) tomato paste stirred
    into $\frac{1}{2}$ cup boiling water to form a
    thick paste, to cook a "tight" sauce
2 cups red table wine (from your own
    wine press, if available)
1 lg. celery stalk, chopped
1 lg. onion, sliced thin
2 garlic cloves, chopped
1-2 carrots, pared, cut into rounds

8-10 small mushrooms, rinsed,
      drained, halved
1 moderately hot Italian pepper (seeded),
    to taste
$\frac{1}{4}$ cup red wine vinegar
    (Sour your own wine.)
$\frac{1}{2}$ tsp. black pepper
1 tsp. salt
1 tbsp. dried rosemary
2-3 bay leaves
1 tsp. dried sage leaves (It is preferable if
      herbs are home-grown.)

   *NOTE: You may substitute chicken, if dressed rabbits are unavailable. Chicken, somewhat close in texture to rabbit, will impart a milder, more refined taste; rabbit has a gamey, smoky taste.

   Heat oil in a large, heavy skillet to moderate high. Lightly brown onion, garlic and rabbit in oil on all sides. Scrape bottom of pan to loosen food particles. In a small bowl, make a thick "tight" sauce with tomato paste and boiling water. Stir in: tomato paste sauce, wine, vinegar, celery, hot pepper, mushrooms, carrots, herbs and spices. Cook to simmer, covered, stirring often, for 35-40 minutes. Remove and discard bay leaves before serving.

   Serve with perciatelli pasta, spooning rabbit stew over pasta. Serves 6.

LAMB STEW
(May be prepared in advance.)

$2\frac{1}{2}$ lbs. lean boneless lamb (shoulder cut), trimmed, cut into cubes

2 tbsp. olive oil

1 onion, thinly sliced

1 carrot, pared, sliced thin

3 garlic cloves, chopped

2 poblano peppers, sliced and cut into thin strips

$\frac{1}{2}$ lb. frozen peas, defrosted

1 can (1 lb.) plum tomatoes, mashed

1 can (1 lb.) corn kernels, drained

1 can (1 lb.) chick peas, drained

1 cup water

1 bay leaf

1 tsp. each: thyme, cilantro, oregano, cinnamon, cumin, turmeric

$\frac{1}{2}$ cup sherry

Heat oil in 4-quart pot with lid. Add and stir in lamb, peppers, onions and garlic and cook at moderate high for 4-5 minutes until lamb is lightly browned. Pour in tomatoes and water; cover and simmer for 20 minutes. Add remainder of ingredients, except sherry, mixing thoroughly. Simmer stew for 10 minutes longer; stir in sherry. Remove and discard bay leaf. Serve with corn bread/rye seeds. Serves 6.

Fall -Winter

Recipes of Our Ancestors
(Continued from page 8)

My ancestors probably ate two main meals a day: breakfast and dinner (or supper); sometimes, they ate a light refreshment in-between. Breakfast may have included flat bread, olives and cheese. Midday, perhaps some bread soaked in sour wine and some grains or fruit. Dinner may have offered a vegetable stew, beans, lentils, bread, fruit and wine.

Nuts (almonds), wild honey from bees, nectar from fruit syrups, were delicacies, as was cake. "He distributed to every person a loaf of bread, a portion of meat, a cake of raisins." (Chronicles 16:3) Figs also made good cakes. Luscious pomegranates were available.

And how did my ancestors cook their food? Mainly, by boiling, in a pot over a fire, or poached in oil. Bread was baked in a fire in a hole in the ground, over hot stones. Wealthy homes had pottery ovens, which were beehive-shaped funnels, fire lit at the base of the oven.

Meals of fellowship cemented friendships, celebrated in gratitude for God-given abundance; or to seal agreements. Dining took place around a low, square table; peasants sat on the floor; the wealthy reclined on low couches around the table. A Roman-style dinner party would serve hors d'oeuvres and wine mixed with honey, and a main course.

Fall -Winter

SALAD OF SPINACH, SHRIMP, RED ONION AND PINEAPPLE
BLEU CHEESE DRESSING
STUFFED MEATLOAF (heirloom)
POTATO PIE
PEAR CRUNCH

SALAD OF SPINACH, SHRIMP, RED ONION AND PINEAPPLE

3 cups baby spinach, rinsed, drained
1 lb. medium shrimp, shelled, cleaned, cooked , drained
1 medium red onion, finely sliced
2 cups fresh pineapple chunks
1 lg. carrot, shredded

Bleu Cheese Dressing (see page 386)

   Prepare Bleu Cheese Dressing. Store in refrigerator if not using immediately. Remove from refrigerator 15 minutes before serving. In a large salad bowl, combine to mix: spinach, red onion, shredded carrot, shrimp and pineapple chunks. Stir the dressing and spoon over salad. Toss the salad to mix thoroughly. Serves 6.

STUFFED MEATLOAF

1 lb. ground beef chuck
3/4 lb. ground lean pork
3/4 lb. ground veal
2 eggs or 1/2 cup egg substitute, beaten
1/4 cup fresh parsley, chopped
1/2 tsp. black pepper
1/2 tsp. salt
2 tbsp. spicy mustard spread

1 tbsp. Worcestershire sauce
1/2 cup prepared tomato sauce or catsup
1/2 cup bran kernels cereal
1/2 cup raisins (optional)
3 hard boiled eggs, shelled
1/2 cup unseasoned bread crumbs
olive oil to coat pan

Brown Gravy (see page 396)

Preheat oven to 350°.

Hard cook 3 eggs (to be used as stuffing). Shell them and set aside. Grease a 9x12x4-inch pan with olive oil. Prepare Brown Gravy. Set aside. In a large bowl, combine ground beef, pork and veal. Make a well in the center of the meat and pour in beaten eggs, parsley, pepper, salt, mustard, Worcestershire sauce, tomato sauce, bran and raisins. Hand-mix the ingredients until well-blended.

Spread crumbs over a sheet of waxed paper on a board. Transfer meatloaf mix to the board, forming a large meatloaf rectangle 8x5x2-inches. Press the 3 shelled eggs in a vertical row, in the center of the rectangle. With the aid of the waxed paper and your hands, roll up the sides of the meatloaf to cover the eggs, forming a bundle. Pat the crumbs all over the outside of the loaf as you form it.

With 2 large spatulas, lift the crumb-coated meatloaf into the greased pan. Roast the loaf in preheated oven 350° for 1 1/2 hours.

Remove pan from oven and pour one cup Brown Gravy over meatloaf. (At serving time, pour remainder of thoroughly heated Brown Gravy over each portion of meatloaf.)

Form a foil tent over the meatloaf and return the pan to the oven. Lower heat to 300° and continue to bake for another 15-20 minutes. Serves 6-8.

POTATO PIE

4-5 medium-size all-purpose potatoes, pared,
    cut into matchsticks, (cover with
    cold water in 2-qt. bowl)
1 yellow onion, finely sliced
1 red chile pepper, seeded
2 tbsp. peanut oil

1 tbsp. canola oil for skillet
6 eggs or 1½ cups egg substitute, beaten
1 tbsp. *lite* ginger soy sauce
1 tbsp. chopped coriander leaves
1 tsp. chili powder, for sprinkling

    Beat eggs, ginger soy sauce and coriander in a bowl. Set aside. Drain potato sticks thoroughly; pat dry with paper towels. Heat peanut oil in a wok or skillet to moderate- high, 320°. Pour potato sticks, onion and chile pepper into wok and stir-fry this mix for 3-4 minutes until potatoes are light golden brown. Remove wok from heat; scrape bottom of wok to be sure potato particles are loosened. Set aside.

    Heat canola oil in a clean non-stick skillet with cover. Pour egg-ginger mix into hot oiled skillet; cover. When omelet starts to firm, add potato mix over eggs in skillet. Cover with lid. Lower heat to low-medium and continue to set the omelet.

    When the top of omelet is firm, gently loosen it from bottom of skillet with a spatula. Remove skillet from burner to work table. Place a large plate over the omelet in the skillet and carefully invert the omelet and the skillet onto the large plate; then slide the omelet back into the skillet to lightly brown the other side.

    Replace the skillet on the burner and continue to cook the omelet for 1-2 minutes on low-moderate. Have serving platter ready. Remove skillet from heat. Again, loosen omelet from skillet with spatula and invert the omelet onto serving platter. Sprinkle with chili powder and serve warm. The omelet may be made a couple of hours in advance and warmed in a low oven 250° for 10 minutes. Cut into wedges. Serves 6.

PEAR CRUNCH
(Prepare in advance, refrigerate.)

6-8 ripe Bartlett pears, pared, cored, sliced
1 tbsp. candied ginger
2 tbsp. orange juice
1 tbsp. grated orange rind
1 tbsp. molasses

vanilla ice cream

TOPPING:
$1\frac{1}{2}$ cups flour
$\frac{1}{3}$ cup dried oats
$\frac{1}{4}$ cup slivered almonds
 2 tbsp. molasses
1 tbsp. cinnamon
$\frac{1}{3}$ cup butter or Smart Balance spread,
      cut into small pieces

Preheat oven 375°.

Lightly grease a 2-quart Pyrex bowl. In a mixing bowl, combine pears, ginger, molasses, juice and rind. Spoon this mix into the prepared bowl. Make the crumble topping by sifting flour into large bowl. Work in the butter with a fork until well blended and the mix resembles fine crumbs. Stir in almonds, oats, cinnamon and molasses. Mix ingredients together until they are well-combined. Sprinkle the topping evenly over the pear and ginger mix in the Pyrex bowl to cover the fruit completely.
Bake casserole in preheated oven at 375° for 30 minutes, until the topping is golden and fruit is tender. Serve with vanilla ice cream. Serves 6.

Fall -Winter

From Mama's Recipe Box
or "How to Treat a Girl-Child"

*I*t would have been a rare Monday lunch hour if Marion's noonday meal was missing a saucer of warmly delicious "Sunday's leftover pasta in sauce"_ and a "Stuffed Artichoke", just waiting for a crust of Italian bread to soak up the garlicky olive oil. That is, if Zie Prevete (my uncle, Father Raphael Orlando) hadn't claimed it for his own lunch.

The pasta treats varied: rigatoni (ridged tubes) in ragout, fusilli (spindles) with a meatball (raisins included) and/or sausages, homemade cheese ravioli (which I had helped Mama to prepare).

We'd spread out clean semolina- floured white sheets over tables, to rest the little "muffs" as they dried. Or my "number 1" favorite _gnocchi (little potato dumplings) rolled off the tines of a fork.

My high school paper bag lunch contained triple-decker sandwiches: BLT's with mayo; egg salad with chopped celery; tuna and chopped onion; and "ordinary" ham and Swiss; OR (how about?) a sautéed crumbed veal cutlet with crisp lettuce leaves. I had attended an academy for young women. Some of those young women who had sported muskrat-fur winter coats hadn't minded in the least, to cozy up to my brown paper bag lunch.

When Mama and I would take our annual Memorial Day trek to the cemetery which was home to my maternal grandparents, Mama would pack a shopping bag: 3 geranium plants, 1 small flat of begonias, a trowel, a watering can (to be filled at the cemetery), and 2 sandwiches with a thermos of hot tea.

When I was 15 years old, and just a tad chubby, my physician (a portly man of Italian descent), suggested that I lose some weight. My Mother was very pleased to cooperate – so she said. Her cooperative suggestion: how about a peanut butter and jelly sandwich as an after school snack? Hmm? "Mama", I retorted, "I want 'real' food". And that's how I cooperated.

Eventually, lots of activity and loads of vanity helped me to achieve the small necessary weight loss. My mother chalked it up to the ubiquitous "baby fat".

Fall -Winter

SPINACH, CARROTS AND BLUEBERRIES
BLEU CHEESE DRESSING
BOSTON BROWN BREAD
BONELESS PORK STEW
BANANA FRUIT CAKE

SPINACH, CARROTS AND BLUEBERRIES

1 lb. baby spinach, washed, drained

1 lg. carrot, pared, shredded

$\frac{1}{2}$ pt. blueberries, carefully rinsed, drained

1 cup grape tomatoes, rinsed, drained

1 cup low-fat herbed croutons

Bleu Cheese Dressing (see page 386)

Prepare Bleu Cheese Dressing. Refrigerate dressing if not serving promptly.

Combine all salad ingredients in a large salad bowl. Just before serving, thoroughly blend the dressing and pour over salad. Toss to mix, and serve in individual bowls. Serves 6.

BOSTON BROWN BREAD

1 cup flour

1 cup whole wheat flour

1 cup coarse cornmeal

$1\frac{1}{2}$ tsp. baking soda

$\frac{1}{4}$ tsp. salt

1 cup raisins

$\frac{1}{4}$ cup dark molasses

2 cups buttermilk (or sour whole milk by adding 2 tbsp. white vinegar to milk)

waxed paper, foil, string

Combine flours, cornmeal, baking soda and salt in a mixing bowl. In another bowl, mix molasses and buttermilk. Stir raisins into flour mix. Grease two 1-pound coffee tins. Add molasses mix to dry ingredients and stir until blended. There is no need to overbeat.

Divide the batter evenly between the 2 greased tins. Cut 2 round pieces of waxed paper to fit tops of cans; grease the waxed sheets and place one each on top of the 2 filled tins. Tear 2 pieces of aluminum foil to fit over cans, 1 sheet for each can. Fit the foil sheets over the waxed paper-covered cans. Tie the foil securely around the cans with string.

Place the covered tins in a large pot with a lid. The pot should be deep enough to hold the cans. Pour enough water in the pot to come halfway up the sides of the upright cans. Cover the pot and simmer (steam) for $1\frac{1}{2}$ to 2 hours. (Add more boiling water during the steaming time.)

Remove cans with mitts on your hands. Remove the foil/waxed paper covers and let the loaves cool slightly in the cans. Then, remove the loaves and allow them to cool completely on wire racks. Makes 2 loaves.

BONELESS PORK STEW

$2\frac{1}{2}$ lbs. lean boneless loin of pork, cut into small chunks

1 lg. onion, thinly sliced

2-3 medium-size sweet potatoes, pared, cut into chunks

1 lg. green pepper, seeded, sliced

1 lg. sweet red pepper, seeded, sliced

2 cups small broccoli florets, rinsed, drained

1 cup prepared tomato sauce

1 cup beef broth (less-salt variety)

1 cup dry light red wine: Chianti or claret

$\frac{1}{2}$ cup pitted Kalamata olives, chopped

1 tbsp. dry mustard

1 tsp. dried sage

a few fresh sage leaves

1 tsp. crushed black peppercorns

$\frac{1}{2}$ tsp. salt

1 tbsp. olive oil for bottom of stew pot

Coat a 4-quart stew pot (with cover) with olive oil. At moderate heat, cook onion and pork chunks in oil for 4-5 minutes, stirring bottom of pot as you cook. Stir in tomato sauce, broth, sweet potato, peppers, broccoli, olives, mustard, sage, fresh sage, peppercorns and salt. Cover pot and simmer stew for 35 minutes or until sweet potato is just tender. Stir in wine. Simmer 5 minutes longer. Serve with seeded rye rolls. Serves 6.

BANANA FRUIT CAKE
(Prepare a day or two in advance.)

$1\frac{1}{2}$ cups self-rising flour

$\frac{1}{2}$ tsp. baking powder

1 cup light brown sugar

2 ripe bananas, mashed

$\frac{1}{4}$ cup chopped candied orange peel

$\frac{1}{4}$ cup chopped nuts

$\frac{1}{2}$ cup dried cranberries

5-6 tbsp. orange juice

2 eggs or $\frac{1}{2}$ cup egg substitute, beaten

$\frac{2}{3}$ cup canola oil

ICING:

$\frac{1}{2}$ cup confectioners' sugar

2-3 tbsp. orange juice

grated rind of 1 orange

Preheat oven 350°.

Grease a large 2-pound loaf tin and line bottom of pan with greased brown paper. In a large bowl, sift flour and baking powder. Stir in sugar, bananas, chopped peel, nuts and cranberries. Stir in orange juice, eggs and oil until well combined. Add this mix to the dry ingredients and mix until blended.

Pour the batter into the prepared pan. Bake in preheated oven at 350° for about 1 hour, until firm to the touch, or when an inserted toothpick removes clean.

Invert cake onto doily-lined cake plate. In a small bowl mix confectioners' sugar with orange juice and drizzle the frosting over the loaf. Sprinkle rind over the top; allow frosting to set before serving. Serves 6-8.

Fall -Winter

Ah! The Romance of the Colorful Italian Language

'SCAROLA IMBOTTIRE – stuffed escarole. Stuffed with chunks of Pecorino Romano, raisins, anchovies, garlic and oil.

BRACIOLE – little arms of top round beef, pounded thin and stuffed with parsley, Italian cheese, raisins, pignola.

UOVA 'MPRIATORIO (eggs in Purgatory) – not too spiced or the dish would be named Uova Inferno.

PASTA PUTTANESCA (whore's style) named because the sauce is spicy and quick to prepare (a whore could prepare this sauce between customers).

POMIDORI AFFUCATI (drowned) – the tomatoes are drowned in their own juicy pulp.

VERDURE – greens in general.

PRIMI PIATTI – the first course, usually a pasta.

MINESTRONE – a mix of vegetables - a soup.

MOZZARELLA IN CAROZZA – little stuffed "carriages" (sandwiches).

ARANCINE – rice balls (little oranges).

CAZZILLI (potato croquettes) - the Italian name refers to the plural diminutive of the male sex organ.

MINNI DI VERGINI (little breasts of St. Agatha, virgin-martyr) – pastry, filled with cream.

DOLCI (sweets) – desserts.

PASTA NAMES - the cuts and designs depict the names:

radiatore – radiators	lasagna – cooking pot (Latin origin)
rigatoni – ridges, large lines	penne – feather pens
macaroni – dumpling (little pillow)	linguine – little tongues
acini di pepe – peppercorns	rotelle – wheels
farfalle – butterflies	fusilli – spindle
ziti – (Sicilian) bridegrooms	orecchiette – little ears
tagliatelli – cuts (of pasta)	spaghetti – a length of cord

ditalini, ditali – little thimbles, big thimbles
gemelli – twins (2 strands of pasta, twisted together)

Fall-Winter

MOZZARELLA IN CAROZZA *(heirloom)*

OSSO BUCCO *(heirloom)*

SAUTÉED SPINACH WITH GARLIC AND OIL

AUNT VIRGINIA'S MOSTACCIOLLI *(heirloom)*

MOZZARELLA IN CAROZZA

1 long loaf Sicilian-style Italian bread
    with sesame seeds

1 lb. fresh mozzarella (not packaged variety)

1 lg. beefsteak tomato

2 eggs, beaten

$\frac{1}{2}$ cup milk

flour for dredging

$\frac{1}{4}$ tsp. black pepper

olive oil for frying

Cut the loaf into 12 slices. Cut cheese into 6 slices; cut the tomato into 6 slices. Form 6 small sandwiches by placing one slice of mozzarella and one slice of tomato between 2 slices of bread. Beat eggs and milk together until thoroughly blended.

Dredge the sandwiches in flour blended with black pepper; then, coat them in egg-milk mix. Heat oil in skillet (about $\frac{1}{4}$-inch deep) and fry sandwiches on both sides to light golden brown. Cheese should start to melt. Drain sandwiches on paper towels and serve them immediately. Serves 6.

OSSO BUCCO
(May be partially prepared in advance.)

5-6 lbs. meaty veal shanks, with marrow in bone, cut through bone in 2-inch-thick sections (should make about 10-12 pieces)

flour for dredging

1 tsp. salt

$\frac{1}{2}$ tsp. pepper

$\frac{1}{4}$ cup olive oil

$1\frac{1}{2}$ cups dry white wine

1 cup chicken broth

2 tbsp. grated lemon peel

$\frac{1}{2}$ cup chopped parsley

1 onion, chopped

3-4 garlic cloves, minced

1 dozen small white mushrooms, rinsed, quartered

Lightly coat shanks in a mix of flour, salt and pepper. In a large (6-quart) Dutch oven, warm oil over medium heat. Add veal to pot, several pieces at a time and brown on all sides. When browned, remove them to a warming platter and brown the remaining veal shanks.

Return all the meat to the pot; add wine and broth, scraping the bottom of the pot for leavings. Reduce heat, cover pot and simmer for $1\frac{1}{2}$ hours or until meat is very tender when pierced with a metal skewer. (You may wish to cool, cover and refrigerate the shanks at this point. Reheat on low heat when ready to continue.)

Combine lemon peel, parsley, onion and garlic. Set aside. Add mushrooms to veal shanks during the last 10 minutes of cooking. With a slotted spoon, transfer meat and mushrooms to a heated platter and keep the dish very warm (in warming oven).

Bring sauce to a boil, scraping bottom of pot for leavings. Add half of the lemon-garlic mix to sauce and allow to simmer just until parsley wilts. Pour sauce over veal shanks and mushrooms and garnish with remaining lemon-garlic mix. Serve with Risotto (see page 66), and Sautéed Spinach (see below). Serves 6.

SAUTÉED SPINACH WITH GARLIC AND OIL

2 lbs. baby spinach

4-6 whole garlic cloves, peeled

$\frac{1}{4}$ cup extra-virgin olive oil

salt and black pepper to taste

In a 4-quart pot with lid, brown garlic in hot oil at moderate high. Stir in spinach and coat with garlic and oil. Cook spinach for only one minute constantly tossing spinach to sauté in oil-garlic mix. Remove from heat immediately. Add salt and pepper to taste. Serve hot. Serves 6.

AUNT VIRGINIA'S MOSTACCIOLLI

(Prepare several days in advance.)

1 cup filberts

1 cup walnuts

$\frac{1}{3}$ cup honey

1 egg white (from a large egg)

1 tbsp. unsweetened cocoa

$\frac{1}{2}$ tsp. cinnamon

$\frac{1}{8}$ tsp. ground cloves

$\frac{1}{2}$ tsp. grated orange peel

pinch of salt

$\frac{1}{3}$ cup flour

about 1 cup confectioners' sugar

FROSTING:

$\frac{1}{2}$ cup confectioners' sugar, sifted

about 5-6 tsp. orange liqueur (eg. Grand Marnier)

Preheat oven 275°.

Finely grind nuts in food processor. Transfer to a mixing bowl. Add honey, egg whites, cocoa, cinnamon, cloves, orange peel and salt; mix thoroughly. Add flour and stir until well blended.

Dust a board with confectioners' sugar. Flatten dough as you place it on top of confectioners' sugared board. Dust thoroughly with additional confectioners' sugar. Flatten dough with your hand or a rolling pin and shape into an 8-inch square. Cut into 16 pieces.

With the aid of a spatula, carefully transfer cookies to a greased baking sheet. Bake at 275° for 25-30 minutes. Remove cookies to cool.

Meanwhile, prepare frosting. Blend $\frac{1}{2}$ cup sifted confectioners' sugar with enough orange liqueur to make a medium-thick icing. Arrange cookies on a flat surface with sides touching. Drizzle the icing from a spoon or pipe it through a pastry bag with a very small tip; separate cookies after icing to prevent sticking together. Makes about 15 cookies.

Fall -Winter

Cooking Is a Prayer

I've always believed that the act of preparing meals has been a blessing which has been gifted to me. A blessing which I must share and gift to others: family, friends, all brethren whoever they may be. Cooking meals enables me to gather folks together to give thanks. When I was a child, I was taught that prayer is the lifting up of our minds and hearts to God. We may pray to adore the Creator, or to praise Him, or to obtain forgiveness, or to ask for favors and blessings for ourselves, – and for others. And, to thank Him. Cooking and sharing of meals is my prayer of thanksgiving and gratitude to God for the gifts of family and friends.

Special Blessings

(A Universal Blessing)
Bless O Lord, these gifts which we are about to receive from Your bounty. Thank you, Lord.

We ask God's blessing on the food we are about to share, on those who gather at this table, and on the cook and the provider.

God bless all who gather around this table of plenty;
God bless those who would be here if they could;
God bless all who do not share at a table of plenty. Amen.

Rub-a-dub-dub, thanks for the grub; Yeah, Lord!
(This lighthearted "blessing" was a gift from a young Jimmy Zukowski who deferred to a certain learned Monsignor's seminarian sense of humor.)

Praise the Lord; bless the cook; pass the roast beef.
AMEN.

Fall -Winter

ICEBERG LETTUCE WEDGES WITH CAPERS
VINAIGRETTE DRESSING
PECAN-PEPPER CRUSTED PORK TENDERLOIN
BAKED EGGPLANT PARMAGIANO WITH RED PEPPER SAUCE
CHOCOLATE STUCCO 2-STORY CAKE

ICEBERG LETTUCE WEDGES WITH CAPERS

1 lg. (or 2 small) head(s) iceberg lettuce, trimmed, washed, drained
1 small jar (or 2 oz.) capers, drained

Vinaigrette Dressing (see page 389)

Prepare Vinaigrette Dressing. Refrigerate dressing if not using within 1 hour.

Have ready: 6 individual salad bowls.

Cut heads of lettuce into 6 wedges; place one wedge into each of the bowls; sprinkle each lettuce wedge with $\frac{1}{2}$ tablespoon of capers. Drizzle Vinaigrette Dressing over each portion at serving time. Serves 6.

PECAN-PEPPER CRUSTED PORK TENDERLOIN

one 3 lb. narrow roll pork tenderloin

2 tbsp. each: freshly ground black pepper, red cayenne pepper,
    white pepper - blended

$\frac{1}{4}$ cup crushed dried sage

$\frac{1}{2}$ cup finely chopped pecans

wine sauce (in recipe, below)

Preheat oven to 450°.

Mix and spread the ground peppers, sage and chopped pecans on a large sheet of waxed paper. Roll the tenderloin in the pepper-nut mix until thoroughly coated. Wipe the bottom of a roasting pan with olive oil. Lay the roast in the pan and cook in center of preheated oven at 450° for 15 minutes. Reduce oven temperature to 350° and continue to roast the meat 30-35 minutes per pound or until meat thermometer registers 185°. Cooking time depends upon the thickness of the tenderloin. Remove from oven and transfer roast to a heat-resistant platter to keep it warm.

If you wish, prepare a pork sauce by pouring 1 cup boiling water into bottom of roasting pan. Scrape the leavings at the bottom of the pan. In a small bowl, stir until smooth: 3 tablespoons flour into one-half cup sweet wine (marsala or sherry or sweet vermouth). Heat the liquid in the roasting pan on the stove burner until it starts to boil. Turn down heat to simmer and slowly whisk in the wine and flour mix until a slightly thickened smooth gravy forms.

Meanwhile cut the roast into slices, $\frac{1}{2}$-inch thick. Lay a piece of foil on the meat and keep it in a warm oven for a few minutes until ready to serve. Pour the hot gravy into a gravy boat at serving time. Serves 8-10.

BAKED EGGPLANT PARMAGIANO WITH RED PEPPER SAUCE

2-3 medium-large eggplant, no more than
    4-5 inches in diameter
    (to cut into 6-8, $\frac{1}{2}$-inch slices per eggplant)
3 eggs, beaten or $\frac{3}{4}$ cup egg substitute

1 cup flour
$\frac{1}{4}$ tsp. black pepper
1 cup fine Italian bread crumbs, unseasoned
1 cup shredded low-fat mozzarella
1 cup grated Parmesan cheese

3 cups Red Pepper Sauce (see page 402)

Prepare Red Pepper Sauce in advance. Reserve 3 cups of sauce for this recipe.

Preheat oven to 400°. Have ready: a 9x15-inch heat-resistant Pyrex casserole dish. Pour and spread $1\frac{1}{2}$ cups Red Pepper Sauce over bottom of casserole. Set aside.

Because eggplant holds water, several hours before preparing the Parmagiano, wash the eggplants under cold running water; cut off the top and bottom ends; pare some of the skin off the eggplant and cut them into slices, $\frac{1}{2}$-inch thick, horizontally. Sprinkle each slice with salt and lemon juice (the latter to prevent discoloration) and stack them on a cutting board, in groups of 6; place a plate on top of each stack and lay a weight on the plate to allow the moisture to be squeezed out of the eggplant. After 2-3 hours, rinse slices and pat dry with paper towels.

Meanwhile beat eggs in a wide, shallow plate; lay out 2 sheets of waxed paper. Over one sheet, spread a mix of flour and black pepper; over the other sheet, spread the crumbs. Dredge each eggplant slice into the flour mix; then, dip the slices into the beaten egg; finally, coat each slice with the crumbs.

Lay 6 to 8 slices on the sauce in the Pyrex dish; divide the mozzarella among the 6 to 8 breaded slices. Repeat the coating procedure with the remaining 6 to 8 slices and place them over the slices in the dish to form "sandwiches". Lightly cover casserole with a sheet of foil. Place the casserole into the center of a preheated oven 400° and bake for 15 minutes. Remove from oven. Turn over "sandwiches" to bake the top side.

Spoon remainder of sauce under and over the eggplant sandwiches; sprinkle Parmesan cheese over the sauce and bake the Parmagiano in oven at 400° for 15 minutes. Lower temperature to 350° and continue to bake until eggplant is tender and bubbly. (Probably another 15-20 minutes.) An inserted toothpick should slip out of the "sandwich" with ease. Serves 6-8.

CHOCOLATE STUCCO 2-STORY CAKE

1 cup canola oil	$1\frac{1}{2}$ cups flour
2 cups sugar	$\frac{1}{4}$ tsp. cinnamon
4 eggs, separated	2 tsp. baking powder
2 oz. melted unsweetened chocolate	dash of salt
1 cup mashed unseasoned potatoes	$\frac{1}{2}$ cup milk (or fat-free evaporated milk)
1 tsp. vanilla	1 cup chopped nuts

Preheat oven 350°.

Grease and flour 2 (9-inch) cake pans. Cream oil and sugar. Add egg yolks, beating well after each addition. Stir in melted chocolate, mashed potatoes and vanilla. Mix flour, baking powder, salt and cinnamon in a bowl. Alternately, add flour mix and milk to chocolate mix, blending thoroughly. Add nuts.

In a clean bowl, beat egg whites to form stiff peaks. Fold stiffly beaten egg whites into batter. Pour batter into 2 prepared pans and bake layers at 350° for 30 minutes or until inserted toothpick tests clean.

Cool cake before removing from pans. Invert one layer onto a decorative cake plate. Frost top of one layer with Caramel Icing (see recipe below). Set other cake layer over bottom layer. Spread remainder of frosting over cake. Garnish with chopped nuts. Serves 8.

CARAMEL ICING

1 cup granulated sugar	1 tsp. vanilla extract
2 cups brown sugar	dash of salt
1 cup sour cream (fat-free available)	$\frac{1}{2}$ cup chopped nuts, for garnish
1 tbsp. butter or Smart Balance spread	

Blend sour cream, granulated and brown sugars and salt in a 1-quart sauce pot. Cook over low heat until sugars dissolve. Then, boil the mix gently until it reaches the slow boil stage or about 240°, on a candy thermometer. Remove from heat. Stir in vanilla and butter. Beat the mixture until it's of spreading consistency. Spread icing between and on top of cake layer. Sprinkle with nuts if desired.

Fall -Winter

"Mama, I Don't Feel So Good."
(For a Sick Day and other related occasions.)

My Mother had a standard menu to serve when we felt "under the weather", or ill, as a result of winter weather. I cannot remember a time when I became ill in the summertime. Probably because school was not in session, there was no good reason to feel sick.

For the first one or two days of our "illness", my mother would feed us very lightly: pastina, applesauce, tea and toast with grape jelly. As our "health" improved, the porridge of the day was a mild chicken broth or "Stracciatella". If a cold was causing our illness, lots of warm fluids were served; her special "Honey and Lemon Tea".

Breakfast wasn't ever my favored meal of the day. But, Mama would never send me off to school without a healthy breakfast. So, she would whip up her special "milk shake". Off I'd go to first grade, with an extra "spark" in my gait. (It had helped that we lived across the street from the school.)

The DelGais children (A few of Jane and Paul Smaldone's 19 grandchildren.) Photo by: Chrissy DelGais

Fall -Winter

A SPECIAL HEIRLOOM MENU

PASTINA AND STRACCIATELLA

BUTTERED TOAST

APPLE SAUCE

HONEY AND LEMON TEA

MAMA'S SPECIAL EGG NOG

FENNEL WATER

BEEF TEA

PASTINA

2 cups water
3-4 tbsp. pastina
dash of salt
1 tsp. butter or 1 tsp. olive oil
1 tsp. grated Romano cheese (optional)

In a small pot, boil the pastina in water for 8 minutes. Drain off half of the water. Transfer pastina in hot water to a serving soup bowl. Add a little salt and stir in butter. Sprinkle Romano cheese over bowl (if desired). Feel better.

BUTTERED TOAST

1-2 portions thin-sliced, white sandwich bread. Lightly toast. Serve with 1 teaspoon butter and 1 tablespoon grape jelly (and remember to save the jelly glass for your Disney collection).

(And when you felt a little better, Mama would graduate you to a richer broth.)

STRACCIATELLA

2 chicken legs with skin

6 cups water

1 tbsp. olive oil

1 tbsp. chopped onion

1 garlic clove, minced

2 eggs, beaten to a foam

2 tbsp. chopped parsley

salt, black pepper to taste

$\frac{1}{2}$ cup grated Romano cheese

Bring 6 cups water to a boil in a 4-quart soup pot. Add chicken legs; cover pot and simmer the chicken for 35-40 minutes. Remove chicken legs from broth to a small mixing bowl. In a small skillet, heat oil and lightly brown garlic and onion in oil. Remove skillet from stove; add 1 cup of chicken broth from the soup pot into the skillet and stir to mix.

Return and stir this mix into the soup pot as soup simmers. Stir in parsley. Remove meat from chicken legs and add to soup pot as soup simmers (discard chicken skin and bones).

In a small bowl, beat eggs to a foam; add salt and pepper to taste; beat in the cheese. Stirring as you go, pour this mix in a steady stream into the simmering broth. Gently stir the simmering soup and cook it a few minutes longer as the egg mix thickens and becomes cooked and firm.

(This soup should be eaten when prepared. Refrigerate leftovers in a clean non-metal bowl, covered with plastic wrap and use within a day.)

APPLE SAUCE

4 Red Delicious apples, pared, cored, cut
    into small chunks

$\frac{1}{2}$ cup water

1 tbsp. brown sugar

$\frac{1}{2}$ tsp. cinnamon or $\frac{1}{4}$ tsp. powdered ginger

1 tbsp. raisins (optional)

Cook the apples in water in a 2-quart pot with lid and simmer them for 20 minutes. Drain juice liquid into a cup. Pour cooked apples into a small bowl and purée with masher. Stir in sugar and spice. Add 1 tablespoon of raisins when you feel better. (Drink apple liquid while it's still warm.)

HONEY AND LEMON TEA

$1\frac{1}{2}$ cups boiling water

juice of $\frac{1}{2}$ lemon, strained

1 tbsp. pure honey

Stir lemon juice and honey into boiling water. (Serve in a large mug with a handle.)

MAMA'S SPECIAL EGG NOG

1 large raw egg, beaten to a foam
   (or use 1 portion egg substitute)
8 oz. cold milk
1 tsp. sugar
1 tbsp. VSOP brandy

Combine all ingredients in a blender or a small bowl; blend on high speed for 10 seconds or use electric or rotary beater for 30 seconds. Pour eggnog into a tall glass. Enjoy!

FENNEL WATER
(For babies who have Colic.)

$1\frac{1}{2}$ cups boiling water
$\frac{1}{2}$ tsp. sugar
$\frac{1}{2}$ tsp. fennel seeds

In a small pot combine water, fennel seeds and sugar. Bring to a boil. Turn off heat. Water will turn golden tan. Strain hot water into a baby bottle. Allow fennel water to cool to room temperature. Give to Baby to alleviate colicky stomach.

BEEF TEA

(My Mother was told by her doctor that she had a slight anemia. She believed in preventive medicine, and attempted to include me in her "blood building". All I shall say is that I did taste the beef tea. I would have preferred Mama to prepare a beef Braciola with the top round steak.)

1 lb. top round steak
2 cups cold water
salt to taste

Cut meat into tiny cubes, about $\frac{1}{2}$-inch square. Soak the beef cubes in cold water for 1 hour. Bring to boil; then cover pot and low-simmer beef for 2 hours. Season with salt; strain liquid.
Sip "tea", warm or cool. (Optional: eat the beef cubes.)

Fall -Winter

"Give Her Something to Eat."

While Jesus was yet speaking, there came some from the house of the ruler of the synagogue, saying, "Your daughter is dead. Why do you trouble the Master further?" But Jesus, having heard what was being said, said to the ruler of the synagogue, "Do not be afraid, only have faith." And he allowed no one to follow him except Peter and James, and John, the brother of James.

And they came to the house of the ruler of the synagogue and the Lord saw a tumult, people weeping and wailing greatly. And going in he said to them, "Why do you make this din, and weep? The girl is asleep, not dead." And they laughed him to scorn. But he, putting them all out, took the father and mother of the girl and those who were with him, and entered in where the girl was lying. And taking the girl by the hand, he said to her, "Talitha cumi," which is interpreted, " Girl, I say to you, arise."

And the girl rose up immediately and began to walk: she was twelve years old. And they were utterly amazed. And he charged them strictly that no one should know of it, and directed that something be given her to eat.

Mark: 5, 35-43

Ryan Goodale
(His Great-grandpa, cousin
Ralph Sanson,
drove my about-to-deliver
Mom to Columbus
Hospital, New York City,
where I was born.)
Photo by: R. Bastien

Fall -Winter

"A Menu in the Greek Tradition"
~ For Angela ~

GREEK SALAD
BALSAMIC VINEGAR AND OIL DRESSING
GREEK BEEF STEW
or
GREEK LAMB STEW
HONEY BOWS (heirloom)

GREEK SALAD

3-4 cups mixed: escarole, romaine, chicory - trimmed, rinsed, drained

3-4 plum tomatoes, cut into $\frac{1}{2}$-inch rounds

1 cucumber, pared, sliced

6-8 radishes, trimmed, sliced thin

$\frac{1}{2}$ cup pitted Kalamata olives

$\frac{1}{2}$ cup cubed feta cheese

$\frac{1}{2}$ cup low-fat croutons

Balsamic Vinegar and Oil Dressing (see page 384)

Prepare Balsamic Vinegar and Oil Dressing in advance and refrigerate it until 1 hour before serving.

Assemble all of the ingredients: greens, vegetables, croutons, olives and cheese into a large salad bowl. At serving, pour dressing over salad; toss to mix. Serve in individual bowls. Serves 6.

GREEK BEEF STEW

$\frac{1}{3}$ cup olive oil

3 lbs. beef boneless round, 1-inch cubes

2 cups red table wine, Burgundy

$\frac{1}{4}$ cup red wine vinegar

1 cup prepared tomato sauce

3 tbsp. tomato paste

3-4 garlic cloves, chopped

3-4 medium-size white onions, quartered

$\frac{1}{2}$ tsp. freshly ground pepper

1 stick cinnamon

2-3 bay leaves

$\frac{1}{2}$ cup feta cheese, crumbled

$\frac{1}{2}$ cup coarsely chopped walnuts

Heat olive oil in a large heavy skillet over high heat. Add beef and brown the meat, stirring occasionally, careful not to overcook. Transfer meat to a bowl and drain fat from skillet. Add wine, tomato sauce and paste, garlic, onions, vinegar, black pepper, cinnamon and bay leaves to skillet. Bring to a boil, stirring frequently. Lower heat to simmer and return beef to the pan. Cover and stew the beef over low heat, for 40-50 minutes until tender. Add feta cheese and walnuts and cook just until feta is soft. Remove and discard bay leaves. Serve over wide noodles. Serves 6.

GREEK LAMB STEW

2 lbs. lean boneless lamb, cubed
  (from shoulder or leg)

2 tbsp. olive oil

6 garlic cloves, whole

1 doz. pearl onions, peeled

8-10 small new potatoes (or med-large, cut into
  chunks - about $2\frac{1}{2}$ cups)

6-8 small white mushrooms, halved

$\frac{1}{2}$ cup Greek olives, pitted and halved

1 tbsp. dried thyme

1 tsp. salt

1 tsp. black peppercorns

1 cup red table wine

$\frac{1}{2}$ cup water

1 cup tomato purée

1 tbsp. chopped parsley, for garnish

4 cups baby spinach, washed, drained

In a large, deep skillet, lightly brown lamb, onion and garlic; scrape bottom of skillet to remove leavings. Add tomato purée, water, wine, potatoes, salt, peppercorns and thyme. Cover pot and simmer for 20 minutes. Stir in mushrooms and olives during last 5 minutes. Serve with steamed baby spinach. (Wash and drain 4 cups baby spinach; cook in steamer for 30 seconds.) Remove pot immediately. Spoon spinach to center of large platter; ladle lamb stew around spinach. Garnish stew with parsley. Serve with hard biscuits, like "frizelle". Serves 6.

HONEY BOWS

(A festive treat anytime. Traditionally used at holidays. Prepare several days in advance. Cover lightly with waxed paper and store in a cool, dry place.)

3 large eggs

½ tsp. salt

1¾-2 cups flour

1 lb. honey

6 tbsp. granulated sugar

corn oil for frying

confectioners' sugar

Use a deep fryer for better results.

Combine eggs, flour, and salt in a large bowl. Use a wooden spoon at first; then, your hands to mix the dough until it leaves the sides of the bowl. Add a little more flour if dough is sticky.

Turn dough onto floured board and knead until dough is smooth and does not stick to fingers. Cut dough into 4 parts and roll each piece on floured board until ⅛-inch thick, the thinner the better. (Keep remaining dough covered with plastic wrap.)

With a sharp knife, cut the thinly rolled dough into strips, about 6 to 8 inches long and 1-inch wide. Form each into a loose knot or twist in middle to make a bow tie.

Meanwhile, preheat 1-inch of oil in deep fryer or skillet to 370°. Fry a few bows and knots at one time, turning if necessary (if using skillet) until the pastry is golden in color. Remove with tongs to a large bowl lined with paper towels to drain.

When all the dough is used, heat the honey and granulated sugar in a 2-quart saucepan until honey mix simmers. With tongs, dip each knot and bow into the hot honey mix and transfer the bows and knots onto a large flat platter, piling the bows and knots to form a mound. Cool thoroughly and sprinkle with confectioners' sugar. Delizioso!

Cousin Garret with a fresh batch.
Photo by: C. Satfield

Fall -Winter

Zie Prevete Goes A-Hunting

For the first six years of my life, we lived in the family's huge Victorian three-story home in Bay Ridge, Brooklyn. My Grandpa Aniello and Uncle Raphael and cousin Ralph shared our beautiful home with its peach and apricot trees, grape arbor and cocozzo trellis. Uncle Raphael, Grandpa's first born son was a priest who made his home with us when he wasn't performing his duties in the Bronx or on Staten Island.

In the Fall, Zie Prevete_(my childish name for my Uncle Raphael, which translated into "Uncle, the Priest"), would take a little trip on the New Jersey Central to enjoy a weekend of hunting rabbits and pheasants and deer at his sister's (Ninella) Hopewell, NJ farm. (Aunt Ninella was cousin Ralph's mother.)

Some of Zie Prevete's quarry would find its way to my Aunt Susie's kitchen in Brooklyn. And that's how I was introduced to Coniglio Cacciatore (Rabbit Stew), Venison Stew and roasted female pheasant. The colorful male pheasants made their way to the taxidermist; then, to the top of my mother's Aeolian upright piano. I can still see them dancing as I practiced my scales.

My oldest paternal uncle,
Fr. Raphael Orlando, "Zie Prevete".
Photo: By Ralph Sanson

Fall -Winter

YELLOW TOMATOES WITH DANDELION GREENS (CICORIA)
LEMON-OIL DRESSING
THREE STEWS:
VENISON STEW (heirloom)
COUNTRY-STYLE STEW
RUSTIC STEW
ICE CREAM AND CRÈME DE MENTHE

Serve this salad with each of the following stews: Venison, Country-Style, Rustic.

YELLOW TOMATOES WITH DANDELION GREENS (CICORIA)

3-4 medium yellow tomatoes, thickly sliced into rounds
3 cups dandelions, trimmed, washed, drained
$\frac{1}{2}$ cup pitted oil-cured olives
1 lg. red onion, sliced thin

Lemon-Oil Dressing (see page 385)

Prepare Lemon-Oil Dressing in advance and refrigerate it until 1 hour before serving.

Have ready: 6 individual salad plates. Just before serving, place the dandelions in a large bowl; pour $\frac{1}{2}$ cup Lemon-Oil Dressing over the greens. Toss to mix. Lay a bed of prepared dandelions on each salad plate. Lay 2-3 slices of tomatoes on top of the greens; garnish with onion slices and olives. Sprinkle 1 tablespoon Lemon-Oil Dressing over each plate. Serves 6.

VENISON STEW

(Boneless beef round, cubed, may be substituted for venison.)

4 lbs. venison steak, trimmed of fat;
   cut into cubes
$\frac{1}{4}$ cup olive oil
3 lg. onions, sliced thin
4-5 garlic cloves, chopped
2 celery stalks, cleaned, chopped
3-4 carrots, pared, cut into chunks
6 medium Red Bliss potatoes, scrubbed, quartered

2 cups beef broth, less-salt variety
$\frac{1}{2}$ cup cider vinegar
1 cup tomato sauce
$\frac{1}{4}$ cup chopped parsley
2 bay leaves
1 tsp. each: dried sage, thyme, mustard powder
1 tsp. salt or more (to taste)
$\frac{1}{2}$ tsp. freshly ground pepper

Preheat oven to 300°.

Heat oil in large Dutch oven on stove burner. Brown cubed venison in oil over moderate heat. Add onions and garlic and cook for about 5 minutes, stirring until soft. Add celery, carrots and potatoes; cook, stirring, for 10 minutes until tender. Stir in broth, tomato sauce and vinegar, herbs, salt and pepper. Cover the pot and cook in preheated oven 300° for 1$\frac{1}{2}$ hours, until meat and potatoes are tender. Remove and discard bay leaves before serving. Serve with slabs of sourdough bread. Serves 6.

COUNTRY-STYLE STEW

(A loose-style stew.)

1 lb. beef chuck, cut into cubes, 1x1-inch
1 lb. sweet pork sausage,
   cut into 6-8 serving portions
1 lb. boneless chicken thighs
2 yellow onions, chopped
4-6 garlic cloves, peeled, leave whole
1 lg. carrot, pared, sliced into narrow rounds
1 lg. celery stalk, scraped, chopped
1 lg. parsnip, pared, chopped

1 sprig each: fresh parsley, fresh oregano,
   fresh cilantro
16 oz. tomato sauce
6 cups water
salt, pepper to taste
extra cilantro for garnish
a pinch of hot red pepper
1 lb. tagliatelle pasta

Place beef, sausages and chicken in a 6-quart soup pot (with lid); cover with 6 cups of cold water. Cover with lid. Bring to a boil; then, skim fat off the surface of the pot. (Suggestion: skim fat with white paper towels, or: chill the pot of meat; then, lift the fat off the top and discard.) Cover the pot; return it to heat; bring to a slow boil. Add onions, garlic, celery, carrot, parsnip and herb bouquet. Simmer for 30 minutes. Add tomato sauce, salt and pepper (hot pepper, if desired), and simmer for another 30 minutes.

Meanwhile, 15 minutes before completion, prepare pasta as directed on package. Drain. Divide tagliatelle among 4-6 pasta-soup bowls. Ladle meats and vegetables with broth over pasta in each bowl. Garnish with tiny sprigs of cilantro. Serves 4-6.

RUSTIC STEW

1½ lbs. boneless pork, cut bite-size

3 boneless and skinned chicken breasts,
    cut bite-size

2-3 hard chorizo sausages (about 1 lb.),
    cut into small chunks

1 can (22 oz.) crushed tomatoes

1 cup water

1 onion, chopped

1 zucchini, chopped

1 carrot, pared, chopped

¼ head cabbage, shredded

1 lg. celery stalk, chopped

1 cup chicken consommé (less-salt variety)

2 bay leaves

6 garlic cloves, chopped

½ tsp. each: chili powder, cumin, cinnamon,
    ginger powder, salt, pepper

1 lg. apple, cored (with skin), cut into bite-size

1 doz. large pitted prunes

1 cup orange juice

grated rind of 1 orange

2 tbsp. olive oil

In a large stew pot with cover, heat 2 tablespoons olive oil. Brown pork on moderately high heat and transfer to a large bowl. Brown chicken pieces and transfer to same bowl. Follow suit with the sausages. Lightly brown onions and garlic, scraping bottom of pan. Return meats to pot; add tomatoes, water, consommé, orange juice, zucchini, carrot, celery, cabbage, bay leaves, spices, salt and pepper. Cover pot and simmer for 30 minutes; add apple, prunes and orange rind and simmer for another 20 minutes. Remove and discard bay leaves. Crusty Artisan bread is a good addition to accommodate the sauce. Serves 6.

ICE CREAM AND CRÈME DE MENTHE

Vanilla Ice Cream drizzled with crème de menthe will make a satisfying statement to these hearty stews. Serve the ice cream in stem goblets, (½ cup size); drizzle liqueur over the ice cream.

Fall -Winter

Secrets of a Fridge

*Y*our refrigerator holds your secrets and freezes them solidly. How old is the butter in that white plastic dish?

One, two, three __ eight large eggs. And when were they tucked so neatly into their cubby holes? I'm talking "dates".

Have you checked the packaged cheese lately?

There are two jars of pickles: one is "Sweet Gherkins"; the other: "Kosher Dill". Sure, they're "preserved" in a vinegar of sorts; but nothing can be preserved forever.

And, how long is "forever" when it comes to the age of foods? Evaluate_ and sanitize your refrigerator AT LEAST once a month: remove and wash trays, glass shelves, bins and drawers_ move the fridge and clean behind and under it!

And we haven't even touched upon the freezer. The snow on some of those packages has formed an arctic tundra.

When it comes to observing rules for refrigeration, remember Rule #1_ When in the slightest doubt, toss it out!

Fall -Winter

SPINACH AND BEAN SOUP

ROASTED CORNISH GAME HENS IN LIME JUICE

WILD RICE STUFFING WITH CRANBERRIES

BRUSSELS SPROUTS WITH BACON AND PIGNOLA

CHOCOLATE CHERRY SPONGE CAKE

SPINACH AND BEAN SOUP
(Soak beans overnight.)

6-8 cups chicken broth (less-salt variety) (*NOTE:)

1 lb. pkg. mixed dried beans, rinse and drain;
    soak beans in cold water in 4 qt. pot, overnight

1 lg. can (20 oz.) chopped tomatoes

1 lg. carrot, pared, chopped

1 lg. celery stalk, chopped

1 onion, chopped

2-3 garlic cloves, slivered

1 lg. all-purpose potato, pared, cubed

2 cups baby spinach, rinsed

2 tbsp. chopped parsley

salt, black pepper, to taste

1 tsp. cayenne pepper

1 tsp. Hungarian paprika

Rinse and soak beans in 4-quart pot (with lid), overnight. Early on the day, rinse beans again and drain. Return beans to 4-quart soup pot. Combine the following and add to beans: broth, chopped tomatoes, chopped carrot, potato, onion, celery and garlic. Stir in parsley, cayenne, paprika, salt and pepper. Cover pot and bring to a slow simmer; cook for $1\frac{1}{2}$ hours, stirring soup occasionally. If the soup is too thick, add up to 1 cup of broth or water. Add spinach during last 5 minutes of cooking. Serves 6.

*NOTE: Prepare homemade chicken broth by simmering legs and wings of chicken in 6 cups water in a 4-quart pot with cover for 35-40 minutes. Remove chicken meat from legs and wings and stir the meat into this soup. It will make a hearty addition. Or add chopped celery and mayo to the chicken meat for a delicious chicken salad sandwich.

ROASTED CORNISH GAME HENS IN LIME JUICE

3-4 Cornish game hens, dressed, rinsed, patted dry
   with paper towels

1 cup flour

2 tbsp. olive oil, (oil for roasting pan)

salt, black pepper to taste

juice of 2 limes

grated rind of 2 limes

$\frac{1}{2}$ cup honey

$\frac{1}{4}$ cup chopped cilantro

Preheat oven to 450°.

Blend lime juice, honey and cilantro in small bowl and set aside. Rinse hens in cold water. Sprinkle salt inside cavities as well as over the exterior. Refrigerate hens, covered with waxed paper for 1-2 hours. Rinse the hens again, in cold water and drain. Pat them dry with paper towels.

With poultry shears, starting at the back end, cut the birds in half, cutting from back end to breast bone and completely around. Brush each half, inside and out, with olive oil; coat hens in flour seasoned with salt and pepper. Arrange the halves, breast side up on a large roasting tray, brushed with oil. Set the tray in the heated oven; lower temperature to 350° and roast hens for 30 minutes. At 20 minutes, brush them with lime juice mix and rind. Continue to roast at 350° for 10 minutes longer or until hens are browned. Serve halves over wild rice stuffing (see recipe below). Serves 6.

WILD RICE STUFFING WITH CRANBERRIES

$\frac{1}{2}$ cup brown rice

$\frac{1}{2}$ cup wild rice

$\frac{1}{2}$ green pepper, finely chopped

1 small onion, chopped

1 celery stalk, trimmed, finely chopped

2 tbsp. fresh parsley, chopped

1 tsp. dried rosemary

1 tbsp. olive oil

1 tbsp. butter or Smart Balance spread

$\frac{1}{4}$ tsp. freshly ground black pepper

2 cups chicken broth, less-salt variety

1 cup chopped fresh cranberries
   (chop in food processor)

In a 2-quart pot with lid, lightly brown onion in olive oil and butter. Pour broth into pot and stir to scrape onions from bottom of pot. Add rice, green pepper, celery, cranberries, parsley, pepper and rosemary. Cover pot and gently simmer for 40-45 minutes until liquid is just absorbed. Add a little more broth, if needed. Serves 6 stuffing portions.

John carves a turkey.

BRUSSELS SPROUTS WITH BACON AND PIGNOLA

4 cups Brussels sprouts, trimmed,
    rinsed, drained (about 1 lb.)
3 slices lean bacon, cooked, crumbled
$\frac{1}{4}$ cup pignola (pine nuts)

2 tbsp. extra-virgin olive oil
$\frac{1}{4}$ tsp. salt
$\frac{1}{2}$ tsp. freshly ground black pepper

    Cook bacon; drain on towels; crumble. Set aside. Steam Brussels sprouts about 14-15 minutes. Do not overcook. Drain. Place in serving bowl. Gently toss with olive oil, salt, pepper and pignola. Garnish with crumbled bacon. Serves 6.

CHOCOLATE CHERRY SPONGE CAKE
(Prepare in advance.)

$\frac{3}{4}$ cup butter or Smart Balance spread, softened
1 cup lt. brown sugar
3 eggs, beaten or $\frac{3}{4}$ cup egg substitute
$1\frac{1}{4}$ cups self-rising flour
$\frac{1}{4}$ cup unsweetened cocoa

1 tbsp. cinnamon
2 tbsp. low-fat milk
1 can (1 lb.) cherries in juice, drain, remove pits
confectioners' sugar, cinnamon – for garnish

Preheat oven to 350°.

    Grease an 8-inch square or round cake pan. Dust the bottom of the pan with flour. In a bowl, cream butter with sugar until fluffy. Gradually add beaten eggs to creamed mixture, beating well after each addition. Sift flour, cinnamon and cocoa into the butter-sugar mix. Fold the batter gently, until all of the ingredients are combined.

    Add the milk, folding it into the batter. Spoon this mixture into the prepared pan. With the back of a knife, level the surface of the batter.

    Arrange the pitted cherries over the top of the batter. Bake the cake in a preheated oven, 350° for 1 hour, until the cake is just firm to the touch. Cool the cake in its pan; then, invert the pan onto a serving plate, lined with a paper doily. When cake is completely cool, sift confectioners' sugar over the top of the cake and sprinkle with cinnamon. Serves 6.

Fall -Winter

Cooking for a Snow Storm

*L*iving on Long Island, one has occasion to survive some mildly wicked snow events. Why is it at the mention of the mere possibility of being "snowed-in", I salivate? Probably, because snowstorms guaranteed my holing-up at home in front of the fireplace, perhaps reading one of the many tomes I've been promising to tackle. Or as a former student and a teacher, maybe it's because I've always equated a snow storm with a day off from school AND a great day to bake a cake.

Well, this one snowstorm in January of 1978 (actually an ice storm), seemed to be a routine matter, except for the ice. Yes, neighbors were skidding here and yon, as they attempted to navigate up our hill; they were going nowhere fast.

The front doorbell sounded five times that snowy afternoon. Actually, it sang its tune three consecutive times. The Westminster chimes had been erased by a power failure.

Our welcomed guests enjoyed grilled hamburgers a la hearth, freshly baked pop corn, and believe it, a slow-heated , previously frozen lasagna (stuffed with tiny meatballs, sausage chunks and creamy cheeses). My husband positioned a spare log grate over the burning logs on the hearth grate, and slow-cooked our dinner.

A picnic in a snowstorm.

P.S. By early morning, our neighbors were able to "dig out" and return to their homes, rather reluctantly.

Fall -Winter

CHICKEN AND EGG SOUP

LAMB MEATBALLS

VEGETABLE ACCOMPANIMENTS

FRUIT TART

CHICKEN AND EGG SOUP

1 full boneless breast of chicken,
    skinned, shredded (*NOTE: below)

1 carrot, pared, shredded

1-2 leeks, trimmed, chop the bulbs

½ cup small broccoli florets

½ cup shitake mushrooms, sliced

¼ cup white rice

4 cups chicken consommé, low-salt variety

2 cups water

1 tbsp. rice wine vinegar

1 tbsp. sherry

1 tiny Thai pepper, seeded, finely chopped
    (wear plastic gloves)

chili powder for garnish

4-6 eggs

In a 4-quart soup pot with cover, bring 4 cups consommé and 2 cups water to a boil. Add shredded chicken; lower heat and simmer, covered, for 20 minutes. Skim top of pot of chicken fat or scum. Add leeks, carrot, broccoli, mushrooms, rice wine vinegar, sherry, Thai pepper and rice. Continue to simmer for 25 minutes. Stir occasionally. Break eggs, one at a time, in a deep plate. Drop eggs into simmering soup. Continue to simmer, covered, for 4-5 minutes. When eggs are lightly firm, remove pot from heat; ladle soup into individual bowls; remove eggs with slotted spoon and transfer eggs to soup bowls. Sprinkle soup with chili powder and serve. Serves 6.

*NOTE: Prepare 15-18 large, shelled and cleaned shrimp may be substituted for shredded chicken.

LAMB MEATBALLS

2 lbs. ground lean lamb

1 pkg. (8 oz.) frozen peas, defrosted
  (run under hot water, drain)

3 scallions with greens, trimmed, chopped

½ red pepper, seeded, minced

2 garlic cloves, minced

1-2 tsp. Thai curry paste (to taste)

1 tbsp. parsley, chopped

1 tbsp. *lite* soy sauce

½ cup fine breadcrumbs

1 egg, beaten or ¼ cup egg substitute

2 tbsp. canola oil

SAUCE:

2 cups stock made from scrapings in wok

2 tbsp. cornstarch stirred into 4 tbsp. water
  (save in a small bowl)

¼ cup *lite* soy sauce

2 tbsp. hoisin sauce

2 tbsp. sherry

1 tbsp. finely chopped fresh gingerroot

2 tbsp. rice wine vinegar

VEGETABLE ACCOMPANIMENTS:

1 lg. Chinese cabbage, trimmed, washed, drained, shredded

1 dozen baby carrots, scraped, trimmed

2-3 leeks, trimmed, sliced

2 large Portobello mushrooms, washed, drained, sliced

Prepare the meatballs. In a large bowl, combine thoroughly: chopped lamb, peas, chopped scallions, red pepper, garlic, curry paste, parsley, soy sauce, crumbs and egg. Form 2-inch meatballs; add canola oil to wok and heat oil to 300°; lightly brown the meatballs. Transfer meatballs to a 2-quart bowl. Set aside. After all of the meatballs are cooked, scrape the bottom of the wok: stir in 2 cups hot water. Make a paste by stirring 2 tablespoons cornstarch into ¼ cup water. Stir this paste into stock liquid in wok. Add and stir in: soy sauce, hoisin sauce, sherry, vinegar and gingerroot. Simmer gently for several minutes until sauce thickens. Return meatballs to sauce in wok and gently toss them with 2 large spoons to coat them thoroughly. Lower heat under wok, and keep meatballs warm. In a 2-quart steamer with basket, lay mushroom slices, carrots, leeks and cabbage (in that order). Add ½ cup water. Cover, close vent and steam vegetables for 4-5 minutes. Turn off heat; remove basket and invert vegetables onto a large round serving platter. Pour hot meatballs over the vegetables and serve. Serves 6.

FRUIT TART
(May be prepared in advance.)

DOUGH:
1¼ cups flour
½ cup butter or Smart Balance spread,
    in tiny cubes
½ cup sugar
1 tbsp. water

FILLING:
¾ cup butter
⅓ cup flour, sifted
1 cup sugar
1½ cups ground almonds
1 egg or ¼ cup egg substitute
4 tbsp. heavy cream
2 egg yolks or ½ cup egg substitute
1 cup fresh cranberries
1 lg. can (1 lb.) apricot halves, drained

PREPARE THE CRUST:

Preheat oven 375°.

In a medium-size bowl, combine flour and sugar and work in butter with a fork. Add water and work the mixture with your hands to form a soft, smooth dough.

Wrap dough in plastic wrap; then, chill dough in refrigerator for 30 minutes.

Roll out dough on a floured board to line a 10-inch pie pan. Lay the dough in the pan and prick the dough with the tines of a fork. Refrigerate crust for 30 minutes.

Line the pie dough in the tin with a sheet of foil and some dried beans (as a weight) and bake in preheated oven 375° for 15 minutes. Remove beans and foil; return pie crust in its tin to the oven and continue to bake pie crust 10 minutes longer.

PREPARE THE FILLING:

Cream together butter and sugar until light and fluffy. Beat in egg and egg yolks; stir in flour, almonds and cream. Arrange apricot halves and cranberries on bottom of pie shell; spoon filling over the top. Bake in oven 375° about 1 hour, or until topping is just set. Cool slightly. Serve warm or cool. Serves 6-8.

Fall -Winter

Healthy Cooking

MENU LOG underwent three revisions before it was published in 2004. The final revision was to offer alternatives to cooking with butter, margarine, solid shortenings, other saturated fats, fatty meats, cholesterol in eggs, excessive amounts of salt and sugar; and for inclusion of varied vegetables, fruits, grains, fish, seafood and lean meats.

LUNCH IS IN THE BAG! continued the quest for healthy cooking in hundreds of luncheon recipes.

And FROM THE TABLE OF PLENTY carries on this tradition in its culinary adventures from the past and into the present.

Fall -Winter

CHICKEN VEGETABLE SOUP
PORK CHOPS WITH FENNEL
STUFFED RED BELLS WITH RISOTTO
TORTA WITH PINE NUTS AND ALMONDS

CHICKEN VEGETABLE SOUP
(May be prepared in advance.)

$1\frac{1}{2}$ lbs. chicken breasts, skinless, boneless,
    cut into small cubes
1 onion, chopped
1 tbsp. olive oil
2 carrots, pared, cut into thin rounds
$\frac{1}{2}$ lb. green beans, trimmed, cut into small pieces
1 can (1 lb.) corn kernels, drained

1 can (1 lb.) lima beans, drained
1 lg. celery stalk, chopped
6 cups boiling water
$\frac{1}{2}$ tsp. pepper
salt to taste
1 tbsp. chopped dill
$\frac{1}{4}$ cup flour

Heat olive oil in a 4-quart pot with lid. Add onion and cook for 2-3 minutes until tender, stirring bottom of pot to loosen particles. Add chicken and 6 cups of boiling water. Cover pot and bring to a boil. Lower heat and simmer chicken for 20 minutes.

Add carrots, lima beans, green beans, corn, celery, pepper, dill and salt to taste. Stir to blend.

Remove 1 cup broth from pot and stir one-quarter cup of flour into this cup of broth. Return the floured broth to the stock pot and stir the soup until smooth. Cover pot and continue to allow the soup to simmer for 10 minutes longer. Serves 6.

PORK CHOPS WITH FENNEL

6 loin pork chops in bone, 1-inch thick,   juice from 2 oranges
   fat trimmed   rind from 1 orange
2-3 fennel bulbs with some fennel grass,   salt to taste
   trimmed, washed, thinly sliced   cracked black pepper
2 tbsp. capers (juniper berries)   olive oil to rub on pan

Grease a 9x15-inch non-stick, oven-proof pan.
Preheat oven to 400°.
Place trimmed chops in the non-stick greased pan. Pour orange juice blended with rind, salt and capers over chops. Grind pepper over chops. Layer sliced fennel over chops and bake, uncovered, in preheated oven 400° for 25 minutes, dependent upon thickness of chops. After 20 minutes, insert meat thermometer in a chop to register about 175°, internally. When cooked, remove pork from oven and transfer, with a spatula and spoon, to serving platter. Spoon fennel sauce with fennel over the chops. Serves 6.

STUFFED RED BELLS WITH RISOTTO

1 cup Arborio rice   1 tbsp. saffron threads
6 red bell peppers, washed   2½ cups chicken stock, less-salt variety
1 small onion, chopped   ½ cup diced pepperoni
2 tbsp. olive oil   ½ cup diced mozzarella
black pepper to taste   olive oil for pan

Preheat grill or broiler to hot (450°-500°).
Cut off tops of washed peppers, about 1-inch below stems; remove seeds from peppers. Reserve stems for later. Lightly brown onion and pepperoni in 2-quart pot with lid. Scrape bottom of pot for leavings. Add and mix thoroughly: rice, pepper to taste, saffron, and chicken stock. Bring mix to a boil; then, to simmer for 20-25 minutes. Remove rice from burner.
Oil the bottom of 9x12-inch pan. Set 6 "topped" peppers in the pan; carefully spoon risotto, evenly among the peppers. Force a little more then 1 tablespoonful of diced mozzarella into the cavities of each of the rice-filled peppers. Top each pepper with a stem.
Grill or broil peppers (5 inches below heat), for 3-4 minutes, until cheese looks bubbly and the peppers' skin begins to shrivel. Serves 6.

TORTA WITH PINE NUTS AND ALMONDS

8 oz. shaved almonds with skins, lightly toasted

2 oz. pine nuts (pignola)

½ lb. unsalted butter (2 sticks) or Smart
   Balance spread at room temperature

1 cup plus 2 tbsp. granulated sugar

3 eggs or ¾ cup egg substitute, lightly beaten

1 tsp. almond extract

1 tsp. vanilla extract

9 tbsp. all-purpose flour

pinch of salt

butter or Smart Balance to grease 8-inch round
   (or square) cake pan

confectioners' sugar

Preheat oven 350°.

Grease pan and line with baking parchment. Food process almonds and pignola to form a mixture which is crumbly. Set aside. (Reserve 1 tablespoonful of each nut for garnish.)

Beat together: butter and sugar in a bowl until smooth and fluffy. Beat in eggs, crumbled nuts, vanilla and almond extracts until well-blended, about 3-4 minutes. Stir in flour and salt and gently mix until flour is just incorporated. Pour batter into greased and parchment-lined pan. Bake torta in preheated oven 350° for 40-50 minutes or until cake is spongy to the touch.

Remove torta from oven and cool on rack. Before serving, dust with confectioners' sugar and garnish with reserved nuts. Serves 6.

Fall -Winter

And Then, the Cake Fell

Cooking and baking have been a part of my life since early childhood. As a five year old, I'd roll the gnocchi off the tines of a fork; crimp the edges of cheese ravioli; roll tiny balls of dough between my child's fingers, hundreds of tiny dough balls which would become my favorite treat, Struffoli, smothered in sweet, sticky honey and nonpareils. Who needed Cracker Jacks?

My first cooking disaster occurred when I was eleven. Chiffon cake. Or should I say, a sunken crater cake. The recipe in the booklet that accompanied Mama's new Dormeyer Mixmaster said: 1 cup corn oil, 5 eggs, separated, etc. My mother stored no corn oil; nor was she about to purchase any. She told me that olive oil would have to make do. After all, wasn't olive oil from a vegetable?

I took the pan of mess out the back door, through the neighbor's broken fence and across to 72nd Street to my Aunt Susie's kitchen (where Aunt Susie would always be found). The spoiled child in me arose to the occasion. Tears streaming down my cheeks found their way into the pan of mess I had extended for her to observe.

Calmly, she took the pan from my oven mitts, placed her chubby foot on the pedal of the chromium garbage pail by the sink, and dumped the mess where it belonged. "Now", she firmly stated, "let's bake some muffins."

Aunt Susie Colantuono, one of my Dad's younger sisters. Photo-courtesty of H. Lewis

Fall -Winter

SOUTHWEST SALAD
HONEY MUSTARD DRESSING
CHEESY VEGETABLE CHOWDER
SAUSAGES AND BEANS
AUNT SUSIE'S BUTTERFLIES (heirloom)

SOUTHWEST SALAD

4 cups mesclun salad greens, rinsed, drained

1 red pepper, seeded, thinly sliced

1 large avocado, peeled, sliced thin
    (sprinkle with lime juice when sliced)

1 small-medium papaya, halved; scoop out seeds;
    then, peel and slice thin

4 tbsp. pumpkin seeds, toasted (*NOTE: below)

2 limes, cut into wedges

Honey Mustard Dressing (see page 384)

Prepare Honey Mustard Dressing in advance and refrigerate it until 1 hour before serving.

*NOTE: Toast pumpkin seeds by spreading seeds on a sheet of foil and roasting them in a hot oven 450° for 2-3 minutes.

Prepare salad on a large flat serving platter. Lay a bed of mesclun; arrange slices of red pepper, avocado and papaya around the platter. Sprinkle with toasted pumpkin seeds. Add wedges of lime. Sprinkle with Honey Mustard Dressing when serving. Serves 4-6.

CHEESY VEGETABLE CHOWDER
(May be made a couple days in advance.)

2 tbsp. olive oil

1 onion, chopped

3 garlic cloves, chopped

2-3 leek bulbs, trimmed, sliced into narrow rounds

8 cups hot water

$\frac{1}{4}$ cup flour

2 lg. carrots, pared, sliced into narrow rounds

2 celery stalks, trimmed, peeled,
    chopped into small chunks

2 medium potatoes, pared, cut into small chunks

2 parsnips, pared, chopped into small chunks

1 tbsp. dried thyme

1 tbsp. fresh parsley, chopped

1-2 bay leaves

1 tsp. salt

$\frac{1}{2}$ tsp. black pepper

1 can (13 oz.) evaporated milk (fat-free available)

1 lb. sharp cheddar cheese, grated

Heat oil in a large 4-quart soup pot with lid. Add onion, garlic and leeks. Cover pot and cook on medium heat for a few minutes, until vegetables are tender.

Add hot water and bring to a boil. Remove 1 cup hot liquid and stir in flour, to form a smooth paste. Spoon flour mix into simmering soup pot, stirring to blend. Add carrots, celery, potatoes, parsnips, herbs and salt and pepper. Cover pot and bring to a boil; lower heat and cook for about 25-30 minutes, until vegetables are tender.

Stir in milk and simmer gently for 5 minutes longer. Add cheese, a handful at a time, stirring constantly after each addition, until cheese is completely melted. Taste the soup and adjust the seasoning, adding a little more salt and pepper, if needed. Remove bay leaf and discard before serving. Serves 8.

SAUSAGES AND BEANS

8-10 links sweet Italian sausages with fennel

1 tbsp. olive oil

1 large onion, chopped

3-4 garlic cloves, chopped

2 Italian green peppers, seeded, sliced

1 red sweet pimiento pepper, seeded, sliced

1 can (8 oz.) chopped tomatoes

1 can (20 oz.) cannellini beans, rinsed in
    cold water, drained

1 tbsp. dried oregano

1 bay leaf

salt, pepper to taste

In a large skillet with cover, heat olive oil to 300° and lightly brown garlic, onion and peppers, scraping bottom of pan to prevent vegetables from sticking. Add sausages, turning often, and brown lightly about 5 minutes. Stir in chopped tomatoes and simmer for 10 minutes, covered. Stir in oregano, pepper and salt and beans. Lay a bay leaf on top of the casserole; cover and heat through (about 4-5 minutes). Remove and discard bay leaf before serving. Serves 6.

AUNT SUSIE'S BUTTERFLIES

(Prepare cupcakes on day before. Prepare custard early on the day needed and chill.)

1 cup Chocolate Cream Filling
1 pkg. (22 oz.) yellow cake mix (follow
*   directions on package for large cupcakes)*
1 cup chocolate mini-morsels (optional)
confectioners' sugar

CHOCOLATE CREAM FILLING:
½ cup confectioners' sugar
6 tbsp. cocoa
⅛ tsp. salt
2 cups heavy cream
1 tsp. vanilla
½ cup chocolate mini-morsels (optional)

Preheat oven to 350°.

Bake cupcakes in greased cupcake pan as directed on cake mix package. Cool them thoroughly. Then, cut out the center of each cupcake and set aside. Fill each cavity with chocolate cream. Split each removed center and set into cream, on top of cupcake, like butterfly wings. Refrigerate.

Sprinkle with confectioners' sugar just before serving.

NOTE: For an added touch, stir 1 cup chocolate mini-morsels into the batter.

FILLING:
Combine confectioners' sugar, cocoa, salt and heavy cream and chill for 2 hours. Then, add 1 tsp. vanilla and whip until cream mix forms stiff peaks. Mound each cupcake cavity with the cream mix. Decorate with cake "wings" and refrigerate. Dust with confectioners' sugar when ready to serve. (Add ½ cup chocolate mini-morsels to the filling, if desired.) Makes 6-7 large "butterflies".

Fall -Winter

"We Don't Hire Skinny Cooks at This Restaurant."

*M*y college pals and I enjoyed the scores of restaurants in Manhattan - town. Before we'd confirm our decision: where to eat before the show, we'd "window shop", and read the menus taped to the entrance doors. At times, there were notices offering jobs as dishwasher, salad chef and counter clerk. The 5x7-inch pale blue card on the little Italian bistro-type eatery caught my eye:

"We Don't Hire Skinny Cooks AT this Restaurant". Our "gang" was curious; the little sign was absolutely correct!!!!

Dick Scaglione, John and Al Canger, DDS.

Fall -Winter

CORN AND SPINACH CHOWDER
MEATBALLS, SPICY-SWEET
WIDE EGG NOODLES IN BUTTER
SOUTHWESTERN FRUIT CAKE

CORN AND SPINACH CHOWDER
(May be prepared several days in advance.)

2 cans (1 lb. each) corn kernels

2 leeks, trimmed, finely sliced

1 lg. onion, finely chopped

1 tbsp. olive oil

1 lg. potato, peeled, diced

2 carrots, pared, chopped

8 cups water

1 can (13 oz.) evaporated milk (fat-free available)

1 tsp. ground nutmeg

1 tsp. ground ginger

2 cups baby spinach leaves, rinsed, trimmed

$\frac{1}{2}$ tsp. salt

$\frac{1}{2}$ tsp. pepper

Heat oil in a large 4-quart soup pot with cover. Add onion and leeks and cook for 3-4 minutes, until vegetables are tender. Add water, carrots, potato, salt and pepper. Bring to a boil and stir in corn kernels.

Reduce heat, cover and simmer for 25 minutes. During last 5 minutes, stir in spinach. Remove pot from heat and allow soup to cool a little.

Transfer half of it to a food processor and purée until smooth. Return puréed soup to a pot; add milk and stir to blend. Season with salt, pepper, nutmeg and ginger. Simmer over low heat for a few minutes. Taste and adjust seasoning, if needed. Serves 8.

MEATBALLS, SPICY-SWEET
(May be prepared in advance.)

½ lb. ground pork

½ lb. ground beef

½ lb. ground veal

1 cup cooked white rice

1 egg, beaten or ¼ cup egg substitute

1 lg. onion, finely chopped

3 tbsp. chopped white raisins

1 tsp. ground cumin

½ tsp. cinnamon

olive oil to grease non-stick skillet

SAUCE:

1 lg. can (1 lb.) crushed tomatoes

1 tbsp. dark brown sugar

2 tbsp. cider vinegar

1 sm. can beef consommé (low-salt variety)

1 tbsp. chili powder

1 tbsp. Hungarian paprika

1 tbsp. each: chopped cilantro, chopped mint

1 tbsp. olive oil

salt, pepper to taste

3 sweet potatoes, peeled, cut into bite-size chunks

Wide Egg Noodles (12 oz.), in butter. Cook as directed on package.

In a large mixing bowl, combine ground meat, cooked rice, onion, raisins, cumin, cinnamon and egg. Mix thoroughly with hands. Form into 2-inch meatballs.

Sauté meatballs in a large, moderately hot, non-stick skillet which has been coated with olive oil. Cook the meatballs on all sides, 8-10 at a time, removing them to a storing bowl as they are cooked.

In the same skillet (if it is large enough – or use a clean skillet which you've coated with olive oil), cook the sweet potato chunks until tender. Avoid having sweet potatoes stick to the bottom of the skillet by constantly moving them with a thin-edged spatula.

In a bowl, blend all of the sauce ingredients, and pour the sauce over sweet potatoes in the skillet. Add meatballs, and gently combine the mix thoroughly. Cover skillet and simmer for 8-10 minutes until the meatballs are heated through. Serve in individual bowls, over wide egg noodles in butter. Serves 6.

SOUTHWESTERN FRUIT CAKE
(Prepare in advance.)

⅓ cup butter or Smart Balance spread, softened
½ cup sugar
1 egg, beaten, or ½ cup egg substitute
⅔ cup sifted flour
1½ tsp. baking powder
⅓ cup fine cornmeal

1 cup dried apricots, chopped
½ cup dried pitted prunes, chopped
½ cup white raisins
½ cup chopped almonds, with skin
grated rind of 1 lemon
juice of 1 lemon, strained
2 tbsp. low-fat milk

Preheat oven to 350°.

Grease one 5x7x4-inch loaf pan. Line base of pan with oiled brown paper. In a large bowl, cream butter and sugar until light and fluffy. Beat in egg. Gently fold the sifted flour, baking powder and cornmeal into the egg mixture, until thoroughly blended. Stir and blend in, all of the dried fruits and nuts. Add lemon rind and juice and milk. Spoon the batter into the prepared pan. Bake loaf in the center of the preheated oven at 350° for 1 hour, or until an inserted toothpick removes clean. Serves 6-8.

Fall -Winter

A Husband's Advice

*W*hen I was in my early 30's, I had decided I would write **MENU LOG**. *The recipes were arranged into seasonal menus. My collection of creatively planned menus was growing rapidly and within ten years our relatives and friends had developed into an inspirational fan club for this Cook. My husband was the in-house gourmet and critic.*

We would occasionally dine at highly-esteemed restaurants. "You could cook that," he'd suggest. Which translated into my experimenting with foods, tastes and techniques until he'd declare – "You've got it!" or "Even better than we ate at Chez Cuisine!!!"

I sensed that I was anticipating his criticisms – waiting for them in fevered anticipation......until one day.

"Honey", he said, "you've really come up with some pretty appealing menus. **MENU LOG** *is going to be a very inviting cookbook! But – there's just one thing."*

I gave him my full attention. "You've got to include a gimmick to sell the book." "A gimmick?", I queried. "Yeah", he continued, "You've gotta include _ some sex in this cookbook. Yeah, that's it _ sex!"

For almost 50 years, Marion fed John a lot more than cake.
Photo by: Bachrach

Fall-Winter

CREAM OF BROCCOLI SOUP
VEAL SALTIMBOCCA (heirloom)
RISOTTO MILANESE (heirloom)
RICE BALLS (ARANCINE) (heirloom)
PIGNOLA COOKIES

CREAM OF BROCCOLI SOUP

$1\frac{1}{2}$ lbs. fresh broccoli, washed, divided into small florets (finely chop the stems)

1 lg. onion, finely chopped

1 carrot, pared, finely chopped

6 cups water

1 can (13 oz.) evaporated milk (fat-free available)

2 tbsp. olive oil

8-oz. pkg. low-fat cream cheese, cut into small chunks

1 tsp. nutmeg

1 bay leaf

$\frac{1}{2}$ tsp. salt

$\frac{1}{2}$ tsp. black pepper

$\frac{1}{4}$ tsp. cayenne pepper

Heat oil in a 4-quart soup pot; add onion, carrot and broccoli stems. Cook for 3-4 minutes, stirring frequently, until vegetables are softened. Add florets and continue to cook, covered, for 20 minutes, until broccoli is tender. Stir in milk and cream cheese chunks. Season soup with nutmeg, bay leaf, salt, black and cayenne peppers. Stir and continue to simmer over low heat for 5 minutes, stirring frequently. Taste and adjust seasoning, if needed. Discard bay leaf. Serve with croutons. Serves 6.

VEAL SALTIMBOCCA

(Literal translation: jump into the mouth. As in: "Oh my-All of the veal rolls are gone; they simply jumped into my mouth!")

6-10 veal cutlets (shoulder cut),
   about 3x6-inches,
   pounded to $\frac{1}{8}$-inch thick (*NOTE:)
6-10 slices shaved prosciutto
1 lb. mozzarella in water; cut into 6-10 slices
$\frac{1}{2}$ cup Parmesan cheese, grated

$\frac{1}{2}$ cup chopped Italian parsley
$\frac{1}{4}$ cup olive oil
$\frac{1}{4}$ cup white wine
salt, freshly ground black pepper to taste
6-10 small metal skewers

Lay pounded cutlets on a cutting board; cover each cutlet with 1 slice prosciutto, Parmesan cheese, slice of mozzarella and chopped parsley.

Roll up each stuffed cutlet, vertically and secure each with a metal skewer. Remember to remove skewers before serving time.

Heat olive oil in a large skillet; cook veal rolls in oil for 4-5 minutes, or until lightly browned. Remove veal from pan to a plate.

Add wine, salt and pepper to skillet and simmer for 2 minutes, scraping bottom of pan. Return veal rolls to skillet and simmer in sauce for an additional 2-3 minutes. Spoon sauce over veal to serve (and watch them "jump into your mouth"). Serves 6-10.

*NOTE: Thin, pounded chicken cutlets may be substituted for veal cutlets.

Banshee with prizes.

RISOTTO MILANESE

(Saffron is a very expensive flavoring, the stigmas of certain fall crocuses. I grow my own saffron crocuses and annually gather the stigmas in the fall and save them in a tiny tin box in my pantry.)

2 tbsp. olive oil

1 yellow onion, finely chopped

1½ cups Arborio rice

about 1 dozen strands saffron

3 cups chicken stock (or use canned,
   low-salt variety) (*NOTE:)

1 cup white wine

6-8 sun-dried tomatoes, cut into strips

6 oz. frozen peas, defrosted

2-3 slices prosciutto, shredded

½ cup grated Romano cheese

¼ cup Romano cheese at serving

pepper, salt, to taste

NOTE: Prepare chicken stock by simmering 2 skinless chicken legs and 2 wings in 3-4 cups boiling water for 45 minutes. Remove chicken meat from bones. Discard bones and add chicken in small chunks to risotto (or save chicken meat for a salad).

Heat oil in a large, deep skillet, about 300°. Lightly cook onion for 2-3 minutes, until softened. Stir in rice and saffron, coating rice in oil and cook for 1 minute. Add stock and wine, a ladle at a time, into the rice mix, stirring and making sure all of the liquid is absorbed before adding the next portion of liquid.

About halfway through, stir in tomatoes. When all of the liquid is incorporated, the rice should be cooked, about 20 minutes. If rice is still crisp, add a little more water and continue to cook a few minutes longer.

Stir in peas, prosciutto, cheese, salt and pepper. Cook 2-3 minutes, stirring until peas are cooked. Turn into serving bowl; sprinkle with more cheese over bowl. Serve hot. Serves 6.

ARANCINE (RICE BALLS)

(An old Sicilian favorite, satisfying and fragrantly delicious – gets its name because it resembles a large orange. Prepare early in the day, or, on day before and warm thoroughly in slow oven before serving.)

2 cups cooked white rice

2 eggs, beaten or egg substitute

$\frac{1}{2}$ cup unseasoned bread crumbs

$\frac{1}{2}$ cup cooked chopped beef

$\frac{1}{4}$ cup cooked peas

1 tsp. onion powder

1 tbsp. chopped parsley

$\frac{1}{4}$ tsp. black pepper

$\frac{1}{2}$ tsp. salt

3-4 drops Tabasco

1 tsp. Worcestershire sauce

fine crumbs for coating

Hungarian paprika

oil for frying

Preheat oil in skillet to 320°.

In a large mixing bowl, combine: cooked rice, beaten eggs, crumbs, salt, pepper, meat, peas, onion powder, parsley, Worcestershire sauce and Tabasco. On a sheet of waxed paper, spread some fine unseasoned crumbs (about 1 cup) and coat crumbs with Hungarian paprika. Form 6 tennis-size balls of the rice mix with your hands, packing them tightly (wet your hands repeatedly). Gently coat rice balls with the crumb-paprika mix. Fry arancine in hot oil in skillet, 3 balls at a time and turn them every 2 minutes to brown all over. Use a spatula and large spoon to turn balls. Transfer to oven-proof serving platter. Serve hot.

PIGNOLA COOKIES
(Prepare a few days in advance. Store in airtight tin.)

1 roll (7 oz.) almond paste

$\frac{3}{4}$ cup granulated sugar

egg white from 1 lg. egg, beaten

1 tbsp. flour

$\frac{1}{2}$ cup pignola (pine nuts) spread on waxed paper

Preheat oven 325°.

Break up paste into little pieces and place into a bowl. Blend with sugar; add beaten egg white and stir until smooth and thickened. Stir in flour. Roll 1 teaspoon of dough between your fingers for each cookie; then roll the ball in the pine nuts.

Set 15 balls on a greased and floured cookie sheet. Bake them in preheated oven, 325° about 12-15 minutes, until lightly golden. Cool thoroughly before carefully removing cookies with a thin spatula. Makes about 15 cookies.

Fall -Winter

"Good News"

Every time I've cooked a meal for someone, I've gained a friend. That's one of the reasons I have written cookbooks. All of those recipes are my written word, the "gospel truth", "little loving messages" straight to the heart via the taste buds.

One of these friends is Father Jim Vlaun, President/C.E.O. of TelecareTV, Diocese of Rockville Centre, Long Island. (Recently honored with the title of "Monsignor.")

He happens to be one of those children of God, a lovable person who, in turn, loves everyone. He has allowed this old cook "to stir her sauce pot", "garnish with basil leaves", "whip into stiff peaks" as a guest on "Good News with Fr. Jim" many times. Thank you, thank you. The least this old cook can do, is to keep on cookin'.

Fall -Winter

TART AND SPICY ZUCCHINI SOUP
POLENTA WITH SHRIMP AND SAUSAGE (heirloom)
ONE HUNDRED VEGETABLES
LUCY CHRISTOPHER'S TARALLI AND HONEY BALLS (heirloom)
TARALLI (MARION CELENZA'S FAMILY RECIPE) (heirloom)

TART AND SPICY ZUCCHINI SOUP

6 cups chicken broth
   (or use packaged less-salt variety)
   (*NOTE: below)

2 tbsp. olive oil

6 garlic cloves, minced

1 large yellow onion, chopped

$\frac{1}{4}$ cup sun-dried tomatoes, soaked in
   1 cup hot water, drain (save tomato water)

1 tsp. chili powder

$\frac{1}{2}$ tsp. ground cumin

salt, pepper to taste (do not add salt if you have
   used packaged chicken broth)

1 tbsp. dried oregano

2-3 medium-size, slender zucchini, scrape the skin,
   and slice into $\frac{1}{4}$-inch rounds

$\frac{1}{4}$ cup long-grain rice

2 limes, washed, sliced into narrow rounds
   with skin

fresh oregano for garnish, if available
   (or, a sprinkling of dried oregano)

*NOTE: Prepare chicken broth by simmering 2 skinless chicken legs and 2 wings into 6 cups boiling water (for this recipe). Cover pot and simmer chicken for 45 minutes. Remove bones from the chicken. Discard bones. You may add chicken, cut into small pieces, into this soup; or reserve the meat for a salad.

In a 4-quart soup pot, cook the garlic and onion in hot oil until tender and lightly browned. Drain tomatoes; save water and add to broth. Add zucchini slices and sun-dried tomatoes and sauté for 1-2 minutes. Pour in 6 cups chicken broth and tomato water. Cover and bring to a slow boil. Stir in rice, salt, pepper, chili powder, cumin and oregano. Cover pot and cook soup for 20-25 minutes, until rice and zucchini are tender. Serve in bowls, over slices of lime. Garnish with sprigs of fresh oregano. Serves 4-6.

POLENTA WITH SHRIMP AND SAUSAGE

(Polenta may be started on day before; follow directions in recipe.)

8 links chorizo sausages

1 lb. extra large shrimp, peeled, cleaned

2 lg. onions, finely sliced

6 garlic cloves, minced

1 red bell pepper, seeded, finely sliced

1 green bell pepper, seeded, finely sliced

1 chile pepper, seeded, chopped
  (wear plastic gloves)

2 cups prepared tomato sauce

¼ cup dry white wine

1 tsp. saffron threads

½ cup water

1 tsp. dried thyme

1 bay leaf

2 tbsp. olive oil

POLENTA:

6 cups water

¼ cup olive oil

1 tsp. salt

½ tsp. freshly ground black pepper

1½ cups yellow cornmeal

½ cup grated Parmesan cheese

In a heavy 4-qt. pot, bring water to a boil with the oil and salt. Add cornmeal in a slow stream, whisking vigorously to avoid forming lumps; simmer polenta, stirring constantly for 30 minutes. (The polenta may spatter.)

Remove pot from heat, stir in cheese and black pepper and pour the mix into a 9x15-inch greased (olive oil) baking pan. Evenly smoothen the surface of the polenta. Allow the polenta to cool, covered, in the refrigerator, for at least 2 hours. (You may prepare it up to this point on the day before.)

On the day, in a large heavy skillet, brown sausage in hot oil. Transfer to platter. In same skillet, brown onion, garlic and peppers, stirring, for 2 minutes. Add tomato sauce, water, wine and saffron, stirring; bring to a boil. Lower heat; add herbs and simmer for 20 minutes. Add more water or wine if sauce becomes too thick. Stir in peeled shrimp during last 5 minutes. Return and stir in the sausage to skillet with rest of ingredients; keep the sauce warm.

Just before serving, grease a clean skillet with olive oil. Cut the cold polenta into 6 squares; at moderate-high heat, sauté the polenta squares for 2-3 minutes on both sides. With a thin spatula, transfer polenta squares to individual plates; spoon the warm stew over the squares. Serves 6.

ONE HUNDRED VEGETABLES

2 cups broccoli florets, trimmed, washed

1 cup white mushroom caps, sliced

1 orange pepper, seeded, thinly sliced

1 red onion, thinly sliced

4 garlic cloves, chopped

1 large fennel bulb, trimmed,
    thinly sliced into rounds

2 cups snow peas, trimmed

2 small zucchini, scrubbed, scraped,
    cut into narrow rounds

1 tbsp. grated gingerroot

2 tbsp. peanut oil

½ cup water

2 tbsp. *lite* soy sauce

2 tsp. brown sugar

Heat peanut oil in wok or skillet to moderate-high, 320°. Stir-fry onion and garlic and gingerroot for 30 seconds. Add broccoli and cook for 2 minutes. Stir in pepper, mushrooms, fennel, zucchini and snow peas and cook for 1-2 minutes. Meanwhile, stir soy sauce and sugar into ½ cup water. Pour this liquid mix into vegetables; lower heat to simmer, tossing vegetables and coating them with the broth. Remove wok from heat. Serve immediately. Serves 4-6.

LUCY CHRISTOPHER'S TARALLI AND HONEY BALLS

(With notes and comments by her granddaughter, Alisa Rietschlin Kahane)

a 5 lb. sack of flour

10 large eggs

1 tbsp. shortening, like Crisco

1 tbsp. vanilla

$\frac{1}{2}$ cup sugar

1 tsp. baking powder

THESE INGREDIENTS PROVIDE ENOUGH DOUGH FOR: TARALLI AND HONEY BALLS

NOTE: *The following original recipe instructions describe Lucy Christopher's "handed down" method of preparing the Taralli-Honey Balls dough. For many years, I have "cheated" and have used a Kitchen Aid mixer _ no more cone-shaped flour bowls and no more endless kneading. – A.R.K.*

Pour flour into a large conical mound on a wood kneading board. Form a well in the center of the mound of flour, the shape of a volcano, into which you will place the liquid ingredients. Break the eggs into the center of this well. You will be using the mound of flour as THE BOWL.

With one hand, gently mix the eggs, avoiding the side walls of flour. Add shortening into the eggs and continue to blend the egg-shortening mix without disturbing the flour. Finally, add baking powder, vanilla and sugar into the well; with one hand make a blend of the liquids.

After all of the liquids are well-blended, with your hand gently begin to gather small amounts of flour into the egg mixture. Now, you may wish to use both hands, working the flour into the dough, equally, around the cone's center, to avoid spilling the liquid egg mixture out of the cone.

When all of the flour has been blended into the egg mixture, you should have a heavy, but moist dough. Knead the mix with your hands to form a smooth, elastic dough, about 10-15 minutes.

Form a large round loaf. Cover the loaf with a clean linen towel and allow the loaf to stand for 15-30 minutes.

Cut the round dough loaf into 6 sections; keep the unused portion of dough covered with the towel as you work on each portion. USE HALF OF THE DOUGH FOR TARALLI; THE OTHER HALF FOR HONEY BALLS.

Cut each section of dough into strips; roll each strip between your hands to form a long rope, $\frac{1}{2}$-inch thick. (Continued on following page)

(Continued from page 72)

FOR TARALLI:

Cut the ropes into 6-inch segments; form each segment into a ring (circle), pinching the ends to meet; seal the ends by pinching them together. Place the rings on ungreased, floured cookie sheets. Bake the Taralli in a preheated oven at 325° until light brown on the bottom, about 15 minutes. Then, turn them over, and bake the other side for another 5-10 minutes.

Cool the Taralli on wire racks. Store them in an airtight container up to 1 month.

FOR HONEY BALLS:

Roll the dough ropes thinner, about ⅜-inch thick. Cut the ropes into small pieces, ⅜-inch wide. Pour enough canola oil into a large deep fry pan or deep fryer to cover the honey balls. When the oil is heated to about 425°, deep fry the balls, a handful at a time, until they are deep golden color.

Remove the Honey Balls with a large slotted spoon or spatula. Place them to drain on paper towels. Heat 4 cups honey mixed with 1 cup granulated sugar in a large skillet, stirring the mix until the sugar dissolves fully and the mixture begins to boil. Add dough balls to the honey mixture. Coat them fully. Spoon them into storing (or serving) dishes; pour extra honey mix over the balls. Garnish with nonpareils and dried fruit. Cool the Honey Balls thoroughly before covering. Store in an airtight container up to 1 month.

NOTE: *My Grandmother wouldn't dare fry the tiny pieces of dough until she had hand-rolled each and every piece into a perfect ball. I gave up on that long ago; therefore, our "honey balls" resemble "honey cubes", but the taste is just the same. — A.R.K.*

TARALLI

(Alisa Kahane's "modern version" of her Grandmother Lucy's Taralli.)

Use a heavy-duty stationary mixer.

$5\frac{1}{2}$-6 cups flour

8 eggs

$\frac{1}{2}$ cup granulated sugar

1 tbsp. vanilla

2 tbsp. baking powder

2 tbsp. (heaping) Crisco

Mix eggs, sugar, vanilla, baking powder and Crisco in mixer at speed #6, with flat blade until well blended.

Gradually, add $5\frac{1}{2}$-6 cups flour, with dough hook on speed #4, until dough is thoroughly mixed, and a soft dough forms. Knead dough with dough hook on speed #2, until smooth and elastic.

PROCEED WITH THIS RECIPE AS IN THE ORIGINAL HEIRLOOM RECIPE.
(SEE BOTTOM OF PAGE 72, WHICH STATES: Form a large, round loaf. Etc.)

Four generations of women: Lucy Christopher's family.
Photo-courtesy of A.R. Kahane.

TARALLI
(Another version of this popular Italian treat.)

4 cups flour
scant ½ cup sugar
½ cup dry white wine
¼ tsp. salt
2 tbsp. olive oil
1 tbsp. anise seeds (optional)

ICING:
1 cup confectioners' sugar
2 tbsp. anisette

Combine flour, sugar, wine, salt and oil. (At another time, at this point, you may wish to add anise seeds to this dough.) Mix thoroughly to form a smooth dough. If necessary, to soften dough, add 1 or 2 more tablespoons of wine. Place dough on a floured board. Divide dough into 6 parts. Cover rest of dough with waxed paper while you work with each section.

Roll each section of dough on the board or between your hands, to form a tube, the thickness of a narrow sausage. Cut the sausage into 6-inch lengths and curl them into doughnut-shaped rings.

Boil 1-quart of water in a 3-quart pot. Drop the dough rings, a few at a time, into the boiling water and cook them for several seconds. (This process will create a shiny surface on the Taralli.) When they rise to the top, remove them with a slotted spoon and drain them on paper towels; allow them to rest for 1 hour.

Preheat oven to 450°.

Place them on baking sheet and bake the Taralli for 20-25 minutes in the center of a preheated oven at 450°, until light golden brown.

Prepare the icing by blending the confectioners' sugar and anisette; spread a little icing on each slightly warm Taralli with a flat knife or a pastry brush. Makes about 4 dozen Taralli. Store in airtight containers; or freeze them before icing.

Fall -Winter

Dinner Parties to Remember

*W*hen John turned 50, fifty-seven family members and friends surprised him with a memorable in-home birthday feast. For a couple of months, prior to this grand occasion, I had busily and secretly organized, prepared and cooked, the "gourmet-extravaganza".

His closest buddy and our son had managed to entice him to commit to a rainy day on the links. Several other close relatives helped to set up rented chairs and tables to accommodate our guests. Our home is only modestly large, but we managed to serve our buffet meal, exclusively from the dining room table and credenza counter. Our kitchen table acted as the "Drinks Bar".

The Buffet included hot and cold appetizers: eggplant rollatini, cheeses and breads, sausage, shrimp and hot dog wraps and deviled eggs. The dinner entrées included: seafood-stuffed flounder fillets, batter-fried colossal shrimp, veal cordon bleu, potato croquettes, ziti al forno, vegetables au gratin and a couple of greens salads (containing home-grown tomatoes, kirbys, mesclun and peppers).

Dessert had taken up an entire shelf in my large upright freezer: a home-made assembled ice cream cake, complete with candles; plus dozens of holiday cookies which I had frozen from the previous Christmas.

Because we are a family who has always given thanks to a Supreme Being, it would have been an oversight not to mention that one of our friends, a clergyman, gathered our inter-faith group around the grand piano (our "altar") for the celebration of a Mass of Thanksgiving.

A Party to remember!

(*The recipes served at this party may be found in* **MENU LOG: A Collection of Recipes as Coordinated Menus** *by Marion O. Celenza.*)

John's "50th". That's John's favorite Aunt Lettie Mandola, seated.

Fall -Winter

VEAL AND MUSHROOM SOUP

VEAL SCHNITZEL WITH ARUGULA AND SPINACH

HONEY MUSTARD DRESSING

GERMAN POTATO SALAD

BREAD PUDDING

VEAL AND MUSHROOM SOUP
(May be prepared in advance.)

1 lb. boneless veal, cut into small chunks

1 onion, chopped

3-4 garlic cloves, minced

2 tbsp. olive oil

2 carrots, pared, shredded

1 doz. small white mushrooms, halved or quartered

1 celery stalk, trimmed, chopped

1 small green bell pepper, seeded, chopped

rind of 1 lemon, minced

juice of 1 lemon

1 bay leaf

2 tbsp. chopped parsley

5 cups water

$\frac{1}{2}$ cup sweet vermouth

1 tsp. salt

$\frac{1}{2}$ tsp. black pepper

1 tsp. nutmeg

$\frac{1}{4}$ cup cornstarch, 1 cup cold water

1 cup evaporated milk, fat-free available

Heat oil in 4-quart pot with lid. Add onion, garlic, pepper and veal; cook on moderate high, tossing meat and vegetables with spatula for 3-4 minutes until veal is lightly browned. Pour in 5 cups of water; stir in carrots, mushrooms, celery, lemon juice and rind of lemon, parsley, salt, pepper, bay leaf and nutmeg. Cover pot; raise heat and simmer for 20-25 minutes. In a small bowl, stir cornstarch into 1 cup of cold water; stir in milk. Pour slowly and stir liquid mix into veal stew as it cooks. Simmer covered for 10 minutes. Blend wine into soup; remove and discard bay leaf before serving. Serves 6-8.

VEAL SCHNITZEL WITH ARUGULA AND SPINACH

six 1-inch thick veal rib chops, trimmed

1 cup flour, seasoned with salt and black pepper

2 eggs, beaten or $\frac{1}{2}$ cup egg substitute

$\frac{1}{2}$ cup fine bread crumbs, unseasoned

2 tbsp. olive oil

2-3 garlic cloves, minced

lemon wedges for garnish

2 cups baby spinach, washed, drained

2 cups arugula, washed, drained

3 Italian plum tomatoes, sliced into rounds

1 carrot, pared, shredded

1 cup herb-seasoned croutons

Honey Mustard Dressing (see page 384)

Prepare the salad dressing. Set aside. Refrigerate if not using within a couple of hours. Pour the prepared greens into a large salad bowl; add tomatoes, shredded carrot and croutons. Toss to mix. Refrigerate salad without dressing while you prepare veal.

Prepare the veal. Pound the meat between sheets of waxed paper to flatten slightly. Place crumbs on a sheet of waxed paper. Place flour seasoned with salt and pepper on a flat dish. Pour eggs in bowl and dredge the chops in seasoned flour; dip them in beaten eggs; coat them in crumbs.

Heat oil in large skillet; cook the garlic in the oil over moderate high heat, stirring, until golden. Add chops and sauté for 4 minutes, turning them over once, until they are golden. Transfer them to paper towels to drain. Lay them on individual platters, one chop per serving; remove salad from refrigerator. Drizzle Honey Mustard Dressing over the salad and toss to mix. Serve with Veal Schnitzel. Garnish veal with lemon wedges. Serves 6.

GERMAN POTATO SALAD

6 medium-size Red Bliss potatoes, cut into
   small chunks, simmered in a covered pot
   for about 8-10 minutes

3-4 slices lean bacon, cooked, drained, crumbled

$\frac{1}{4}$ cup chopped parsley

2 tbsp. fresh chopped dill or 1 tsp. dried dill

2-3 scallions, trimmed, chopped (include greens)

1 celery stalk, chopped

$\frac{1}{2}$ cup beef broth (mash 1 beef bouillon cube
   in $\frac{1}{2}$ cup boiling water)

$\frac{1}{4}$ cup cider vinegar

1 tbsp. Worcestershire sauce

$1\frac{1}{2}$ tbsp. brown sugar

1 tbsp. mustard spread

$\frac{1}{4}$ tsp. salt

$\frac{1}{2}$ tsp. freshly ground pepper

Hungarian paprika for garnish

Drain potatoes; briefly, run cool water over them and drain them again. Place potatoes in a large bowl. In a small bowl, blend parsley, dill, scallions, sugar, celery, vinegar, broth, Worcestershire sauce, mustard, salt and pepper. Stir in crumbled bacon. Pour over warm potatoes; toss to mix thoroughly. Transfer into serving bowl; sprinkle with paprika. Serve warm. Serves 6.

BREAD PUDDING

1-2 tbsp. sweet butter or Smart Balance spread

4 Granny Smith apples, peeled, cored, sliced into thin rings

1 cup brown sugar

1 tbsp. ground cinnamon

$\frac{1}{4}$ cup sweet white wine

6 slices white bread, cut off crusts (save to stale for crumbs)

1 can (13$\frac{1}{2}$ oz.) evaporated milk, fat-free available

3 eggs, beaten or $\frac{3}{4}$ cup egg substitute

$\frac{1}{2}$ cup white raisins, soaked for $\frac{1}{2}$ hour in 2 tbsp. rum

rind of 1 orange

Preheat oven 350°.

Grease a 9x15-inch oven-proof glass casserole dish with butter. Arrange apple rings over bottom of dish. Sprinkle $\frac{1}{2}$ cup (half) brown sugar and $\frac{1}{2}$ tablespoon cinnamon over apples. Pour wine over apple slices; add and layer bread slices, pressing them down with your hands to flatten.

Beat together: evaporated milk and eggs, remaining brown sugar/cinnamon, orange rind and rum-soaked raisins; pour this mixture over the bread. Allow the casserole of bread to soak for 30 minutes in refrigerator. Bake in preheated oven, 350° for 25-30 minutes until golden and set. Serve warm. Serves 6.

John's "65th". (John with Marion, Lena Zukowski and Kay Harms.)

Fall - Winter

Cooking for Your Mother-In-Law

*N*ot long into the marriage, I quickly was introduced to a most challenging contest: new promising cook vs. "no holds barred", "who're you kidding?", "one hand tied behind my back", "intimidating matriarch chef".

My mother-in-law assured all of us she was a classical artist at the stove. Yeah, sure. But why did her husband empty a bowl of unfulfilled escargots over the dear lady's head, in a fit of pique?

When her first-born proudly informed his mother of his new wife's culinary prowess and boasted the caption: "And she's writing her recipes in a cookbook!!", dear mother-in-law, left hand on hip, right eyebrow arched, sneered, as her right index digit marked time against her temple: "Hmph!! I've got 300 recipes – ALL-IN-HERE!!"

A few thousand bake-offs later, at my dining room table, she took great pleasure to point out to everyone present: two obviously unopened mussels, protruding from her husband's bowl of "Mussels in White Wine Sauce". I think my eyes rolled back into my head. The message was clearly delivered.

Nevertheless, he kindly and respectfully refused the gauntlet. Thank the Lord!

Frances and Silvio Celenza.

Fall -Winter

TUNA CURRY CHOWDER
MUSSELS IN BEER
SEAFOOD ROAST
DOUBLE CHOCOLATE FUDGE SHEET CAKE

TUNA CURRY CHOWDER
(May be prepared in advance.)

1 lg. onion, chopped

6 garlic cloves, chopped

1 carrot, pared, chopped

2 tbsp. olive oil

6 cups water

2 cans (7 oz. each) flaked tuna

1 lb. can Italian plum tomatoes in juice, mashed

$\frac{1}{2}$ cup white rice

1 tbsp. curry powder

1 tsp. coriander

1 tbsp. chopped fresh parsley

1 tsp. salt

$\frac{1}{2}$ tsp. black pepper

$\frac{1}{2}$ pt. sour cream, fat-free available

Heat oil in 4-quart pot with lid. Cook onion and garlic at moderate-high until tender, scraping the bottom of the pot to loosen vegetable particles. Pour in and blend 6 cups water, tomatoes, carrots, herbs and spices. Cover pot and bring to a boil. Lower heat and simmer for 15-20 minutes. Stir in rice; cover and continue to simmer for 20-25 minutes until rice is tender. Stir in tuna during the last 5 minutes. Decant 2 cups broth only, and stir sour cream into the broth until smooth. Return creamed broth to the pot as the soup continues to simmer. Blend the soup thoroughly. Serves 6.

Cousin Ralph Mazza prepping a favorite seafood dish.
Photo-courtesy of Mazza Family

MUSSELS IN BEER

4 lbs. fresh mussels

1 pt. beer

1 lg. onion, chopped

6 garlic cloves, chopped

1 chile pepper, seeded, finely chopped (wear plastic
  gloves when working with hot pepper)

1 cup ripe tomatoes, diced

$\frac{1}{4}$ cup chopped cilantro

1 bay leaf

Remove and discard any mussels which do not close when sharply tapped with a knife. Scrub mussels under cold running water; cut away any remnant "beards" from the shells.

In a heavy-duty pan with cover, pour tomatoes, onion, garlic, bay leaf, pepper and beer. Bring to a boil. Add mussels; cover and cook at medium-high heat for about 8-10 minutes, or until mussels open. Discard any mussels which do not open. Remove and discard bay leaf. Ladle mussels into individual bowls; sprinkle with cilantro. Pepper frizelles make a tasty accompaniment. Serves 4-6. (Do not save leftovers.)

SEAFOOD ROAST

10-12 small Red Bliss potatoes, scrubbed, halved

$1\frac{1}{2}$ doz. pearl onions, skinned,
  (halved, if necessary)

6 garlic cloves, chopped

2-3 small-medium zucchini, scrubbed,
  sliced into rounds

$1\frac{1}{2}$ doz. extra large shrimp with
  shell on, uncooked

4 small squid, cleaned, sliced into rings
  (or ready-cleaned and sliced)

6 plum tomatoes, quartered

2 red pimiento peppers, seeded, chopped

2 lemons, quartered into wedges

3-4 sprigs rosemary

$\frac{1}{4}$ cup olive oil

salt, black pepper, cayenne pepper - to taste

Preheat oven to 400°.

Place potatoes in 9x15-inch roasting pan. Mix in: onions, garlic, pimientos, zucchini, lemons and rosemary. Pour oil and seasonings to coat vegetables. Roast vegetables at 400°, uncovered, for about 40 minutes, until potatoes are barely tender. Stir in shrimp, squid, tomatoes, tossing to coat them in the oil. Roast the seafood mix for another 10 minutes. Vegetables should be cooked through and slightly charred. Serve from pan. Serves 6.

DOUBLE CHOCOLATE FUDGE SHEET CAKE
(Prepare a day or two in advance.)

1 cup butter or Smart Balance spread

$\frac{1}{2}$ cup Ghiradelli semisweet chocolate morsels

$\frac{2}{3}$ cup low-fat milk

$2\frac{1}{2}$ cups flour, sifted

2 tsp. baking powder

$1\frac{2}{3}$ cup lt. brown sugar

$\frac{2}{3}$ cup sour cream, available low-fat and fat-free

2 eggs, beaten or $\frac{1}{2}$ cup egg substitute

FROSTING:

8 oz. Ghiradelli semisweet chocolate morsels

3 tbsp. evaporated milk, available fat-free

1 tbsp. butter or Smart Balance spread

Preheat oven 375°.

Grease a 9x12-inch cake pan. In a small saucepan, melt chocolate morsels with butter and milk over low heat, stirring frequently. Sift flour and baking powder into a mixing bowl and stir in sugar. Pour the hot chocolate liquid into the bowl and then beat well until all of the ingredients are thoroughly mixed. Stir in sour cream followed by the beaten eggs. Pour this mix into the prepared pan to bake in center of preheated oven at 375° for 40-45 minutes. Allow the cake to cool thoroughly in pan for several hours.

Then, cut the sheet cake into $4x4\frac{1}{2}$-inch pieces. Run a knife around the inside edge of the pan to loosen cake from sides. Gently, with a spatula, lift sections onto a serving platter, lined with paper doilies.

While the cake is cooling, prepare the frosting. Place chocolate morsels, butter and evaporated milk in top half of small double boiler. Add 1 cup water to bottom half. Turn heat to high and set the water to boil. Then, lower to simmer and melt the chocolate over the hot water, stirring frequently until the frosting is smooth and shiny. Remove frosting from heat. Let stand for a few minutes. Then, spoon a little icing over each cut section of cake. Smoothen with frosting spreader or flat knife. Be neat. Serves 6 generous portions.

Potato Pie, page 16

Chicory, Dandelions and Grapes Salad, page 333

Three Muffins (Cranberry Pecan Muffins, Pumpkin Apple-Cinnamon Muffins, Blueberry Orange Muffins), pages 231-232

Orange Pumpkin Soup, page 215

Cantaloupe Sundae, page 359

Vegetable Mélange, page 152

Lamb Chops in Tomato Prune Sauce, page 143

Soybean and Pepper Salad, page 212

Black Bean and Sausage Chili, page 89

Mandel Bread, page 281

Pecan Pie, page 352

Arugula, Prosciutto and Figs Salad, page 104

Strawberries and Cherries with Chocolate Sauce, page 161

Filet Mignons with Artichokes, page 205

Mashed Sweet Potatoes, page 220   Grilled Asparagus and Apples, page 221
Grilled Honey Ginger Salmon, page 221

Ravioli with Red Pepper Vodka Sauce, page 402

Spring-Summer

Bless the Cook, O Lord; I Need It!

*M*y family has always given thanks for the food we are about to eat. My uncle, Zie Prevete, gave thanks in Neapolitan Italian. As time flies by, and our friendships have grown, many blessings have been bestowed: upon those who gather around the table of plenty; those who would be present if they could; those who are with us in their spirit; upon the victims of world terror and strife; for the newborn, the newly wedded, those about to graduate to higher levels, and the birthday children of all ages. We pray for them, and ask God to grant them blessings.

And, if you raise your prayerful, downcast eyes, just a speck, you will notice: everyone, young and old, sincerely asks for these gifts to be bestowed.

Marion's cookin'.

CREAMED TOMATO SOUP
GLORIA'S STUFFED CABBAGE
RICE (Select a Rice Recipe from this Book)
BLACK AND WHITE DROP COOKIES

CREAMED TOMATO SOUP
(May be prepared a couple of days in advance.)

1 lg. can (20 oz.) plum tomatoes, mashed
6 cups hot water (or packaged less-salt vegetable stock)
    (You may prepare your own vegetable stock by simmering
    1 celery stalk chopped, 1 carrot chopped and 1 seeded, green pepper chopped
    in 3 cups water for 30 minutes; purée vegetables and return them to the stock pot;
    add several or more cups of water.)
1 can (12 oz.) evaporated milk, fat-free available
$\frac{1}{4}$ cup puréed almonds
$\frac{1}{2}$ cup shredded basil leaves (or use mint leaves, if available)
salt, black pepper to taste

Add tomatoes to stock; bring pot to boil; cover pot and simmer soup for 20 minutes. Stir in evaporated milk, almonds, basil, salt and pepper and continue to gently simmer for 15 minutes longer. Stir occasionally. Serves 6. May be frozen in containers.

GLORIA'S STUFFED CABBAGE

1 lg. head green cabbage, remove outer
    leaves, remove as much core as possible,
    while keeping the cabbage whole
1 lb. chopped sirloin
2 cups cooked white rice
$\frac{1}{4}$ cup chopped parsley
1 small onion, finely chopped

$\frac{1}{2}$ tsp. salt
$\frac{1}{4}$ tsp. black pepper
$\frac{1}{4}$ lb. chopped prosciutto
2 cups prepared tomato sauce
$\frac{1}{2}$ cup Parmesan cheese
2 tbsp. olive oil (plus olive oil for
    bottom of casserole)

Preheat oven 350°.

Prepare a 9x15-inch Pyrex casserole by coating the inside with olive oil. Place the cabbage in a large pot with lid. Add enough water to reach half way up the side of the cabbage. Cover pot; bring to a boil and simmer for 30-35 minutes or until a thin metal tester slips easily in and out of the center of the cabbage. Meanwhile, sauté chopped sirloin and onion in olive oil, stirring the mix, to cook evenly. Transfer meat mixture to a large bowl. Add cooked rice, parsley, salt, pepper, prosciutto and mix thoroughly. Set aside.

Do not overcook the cabbage. Drain the cabbage and gently spray cool water over it, for easier handling. Drain cabbage again; lay it on a board. Cut the large leaves off the cabbage and lay them open on the board. Pack about one-quarter cup (or less) of the chopped beef mix on one end of each cabbage leaf. Carefully, roll up the leaves; lay the rolls seam-side down in oiled casserole. You should form about 10-12 rolls.

Pour tomato sauce over the cabbage rolls. Sprinkle them with cheese and cover lightly with a sheet of foil. Bake casserole in preheated oven 350° for 10 minutes; remove foil and continue baking for another 10 minutes, until top crust is lightly golden. Spoon sauce over cabbage rolls. Serve with a side of white rice. (Or, select a rice recipe from this book.) Serves 6.

BLACK AND WHITE DROP COOKIES

1 cup butter or Smart Balance spread, softened

1¾ cups sugar

4 eggs or 1 cup egg substitute

1 cup milk (or fat-free evaporated milk)

1 tsp. vanilla extract

1 tsp. lemon juice

1 tsp. grated lemon peel

2½ cups all-purpose flour

2½ cups cake flour

1 tsp. baking powder

dash of salt

FROSTING:

4 cups confectioners' sugar

½ cup boiling water

1 oz. semisweet chocolate

1 tbsp. fresh lemon juice

Preheat oven 375°.

Grease two 9x15-inch baking sheets. Prepare the drop cookies. In a large bowl, combine sugar and butter. Beat until mix is fluffy. Add eggs, milk, vanilla extract, lemon juice and rind and mix until smooth.

In another bowl combine flours, baking powder and salt and stir to blend. Add the dry ingredients to the butter-egg mix in three portions, mixing thoroughly after each addition. Drop heaping tablespoonfuls of the batter 2 inches apart on the prepared baking sheets. Bake cookies in preheated oven at 375° for 20-30 minutes, until edges begin to brown. Remove from oven and allow cookies to cool completely on the trays.

Meanwhile, prepare the frosting:
Pour confectioners' sugar in a large bowl. Add boiling water, a little at a time, stirring constantly, until frosting mix is thick and easily spread.

Spoon half of the frosting to the top half of a double boiler (1 cup water in bottom half) and set pot to simmer. Add the chocolate. Warm the chocolate frosting mix, stirring until the chocolate is melted and the frosting is creamy. Remove pot from heat. Stir 1 tablespoon of lemon juice into the white frosting.

Frost half of each cookie with chocolate frosting and the other half with white (lemon) sugar frosting. A thin butter knife or a thick pastry brush will help to do the job. Makes about 2 dozen drop cookies.

Spring-Summer

When Is It Ripe?_____ And Other Helpful Hints

I confess ___ I used to store tomatoes in the refrigerator. The farmers in my family told me "never" to house tomatoes in areas cooler then 55-60 degrees. My son, the geneticist, informed me that too cool a temperature cuts off the aroma – creating substances in the tomato.

Photos on this page
by: C. and G. Sinibaldi

Keep corn in its husk to preserve the moisture in the kernels; and eat corn as soon as it is picked. This is okay for my cousins on the farm, but most of us who have no local farm stand should try to use corn as soon as possible after you bring it home from the green grocer. If you can't eat the corn the same day you buy it, wrap the unshucked corn in a wet paper bag; place the bag into a plastic bag and place the plastic bag into the refrigerator. To maintain freshness, trim the bottom ends of asparagus, and store the stalks upright in cool water in the refrigerator; do the same for celery and broccoli.

Believe it or not, most fruits, like apples, bananas, avocado, peaches, pears and plums actually will ripen if you just let them sit in a paper bag on the counter for a couple of days. Refrigerate only when ripened. When dealing with melons (but not cantaloupes) the usual rule to follow is: what you see and SMELL is what you get. Regarding melons, prolonged refrigeration makes for rind decay.

Select slender "young" eggplants, free of bruises and taut of skin. Smaller, slender and firm zucchini and squash are the best.

It is important to wash fruits and vegetables with cool water before eating. However, some produce may spoil faster if you pre-wash it. Even fruits whose skins you're definitely not eating, such as bananas, pineapples, mangoes or melons, should be washed.

Nutritionally speaking, when it comes to fruits and vegetables with edible skin – go for the skin (it's loaded with vitamins!).

The Sansone Farm in Hopewell, New Jersey. Tended by 4 generations of Sansones: Uncle Frank and Aunt Caterina and their children; their children; and their children's children and more.

Spring-Summer

BLACK BEAN AND SAUSAGE CHILI
BATTERED SEAFOOD WITH FRUIT
FRAGRANT RICE
ARLINE'S LEMON SQUARES

BLACK BEAN AND SAUSAGE CHILI
(Start night before.)

1 lb. pkg. dried black beans: rinse,
    then soak the beans overnight
2 tbsp. olive oil
4-6 links pork fennel sausage
    (include 1-2 spicy pork sausages)
1 lg. yellow onion, chopped
1 lg. celery stalk, chopped
1 lg. carrot, pared, chopped
6 garlic cloves, chopped

1 red bell pepper, seeded, diced
6-8 ripe plum tomatoes, diced OR
    (1 lb. canned chopped tomatoes)
½ cup fresh cilantro, chopped
1 tsp. ground cumin
1 tsp. chili powder
salt and pepper to taste
1 cup long grain rice, cooked OR
    (1 cup orzo, cooked)

Drain the beans (which you've soaked overnight). Pour beans into a 2-quart pot with lid; cover with water and bring to a low boil. Cover; lower heat and simmer for 1½ hours until beans are tender, not mushy. Meanwhile, in a large skillet, brown sausage, onion and garlic in hot olive oil on moderate-high about 4-5 minutes. Slice sausage into rounds. Set aside.

When beans are cooked, drain them well, reserving 1 cup of cooking liquid. In the large skillet with the sliced sausages, pour cooked beans, tomatoes, carrot, red pepper, celery, cilantro and all of the seasonings. Stir in the reserved liquid. Cover and simmer chili for 30-35 minutes. Add cooked rice in last 5 minutes. Taste and adjust the seasonings. Serves 6.

BATTERED SEAFOOD WITH FRUIT

12-14 prawns or colossal shrimp, peeled,
    cleaned, leave on tail
12-14 large sea scallops
4-6 medium-size tilapia fillets (or cut
    4 large fillets into 2 portions each fillet)
2 green peppers, seeded, quartered
1 red pepper, seeded, quartered
6 prune plums, pitted, halved
4 peaches, pitted, skin peeled, quartered
    (*NOTE: directions at end of recipe)
1 small can (8 oz.) pineapple chunks (save juice)

SAUCE:
1 tbsp. gingerroot
2 garlic cloves, minced
2 scallions with greens, chopped
2 tbsp. sherry
2 tbsp. lemon juice
2 tsp. sesame oil
1 tbsp. *lite* soy sauce
juice from pineapple
2 tbsp. plum sauce

BATTER:
6 egg whites
    (or use 8 oz. container egg substitute)
4-5 tbsp. cornstarch
2-3 tbsp. flour
canola oil for frying

Clean and drain seafood. In a small bowl, blend all ingredients for the sauce. Set aside.

In a large, low and wide bowl, with electric beater, beat egg whites (or egg substitute) until foamy; fold in cornstarch and flour. Meanwhile heat a couple of inches of canola oil in a large skillet (or use deep fryer). Heat to 340°.

When the skillet is heated, fry the seafood by dipping several pieces at a time into the batter and laying them in the hot oil. Turn each piece, using 2 spatulas and fry the other side; the crust should be pale gold.

Transfer the cooked seafood to drain on paper towels; then, onto a large serving oven-proof platter. Place platter of fish in warming oven.

After all of the seafood is fried, collect all of the oil and residue in the skillet and pour it into a disposable container to discard. Wipe the inside base of the skillet with paper towels and discard the towels.

Grease the bottom of the same skillet with 1 tablespoon canola oil. In a large bowl, pour peppers and fruits. Pour the sauce mix over the peppers and fruits and toss to coat.

Turn up the heat in the skillet to 300° and cook the mix of vegetables, fruits and sauce for 5 minutes, stirring the ingredients in the skillet frequently. Pour this sauce with vegetables and fruit over the warm seafood platter. Serve immediately or keep platter warm, uncovered, in a low oven for a few minutes. Serves 6.

*NOTE: Remove peach skin by resting the whole peach in a bowl of boiling water for 1 minute. Remove peach. Skin should easily peel with your fingers.

FRAGRANT RICE

2 tbsp. olive oil

1 cup long grain rice

1 sm. red bell pepper, seeded, thinly sliced

1 sm. green bell pepper, seeded, thinly sliced

3-4 scallions, thinly sliced, including greens

4 garlic cloves, chopped

1 small onion, chopped

2 tbsp. cumin seeds, crushed

1 tsp. each: dried oregano, chopped fresh basil

2½ cups canned chicken stock, less-salt variety

(salt), pepper to taste

Heat oil in a 2-quart pot with lid. Cook on low heat until tender: onion, garlic, peppers and scallions for about 5 minutes. (Set aside 2-3 tablespoons of raw scallions for garnish.)

Add and thoroughly mix: rice, stock, cumin, oregano, basil and (salt)/pepper. Cover pot and simmer for 20 minutes, until most of liquid is absorbed and rice is tender. Pour into serving bowl; garnish with chopped scallions. Serve hot. Serves 4-6.

ARLINE'S LEMON SQUARES

2 cups flour

½ cup confectioners' sugar

1 cup butter, softened

4 eggs, beaten

2 cups granulated sugar

⅓ cup lemon juice

grated rind of 1 lemon

¼ cup flour

1 tsp. baking powder

additional confectioners' sugar for dusting

Preheat oven 350°.

You will need a 9x13-inch cake pan. Sift flour with confectioners' sugar. Cut in butter until mix clings together. Press this mix into a 9x13-inch pan. Bake in a preheated oven 350° for 20-25 minutes or until lightly browned. Beat together: eggs, granulated sugar, lemon juice and rind.

Sift together: flour and baking powder and stir the flour mix into the egg mixture. Spoon the mix over baked crust. Bake the pastry at 350° for 25 minutes longer. Sprinkle with additional confectioners' sugar. Cool thoroughly; then cut into squares. Yield: about 2 dozen.

Spring-Summer

Our Hostess with the Mostest

*O*ver the years, I have attempted to remain a humble person. It became increasingly difficult to place pride completely in the shadows. Especially when I continued to host one dinner party after another _____ and it has been so much fun!

Nevertheless, just in the nick of Father Time, my daughter-in-law's sister, Paula, has emerged from the kitchen's shadows, has accepted the traditional wooden spoon, and has become, without a doubt, "Our hostess with the mostest". An exceptionally talented "Fine Artist", Paula has also developed into a culinary artist.

From The Table of Plenty includes one of her creative menus.

Fine Artist Paula Shea Barbarotto.
Photo by: J. Barbarotto

Spring-Summer

PAULA'S TOSSED SALAD WITH RICOTTA SALATA

PAULA'S DRESSING

OLD FASHIONED ROAST BEEF WITH GRAVY

MUSHROOMS AU GRATIN

ROASTED RED BLISS POTATOES

STEAMED ASPARAGUS

PAULA'S ALMOND BISCOTTI

A DEVIL OF A CHOCOLATE CAKE

FRESH STRAWBERRIES

PAULA'S TOSSED SALAD WITH RICOTTA SALATA

(Trim, rinse and drain all lettuces; dry in salad spinner.)

2 cups romaine, torn bite-size

2 cups red leaf lettuce, torn bite-size

2 cups arugula

1 cup radicchio, torn bite-size

1 small endive cut into thin rings

$\frac{1}{2}$ cup pitted black olives (if canned olives are used, rinse and drain them)

1 Kirby cucumber, scrubbed, trimmed, sliced

$\frac{1}{4}$ lb. ricotta salata, shaved (use a peeler)

PAULA'S DRESSING:

$\frac{1}{2}$ cup extra-virgin olive oil

$\frac{1}{4}$ cup fresh lemon juice

$\frac{1}{4}$ cup honey

Prepare dressing. Blend honey and lemon juice in a small pot. Gently heat the mix until honey shows thin. Cool and add olive oil. Mix thoroughly. Store unused dressing in refrigerator.

Combine romaine, red leaf, arugula, radicchio and endive in a large salad bowl. Add sliced Kirby and pitted olives. Toss ingredients to mix thoroughly. Drizzle $\frac{1}{2}$ cup dressing over the salad and toss again to mix. Garnish salad with shaved ricotta salata and serve. Serves 6-8.

OLD FASHIONED ROAST BEEF WITH GRAVY

a 5-6 lb. eye round beef roast, at room temperature
garlic powder, black pepper, Kosher salt, to taste
2 large yellow onions, thinly sliced

roasting pan with rack
water for bottom of roasting pan

Preheat oven 475°.

Allow meat to come to room temperature. Season the roast with garlic powder, freshly ground black pepper and Kosher salt to taste.

Place the roast on the rack in the pan, fat side up. Add about $\frac{1}{4}$ inch tap water into the bottom of the pan. Roast the beef in a preheated oven at 475° for 15 minutes. Reduce temperature to 350° and continue to roast the beef at 15 minutes per pound. Add the sliced onions around the roast during the final 30 minutes of cooking time. (Use meat thermometer to test for doneness: 120° internal temperature = rare.)

Remove the pan from the oven and transfer the roast to a carving board to stand for 10-15 minutes before carving. Meanwhile, have ready: 2 tablespoons flour stirred smoothly into $\frac{1}{2}$ cup cool water. Strain the liquid and onions from the pan into a bowl. Return the strained liquid into the same roasting pan and place the roasting pan on stove burner.

Set burner temperature to medium-high. As soon as the beef liquid begins to simmer, lower the heat under the pan and add the floured water, stirring as you pour. Continue to stir and scrape the bottom of the roasting pan as the gravy begins to thicken. You may wish to re-strain the gravy through a wider sieve, as you pour the hot gravy into a gravy bowl. Slice the roast and arrange the slices on a large platter; accompany the roast beef with the hot gravy. Crusty bread or rolls make a nice accompaniment to this hearty party meal. Serves 8 or more.

MUSHROOMS AU GRATIN
(Handed down from Paula's mother-in-law, Rose.)

3 lbs. white mushrooms, trimmed,
    scrubbed, quartered
5-6 slices white bread (or use wheat bread)
4-5 garlic cloves, minced
$\frac{1}{2}$ cup grated Romano cheese

$\frac{1}{3}$ cup fresh parsley, chopped
    (or use dried parsley)
Kosher salt and black pepper to taste
$\frac{1}{4}$ cup olive oil (or a little more)

Preheat oven 350°.

Food process the bread to form crumbs. Par-boil mushrooms for 5 minutes; drain. In a large bowl combine bread crumbs, minced garlic and grated cheese, parsley, salt and pepper.

Form a layer of mushrooms on the bottom of a large baking dish; sprinkle with $\frac{1}{4}$ of the bread crumb mix; drizzle 2 tablespoons olive oil over this mix. Repeat with a layer of mushrooms, another quarter of the crumb mix and a sprinkling of olive oil. Repeat this procedure once or twice more, using all of the ingredients and ending with a sprinkling of olive oil.

Roast mushroom casserole, uncovered, in a preheated oven at 350° for 15-20 minutes or until lightly browned. Serves 8 or more.

ROASTED RED BLISS POTATOES
(You can roast the potatoes and mushrooms simultaneously.)

4 lbs. Red Bliss potatoes, scrubbed,
    quartered or eighth
1 tsp. paprika
1 tsp. garlic powder

$\frac{1}{4}$ cup chopped parsley
$\frac{1}{4}$ tsp. black pepper
salt to taste
$\frac{1}{4}$ cup olive oil

Preheat oven to 350°.

Place potatoes into a large bowl. Blend all of the seasonings in small bowl and sprinkle the mix over the potatoes; drizzle with olive oil and toss together to mix thoroughly. Pour the potato mix into a roasting pan and spread the potatoes to fit evenly in the pan. Roast the potatoes in a preheated oven 350° for 45 minutes. Occasionally, stir the potatoes as they roast. Test potatoes with a fork for tenderness. Serves 8 or more.

STEAMED ASPARAGUS

2 bunches asparagus, trimmed, rinsed and drained
2 garlic cloves, chopped
olive oil (optional), salt

Lay asparagus and chopped garlic in the basket of a steamer pot with cover. Add an inch of water to the pot under the basket. Season with a little salt. Steam the asparagus and garlic for 4-5 minutes until desired tenderness. Remove asparagus to a platter and serve. Drizzle asparagus with a little olive oil (optional). If not serving immediately, place asparagus in a quick ice bath to stop the cooking. Serves 8 or more.

PAULA'S ALMOND BISCOTTI

$2\frac{1}{4}$ cups all-purpose flour
2 tsp. double-acting baking powder
$\frac{1}{2}$ cup granulated sugar
5 tbsp. unsalted margarine

2 eggs
$1\frac{1}{2}$ tsp. grated lemon zest
1 tsp. vanilla extract
1 cup slivered, skinless almonds, freshly chopped

Preheat oven to 350°.

Combine flour and baking powder in a bowl. In a large bowl, with electric mixer at high speed, beat sugar and margarine until light and fluffy. Beat in eggs, lemon zest and vanilla extract. Set mixer to low and gradually add flour mix and almonds. Stir to combine. Do not overbeat.

Divide dough in half. With moistened hands form each half into a $12x1\frac{1}{2}$-inch log. Lay both logs on a nonstick baking sheet. Moisten the surface of a rolling pin and flatten each log to $\frac{1}{2}$-inch thickness. Bake the logs in preheated oven at 350° for 18 minutes, until dough is firm. (Do not turn off oven.)

With the aid of 2 long spatulas, carefully transfer the baked logs to a cutting board. Dip a serrated knife into water before each cut. Cut each log into 12 slices on a diagonal. Lay the slices, cut-side down, on the baking sheet and bake in oven at 350° for 10-12 minutes, until lightly browned.

Remove sheet from oven and completely cool the biscuits on a rack. When thoroughly cooled, store in an airtight container for up to 1 week; or wrap in foil and freeze up to several months. Makes 2 dozen biscotti.

A DEVIL OF A CHOCOLATE CAKE

(Haven't you ever wondered what the difference is between "chocolate cake" and "devil's food cake"? After years of pondering this question, I've come to the conclusion that there is more cocoa and fat in devil's food - it's richer and more "sinful". Then, there's "red devil's food" which adds the fire-red food coloring.)

1 cup unsalted butter, bring to room temperature	2 tsp. baking soda
2¼ cups dark brown sugar, packed	½ tsp. salt
3 oz. unsweetened chocolate	½ cup buttermilk
3 eggs	1 cup boiling water
2¼ cups cake flour	2 tsp. vanilla extract

Preheat oven 375°.

Grease and flour two 9-inch cake pans; set aside. Place chocolate in a small heavy saucepan, melting it over low heat; set aside. In a bowl, cream butter and brown sugar together with an electric mixer. Set the mixer on low speed and add eggs, one at a time, beating well after each addition. Stir in melted chocolate.

Combine cake flour, baking soda and salt. Add the flour mix and buttermilk, alternately, in 3 stages, into the chocolate mixture, ending with the flour. Slowly, stir in boiling water and vanilla. Pour the batter into the 2 prepared pans; bake in center of oven at 375° for 30 minutes, or until inserted toothpick removes clean.

Remove cake pans from oven and allow to cool for 5 minutes. Then, invert pans over wire racks to cool completely. Remove one layer to a serving plate.

Prepare the Chocolate Frosting (see recipe on the following page).

Using a frosting spreader, cover the top of this layer with chocolate icing; place second layer on top and frost the top of this layer; then frost the sides of the cake. Serves 8-10. (This cake may be stored in a cake server and refrigerated. Remove from refrigerator ½ hour before serving.)

CHOCOLATE FROSTING

1½ cups semisweet chocolate morsels
½ cup unsalted butter, at room temperature
⅔ cup milk
1 tsp. vanilla extract
1 cup confectioners' sugar

Combine chocolate morsels and butter, and melt this mix in a 1-quart heavy saucepan over very low heat, stirring occasionally. Remove pot from heat; stir in milk and vanilla; then, spoon this mix into a bowl. Gradually add confectioners' sugar, beating with an electric mixer until smooth and creamy (mixture will be runny). Refrigerate the chocolate frosting for 1 hour, beating occasionally (the frosting will stiffen). Spread frosting on cake as directed in recipe on page 97.

FRESH WHOLE STRAWBERRIES

2 lbs. large strawberries, hulled, washed, drained

Arrange strawberries on a large, flat plate. Serve them at time of dessert. Serves 8 or more.

Spring-Summer

Green, White and Red

*I*talians are very food oriented. Simply, contemplate the colors in their flag: green, white, red. There are several theories regarding the history behind the colors. For example: my Uncle Raphael (a Catholic priest) believed green represented "hope"; white stood for "faith"; and red connoted "charity". I stand behind my family's "historical" interpretation, "both sides of my family, including in-laws."

Green is the GRASS of Italy: basilico-basil

White represents creamy MILK: formaggio-cheese

Red stands for the TOMATO: salsa di pomodori-cooked plum tomato sauce

Check out Pantone®, Inc. I still believe my family speaks the truth!

Spring-Summer

ITALIAN FLAG SALAD
ITALIAN DRESSING
STUFFED SHELLS
VEAL CUTLET PARMAGIANO IN A SAUCE CRUST
VANILLA BEAN ICE CREAM WITH ASSORTED LIQUEURS
CAFFÉ ESPRESSO

ITALIAN FLAG SALAD

Bed of salad greens: select from green leaf, red leaf, romaine, escarole, chicory, endive, arugula - several or all (about 5 cups)

1 cucumber, scrubbed, scraped (do not pare), finely sliced

12 pimiento olives, thinly sliced

12 cherry tomatoes or 6 plum tomatoes, quartered

1 medium green bell pepper, seeded, thinly sliced

1 medium red bell pepper, seeded, thinly sliced

Italian Dressing (see page 384)

Prepare Italian Dressing. Refrigerate dressing if not using within 1 hour.

Prepare chilled salad by trimming, rinsing and draining. Place into a large salad bowl. Add dressing at serving time and toss to mix. Serves 6.

STUFFED SHELLS

(Prepare several days in advance and freeze in 9x15x3-inch baking dish, with sauce only on bottom of dish. On the day needed, remove from freezer and let stand 30 minutes. Ladle a light coating of sauce over the shells and bake as directed.)

1 lb. jumbo shells pasta

2 lbs. ricotta

8 oz. mozzarella cheese, diced

$\frac{1}{2}$ cup grated Parmesan cheese
   (plus extra cheese for casserole)

2 eggs beaten, or egg substitute

1 tbsp. chopped parsley

$\frac{1}{2}$ tsp. salt

$\frac{1}{4}$ tsp. black pepper

$\frac{1}{4}$ tsp. nutmeg

4-5 cups Chopped Beef Tomato Sauce (see page 397), prepared several days in advance and refrigerated, or several weeks in advance and frozen. If frozen, defrost sauce in refrigerator overnight.

Prepare shells as directed on package (about 7 minutes parboiled). Drain and rinse with cool water; drain again and set aside.

In a 2-quart bowl, combine ricotta, diced mozzarella, Parmesan, eggs, parsley and seasonings. Evenly spread 1 cup Chopped Beef Tomato Sauce on bottom of 9x15x13-inch baking dish. Stuff each jumbo shell with 1 tablespoon of cheese mix. Place them side by side in dish. Spoon 1 cup of sauce over the shells when ready to bake. (Or refrigerate or freeze as desired.)

Preheat oven at 350°.

Sprinkle more Parmesan cheese over casserole and bake 30 minutes until bubbly. Serve with remaining hot sauce. Serves 6-8.

VEAL CUTLET PARMAGIANO IN A SAUCE CRUST

2-3 cups Marinara Sauce (see pages 398-9)

6-8 large veal cutlets (do *not* pound thin)
1 cup grated Parmesan cheese
4 beaten eggs or 1 cup egg substitute
¼ cup fresh finely chopped parsley
¼ tsp. black pepper
dash of salt
1 cup flour

2 cups unseasoned Italian bread crumbs, combined
    with another ½ cup grated Parmesan cheese
1 cup shredded low-fat mozzarella
enough canola oil in large skillet, to cover ¼ inch
    on bottom of pan

Lay out one sheet waxed paper onto which you pour flour mixed with pepper and salt. Spread crumbs mixed into grated Parmesan cheese on another sheet of waxed paper. Pour 2-3 cups tomato sauce in a wide, shallow dish; pour eggs and parsley into another wide shallow dish; beat eggs mixture until foamy. Preheat canola oil (300°) in a large skillet.

Lay veal cutlets, one at a time, into the flour to coat on each side; then dip the cutlets into beaten eggs to coat on each side; coat the cutlets with the tomato sauce and quickly lay them on the crumbs-cheese mix to coat on both sides. Sauté cutlets on both sides, one or two at a time as you complete coating them.

Transfer cooked cutlets to heat-resistant serving dish.

Preheat oven to 350°.

Sprinkle more Parmesan cheese and shredded mozzarella over the cutlets and bake in preheated oven at 350° for 15-20 minutes or until cheese is melted and cutlets turn light brown. NOTE: Do not bake the cheese-covered cutlets until you're ready to serve them. (Keep the unbaked tray in an unheated oven, up to a few hours; or refrigerate the casserole until ready to bake and serve.) Serves 6-8.

VANILLA BEAN ICE CREAM WITH ASSORTED LIQUEURS

1 qt. vanilla bean ice cream
6 individual serving bowls
assorted liqueurs, such as: Crème de Menthe, Kahlua, Cherry Heering...and Caffé Espresso.

Prepare individual portions of vanilla ice cream in small serving bowls. Drizzle 1-2 tablespoons of a liqueur over ice cream in bowls. Serve immediately. Caffé Espresso makes a nice accompaniment.

Spring-Summer

"Yes! I Do Care a Fig."

The 18th century English humorist, Edward Lear, in his Book of Nonsense has Mr. & Mrs. Discobbolas end their dizzy rhyme:

"But we don't care a button!   We don't care a fig!"

Each Autumn, for at least 50 years, my father-in-law deftly and expertly pruned his two fig trees. His aim was to prune the limbs at the joinings of new and old wood. Then he would wrap his prizes in thick tar paper and twine. People in temperate climates plant fig trees. In colder climates, people have been known to bring the tree indoors during the dormant winter, its roots wrapped in burlap. Fig trees are very much loved and quite loveable.

The Ficus tree is deciduous, with rough textured leaves which form three lobes. Figs appear in earliest recorded history. Greek poets, Chinese dynasties, Roman leaders, Egyptian queens (remember, Cleopatra ended her life with an asp brought to her in a basket of figs!). I would be remiss not to remind you of Adam & Eve in the old Bible story.

The fig tree probably originated in Asia Minor and is native to the Mediterranean region. The fruits of these trees are known to assist in the digestive process, having mild laxative qualities. Figs are rich in calcium, iron, phosphorus, potassium and Vitamins B & C. They are fat-free, sodium-free and cholesterol-free.

Ants are the chief pollinators for fig trees: the tiny insects search out the sweetness in the flower, pick up pollen on their feet and carry the pollen to their next conquest flower.

Figs happen to be my favorite of all fruits (a difficult but honest statement). I've had the pleasurable experience of savoring many varieties: Black Mission, Calimyrna, Kadota, and Wild Turkey. My father-in-law in the 30 years I had known him, never failed to remember his favorite daughter-in-law in the late August of each year _ with a dinner plate, piled high with small dark purple treasures _ figs (probably a variety of Black Mission).

Spring-Summer

ARUGULA WITH PROSCIUTTO AND FIGS
HONEY ORANGE DRESSING
BRACIOLE
SWEET AND SOUR RATATOUILLE
WARM BLACKBERRY COMPOTE

ARUGULA WITH PROSCIUTTO AND FIGS

3 cups arugula, trimmed, rinsed, drained
6-8 fresh figs, (Kadota, Brown Turkey, Calimyrna)
6-8 slices prosciutto
1 cup shredded provolone
12-15 cherry tomatoes
$\frac{1}{2}$ cup of chopped walnuts

HONEY ORANGE DRESSING:
$\frac{1}{4}$ cup extra-virgin olive oil
$\frac{1}{4}$ cup orange juice
1 tbsp. honey
1 small red chile pepper, seeded, chopped, to taste
1 tsp. dried oregano

   On a large glass platter, arrange a layer of arugula. Quarter the figs and place them around the bed of arugula. Scatter the tomatoes. With a pair of kitchen shears, cut the prosciutto into strips. Scatter the prosciutto strips, provolone and walnuts over the arugula and figs.
   Combine dressing ingredients in a jar. Refrigerate dressing if not using within an hour. (When handling hot pepper varieties, wear plastic gloves. Wash your hands thoroughly; avoid touching face and eyes.)
   Shake jar of dressing to blend thoroughly. Drizzle dressing over salad before serving. Use a spatula and spoon to serve. Serves 6.

BRACIOLE

(May be prepared ahead of time and reheated in warm oven.)

1 lg. can or jar prepared marinara tomato sauce
1 small onion, finely chopped
1 garlic clove, minced
$\frac{1}{4}$ cup grated Parmesan cheese
several basil leaves, torn
$\frac{1}{2}$ cup red table wine – optional
olive oil to coat skillet
2-3 slices of beef top round or flank steak
    for braciole; meat should be placed
    between 2 sheets of waxed paper and pounded
    thin with mallet
2-3 thin slices veal (from shoulder), pounded thin
    as directed above
2-3 slices pork tenderloin, pounded thin
    as directed above

Filling for beef: $\frac{1}{4}$ cup chopped parsley,
    $\frac{1}{4}$ cup chopped provolone cheese,
    salt and pepper to taste
Filling for veal: $\frac{1}{4}$ cup chopped green pepper,
    $\frac{1}{4}$ cup (about 2-3 thin slices) prosciutto,
    shredded, $\frac{1}{4}$ cup grated Parmesan cheese
Filling for pork: $\frac{1}{4}$ cup dried oregano,
    2 tbsp. pignola (pine nuts), $\frac{1}{4}$ cup raisins

about 1 dozen thin small metal skewers

Combine each of the fillings into separate small bowls. Lay a sheet of waxed paper on a board. Prepare the beef braciole first. The pounded slices of beef will probably be as large as a dinner plate. After preparation, each braciola can provide 2-3 servings. Use work board as your base.

Spread the beef filling over the slices of beef. Roll up, lengthwise, and knit to fasten with a thin metal skewer. Set aside on a platter.

Spread veal filling over pounded slices of veal. Roll up lengthwise as directed above.

Spread pork filling over pounded tenderloin. Proceed as directed above.

Heat oil in large skillet to moderate. Lightly brown onion, garlic and braciole on all sides. When cooked, transfer them to a platter. Scrape bottom of skillet with spatula to loosen any leavings. Pour sauce into skillet; stir in cheese and basil and simmer for 5 minutes. Arrange braciole in skillet with sauce. Stir in red table wine (or a little water) to loosen the sauce and enhance the flavor of the sauce. Warm on low simmer for 5 minutes or so. Cut braciole into segments when serving. Spoon sauce over them. Crusty artisan bread goes well with this entrée. Serves 6.

SWEET AND SOUR RATATOUILLE

(Prepare on day before.)

2 tbsp. olive oil

4 baby eggplants, washed, ends trimmed, cubed

2 celery stalks, chopped

1 green bell pepper, seeded, thinly sliced

1 can (1 lb.) whole peeled plum tomatoes, mashed

1 medium onion, chopped

3-4 garlic cloves, chopped

$\frac{1}{2}$ cup assorted pitted olives, chopped

sm. jar (1 oz.) capers, drained

2 tbsp. Italian parsley, chopped

2 tbsp. granulated sugar

$\frac{1}{4}$ cup red wine vinegar

$\frac{1}{4}$ cup extra-virgin olive oil

salt, pepper

Blend extra-virgin olive oil, wine vinegar and sugar in a cup. Set aside.

Coat a large skillet with 2 tablespoons olive oil. On medium high, lightly brown onion, garlic, pepper and celery for 2-3 minutes. Add eggplant cubes and sauté for 3-4 minutes until golden. Pour tomatoes in skillet; stir and cook for 5 minutes. Add olives, capers, parsley, oil/wine vinegar mix, sugar, salt and pepper. Lower heat to simmer and cook 5 minutes longer.

Transfer stew to serving bowl. Refrigerate, covered. Remove from refrigerator 2-3 hours before serving. Bread crisps make a tasty accompaniment. Serves 6.

WARM BLACKBERRY COMPOTE

(Prepare in advance.)

1 quart blackberries, gently rinsed, drained
$\frac{1}{3}$ cup sugar
1 egg or $\frac{1}{4}$ cup egg substitute
$\frac{1}{3}$ cup light brown sugar
juice of 1 lemon
6 tbsp. sweet butter or Smart balance spread, melted
$\frac{1}{2}$ cup evaporated milk, fat-free available
1 cup self-rising cake flour
decorator's sugar for sprinkling

Preheat oven to 350°.

Grease a large 1-quart round Pyrex oven-proof baking dish. In a large mixing bowl, gently toss together blackberries, white sugar and lemon juice until thoroughly combined. Pour this mix into the prepared dish.

In a bowl, on low speed, beat together: egg and brown sugar until well-combined. Stir in melted butter and milk. Sift flour into the egg/butter mixture and fold gently to form a smooth batter.

Spread this batter over the blackberry mix in the baking dish to cover the fruit. Bake in preheated oven 350° for 25-30 minutes, until topping is firm and golden. While hot, sprinkle crust with decorator's sugar, if desired, and serve warm. Serves 5-6.

Spring-Summer

From My Mother's Box
Of Kitchen Secrets

*S*ometimes we wish that "someone" had shared their kitchen expertise. For example, cream mixes may curdle as you stir lemon juice into the cream. To prevent curdling: (1) add wine and/or lemon juice BEFORE, not after the eggs and cream, AND (2) gradually stir in the cream (mix), and (3) add just a little EXTRA bit of cream when separation threatens.

When you substitute oils for fat solids, a little less liquid is needed in the conversion. For example: $\frac{1}{4}$ cup butter converts into 3 tablespoons canola oil or olive oil. (1 teaspoon butter= $\frac{3}{4}$ teaspoon oil; 1 tablespoon butter= $2\frac{1}{4}$ teaspoons oil; $\frac{1}{2}$ cup butter= $\frac{1}{4}$ cup + 2 tablespoons oil.)

Don't sift flour unless the recipe requires pre-sifting. Today's packaged flour isn't as compacted as it was 100 years ago (you also had the threat of insects and other impurities residing in the sack of flour). However, we still should "pick over" the split peas and beans.

And always preheat the oven to the required temperature before inserting the prepared pan. Circulating air around the cake or cookie pan(s) is very necessary for a complete baking. Don't over-load the oven. Usually, cakes and cookies do best if the pans are placed in a clean oven, slightly above-center.

Spring-Summer

SPINACH, ARUGULA, CARROTS AND MOZZARELLA
PARMESAN CHEESE DRESSING
CHICKEN FRANCESE FOR AHIDA
TAGLIATELLE WITH PARMESAN CHEESE
CHOCOLATE TORTE WITH ALMONDS

SPINACH, ARUGULA, CARROTS AND MOZZARELLA

2 cups baby spinach, rinsed, drained

2 cups arugula, rinsed, drained

    (or use 4 cups of one: baby spinach or arugula)

1 lg. carrot, pared, shredded

$\frac{1}{2}$ cup shredded mozzarella (low-fat available)

2 garlic cloves, finely chopped

$\frac{1}{2}$ cup pitted Kalamata olives

Parmesan Cheese Dressing (see page 388)

    Prepare Parmesan Cheese Dressing. Refrigerate dressing until one hour before serving; shake or stir well before using.

    In a large bowl, add and toss together: spinach, arugula, carrot, mozzarella, garlic and olives. At serving time add dressing to salad; toss and serve. Serves 6.

CHICKEN FRANCESE FOR AHIDA

6-8 chicken cutlets, boneless, skinless, rinsed, patted dry with paper towels

1 lg. yellow onion, thinly sliced

2 cups (about 8-10 oz.) white mushrooms, rinsed, patted dry with paper towels, sliced thin

1 cup flour (remove 1 tbsp. flour and save for sauce)

¼ cup chopped parsley

¼ cup olive oil

¼ cup water

½ cup dry white wine

strained juice of 1 lemon

½-1 cup light cream (or half-and-half, fat-free available)

½ tsp. black pepper

¼ tsp. salt

½ cup grated Parmesan cheese

1 lemon, thinly sliced into rounds for garnish (remove seeds)

Heat oil in a large non-stick skillet to moderate 320°. Spread flour, pepper and salt on a sheet of waxed paper. Dredge the chicken in the flour mix and set aside on a large plate. Sauté the chicken in the skillet, about 3-5 minutes on each side, depending on the thickness of chicken. Do not overcook chicken. Briefly, lay chicken on paper towels to drain; transfer them to, and arrange the sautéed chicken on a large oven-resistant casserole pan from which you'll serve the chicken. Add more oil to the skillet if necessary.

Sauté onion in oil for 4-5 minutes, adding the mushrooms half-way through the cooking. Stir the bottom of the skillet to loosen any residue mushroom-onions and cook them until onions are golden; stir in parsley. Combine water, wine and lemon juice into a small bowl and gradually stir this liquid into the simmering onion mix in the skillet. Stir 1 tablespoon flour into ½ cup light cream to dissolve; stir the cream mix into the skillet; stir in ¼ cup Parmesan cheese; keep stirring to blend thoroughly. The sauce should be slightly thickened.

Preheat oven to 350°.

Carefully, pour the sauce evenly over the chicken in the casserole dish; sprinkle remainder of cheese over the dish. Garnish with slices of lemon; bake casserole in preheated oven at 350° for 10-15 minutes. Serve very warm with a side of tagliatelle in butter and Parmesan cheese. Serves 6.

CHOCOLATE TORTE WITH ALMONDS

(Prepare in advance.)

8 oz. Ghiradelli semisweet chocolate morsels

1 cup light brown sugar

$\frac{3}{4}$ cup butter or Smart Balance spread, softened

$\frac{1}{4}$ cup ground almonds

$\frac{1}{2}$ cup sifted flour

1 tsp. baking powder

5 eggs, separated (or $1\frac{1}{4}$ cups egg substitute plus 1 cup "egg whites only" - egg white substitute found in dairy or baking departments)

$\frac{1}{4}$ cup blanched almonds, finely chopped

confectioners' sugar to garnish torte

Preheat oven to 350°.

Grease and flour a 9-inch spring-form pan. Melt chocolate morsels in top half of double boiler (1 cup water added to bottom half). Place double boiler on burner. Raise heat to boil; then lower to simmer, stirring chocolate frequently, until melted.

Remove pot from burner and stir sugar into melted chocolate until dissolved. Add butter to the mix, stirring to melt. Gently stir in ground almonds, flour and baking powder. Pour and scrape out the chocolate mix into a large bowl. Add the egg yolks, a little at a time, beating well after each addition.

In another clean large bowl, beat the egg whites at high speed until they form soft peaks. Fold the whites into the chocolate mixture. Stir in chopped blanched almonds. Pour the mixture into the prepared pan. Bake in preheated oven 350° for 40-45 minutes, until cake has risen and is firm to the touch (cake will form surface cracks during baking).

Let the cake cool in its pan for 1 hour. Run a knife around inside edge to loosen. Gently, remove outer ring of spring-form pan. Do not remove cake from base of pan. Place cake (on its base) on serving platter, lined with a paper doily. Before serving, dust cake with confectioners' sugar. Serves 8.

Spring-Summer

"I Knew You When You Drank Manischewitz."

*A*nd now, I drink Montepulciano d'Abruzzo, Australian Shiraz, Spanish Rioja, St. Emilion Bordeaux, Rosso di Toscana and the Pinots: Grigio and Noir. Let's face it: "I'm a "Wino". I've never met a wine (especially red wine) I haven't enjoyed. Many years ago, I bragged about the modest Folonari, a light red wine, for $1.00 a bottle. To me, it was delicious; a little "easy", perhaps. Hey - I was young and a novice. Wish I could boast about a $5.00 bottle of "easy" wine, today.

Ah! Wine _ nectar for the gods!

Spring-Summer

VEGETABLE BEEF NOODLE SOUP
STUFFED CHICKEN BREASTS IN A WRAP
POTATO SALAD
ORANGE CHIFFON CAKE

VEGETABLE BEEF NOODLE SOUP

1 lb. lean beef cubes	1 cup broccoli florets
2-3 garlic cloves, minced	4-6 baby ears of corn, halved lengthwise
3-4 scallions, chopped, include greens	8 oz. thin egg noodles
4 tbsp. *lite* soy sauce	7 cups beef consommé, low-salt variety
1-2 tbsp. sesame oil	$\frac{1}{4}$ tsp. chili powder
1 leek, chopped	1 cup light dry red wine: Chianti or Folonari

In a 6-quart soup pot, heat oil and cook beef cubes, scallions, leek and garlic until tender, about 5-6 minutes. Scrape bottom of pot to loosen particles. Stir in soy sauce.

Pour beef consommé into pot; add broccoli and baby corn. Bring to a boil; stir in wine; stir in noodles. Cook for 7-8 minutes.

Ladle soup into individual bowls. Before serving, sprinkle soup with chili powder. Serves 6-8.

STUFFED CHICKEN BREASTS IN A WRAP

4 chicken breasts, each halved, bones and skin removed
8 slices prosciutto
8 oz. semi-soft cheese (brie, camembert)
$\frac{1}{4}$ cup chopped parsley
$\frac{1}{2}$ cup white mushrooms, chopped
1 small onion, finely chopped
$\frac{1}{2}$ cup red table wine
1 cup prepared chicken stock, less-salt variety
1 tbsp. brown sugar
freshly ground black pepper, to taste

8 small metal skewers

Wash chicken thoroughly; pat dry with paper towels. Cut a horizontal slit (pocket) through the thickest part of each half chicken breast. Set chicken aside on tempered glass board. In a small bowl, chop cheese into very small chunks. Add parsley, mushrooms, onion and mix thoroughly. Divide the cheese mix to stuff the 8 halves of chicken breasts.

Wrap each half-breast with 1 slice prosciutto; hold together with small metal skewers.

Pour wine and stock into a large skillet; bring to a boil and stir in brown sugar to dissolve. Add chicken breasts to skillet; cover and lower heat to simmering for 10-12 minutes, depending on the thickness of chicken.

Insert a skewer into the thickest part of the chicken to test for doneness: juice will run clear when skewer is inserted.

With a spatula and spoon, remove chicken from pan and transfer to a heat-resistant platter. Keep chicken in warming oven.

Reheat sauce in skillet to a boil; then lower to simmer and cook until sauce is reduced and thickens. Gently, remove skewer from chicken. Cut each stuffed half chicken breast in half, and arrange the pieces around the platter. Grind fresh black pepper over platter; pour sauce over chicken to serve. Serves 6.

POTATO SALAD

6 medium-large California white potatoes,
    scrubbed
1 small yellow onion, chopped
$\frac{1}{2}$ green bell pepper, seeded,
    sliced into slivers
optional: (1 small red cayenne or
    chile pepper, seeded, chopped -
    use plastic gloves)
$\frac{1}{2}$ cup sun-dried tomatoes,
    cut into thin strips
4 tbsp. cilantro, chopped

SAUCE:
$\frac{1}{2}$ cup light mayonnaise
1 tbsp. fresh lemon juice
$\frac{1}{2}$ cup light sour cream
black pepper and salt

    Boil potatoes for 20-25 minutes in a 4-quart pot with just enough water to cover. Insert a thin knife to test for tenderness. Potatoes should be firmly tender. Run cold water into pot; drain. When cooled enough to handle, peel off potato skin. Slice potatoes into rings and place in 4-quart mixing bowl. Add peppers, onions, sun-dried tomatoes and cilantro (reserve 2 tablespoons for garnish).

    In a small bowl prepare the sauce. Blend mayonnaise, sour cream, lemon juice and a sprinkling of pepper and salt. Pour dressing into potato bowl; use 2 spoons and toss potatoes to mix thoroughly. Pour potato salad into a decorative 4-quart serving bowl. Sprinkle cilantro to garnish. Cover tightly with plastic wrap and refrigerate until 30 minutes before serving. Serves 6.

ORANGE CHIFFON CAKE

¾ cup canola oil

1 cup sugar

4 eggs, separated

3¾ cups flour, sifted

3 tsp. baking powder

pinch of salt

1¼ cups orange juice, no pulp

1 tsp. grated orange rind

1 tbsp. orange water (sold in pharmacy and specialty food stores)

SYRUP:

¾ cup orange juice

1 cup sugar

extra confectioners' sugar for dusting cake

Preheat oven to 350°.

Grease and flour a 10-inch Bundt pan. Cream together: canola oil and sugar until light and fluffy. Add egg yolks, one at a time, whisking well after each addition. Sift together flour, baking powder and salt. Fold dry ingredients and orange juice alternately into the egg mixture with a spoon. Stir in orange water and rind.

Beat the egg whites at high speed until they form soft peaks and fold them into the batter. Pour batter into the prepared Bundt pan and bake the cake in a preheated oven at 350° for 50-55 minutes or until inserted toothpick removes clean.

In a small saucepan, bring orange juice and sugar to a boil and simmer for 5 minutes, until sugar is dissolved. Remove cake from oven and cool in pan for 10 minutes. Prick top of cake with metal baking nail or tines of a serving fork. Brush ½ amount of syrup over the top of the warm cake. Allow cake to cool another 10 minutes.

Invert cake on a serving platter. Remove pan from cake and prick inverted cake with metal baking nail. Brush the remainder of the syrup over the cake. Allow to cool. Just before serving, generously dust cake with confectioners' sugar. Serves 6-8.

Spring-Summer

Cookin' with Ludwig, Pete and Freddie

Truly, I cannot tell you (with authority) what's first to hit the a.m. scene: my bare feet on the bedroom floor or my right index digit against the Bose on/off. Classical music has become a necessary background in my daily life, especially in the kitchen while I wear my chef's toque.

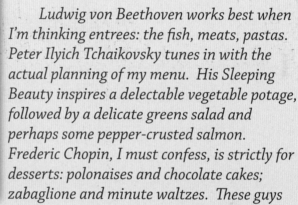

Ludwig von Beethoven works best when I'm thinking entrees: the fish, meats, pastas. Peter Ilyich Tchaikovsky tunes in with the actual planning of my menu. His Sleeping Beauty inspires a delectable vegetable potage, followed by a delicate greens salad and perhaps some pepper-crusted salmon. Frederic Chopin, I must confess, is strictly for desserts: polonaises and chocolate cakes; zabaglione and minute waltzes. These guys are my top three faves, not necessarily in the order I have placed them. It depends upon the weather of the day.

Of course, I'm quite eclectic in my choice of composers and their compositions, as I am in my tastes for various cuisines. Listen to Max Bruch's Violin Concerto in G minor and I lower to simmer, and weep salty tears into the cassoulet. A little twist of Ravel, a dash of Rachmaninoff, a rub of Gershwin's blue tones, Vivaldi's Seasons-ings..............You get my message?

Spring-Summer

TOMATO SOUP WITH FENNEL AND SHRIMP
EARLY SPRING SALAD
LEMON-OIL DRESSING
SHEPHERD'S PIE
CATHERINE'S IRISH SODA BREAD
TANGY LEMON CAKE

TOMATO SOUP WITH FENNEL AND SHRIMP

1 lb. uncooked, peeled shrimp

1 lg. can (22 oz.) chopped tomatoes

6 cups water

2 tbsp. olive oil

1 large onion, chopped

1 large fennel bulb, chopped

2 large all-purpose potatoes, pared, cut into chunks;
    simmer in small pot for 8-10 minutes
    until tender; set aside

1 bay leaf

1 tsp. salt

freshly ground pepper

sprigs of fennel grass for garnish

Heat oil to moderate-high in a 4-quart soup pot with cover. Cook onion and fennel in oil for 3-4 minutes until fennel is tender. Scrape bottom of pot; add tomatoes and 6 cups water, bay leaf, salt and pepper. Cover pot and simmer soup for 30 minutes.

Mash the potatoes just after they are cooked, while still hot. Spoon mashed potatoes into soup pot and stir thoroughly to blend. Add shrimp.

Simmer soup for 10 minutes to allow tastes to blend. Taste and adjust amounts of salt and pepper. Before serving, remove and discard bay leaf. At serving, float a sprig of fennel grass in each bowl. Serves 6-8.

EARLY SPRING SALAD

2 cups dandelions, trimmed, washed, drained

2 cups arugula, trimmed, washed, drained

1 Vidalia onion, sliced thin

1 dozen cherry (or grape) tomatoes, washed, halved

½ pt. blueberries, rinsed, drained

Lemon-Oil Dressing (see page 385)

Trim, wash, thoroughly drain greens. Place greens in serving bowl; cover lightly with a sheet of waxed paper; chill salad on bottom shelf of refrigerator for 1 hour.

Meanwhile, prepare dressing in a small jar. Refrigerate dressing if not using within an hour. Slice onion, prepare blueberries and wash and drain tomatoes. Just before serving, halve tomatoes and assemble salad in serving bowl. Drizzle dressing over salad; toss to mix. Serves 4-6.

SHEPHERD'S PIE

2 lbs. all-purpose potatoes (4 large), peeled, cut into chunks

¼ cup olive oil

¼ cup light cream or evaporated milk

2 tbsp. canola oil

1 lg. onion, finely chopped

1½ lbs. lean ground lamb

3-4 medium-size carrots, pared, thinly sliced into rounds

¼ cup chopped parsley

½ tsp. salt

½ tsp. freshly ground pepper

2½ cups beef broth (less-salt variety)

Preheat oven 350°.

Cook potatoes in a medium-size pot with enough water to cover. Bring water to a boil and simmer for 10-12 minutes until potatoes are tender. Drain and mash them with olive oil and milk (or cream). Set aside.

Heat canola oil in a large skillet over moderate heat. Add onion and 1 cup broth and cook until softened, not browned. Add ground lamb to pan and cook 6-8 minutes, stirring continuously, until meat is no longer pink. Drain off excess fat from skillet. Add carrots, salt, pepper and parsley. Bring pot to boil, lower heat, and simmer for 8-10 minutes until carrots are tender.

Remove skillet from heat and transfer lamb mix to a large, deep oven-proof casserole dish. Add enough of the remaining broth to moisten the meat mix. Spread mashed potatoes over meat and vegetables. Bake casserole in preheated oven at 350° for 40 minutes or until mashed potato is golden brown. Serves 6.

CATHERINE SHEA'S IRISH SODA BREAD

$\frac{2}{3}$ cup raisins

2 cups sifted all-purpose flour

$1\frac{1}{2}$ tsp. baking powder

$\frac{3}{4}$ tsp. baking soda

1 tsp. salt

3 tbsp. granulated sugar

$1\frac{1}{2}$ tsp. caraway seeds

3 tbsp. white shortening – like Crisco

1 cup buttermilk

melted butter and a sprinkling of granulated sugar for top of loaf

> Grease a cast-iron fry pan or 8-inch cake pan.
> Preheat oven to 350°.

In a large mixing bowl, sift flour, baking powder, baking soda, salt and sugar. Stir in caraway seeds. Cut shortening into the flour mix by using 2 kitchen knives. Pour buttermilk into the dough; fold in raisins. Mix the batter thoroughly; the dough will be sticky.

Turn out dough onto a floured board and gently knead a few strokes. Shape the dough into a round loaf and fit it into the greased cast-iron fry pan (or cake pan). Make crosswise cuts into the dough, cutting about two-thirds deep into the dough. Brush top of loaf with melted butter and sprinkle with granulated sugar. Bake loaf in preheated oven 350° for 30-45 minutes or until inserted toothpick removes clean. Makes one loaf. Serves 6-8.

Catherine Shea at daughter Cathy's bridal shower.

TANGY LEMON CAKE

2 cups flour, sifted

2 tsp. baking powder

1 cup sugar

4 eggs

$\frac{2}{3}$ cup sour cream

grated rind of 1 lemon

$\frac{1}{4}$ cup fresh lemon juice

$\frac{2}{3}$ cup canola oil

SYRUP:

$\frac{1}{4}$ cup confectioners' sugar

2-3 tbsp fresh lemon juice

(extra confectioners' sugar for garnish)

Preheat oven to 350°.

Lightly grease an 8-inch spring form cake pan with butter or Smart Balance spread. Lightly flour the bottom of the pan. Sift flour and baking powder into a bowl and stir in sugar.

In a separate bowl, beat eggs until they are thick and foamy. Add sour cream, lemon juice, oil and rind and continue to beat until thoroughly blended. Pour and fold the egg mixture into the flour mix until evenly combined.

Pour the batter into the prepared pan and bake cake in preheated oven at 350° for 45-50 minutes, until light golden brown and inserted toothpick removes clean.

As the cake bakes, prepare the syrup: blend confectioners' sugar and lemon juice in a small saucepan. Stir syrup over low heat until mixture starts to bubble and thickens. As soon as cake comes out of the oven, prick the surface with the tines of a fork all over the top of the cake - about 12 inserts. Brush the syrup a little at a time over the top of the cake.

Let the cake cool completely in the pan. Run a knife around the cake's edge. Remove sides of pan and place cake on serving dish. (Do not remove cake from bottom of pan.) Just before serving, generously dust cake with confectioners' sugar. Serves 8.

Spring-Summer

Patron Saints of Cooks

I can readily understand the connection between St. Martha, the sister of Mary and Lazarus (whom the Lord had brought back from the dead), and her sobriquet, "patroness of cooks".

While her sister, Mary, attentively listened to the Lord's teachings, Martha prepared the dinner. When she asked the Lord to rebuke Mary for not assisting her in the kitchen, the Lord informed them that Mary had chosen the good part.

St. Lawrence, a third century deacon was martyred by being slowly roasted on a gridiron. Hence, some lives of saints have recognized him to be the patron saint of grillers and chefs of the barbecue.

Not exactly appetizing.

Spring-Summer

SANTA FE MINESTRONE
PORK FILLETS WITH APRICOTS, ALMONDS AND PROSCIUTTO
ROASTED POTATOES AND MUSHROOMS
ITALIAN PUDDING

SANTA FE MINESTRONE

1 large yellow onion, chopped

6 garlic cloves, sliced

1 large carrot, pared, thinly sliced into rounds

1 medium all-purpose potato, pared, cubed

4-6 plum tomatoes, washed, diced

1 medium zucchini, scraped, diced

½ small green cabbage, washed, shredded

1 small can (3-4 oz.) corn kernels

1 cup green beans, trimmed, washed,
   cut into small pieces

6 cups canned chicken broth, less-salt variety
   or: prepare homemade chicken broth
   (see page 44)

2 tbsp. olive oil

salt, black pepper to taste

½ tsp. cumin

1-2 tsp. chili powder

2-3 tbsp. chopped cilantro

In a 6-quart soup pot, lightly brown onion and garlic, scraping bottom of pot to prevent sticking. Pour in 6 cups chicken broth. Stir in carrot, potato, tomatoes, zucchini, cabbage, green beans and corn kernels. Stir in salt, pepper, cumin, chili powder and cilantro. Raise heat under pot; cover pot and bring soup to a slow simmer. Cook for 45 minutes. Taste soup; add more chili powder if desired. Serve with nacho chips. Serves 5-6.

PORK FILLETS WITH APRICOTS, ALMONDS AND PROSCIUTTO

6 pork tenderloin, 1-inch thick (make a pocket in each chop by cutting a 2-inch horizontal
    center slit around edge of each chop)

½ cup chopped dried apricots   6 shallots, finely chopped

¼ cup finely chopped almonds   ½ cup marsala wine

1 tbsp. dried oregano   1 tbsp. olive oil

salt, black pepper

2 garlic cloves, chopped   6 slices prosciutto

2 tbsp. olive oil   olive oil to coat pan

    Make a slit in side of tenderloin (see directions above).
    In a small bowl, combine apricots, almonds, oregano, garlic, 2 tablespoons olive oil, salt and pepper to taste. Finely chop shallots and place in small bowl; toss with 1 tablespoon olive oil and marsala wine. Set aside.
    Stuff each chop by forcing one portion of apricot-almond mix equally into 6 pockets. Wrap each chop with one slice of prosciutto and place chops seam-side down into oil-coated 9x12-inch pan.
    Preheat oven to 375°.
    Spoon shallots-wine mix over pork fillets and bake them at 375° for 25-30 minutes. Lightly cover pork with foil after 20 minutes. Do not overcook. Serves 6.

ROASTED POTATOES AND MUSHROOMS

8 medium Red Bliss potatoes, scrubbed,   1 garlic clove, minced
    each cut into 4-6 wedges   ½ tsp. black pepper

2 cups white mushrooms, halved and quartered   6 basil leaves, torn into small pieces

½ cup spicy mustard spread   3 tbsp. olive oil

1 tsp. Italian seasoning   oil for greasing 9x12x2-inch pan

    Preheat oven 425°. Oil a 9x12x2-inch pan.
    Place potato chunks and mushrooms into large bowl.

    In a small bowl, blend mustard, garlic, oil, seasonings and basil. Spoon this mix into potatoes and mushrooms and toss to mix. Pour potato mix into the oiled pan to roast in oven 425° for 35-40 minutes, or until potatoes are fork-tender. Stir vegetables, occasionally, as they roast. Serves 6.

ITALIAN PUDDING

6 individual oven-proof pudding dishes (or ramekins),
$\frac{1}{2}$ cup-each
butter or Smart Balance spread for coating the cups
$\frac{1}{2}$ cup candied, dried fruit cake mix, warm water to cover
$1\frac{1}{2}$ cups low-fat ricotta cheese
3 egg yolks or $\frac{3}{4}$ cup egg substitute
2 tbsp. granulated sugar
1 tsp. ground cinnamon
grated rind of 2 lemons (save half amount for garnish)
1 pt. sour cream, fat-free available

Preheat oven to 350°.

Lightly grease 6 pudding dishes ($\frac{1}{2}$ cup-each). Spoon fruit cake mix into a small bowl and cover with warm water. Leave fruit cake mix to soak for 10 minutes.

Beat ricotta with yolks in a 2-quart bowl. Stir in sugar, cinnamon and lemon rind. Mix to combine.

Drain the dried fruit through a colander. Mix the drained fruit with the ricotta mixture. Spoon this mix into the oven-proof pudding dishes.

Place pudding cups on a metal tray and bake in preheated oven at 350° for 15-20 minutes. Tops should be firm to the touch, but not brown. Garnish with lemon rind and a dollop of sour cream. Good either warm or chilled. Serves 6.

Spring-Summer

His First Word Was..."Cheese".

That shiny, slippery "fake" plastic-wrapped, packaged cheese product. At first, tiny specks of the orange stuff; then, narrow, wormy strips, tightly clutched in his chubby little fists.

My two-fisted eight-month old was hooked on food substitutes! His future terrified me. What next? Those 3x7x1-inch boxes of macaroni and whatever? Or, gummy squares of this orange stuff to lay on gummier squares of so-called "sandwich" bread?

Turns out, his taste for cheese quickly graduated to creamy mozzarella in carozza, aged gorgonzola, Wisconsin cheddar wheels and any and all types of cultures, enzymes and curds.

Young Chip is wishing
for goat cheese.

Spring-Summer

SUMMER PASTA SALAD
WALNUT-PEPPER CRUSTED SALMON
BLUEBERRY CRUMB CAKE

SUMMER PASTA SALAD
(May be prepared a day in advance.)

12 oz. small-size pasta, (eg.: tri-color rotini, cut ziti, elbows, cooked as directed on package)

1 cup light mayonnaise

1 cup large pepperoni slices, cut into narrow strips

1 cup sharp provolone, sliced into narrow strips

½ cup red bell pepper, seeded, diced

¼ cup green jalapeño, seeded, diced
 (or: substitute ¼ cup green fryer, seeded, diced)

6 small white mushrooms, rinsed, quartered

½ cup pitted calamata olives, coarsely chopped

½ cup grated Parmesan cheese

2 tbsp. extra-virgin olive oil

2 tbsp. white wine vinegar

1 tbsp. dried oregano

½ tsp. salt (to taste)

½ tsp. freshly ground black pepper

2 tbsp. fresh Italian parsley, chopped – for garnish

2 hard-cooked eggs, vertically sliced into 8 wedges – for garnish

In a small jar, blend oil, vinegar, oregano, salt and pepper. Store in refrigerator, if not serving within the hour. (Remove from refrigerator about 1 hour before serving.)

Cook the pasta as directed. Drain pasta; rinse with cool water. Drain again, thoroughly. Pour pasta into a large serving bowl. Add peppers, mushrooms, provolone, olives and pepperoni. Toss to mix. Sprinkle Parmesan over bowl. Toss again.

In a small bowl, whisk and blend the jar of oil and vinegar dressing into 1 cup of light mayonnaise, until smooth and creamy. Pour dressing over the pasta salad. Toss to mix. Garnish with hard-cooked egg slices and Italian parsley. Refrigerate salad, covered with plastic wrap, if not serving promptly. Serves 6.

WALNUT-PEPPER CRUSTED SALMON

2 lbs. salmon fillets, center-cut, skinned, cut into 6 portions

2 tbsp. olive oil

3-4 garlic cloves, minced

$\frac{1}{4}$ cup fresh lemon juice

$\frac{1}{4}$ cup soy sauce, less-salt variety

2 tbsp. honey

2 tbsp. mustard spread

$\frac{1}{4}$ cup coarse cracked black pepper

$\frac{1}{4}$ cup finely chopped walnuts

2 tbsp. chopped dill

2 tbsp. finely chopped sweet red pepper

$\frac{1}{2}$ cup grated Parmesan cheese

Preheat oven to 375°.

In a small bowl, combine and mix: soy sauce, garlic, lemon juice, mustard and honey. Spread this mix over the top of the salmon.

On a sheet of wax paper, blend a mix of cracked black pepper, finely chopped walnuts, chopped red pepper and dill. Coat the honey-glazed fillets with this pepper-nut mix to form a crust.

Lay the prepared portions of salmon on an oiled 9x15-inch oven-proof pan. Sprinkle the salmon with grated Parmesan and bake the fish in a preheated oven at 375° for 20-25 minutes, depending upon thickness of fillets. Remove salmon portions with a spatula to individual plates. Serves 6.

BLUEBERRY CRUMB CAKE

$\frac{1}{2}$ cup butter or Smart Balance spread, softened
$\frac{2}{3}$ cup sugar
2 large eggs or $\frac{1}{2}$ cup egg substitute
1 cup flour
$\frac{3}{4}$ tsp. baking powder
$\frac{1}{2}$ tsp. salt
1 pt. blueberries, rinsed, drained

TOPPING:
1 cup flour
$\frac{1}{2}$ cup firmly packed brown sugar
6 tbsp. butter or Smart Balance spread, softened
1 tsp. cinnamon

Prepare crumb topping. With 2 forks, toss and combine: flour, brown sugar, butter and cinnamon until well-blended and crumbly. Set aside.

Preheat oven to 350°.

Butter and flour an 8-inch pan, square or round.

In a large bowl, cream together: butter and sugar, until mix is light and fluffy; beat in eggs, one at a time. Sift in flour, baking powder and salt. Beat the batter until it is just combined. Spoon and spread batter evenly into prepared pan. Arrange blueberries over the top of the batter. Sprinkle the crumb mix over the berries. Bake cake in middle of oven at 350° for 50-60 minutes, or until a toothpick tests clean. This cake is delicious when served warm or at room temperature, directly out of the pan. Serves 6.

Spring-Summer

Grandpas Are Good Teachers

When my paternal grandparents arrived in New York City (circa 1904), they made their first home among paisanos on Carroll Street, Brooklyn. Grandpa Aniello (Neil) opened a restaurant-bar under the large apartment where he and my grandmother Theresa and their nine children called home. Every day Grandpa Neil would serve the changing "menu of the day": a soup, a pasta, Italian bread, wine and beer.

When the family moved to Fort Hamilton Parkway, Brooklyn, (eventually, my first home), we lived in a huge Victorian frame cottage with a wrap-around porch. A garden of fruit trees, flowers and vegetables encircled our beautiful home.

Grandpa Neil continued to play "host". Every Saturday evening, Grandpa would preside over a caffé around the dining room table which happened to rest beneath a 1x3-foot stained glass chandelier, depicting a lively hunt scene. Paisanos would gather at our home. Grandpa would read from the latest Italian novella; or he would dramatically retell some human interest stories from the latest IL PROGRESSO. Mama served pastry and espresso.

After a couple of entrancing hours, and usually at a climax in the narration, Grandpa would slowly savor a final sip from his coffee cup. His radiant and caressing smile cast its glow upon everyone present. "To be continued, next week."

Grandpa Vincenzo had arrived in New York a few years earlier (my mother, child number three, had been born in New York City; three other children arrived in quick succession). Grandpa Vincent and Grandma Alfonsina eventually made their home on Fifteenth Avenue and Seventy-Third Street in Brooklyn. Every Sunday, Grandpa Vincent, who had labeled himself a gourmet cook, arranged his dining room buffet with home-grilled sirloin steaks and potatoes, pasta and a salad - and lots of fresh fruits.

As you can see, I've had exemplary teachers.

P.S. Grandma Theresa and Grandpa Neil were parents of nine children; Grandma Alfonsina and Grandpa Vincent gifted our family with six children; Grandpa Vincent's second wife, Ines, added another pair.

Grandpa Aniello Orlando
(sons, Uncle Emil and my Dad, Dominick,
on each side of Grandpa).

Spring-Summer

TUSCAN GREENS SALAD
OIL AND WINE VINEGAR DRESSING
CLAMS ON THE BARBEQUE WITH SALSA
SAUSAGE AND EGGPLANT PARMAGIANO (heirloom)
APRICOT-BLUEBERRY COBBLER

TUSCAN GREENS SALAD

2 cups arugula, trimmed, rinsed, drained

3 cups baby romaine, trimmed, rinsed, drained

$\frac{1}{2}$ cup torn basil

3-4 garlic cloves, chopped

$\frac{1}{2}$ cup pitted green olives

$\frac{1}{2}$ cup shelled pistachio nuts

6 slices crusty artisan bread

2 tbsp. olive oil

$\frac{1}{4}$ cup grated Romano cheese

Oil and Wine Vinegar Dressing (see page 384)

Pour greens into a large salad bowl; add basil, garlic, olives and nuts; toss to mix. Refrigerate salad with a light plastic covering, until serving.

Prepare dressing in a jar; refrigerate dressing until 30 minutes before serving. At that time, heat 2 tablespoons olive oil in a small non-stick skillet. Cut 6 slices of artisan bread, $\frac{1}{2}$-inch thick. Brush one side of each slice with oil and wine vinegar dressing; sprinkle the bread with cheese and place the bread dressing side down, in the heated oil. Raise heat to moderate high and quickly toast the bread.

Add remaining dressing to salad and toss to mix.

Turn over slices of bread to toast their other side for one minute. Remove bread and insert slices of toasted bread into the salad, around the inside of the bowl. Serve immediately. Serves 6.

CLAMS ON THE BARBEQUE WITH SALSA

4 lbs. Little Neck or cherrystone clams; rinse clams in cold water; place them in a large bowl and sprinkle with $\frac{1}{2}$ cup salt; cover clams with cold water and refrigerate them for 1 hour to extract grit and waste. Rinse clams again and drain. Use quickly.

SALSA:

1 can (1 lb.) chopped tomatoes

6 small baby bella mushrooms, rinsed, chopped

4 garlic cloves, chopped

1 large red onion, chopped

1 can (1 lb.) corn kernels

4 scallions, trimmed, chopped, include greens

1 small chile, finely chopped (add to taste)

1 tsp. ground cumin

salt to taste

2 tbsp. cilantro, finely chopped

sprigs of cilantro, for garnish

2 limes, cut into wedges

juice of 2 limes

Prepare the salsa. In a 2-quart decorative bowl, combine tomatoes, garlic, mushrooms, onion, corn, scallions, chile, cumin, salt, cilantro and lime juice. Refrigerate.

Drain clams for the last time; spread them on a perforated metal tray with a fireproof handle and place the tray directly over hot coals of a grill cooker. Grill the clams for about 5-10 minutes. Wearing a fire-resistant mitt, grab the tray by the handle and occasionally shake the metal tray to toss around the clams in shells. Use a metal spatula to assist you.

The clams will open; immediately remove the tray from the grill; spoon clams directly into individual serving dishes (discard clams which haven't opened). Squeeze a wedge of lime over each portion and top with salsa. Add sprigs of cilantro for garnish. Corn nachos make a tasty accompaniment. Serves 6.

SAUSAGE AND EGGPLANT PARMAGIANO

(About Eggplant: Select medium-size, firm, young eggplant. After slicing eggplant, layer the slices; sprinkle them lightly with salt. Place a dinner plate on top of the piled slices, and place a weight on top of the plate. Apply this pressure for 1 hour. This method will help to squeeze out any bitterness. Then rinse each slice under cold water. Shake off excess water from the slices and proceed as directed below.)

*3-4 eggplant, medium-size, washed, cut vertically
    into ¼-inch slices, about 16-18 slices*

3-4 eggs, beaten, or 1 cup egg substitute

1 cup all-purpose flour

salt, black pepper to taste

¼ cup canola oil

4 links sweet Italian sausage with fennel seed

1 tbsp. olive oil

2 cups prepared marinara sauce (in a bowl)

¼ cup grated Parmesan cheese

1 lb. low-fat mozzarella, cubed

9x15-inch non-stick lasagna pan

Heat 1 tablespoon olive oil in a skillet at moderate heat; add sausages and brown them on all sides. Remove sausages to plate and refrigerate them. (It will be easier to slice sausages when they are cold.)

Lay out a sheet of waxed paper and spread on it: flour blended with salt and pepper. Add and beat eggs into a wide, flat dish with an edge. Add one-quarter cup canola oil into a clean skillet. Heat oil to moderate (about 300°).

Dip rinsed eggplant slices into flour; then, into beaten egg mix; then, re-coat with flour. Sauté prepared eggplant slices in hot oil, a few slices at a time. Drain the slices on paper towels. Return sausages from refrigerator to cutting board. Slice the sausages into ½-inch rounds.

Preheat oven to 350°.

Using a 9x15-inch non-stick lasagna pan, line the bottom with one layer of cooked eggplant slices, vertically and overlapping. Spread 1 cup of prepared marinara sauce over the layer of eggplant. Add another layer of cooked eggplant, vertically and overlapping. Use all of the remaining eggplant slices. Spread all of the sausages over the eggplant casserole; spoon the rest of the sauce over the sausages and sprinkle the casserole with Parmesan cheese and mozzarella cubes.

Bake the parmagiana at 350° for 30-35 minutes, or until cheese melts and starts to turn light golden brown. If not serving immediately, the casserole may be prepared up to baking, wrapped in plastic, and refrigerated up to a couple of days. Then, proceed as directed. Best when served very warm and accompanied by crusty Italian bread. Serves 6-8.

APRICOT-BLUEBERRY COBBLER

(Prepare a day or two in advance.)

2 lbs. apricots, washed, pits removed, sliced into strips
   (if using canned apricots, drain apricots thoroughly)
1 pt. blueberries, rinsed, drained
$\frac{1}{3}$ cup sugar
$\frac{1}{4}$ cup flour
1 tsp. cinnamon
juice of 1 lemon
grated rind of 1 lemon

TOPPING:
$2\frac{1}{4}$ cups flour
1 egg or $\frac{1}{4}$ cup egg substitute, beaten
$\frac{1}{3}$ cup sugar
$\frac{2}{3}$ cup buttermilk
2 tsp. baking powder
6 tbsp. butter or Smart Balance spread, melted

1 pt. heavy whipping cream (whipped into stiff peaks) for garnish

Grandpa Vincenzo Capriglione.

Preheat oven to 375°.

Grease a 9x12x3-inch oven-proof Pyrex baking dish. In a large bowl, mix together: blueberries, apricots, sugar, lemon juice, rind, cinnamon and $\frac{1}{4}$ cup of flour.

Pour the fruit mix into the bottom of the greased baking dish.

Prepare the topping. In a large bowl, at low speed, beat together until well combined: remaining $2\frac{1}{4}$ cups flour, sugar, baking powder. Beat in egg, buttermilk and melted butter. Mix to form a soft dough. Spoon the batter on top of the fruit mix until it is almost covered. Bake the cobbler in a preheated oven at 375° for 35-40 minutes, until golden and bubbly. Serve warm with dollops of whipped cream. Serves 6.

Spring-Summer

Moses and the Exodus from Egypt

The Second Book of the Pentateuch, the Book of Exodus (in the Torah and the Old Testament), narrates the courageous history of the sufferings and the deliverance of the Chosen People from Egypt into the land which flows with milk and honey.

In this exciting and graphic tale, which historically is placed in the 13th century B.C., God tells Moses to lead the Israelites across the desert into the Promised Land. Apparently, Moses who is said to have had a speech impairment, lacked confidence in his ability to undertake this tremendous task he had been given.

Nevertheless, with support from his brother Aaron, the Levite (priest), we are allowed the opportunity to read and to vicariously live through, the horrendous experiences of these people. For over forty years, the Israelites would suffer ten plagues, encounter blessings and miracles, receive the Ten Commandments, establish their Covenant and laws, build their sanctuary and achieve the Promised Land.

One of these miracles depicts the gifts of food – the quails and manna. Manna was the miraculous food with which God fed the Israelites for 40 years in the desert. This manna was creamy white, grainy flakes and tasted like milk and honey. The manna was prepared by grinding and boiling the fine flakes and making a dough. It became as a continuous dough starter which nourished these people and was preserved in gomers, 2-quart containers.

Spring-Summer

MUSHROOMS AND ANCHOVY
LEMON-OIL DRESSING
ALMOND CRUSTED CHICKEN WITH PEARS IN GORGONZOLA
ORZO SALAD
STEAMED ASPARAGUS
STRUFFOLI (heirloom)

MUSHROOMS AND ANCHOVY

6 large Boston lettuce leaves, rinsed, drained

$1\frac{1}{2}$ doz. small white mushrooms, rinsed, drained, thinly sliced

$\frac{1}{2}$ tin (2 oz.) anchovy fillets, drained and chopped (add more if you love anchovy)

1 cup shredded Genoa salami, about 12 slices

1 tbsp. oregano

2-3 garlic cloves, chopped

Lemon-Oil Dressing (see page 385)

Prepare Lemon-Oil Dressing. Refrigerate dressing until 1 hour before using.

Line 6 individual salad bowls with lettuce. In a 2-quart bowl, mix sliced mushrooms, chopped anchovy, salami, oregano and garlic. Drizzle dressing over mushroom mix. Toss and coat mushroom mix thoroughly, using 2 spoons. Divide into 6 portions and spoon over lettuce in bowls. Serves 6.

ALMOND CRUSTED CHICKEN WITH PEARS IN GORGONZOLA
(*NOTE: at end of recipe)

6-8 chicken breast halves, skinless, boneless

SAUCE:
$\frac{1}{2}$ cup Rose's lime juice
$\frac{1}{4}$ cup - 6 tbsp. honey mustard spread
$1\frac{1}{4}$ cup honey

CRUST:
1 cup sliced almonds with skins
$\frac{1}{2}$ tsp. cracked black pepper

2 ripe Bartlett pears, each quartered, seeds removed
$\frac{1}{4}$ cup - 6 tbsp. crumbled Gorgonzola cheese
slices of lime for garnish

Preheat oven to 375°.

In a wide shallow bowl, blend lime juice, honey mustard and honey. Scatter almonds and black pepper on a sheet of waxed paper. Lightly coat with olive oil, a large 9x15x2-inch heat-resistant oven pan.

Coat the chicken on both sides with lime-honey mustard sauce; coat the breasts with pepper-almonds and lay the chicken pieces on the oiled pan. Spoon leftover sauce and almonds over the chicken.

Arrange the quartered pears around and between the chicken pieces. Lay a loose sheet of foil over the tray. Bake the chicken in a preheated oven at 375° for 20-25 minutes, until juices run clear. Do not overcook. Remove tray from oven and dress the pears in Gorgonzola cheese. Garnish with slices of lime. Serves 6.

*NOTE: You can prepare PECAN CRUSTED PORK TENDERLOIN by following these directions:
1. substitute - 6 boneless pork tenderloins, $\frac{1}{2}$-inch thick, for chicken
2. substitute - chopped pecans for almonds
3. substitute - apples for pears

ORZO SALAD

(Prepare on day before.)

1 cup orzo
4 oz. feta cheese, diced
¼ cup chopped parsley
¼ cup chopped basil
1 tbsp. chopped dill
1 large beefsteak tomato seeded, coarsely chopped

3 cups shredded iceberg lettuce for lettuce beds

Lemon-Oil Dressing (see page 385)

Prepare Lemon-Oil Dressing in advance. Refrigerate dressing until 1 hour before using.

Cook orzo according to package directions: drain; rinse with cold water; drain again.

Combine and toss to mix: feta cheese, parsley, basil, dill and chopped tomato. Spoon over orzo and gently toss the mix to coat thoroughly.

Shake the Lemon-Oil Dressing thoroughly. Pour about one-half cupful over orzo mix. Toss to coat the mix. Cover bowl with plastic wrap and refrigerate orzo mix for several hours or overnight. Just before serving, toss the mixture, again. Serve on individual beds of lettuce. Serves 6.

STEAMED ASPARAGUS

about 2 dozen to 30 thick asparagus spears, trimmed, rinsed, drained
6 garlic cloves, leave whole
pepper and salt to taste
olive oil

Steam asparagus and garlic in a small amount of water for 7-8 minutes; use an asparagus steamer (upright steamer) if you have one. Drain liquid and arrange asparagus on a serving platter; season with pepper and salt to taste; drizzle with olive oil. Serve warm or at room temperature. Serves 6.

STRUFFOLI

(In Italian homes this delectable confection is a special traditional treat. When thoroughly cooled, lay a sheet of waxed paper over the entire platter. It will keep for several weeks in a cool place.)

$3\frac{1}{2}$ cups flour

6 whole eggs, beaten

$\frac{1}{4}$ tsp. salt

$\frac{1}{4}$ tsp. baking powder

6 tbsp. granulated sugar

6 tbsp. pure honey

2 oz. pignola nuts

3 tbsp. nonpareils

$\frac{1}{4}$ cup candied cherries, halved

corn oil for frying, about 2 quarts

Pour corn oil into deep fryer or frying pan and preheat to 370°.

In a large bowl mix flour and eggs together with wooden spoon. Add salt and baking powder and continue mixing and kneading. Add more flour, up to 1 cup if necessary if dough is sticky. Use hands to knead dough on floured board. Knead about 8 to 10 minutes until dough is smooth. Cut small pieces from dough and roll into narrow ropes. Keep rest of dough covered with waxed paper as you roll ropes. After all the ropes are rolled, with a small knife, cut $\frac{1}{4}$-inch pieces from all the ropes. Roll each small piece between your floured fingers and spread the dough balls on the board.

By this time the oil should have heated to 370°. Using a large, flat, perforated spoon, lay a handful of dough balls onto the spoon and gently empty them into the hot oil. Fry a handful at a time for a few minutes, until golden brown. With same perforated spoon remove the cooked honey balls and place them into a very large paper towel lined bowl. For every several handfuls add another sheet of towel to drain the oil. When completed, pull out all paper towels.

In a 2-quart heavy pot, pour honey and granulated sugar. Cook on medium-high temperature. When the honey mix starts to bubble remove from heat and pour over cooked dough balls. Toss balls into honey mix to coat thoroughly. Meanwhile, have a large glass or crockery platter ready to accept the honey balls. With hands, form a ring of honey balls on platter. Sprinkle with pignola nuts, cherries and nonpareils. Cool. May be saved by laying a sheet of waxed paper atop the honey balls. Will keep about 3 weeks at room temperature.

Spring-Summer

2000 Years in the Making _
(A Suggested Script for Food Network TV)

SCENE: (Passover, the feast of Jews, was near. When therefore, Jesus had lifted up his eyes and seen that a very great crowd had come to him.)

JESUS: Philip, take two hundred denarii. Stop at the market place and buy bread to feed this crowd.

PHILIP: "Two hundred denarii worth of bread is not enough for them."

ANDREW: "Lord, there is a young boy here who has five barley loaves and two fishes; but what are these among so many?"

JESUS, THE LORD: "Make the people recline."
(Now there was much grass in the place. The men therefore reclined, in number about five thousand. Jesus then took the loaves, and when he had given thanks, distributed them to those reclining; and likewise the fishes, as much as they wished. And when they were filled, he said to his disciples:)

JESUS, THE LORD: "Gather the fragments that are left over, lest they be wasted."
(And they filled twelve baskets with the fragments of the five barley loaves.)

A miraculous banquet! And with leftovers!

THE BIBLE (The NEW TESTAMENT),
St. John: 6, 1-15

Spring-Summer

WILD ARUGULA WITH SHRIMP VINAIGRETTE
VINAIGRETTE DRESSING
CHAROSETH (HAROSET) (heirloom)
CAPUZZELLE DI AGNELLI (heirloom)
LAMB CHOPS IN TOMATO-PRUNE SAUCE
ASPARAGUS, MUSHROOMS AND ALMONDS
PASTIERA DI GRANO (heirloom)

WILD ARUGULA WITH SHRIMP VINAIGRETTE

4-5 cups wild arugula (or cultivated arugula), gently rinsed, thoroughly drained
1 cup tiny cooked shrimp, shelled, minced

Vinaigrette Dressing (see page 389)

Prepare Vinaigrette Dressing in advance. Refrigerate dressing until 1 hour before serving. Place arugula in a large salad bowl. Just before serving, empty dressing into a 1-quart bowl. Stir in minced cooked shrimp. Ladle $\frac{1}{2}$ cup of vinaigrette with shrimp over the salad of greens; toss well to mix. Prepare individual salad portions and top salads with an additional 1-2 tablespoons of dressing with shrimp. Serves 6.

CHAROSETH (HAROSET)

(Charoseth comprises part of the Seder of the Passover meal which celebrates Israel's release from Egyptian bondage. It symbolizes the mortar (or clay) which the enslaved Israelites used to make bricks when they were building storehouses for the Pharaohs in the cities of ancient Egypt. The sweet taste imparts a reflection upon the gift of freedom.)

*4-6 red delicious apples, peeled,
    cored, finely chopped
1 cup chopped pitted dates
2 cups almonds (or walnuts), shelled, chopped*

*$\frac{1}{4}$ cup honey
1 tbsp. lemon juice
$2\frac{1}{2}$ tsp. ground cinnamon
1 cup Kosher red wine*

In a large wood bowl mix apples, nuts, dates, honey, lemon juice and cinnamon. Add wine and toss to mix thoroughly. Apportion $\frac{1}{4}$ cup serving for each place setting. Reserve remainder for Seder dish. Serve on or with matzoh. Serves 6 or more.

CAPUZZELLE DI AGNELLI

(In many Italian homes, Easter preparations began after the noon hour on Holy Saturday. Roasted sheep's (lamb's) head was the traditional food to "break the fast". In addition to the lamb's head, boiled eggs were served for Italians to celebrate the end of the 40 days of fast and abstinence. Actually, Christian Easter, originally a Pagan celebration, saw the Risen Christ as the symbol of rebirth and new beginnings for God's human creations, as in the baby lamb and the symbolical eggs.)

Different nationalities display unique traditions in their Easter celebrations; many of these traditions display special foods as their centerpiece.

2-3 sheep heads (or lambs' heads)	6 all-purpose potatoes, pared, cut into
½ cup olive oil	medium-size chunks
1 doz. garlic cloves, minced	3-4 carrots, pared, cut into thick chunks
¼ cup dried oregano	2 celery stalks, trimmed, cut into large chunks
1-2 tsp. salt	2 lg. onions, quartered
1 tsp. black pepper	

Preheat oven 400°.

Split the heads, leaving the brains, eyes and tongues in place. Brush the heads with a mix of olive oil, garlic, oregano, salt and pepper. Lay them, eyes up, in a large roaster.

Combine potatoes, onions, carrots and celery in a bowl and toss to coat with remaining oil mix. Surround the capuzzelles with the vegetables.

Roast them in preheated oven, at 400° for 15 minutes. Reduce heat to 350° and roast lamb for another 20-25 minutes. Serve with an accompaniment of hard-cooked eggs. (Brains have consistency of peanut butter and display a pungent smoky taste.)

LAMB CHOPS IN TOMATO-PRUNE SAUCE

8-10 small thick loin lamb chops, trimmed

1 large onion, thinly sliced

8 fresh prune plums, pitted, halved

1 tbsp. olive oil

salt and freshly ground black pepper to taste

1 lg. can (20 oz.) crushed tomatoes

1 tsp. ground cinnamon

1 tsp. ground cloves

$\frac{1}{2}$ tsp. saffron threads, crushed

$\frac{1}{4}$ cup water

$\frac{1}{4}$ cup dry sherry

In a 2-quart saucepan, combine tomatoes, cinnamon, cloves, saffron, water and wine. Simmer this mixture, stirring occasionally for 20 minutes. Season the sauce with salt and freshly ground black pepper to taste.

In a heavy skillet, warm oil over moderate heat. Add chops, sliced onion and prune plums. Season with salt and freshly ground black pepper. Sauté chops for 3-4 minutes on each side for medium-rare, as you brown onions and plums. Pour sauce over chops in skillet and cook for 1-2 minutes longer.

Transfer chops to a large oven-proof serving platter. Pour tomato-prune sauce over them. If not serving immediately, cover lightly with foil and place platter in warming oven 200° for 20 minutes before serving. Do not overcook. Serves 6.

ASPARAGUS, MUSHROOMS AND ALMONDS

30 asparagus stalks, washed, trimmed

2 cups porcini mushrooms, washed, drained

4 garlic cloves, chopped

$\frac{1}{2}$ cup sliced almonds with skins

1 small red chile pepper, chopped (seeded)

2 tbsp. peanut oil

2 tbsp. honey

1 tsp. sesame oil

3 tbsp. *lite* ginger soy sauce

2 tbsp. sliced almonds with skins for garnish

Blend ginger soy sauce, honey and sesame oil in a cup. Set aside.

Heat peanut oil in a large wok or skillet to moderate high 320°. Stir-fry garlic and asparagus for 2 minutes; stir in mushrooms and cook for 1 minute; add chile pepper and almonds and cook 1 minute longer.

Sprinkle sauce over vegetables; cook 30 seconds more and toss the vegetables to coat thoroughly, with the sauce. Remove wok from heat; garnish with almonds. Serves 6.

PASTIERA DI GRANO I
(Part 1A- prepare 2 days prior to baking the pie.)

PART 1A - FILLING:

¼ lb. wheat berries (grain)

½ cup milk

2 tbsp. butter

1 tsp. salt

½ cup sugar

½ tsp. each: ground cinnamon,
grated lemon rind, grated orange rind

PART 1B - FILLING, cont:

1½ lbs. ricotta

4 large eggs

½ cup sugar

1 tsp. vanilla extract

¼ cup chopped citron

1 tbsp. orange water (You may purchase orange
water at a pharmacy.)

PART 2 - CRUST: (Pasta Frolla: a sweet pie crust)

2 cups sifted flour

½ cup sugar

pinch of salt

¼ cup butter

3 egg yolks

1 tbsp. milk

confectioners' sugar for dusting (optional)

Have ready: a 10-inch pie plate (pan)

Prepare the crust. Sift flour, sugar and a pinch of salt in a medium-size bowl. Cut in butter with a pastry blender or with finger tips to distribute butter evenly through the flour. Stir in egg yolks, one at a time, mixing with wooden spoon.

Work with your hands until dough is easy to manage. Add milk and work in to blend thoroughly. Turn dough onto a lightly floured board and with your hands, knead the dough until smooth, forming it into a ball; (wrap the dough in plastic and chill dough for one hour). Divide dough ball into 2 parts. Cover one part with plastic while you roll out a crust on the lightly floured board. Crust should be about ⅛ to ¼-inch thick, to line a deep 10-inch pie plate or pan.

Grease the pan with butter; line the pan with crust, allowing a ½-inch overhang. Roll out the other half of the dough. Cut 1-inch wide strips for a lattice-work top crust.

PART 1A:

In a medium bowl, soak the grain in cold water for 2 days and nights, changing the water daily. Then, drain the grain, thoroughly.

Boil the grain in 4 cups water for 15 minutes. The grain should crack and soften. Drain the grain and return them to a clean 2-quart saucepot.

Add milk, butter, sugar, salt, cinnamon, lemon and orange rinds and bring to a boil. Reduce heat to low, and simmer until grain absorbs the milk, about 1 hour.

Preheat oven 375º.

When the grain is ready, continue to make the filling.

In a bowl, beat ricotta until smooth. Beat in eggs, 1 at a time; stir in grain mix, sugar, citron, vanilla and orange water. Pour the filling into the pie shell and arrange the dough in lattice strips to cover top of pie. Roll bottom overhang up and over the strips to make a fluted edge around the pie pan.

Bake pie in preheated oven 375º, for 50 minutes, or until a toothpick inserted into the center of the pie slips out clean. When cooled, dust pie with confectioners' sugar, if desired. Serves 6-8.

PASTIERA DI GRANO
(Simple Version)

1 pie shell (sweet pie crust; see previous recipe for Pastiera Di Grano I)
(Or you may purchase 2 prepared pie shells; use one for bottom crust and another for lattice-top crust.)

1 can (about 1 lb.) cooked wheat grain (You may purchase canned wheat grain in Italian
    specialty food shops.)
$\frac{1}{2}$ cup scalded milk
1 tsp. salt
$\frac{1}{2}$ cup sugar
$\frac{1}{4}$ cup chopped citron
grated rinds from 1 orange and 1 lemon

$1\frac{1}{2}$ lbs. ricotta
$\frac{1}{2}$ cup sugar
4 egg yolks, beaten
1 tbsp. orange water (You may purchase orange water at a pharmacy.)
1 tsp. vanilla extract
4 egg whites, stiffly beaten

confectioners' sugar for garnish

    Preheat oven to 375°.
    Scald milk in a 1-quart pot; add 1 can of wheat grain, salt and sugar. Boil the mix for 5 minutes. Remove pot from heat; add citron, orange and lemon peels and set aside.
    In a large bowl, cream ricotta and $\frac{1}{2}$ cup sugar. Add 4 egg yolks, vanilla and orange water to blend well. Stir in prepared grain mix. Fold in stiffly beaten egg whites. Pour mix into prepared pie shell.
    Arrange the top crust dough in lattice strips to cover the pie. Roll bottom overhang up and over the strips to make a fluted edge around the pie pan.
    Bake pie in preheated oven 375° for about 50 minutes, or until toothpick inserted into the center of the pie slips out clean. When pie is thoroughly cooled, dust pie with confectioners' sugar, if desired. Serves 6-8.

Spring-Summer

Washing Dishes May Be Beneficial to Your Health.
(Not to Mention What Scrubbing Pots and Pans Can Do.)

*M*y family's large appliances never included a dishwashing machine. When Mama was "forced" into living her last years in a lovely garden apartment, complete with a Hotpoint dishwasher, the machine went unused for eight years.

Our present home has sported two dishwashing machines in 45 years. Dishwasher#1 lived with us for over 30 years (hadn't operated as a dishwasher for 22 of those 30-plus years). Dishwasher #2 has celebrated its fifteenth birthday; I use it occasionally.

Actually, "the lady of this house" rarely uses her dishwasher. "She" is the dishwasher, as was her own mother before her. I find that washing the dishes and scrubbing the pots and cleaning the ovens are very beneficial to my health. I don't believe that my Mother ever analyzed this matter with as much investigative research as her daughter.

Working around the kitchen after dinner is similar to "the walk around the block" with the dog. It aids the digestion. Although walking the dog on a clear, starlit evening, tends to aid not only my digestive functions; it uplifts my spirits.

Come to think of it, after some careful consideration, walking the dog may be much more beneficial to your health. Leave the dishes to the dishwashing machine.

Chip washes dishes.

146

Spring-Summer

FENNEL, CUCUMBER AND EGG CITRUS SALAD

LEMON-OIL DRESSING

CITRUS CHICKEN

STEAMED BROCCOLI

NEAPOLITAN LEMON AND ORANGE ALMOND CAKE

FENNEL, CUCUMBER AND EGG CITRUS SALAD

greenleaf lettuce leaves for salad beds, washed, drained

2 large fennel bulbs, trimmed, washed

1 medium-to-long cucumber, scraped, sliced into rounds

2 navel oranges, washed, sliced into rounds

3 hard-cooked eggs, quartered

2 roasted red peppers, sliced thin; (*NOTE: "How to Roast Peppers", page 148)

several sprigs of mint, washed

cracked black pepper

lemon juice

Lemon-Oil Dressing (see page 385)

   Prepare dressing and refrigerate it if not using within a couple
of hours.
   Roast the peppers as directed on page 148; or you may use 1 jar
(12 oz.) Italian style roasted peppers in water. (Slice peppers into narrow
strips after roasting.)
   Hard-cook the eggs. Remove shells; cool eggs in refrigerator.
   Assemble the salad. Arrange 6 large lettuce leaves to cover a
15-inch glass or ceramic serving platter. Slice fennel bulbs into ½-inch
rounds. Around the platter, lay sliced fennel, cucumber rounds, navel
orange slices, red pepper strips and egg wedges. Sprinkle the mix
with lemon juice. Grind black peppercorns over the entire dish. Drizzle
platter with Lemon-Oil Dressing. Garnish with mint sprigs. Serves 6.

Aunt Helen Capriglione, Marion and
cousin Ruthie Sanson Bastien,
know how to wash dishes.

*NOTE: "How to Roast Peppers"

(1) If you're roasting more than 2 peppers, preheat oven to 450°. Lay 4-6 peppers on a cookie sheet lined with a sheet of foil. I remove the seeds before I roast the peppers, by coring the peppers and removing the stem with the ribs and seeds. Insert a clove of peeled garlic into the cavity of each pepper. Roast peppers 15-20 minutes on each side (turn twice). The skin will char. Remove the tray from the oven, wrap the peppers in the foil, and allow them to steam, covered, until they're cool enough to handle. Then, you can peel off the skin (starting from blossom end). You may serve them (with the garlic) as a whole pepper or sliced into strips.

(2) OR: If you're roasting 1 or 2 peppers, use a long-handled fork and char the peppers over an open flame, turning them every 2-3 minutes, until skins are charred. Then, proceed to remove skin as in Method (1). Also, cut off ends and discard seeds and ribs.

(3) OR: Broil peppers by laying them on a cookie sheet lined with foil as in Method (1). (You may remove seeds before broiling.) Broil in preheated broiler-oven about 3 inches from heat, turning peppers every 5 minutes for 20 minutes or so, until skins are charred. Proceed as directed in Method (1). (If preparing chiles, use protective gloves.) IN ANY CASE, DO NOT LEAVE PROCEDURE UNATTENDED.

CITRUS CHICKEN

10 to 12 portions of boneless, skinless chicken breast-halves and thighs
2 tbsp. olive oil, 3-4 garlic cloves, minced

MARINADE:

1 tbsp. mild chili powder	juice and grated rind of 1 orange
1 tbsp. Hungarian paprika	(wash skin of all fruit
$\frac{1}{2}$ tsp. ground cumin	before eating)
$\frac{1}{2}$ cup chopped cilantro	juice of 2 limes
	juice of 2 lemons
	$\frac{1}{2}$ cup pineapple juice
	salt, black pepper to taste

Preheat oven to 400°.
Make a marinade with chili powder, cilantro, paprika, cumin, orange juice and rind, lemon, lime and pineapple juices, salt and pepper.
Heat olive oil in a large oven-proof skillet with a handle. Brown garlic; scrape bottom of skillet and add pieces of chicken to fill the pan.
Pour marinade over the chicken. Bake chicken, uncovered, at 400° for 30-35 minutes or until chicken is lightly browned and juices run clear when chicken is pierced. Baste chicken frequently as it roasts. Serves 6.

STEAMED BROCCOLI

Serve STEAMED BROCCOLI as a vegetable side. Steam 4 cups of broccoli florets for 4-5 minutes. Drain. Sprinkle broccoli with a little extra-virgin olive oil and lemon juice at serving. Serve warm or at room temperature.

NEAPOLITAN LEMON AND ORANGE ALMOND CAKE

3 eggs or $\frac{3}{4}$ cup egg substitute

$\frac{1}{3}$ cup canola oil

1 pkg. (22 oz.) yellow cake mix

$\frac{3}{4}$ cup low-fat milk

2 tbsp. orange liqueur

finely grated rinds and juices of 1 orange and 1 lemon

$\frac{1}{4}$ cup ground almonds

1 tsp. ground cinnamon

$\frac{1}{4}$ cup sliced almonds with skin and confectioners' sugar for garnish

Preheat oven to 350°.

Grease and flour an 8-inch tube pan.

In a large bowl, beat together: eggs, milk and oil. Add cake mix, a little at a time, beating after each addition. Stir in liqueur, rinds, juices, ground almonds and cinnamon. Beat batter at medium speed for 2 minutes. Pour batter into prepared pan and bake the cake in a moderate oven at 350° for 35 to 40 minutes until golden, and inserted tester removes clean.

Allow cake to cool in pan for 10 minutes. Turn cake onto a serving dish. Garnish cake with sliced almonds. When cake is thoroughly cooled, sift confectioners' sugar over top, just before serving. Serves 6-8.

Original ink sketch of Banshee, Jet, Teller and Luci by talented Brian McCabe.

Spring-Summer

Planting and Growing a Vegetable Garden

A plant is a living thing. Plants make their own food through the process of photosynthesis. Leaves are green because of the plants' own food factories, chloroplasts. Using the sun's energy, plants combine water and carbon dioxide to make food. The soil provides minerals for plants, not food. The roots are the transportation system of the plant, carrying water and minerals using tubes, called xylem; and plants transport food from the leaves to the rest of the plant through tubes called phloem. Plants absorb carbon dioxide and give off oxygen through tiny pores called stomata.

So, why do my tomato plants have dry and withered leaves? Why are there rotten areas at the blossom end? Why did the basil shrivel up and expire after one "cool" night? And then, there's those slugs, bugs and other plant predators.

Food plants and farmers don't stand a chance! Yet, look around and behind? Apparently, human kind has been quite successful in continuing its generations. Perhaps, it's because we have our obligation to assist Nature in her quest to feed the world. We must sow the seed on fertile soil; obey the laws of the seasons; add water if the clouds take a vacation; and pray for sunshine.

Spring-Summer

CAPRESE SALAD
SEAFOOD GENOESE
GRILLED VEGETABLE MÉLANGE
CHOCOLATE MERINGUES AND RASPBERRIES

CAPRESE SALAD

3 large firm beefsteak tomatoes, sliced into thick rounds
   (You will need at least 12 slices of tomatoes.)
1 (1 lb.) fresh smoky mozzarella, cut into 12 slices
1½ dozen large basil leaves
2 dozen pitted oil-cured olives
1 tbsp. balsamic vinegar
2 tbsp. extra-virgin olive oil
salt to taste, freshly ground black pepper

Preheat broiler to 500°.

Blend vinegar and oil in a small jar or a cup.

On a 9x12-inch metal tray, place 6 slices of tomatoes; top each with one basil leaf and a slice of mozzarella. Cover each with another slice of tomato, one basil leaf and a slice of mozzarella.
Press 4 olives into each top slice of cheese.

Grill the tomato-cheese tiers in preheated broiler, 5 inches away from heat, for 2 minutes, until cheese starts to bubble and turns golden.

Remove tray from broiler; drizzle the servings with oil/balsamic vinegar mix. Add salt to taste and grind black peppercorns over the tray. Garnish with basil leaves. Serve with a spatula onto individual serving salad dishes. Serves 6.

SEAFOOD GENOESE

1½ cups arborio rice

3 cups seafood stock (prepared by simmering
    1 doz. raw jumbo shrimp, in shell,
    in 1 cup water for 5 minutes, until shrimp
    become opaque)

1 dozen Little Neck clams in shell, scrubbed
    with seafood brush under running cold water

1 dozen mussels, scrubbed with brush under
    running cold water

1 small onion, chopped

2 garlic cloves, minced

2 tbsp. olive oil

1 tsp. saffron threads

1 tbsp. dried oregano

salt, pepper to taste

½ cup grated Pecorino Romano cheese

Simmer shrimp in shell in 1 cup water for 5 minutes or until shrimp turn opaque or slightly pink in color. Drain liquid into a small bowl. Set aside cooked shrimp.

In a wide 4-quart pan with cover, lightly brown onion and garlic in olive oil for 2 minutes. Scrape bottom of pot to remove leavings. Pour in seafood stock (about 1 cup); add 2 additional cups of water to pot. Pour in rice, salt and pepper to taste, saffron and oregano. Stir to mix thoroughly.

Cover pot and bring to boil; lower heat and simmer gently for 15 minutes. Float clams and mussels in rice and simmer for an additional 5-10 minutes, or until shells open. (Discard any shells which do not open.)

Add and stir: bowl of cooked shrimp in shell. Cook for 2-3 minutes; transfer seafood risotto to a large warmed ceramic serving platter. Sprinkle entire dish with Pecorino Romano cheese. Serve hot. Serves 6.

GRILLED VEGETABLE MÉLANGE

1 dozen spears slender asparagus, trimmed, rinsed

2 cups sliced mushrooms

1 small onion, thinly sliced

2 tbsp. olive oil

¼ cup seeded, chopped red pepper

¼ cup seeded, chopped poblano pepper

8 very tiny red potatoes, scrubbed, halved

1 can (12 oz.) corn kernels, rinsed, drain

2-3 torn basil leaves

1 tbsp. dried oregano

¼ tsp. black pepper

salt to taste

¼ cup pitted oil-cured olives

In a large skillet or solid metal grill pan, heat oil to moderate high and cook onions and potatoes until tender; add asparagus and mushrooms and cook for 5 minutes longer, stirring vegetables with a spatula. Stir in red pepper, poblano and basil leaves. Empty can of corn into the mix; season with pepper, salt and oregano, tossing the mix, and cook for 2 minutes, until corn is hot. Transfer the mélange to a serving platter; sprinkle with olives. Serve warm. Serves 6.

CHOCOLATE CHIP MERINGUES AND RASPBERRIES

6 egg whites
1½ cups granulated sugar
1 tsp. cinnamon
2 cups tiny dark chocolate chips (Use a dark chocolate with at least 60% cacao.)
½ cup dark cocoa (Use a dark chocolate cocoa with at least 60% cacao.)
1 cup chopped almonds
1 cup grated coconut
cinnamon for sprinkling

Prepare 3 baking sheets, 9x15 inches by lining them with aluminum foil. Set aside.

Preheat the oven to 375° for 3 hours prior to baking.

Beat egg whites in a large bowl with electric mixer on high. Gradually, add sugar and continue to beat until meringue is stiff and holds peaks. Do not underbeat.

Using electric mixer, beat in cinnamon and cocoa, just until blended. Fold in chocolate chips, chopped almonds and coconut. Drop by heaping tablespoons onto the foil-lined tins. Lightly sprinkle cookies with cinnamon

Open the oven door(s) and place all the trays into the oven(s) on separate racks; quickly, close the door(s); then, TURN OFF the oven(s).

Allow the cookies to slow bake IN THE OVEN OVERNIGHT (or at least for 8-9 hours).
And forget it!!! After at least 8-9 hours, remove trays from oven and gently peel the cookies off the foil onto clean trays.

Treat the cookies gingerly. They are very fragile. You may wish to arrange layers of cookies on trays, with tissue paper in between layers. (These cookies are well worth the effort.) Serve with fresh raspberries. Yields about 5 dozen.

Spring-Summer

Not Everyone Eats Cheerios for Breakfast

*H*ave you ever wondered what people in other countries eat for breakfast? The American way of breaking fast can include a simple bowl of cheerios or oatmeal; or a cup of coffee sold at a fast food rest stop; or, juice, bacon, eggs. rolls, potatoes and a pot of coffee, plus a donut. A few of my relatives and friends from other nations were happy to share their experiences on this topic.

In China, breakfast is quick, even on weekends! Street vendors offer inexpensive and quick pick-me-ups. At home, breakfast usually is a bowl of rice porridge or noodles or soybean milk soup. However, the Chinese have a "sweet tooth" for pancakes, doughnuts and buns. And tea, believe it, is not usually the beverage of choice at breakfast. Soups provide the liquid (or milk, for the younger folks).

Russians like open-faced sandwiches with cheese, salami or ham and tea. Children, however, may start their day with boiled eggs, Kasha (cooked grains) and milk.

Italians prefer a "continental" breakfast of coffee/tea/ hot cocoa with bread and butter or jam. France has its own version of a "continental" breakfast with croissants and jam, dipped into a large mug of coffee, no butter!

Traditionally, in Great Britain, BIG breakfasts are for weekends only. These breakfasts include sausage, bacon, eggs, baked beans, fried bread and tomatoes. Most Brits, however, start the morning with cereal and milk, toast with jam or marmalade, and tea (or coffee).

Chip prepares for school.

Spring-Summer

⬥

SHRIMP WITH CASHEWS
EGG FOO YUNG
CHINESE FRIED VEGETABLES
ORANGES AND BERRIES IN LIME

SHRIMP WITH CASHEWS

2 lbs. jumbo shrimp, peeled, deveined, leave tail on

$\frac{1}{2}$ cup cornstarch

cayenne pepper (to taste)

4 tbsp. canola oil

SAUCE:

2 leeks, thinly sliced	1 can (15 oz.) evaporated milk (fat-free available)
2 garlic cloves, minced	2 tbsp. cornstarch, stirred into $\frac{1}{2}$ cup water
2 cups broccoli florets	2 tbsp. rice wine vinegar
1 red bell pepper, seeded, thinly sliced	a few dashes Tabasco
1 can (1 lb.) pineapple chunks	$\frac{1}{2}$ cup chili sauce
$\frac{1}{2}$ cup unsalted cashews, chopped	2 tbsp. chopped parsley for garnish

Heat 4 tbsp. canola oil in a large skillet. Pour $\frac{1}{2}$ cup cornstarch, mixed with cayenne pepper, in a small bowl. Coat each shrimp in this mix and fry on both sides in skillet at 320°. You may have to cook 6 shrimp at a time. Transfer cooked shrimp to a paper towel-lined platter and set aside. After the shrimp are cooked, add another tablespoon canola oil to skillet, if necessary. Add leeks, garlic, broccoli and pepper to the pan and stir fry at 320° for 2-3 minutes. Mix in pineapple and cashews during last minute.

In a small bowl, combine 2 tablespoons cornstarch stirred into $\frac{1}{2}$ cup water with 2 tablespoons rice wine vinegar, chili sauce and Tabasco. Slowly stir and blend evaporated milk into the paste. Pour this mix into the skillet with the vegetables. Stir to mix. Continue to simmer while stirring. Sauce will thicken (in a few minutes).

Return shrimp to skillet; spoon sauce over shrimp and cook for a couple of minutes until shrimp are heated through. Sprinkle shrimp with parsley and serve directly from the skillet. Serves 6.

EGG FOO YUNG

1 doz. eggs or egg substitute

2 cups cooked chicken breast, shredded

1 doz. ex-large shrimp, peeled, cleaned

1 tbsp. chopped gingerroot

2 scallions, chopped, including greens

1 tbsp. chopped coriander

2-3 tsp. *lite* soy sauce

a few dashes of Tabasco

4-6 small mushrooms, chopped

2 tbsp. peanut oil

In a large bowl, beat eggs. Add and mix: gingerroot, scallions, mushrooms, coriander, soy sauce and Tabasco.

Heat oil, 320° in a very large non-stick skillet, preferably electric. Pour beaten egg mix in heated skillet, tilting the pan to coat the base completely. As the omelet sets, arrange shrimp and shredded chicken over egg mix. Cover and continue to cook over medium heat (lower to 280°) until the surface is set and the underside is a golden brown in color, when moved with a spatula.

Turn off heat and remove skillet from heat and allow to set for a few minutes. With a long spatula, loosen omelet around and under the pan. Place a large serving plate (about 15 inches in diameter) over the omelet, surface-side facing omelet. Hold plate in place with one hand and invert skillet onto plate. Remove skillet carefully over the platter which you've placed on counter.
Now, you can use a spatula to assist the omelet to slide onto the platter.
Cut omelet into squares or wedges. Serves 4-6.

CHINESE FRIED VEGETABLES

2 tbsp. peanut oil

1 bunch broccoli florets, washed, drained

1 large onion, thinly sliced

3 celery stalks, trimmed, cut into small chunks

10 oz. baby spinach, rinsed, drained

6 oz. snow peas, trimmed

3-4 scallions, including greens, trimmed, chopped

1 dozen baby carrots, scraped, trimmed

2-3 garlic cloves, chopped

1 tbsp. gingerroot

ASIAN DRESSING II:

$\frac{1}{4}$ cup sherry

2 tbsp. *lite* soy sauce

2 tbsp. hoisin sauce

Chinese 5-spice powder

Prepare dressing. In a cup, blend sherry, soy sauce, hoisin sauce and 5-spice powder. Set aside. Heat peanut oil in large wok or skillet at 300°. Cut broccoli into small florets. Cook broccoli, onion, celery, scallions, snow peas, carrot, garlic, gingerroot for 2-3 minutes. Add spinach and cook for another minute.

Remove from heat and place a lid on top while you stir the dressing. Remove cover and drizzle sherry mix over vegetables. Toss with 2 spoons to coat thoroughly. Serve directly from wok. Serves 5-6.

ORANGES AND BERRIES IN LIME

3-4 navel oranges, skin removed, cut into sections

1$\frac{1}{2}$ dozen strawberries, hulled, washed, drained, halved

8 oz. blueberries, washed, drained

grated rind and juice of 1 lime

$\frac{1}{4}$ cup strawberry liqueur (or cherry)

orange peel twirls, mint sprigs, for garnish

Wash all skins and fruits gently and thoroughly. Pat dry with paper towels or drain.

In a decorative serving bowl, combine orange segments, strawberries and blueberries. Sprinkle grated rind, juice of lime and liqueur. Toss fruit gently with 2 large spoons to coat with sauce. Garnish with orange peel and a sprig of mint. Serves 4-6.

Spring-Summer

The Doggie Bag or
"2 for the Price of 1"

When relatives and friends shared a special supper at our home, they were certain to go home with a "doggie bag". In fact, habits had been formed, and the doggie bag was expected and welcomed.

Mama's doggie bags weren't what you couldn't consume at our dinner table; they were P.S.'s for you to enjoy at your table the next day. My mother set a beautiful table; she also set a generous example for her daughter to follow.

Only one negative: I am constantly shopping for storage containers.

Spring-Summer

CHINESE CHICKEN SALAD
MME. ELIZABETH KOSMACH'S SUPERB GOLDEN CRESCENTS
STUFFED ZUCCHINI FLOWERS FROM THE FARM
STRAWBERRIES AND CHERRIES WITH CHOCOLATE SAUCE

CHINESE CHICKEN SALAD

3 full chicken breasts, skinless, boneless, sliced into
    narrow strips after you marinate the chicken

2-3 tbsp. canola oil

1 small can baby whole corn, drained,
    each tiny ear, cut in half, lengthwise

1 red pepper, seeded, thinly sliced

1 carrot, pared, cut into narrow sticks

1 small can (8 oz.) sliced water chestnuts, drained

1 can (6 oz.) bean sprouts, drained

3-4 scallions, trimmed, sliced vertically like straws

MARINADE:

2 tbsp. sesame seeds

1 tbsp. sesame oil

2 tbsp. *lite* soy sauce

SAUCE:

2 tbsp. rice wine vinegar

4 tbsp. *lite* soy sauce

a few dashes of Tabasco

Wash chicken in cold water; drain and pat dry with paper towels. Lay chicken in a shallow dish.

Stir soy sauce and sesame oil in a small bowl. Drizzle this mix over the chicken; sprinkle sesame seeds over chicken. Lay chicken on glass board and thinly slice into strips.

Heat canola oil in a large wok or skillet, 320°. Sauté chicken pieces on both sides for 4-5 minutes. Remove with slotted spoon to a large serving platter. Allow chicken to cool.

Add sprouts, pepper, carrot, water chestnuts and corn to the wok and cook for 2-3 minutes. Remove vegetables to serving platter with slotted spoon. Place vegetables in center of platter; arrange chicken in a circle around the vegetables. Arrange scallion sticks to garnish vegetables.

Meanwhile, combine sauce ingredients. Spoon sauce over the chicken salad and serve at room temperature. Serves 6.

MME. ELIZABETH KOSMACH'S SUPERB GOLDEN CRESCENTS

(Elizabeth Kosmach was the mother of my dear friend, Lena Zukowski.
This delightful lady enriched us with her love, kindness and sense of humor for over 102 years.)

$\frac{1}{2}$ cup sugar

$\frac{1}{4}$ lb. butter or Smart Balance spread, melted

1 tsp. salt

2 eggs

$\frac{1}{2}$ cup lukewarm milk

2 pkgs. dry yeast

$\frac{1}{2}$ cup very warm (not hot) water

$3\frac{1}{2}$-4 cups unsifted flour

Preheat the oven to 350°.

In a large bowl, beat until smooth: sugar, melted butter, salt and eggs. Stir in lukewarm milk. Dissolve yeast in very warm water. Add and blend yeast mixture to egg mixture. Stir in unsifted flour until well blended. Scrape down sides of bowl.

Cover the dough with a tea towel and allow dough to rise in a warm place until doubled, about $1\frac{1}{2}$ hours. Divide dough into 2 portions.

On a floured board, roll out each portion in a 15-inch circle and cut this "pie" into 8 wedges. Do the same with the other portion.

Have ready: two 9x15-inch greased cookie sheets. Roll up each wedge (triangle) of dough from its wide edge, securely pinching the point to the middle section of the roll. Shape each roll into a crescent (tighter than a half-circle) and lay each crescent on a greased baking sheet with the sealed point down; allow about a $1\frac{1}{2}$-inch space around the crescents.

Cover each pan with tea towels and allow the rolls to rise in a warm place, for about 45 minutes, until they are fluffy and puffed-looking.

Bake the crescents in a preheated oven 350° in the center of the oven for 10-15 minutes, one tray at a time. It would be a rewarding experience just to view these ethereal crescents behind a clear glass oven door. Makes 16 superb crescent rolls.

STUFFED ZUCCHINI FLOWERS FROM THE FARM

1 dozen zucchini flowers, rinsed, drained well, and patted dry with paper towels; remove stamens

$\frac{1}{2}$ cup gorgonzola, chopped

$\frac{1}{2}$ cup mozzarella, cubed

In a small bowl, mix gorgonzola and mozzarella cheeses. Spread open the zucchini flowers (remove stamen) and insert 1 tablespoon of the cheese mix into each flower. Set aside.

COATING:

3 eggs, beaten with $\frac{1}{4}$ cup cold water
   (or use egg substitute in place of whole eggs)

$\frac{1}{2}$ cup grated Romano cheese

$\frac{1}{4}$ tsp. black pepper

dash of salt

1 cup sifted flour

canola oil for frying

In a wide plate with a rim, beat together: eggs, water, Romano cheese, pepper and salt. Sift flour onto a sheet of waxed paper. Heat to moderate-high, $\frac{1}{4}$-inch of oil in a skillet.

Dredge filled flowers in flour; dip them to coat with egg mix; fry them in hot oil on both sides until golden in color, about 3-4 minutes. Drain them on paper towels; keep them in a warm oven. Serves 6.

STRAWBERRIES AND CHERRIES WITH CHOCOLATE SAUCE

2 lbs. large strawberries with stems, washed, drained thoroughly

2 cups Bing and/or Queen Anne cherries, washed and drained, leave stems

8 oz. Ghiradelli (or other gourmet brand) semisweet chocolate morsels

1 tbsp. Chambord (strawberry liqueur) or Cherry Heering

Pour chocolate morsels into top half of a small double-boiler. Add 1 cup water to bottom half. Place double boiler on stove burner; bring water to a boil; then, lower to simmer for 5 minutes, until chocolate melts. Stir chocolate frequently.

Remove pots from burner; remove top pot with chocolate from lower pot of hot water. Stir 1 tablespoon of liqueur into the melted chocolate. Spoon the sauce into a small serving bowl which will be set in the center of a 12-inch serving platter.

Arrange the prepared strawberries and cherries around the dip bowl on the serving platter. Refrigerate platter of fruit until needed; however, remove bowl of chocolate and maintain sauce at room temperature. Serves 6-8.

Spring-Summer

Shake Vigorously, and
Other Cooking Instructions

ookbook and recipe instructions give me a chuckle. Whether a word is misspelled or misused – or a letter or word omitted or transposed, the phraseology certainly can tickle the risibilities. I'm thinking especially of:

"Blend oil and vinegar with herbs and shake vigorously"; or "blend oil and vinegar with herbs; shake vigorously".

"Break an egg and beat it" as in "break an egg; beat it". (And away I go!)

"Cook for 1 hour at 3:25" (and don't even attempt cooking it at any other time.)

"Allow cake to cool thoroughly on a rake before removing from pan."

"Cook the broccoli in a pot of bowling water for 4-5 minutes."

"Chow mein needles make a fine accompaniment." (very, very fine)

"Paste chicken in roasting pan."

*"1 tsp. ground cinnamon
$\frac{1}{2}$ tsp. ground gloves"*

"Check doneness with a tooth; if it comes out clean, cake is ready."

"Serve warm with ice cream scoop on top."

"Cover pot and turn up the heat."
(I always knew that the kitchen was the warmest room in the house.)

How many chuckles does THIS COOKBOOK offer the reader?

Spring-Summer

SCALLOPS IN GINGER SAUCE
VEGETABLE FRITTO MISTO (heirloom)
LIME RICE
LEMON MOUSSE

SCALLOPS IN GINGER SAUCE

2 lbs. sea scallops, washed in cold water, drained

2 tbsp. peanut oil

4 garlic cloves, minced

3-4 leeks, trimmed, chopped

3-4 scallions with greens, trimmed,
    cut into lengthwise strips

1-inch piece gingerroot, peeled, grated

1 cup shitake mushrooms, in small pieces

1 can (6 oz.) bamboo shoots, drained

2 cups snow peas, trimmed

GINGER SAUCE:

$\frac{1}{4}$ cup *lite* soy sauce

1 tsp. Chinese 5-spice powder

$\frac{1}{2}$ cup orange juice

grated rind of 1 orange

1 navel orange, cut into 6 wedges for garnish

Prepare Ginger Sauce. In a small bowl blend soy sauce, orange juice, 5-spice powder, rind; set aside.

Heat peanut oil 320° in a large wok; sauté scallops, garlic, leeks, scallions, gingerroot for 3-4 minutes; add snow peas, mushrooms, bamboo shoots and stir fry for another 2-3 minutes. Lower heat to moderate 300° and stir in sauce to coat scallops and vegetables. Cook for another 2-3 minutes. Garnish with orange wedges. Serve hot. Serves 4-6.

VEGETABLE FRITTO MISTO
(May be warmed in oven before serving.)

1/4 cup canola oil for a large skillet
(plus more oil as needed)

8 eggs beaten with 1/4 cup water, or
2 cups egg substitute, beaten

1/4 cup finely grated Parmesan cheese

1 cup sifted flour

salt and pepper to taste

1 cup unseasoned bread crumbs

1 tbsp. finely chopped parsley

4 small-medium zucchini, scrape skin, trim ends,
quarter into lengthwise strips

1 medium-size eggplant, pared, 1/2-inch
thick slices (cut the slices in half)

1 jar (16 oz.) seasoned artichoke hearts, drained

15-18 asparagus spears, medium-size thick

1 small-medium cauliflower, rinsed, drained,
separated into small florets

3-4 broccoli spears, rinsed, drained,
separated into small florets

3 lemons, quartered, for garnish

Break eggs into a 2-quart bowl; add cheese and water and whisk to blend thoroughly.

Lay 2 sheets of waxed paper, side-by-side on a board. Spread sifted flour, blended with salt and pepper on one sheet; spread crumbs, mixed with parsley on the other sheet of waxed paper.

Set out 2 large plates; sprinkle a coating of flour on each. Pour 1/4 cup canola oil into bottom of a large skillet and have it ready for frying the breaded vegetables.

Bread the zucchini strips and eggplant slices by first coating each piece with flour mix; then by dipping them into beaten eggs; then by coating with crumbs mix. Lay them neatly on one of the platters; leave a space for the asparagus.

Next, coat asparagus in flour mix, dip each stalk into the egg mix; then roll the spears into the crumb mix. Set on plate. Do the same with drained artichokes.

Finally, stir and blend remaining flour into the eggs. Add a tablespoon or two of water if batter is too thick; or add a tablespoon or two of flour, if batter is too thin to coat the cauliflower. Dip the cauliflower segments into the batter, shaking off excess batter. Lay them on a clean plate, leaving room for broccoli.

Scrape the rest of the crumbs mix into the bowl of batter and stir to blend. Dip the broccoli florets into this crumb batter and lay them next to the cauliflower on the plate.

Sauté the vegetables in oil in a preheated skillet, starting with zucchini, eggplant, asparagus, cauliflower and broccoli. Replenish skillet with more oil as necessary, lightly browning zucchini and eggplant on both sides and lightly crisping the asparagus. Cooking the cauliflower and broccoli florets will take a little longer, especially the cauliflower. Work with vegetable tongs, or a spatula and large spoon to assist you.

Transfer the cooked vegetables to the board which you've lined with paper towels to absorb the oil residue. Have ready: a large heat-resistant platter, 9x15 inches. With tongs, carefully transfer all of the fried vegetables to the platter. Offer lemon wedges in a separate small bowl. Serve warm. Serves 6.

LIME RICE

½ cup brown rice
½ cup wild rice, pre-soaked in hot water
    for 1 hour
2 tbsp. olive oil
1 small sweet red pepper, chopped
1 yellow onion, minced

4 garlic cloves, minced
3 cups canned chicken stock, less-salt variety
1 can (8 oz.) corn kernels
juice of 2 limes
¼ cup chopped fresh cilantro (for garnish)

Heat oil in 2-quart pot with lid. Brown garlic, onion and pepper; scrape bottom of pot to loosen leavings. Add brown and wild rice and stock. Cover, bring to a boil; then, simmer for 20-25 minutes, or until liquid is almost absorbed and rice is tender.

Stir in corn and juice of 2 limes. Pour rice mix into serving bowl; garnish with cilantro. Serve hot; serves 4-6.

LEMON MOUSSE

1 cup heavy cream
1 envelope unflavored gelatin
¼ cup water
4 eggs, separated (or 1 cup egg substitute,
    whites only from 4 eggs)

⅔ cup sugar
¼ cup fresh lemon juice, strained
2 tbsp. grated lemon rind
lemon slices for garnish

Beat cream until it forms peaks, refrigerate it, uncovered. Soften gelatin in water over a pot of hot water. Beat egg yolks; add sugar a little at a time and beat until frothy. Beat egg whites in a separate, clean bowl until stiff peaks form and set aside. Add lemon juice, rind, and gelatin to yolks mix. Fold in egg whites and whipped cream. Garnish with lemon slices. Chill for several hours. Serves 6.

Spring-Summer

Food for Thought

*F*ish and seafood are good for us. Omega-3 fatty acids are good guys. Salmon is king among fish when it comes to those "good- guy", heart-saving fatty acids. So are mackerel, tuna, sardines. Trout, herring (not creamed), and shrimp make a good grade.

Fish is a tasty food and usually broils, grills and steams in a short cooking time.

Now that's food for thought _ FISH.

Cousins Glenn, Austin and Jan Miller go fishing for their dinner.(Aunt Anna Capriglione Mazza's grandchildren and great-grandchildren.)
Photo-courtesy of The Millers

Spring-Summer

MARINATED SHRIMP WITH GUACAMOLE
MEDITERRANEAN BAKED SWORDFISH
BRUSCHETTA DI POMIDORO
MOCHA MOUSSE

MARINATED SHRIMP WITH GUACAMOLE

2 lbs. jumbo shrimp, shelled, cleaned, leave on tail

1 tsp. ground cumin

1 tsp. mild chili powder

$\frac{1}{2}$ tsp. Hungarian paprika

$\frac{1}{4}$ cup orange juice

grated rind of 1 orange

2 tbsp. extra-virgin olive oil

2 tbsp. chopped cilantro

salt, pepper to taste

6 metal skewers

Thread 6 metal skewers with prepared shrimp. In a small bowl mix all of the basting ingredients: orange juice, cumin, chili powder, paprika, rind, oil, cilantro, salt and pepper. Brush this mix on skewered shrimp. Cook on hot grill, basting and turning, a few minutes on each side. Serve immediately with a portion of chilled guacamole (see below), and small, split, grill-toasted rolls. Serves 6.

GUACAMOLE:

1 large ripe avocado

2 tbsp. chopped cilantro

1 small red chile pepper, seeded, finely chopped

1-2 tbsp. finely chopped tomato

1 small onion, finely chopped

juice of 1 lime

salt, black pepper to taste

Carefully peel skin off avocado; cut avocado in half and remove stone (discard stone). Place avocado pulp in bowl. Mash with hand masher and add/mix cilantro, tomato, onion, chile, lime juice, salt and pepper. Cover and refrigerate the guacamole.

MEDITERRANEAN BAKED SWORDFISH

6 medium-size swordfish steaks,
    about ¾-inch thick
2-3 fennel bulbs, trimmed, cut into
    ¼-inch rounds, including some fennel grass
2 tbsp. olive oil
¼ cup Kalamata olives, pitted, chopped

1 tsp. grated lemon rind
¼ cup dry white wine
1 tbsp. fresh lemon juice
1 large navel orange, washed,
    thinly sliced into rounds

Preheat oven to 450°.

Heat oil in a skillet to moderate-high. Cook fennel in oil for 3-4 minutes, stirring constantly. Add wine, olives, lemon juice and rind. Cook 1 minute longer. Remove skillet from heat.

Arrange swordfish steaks in a greased, oven-proof baking pan. Lay orange rounds on top of fish. Spoon fennel mix over swordfish. Cover with foil and roast fish in preheated oven 450° for 10 minutes. Remove foil; spoon fennel sauce over fish and continue to roast fish 10 minutes longer. Serves 6.

BRUSCHETTA DI POMIDORO

about 3 doz. or more cherry or grape tomatoes,
    halved
4 garlic cloves, chopped
1½ doz. basil leaves, shredded

¼ cup extra-virgin olive oil
salt, freshly ground black pepper
6-8 slices ciabatta

Place halved tomatoes in a bowl. Add basil, oil, salt and pepper. Sprinkle garlic on ciabatta slices; lightly toast ciabatta in toaster oven or under broiler. This procedure should take only 1 minute or so. Do not leave toasting bread unattended.

Arrange toasts around a 15-inch glass plate. Spoon tomato mix over bread and serve immediately. Serves 6.

MOCHA MOUSSE

1 pkg. (6 oz.) semisweet chocolate morsels

5 tbsp. boiling liquid coffee (you may use decaffeinated coffee)

4 eggs, separated (or 1 cup egg substitute and whites only, from 4 eggs)

2 tbsp. rum

Combine morsels, with coffee, in blender. Cover blender jar, and set at high speed for 10 seconds, or until chocolate-coffee mix is smooth. Add 4 yolks and rum, and cover to blend for 5 seconds, or until smooth. In a clean bowl, beat egg whites until stiff peaks form. Fold the chocolate mix into the meringue. Spoon the mousse into serving bowls to chill in refrigerator for several hours. Serves 6.

Spring-Summer

It May Not Be the Slightest Gourmet; But It's Totally Ergonomic.

*W*ithin the past five years, "everyone" in my neighborhood has refurbished their kitchen. These new additions, "the most important room in the house" (as far as I'm concerned) are truly breathtaking. One envies the restaurant-size stainless refrigerators; gas stoves (with at least 6 burners), which weigh in at 3,000 pounds apiece; marble-inlaid counters which extend beyond the imagination; recessed lighting EVERYWHERE.

From what I'm told, some day soon, these gorgeous centerpieces will be utilized as they're intended: as rooms, furnished with enough equipment to cook small or large meals, for a gathering of family and friends to enjoy.

Cathy and Chip's new kitchen.

Spring-Summer

SPINACH, ROASTED POTATOES AND CORN SALAD
HONEY MUSTARD DRESSING
GINGER SOY CHICKEN IN WINE
SESAME GREEN BEANS
POTATO AND APPLE CHEDDAR PANCAKES
PUMPKIN SPICE PANCAKES
CHOCOLATE SPICE APPLES

SPINACH, ROASTED POTATOES AND CORN SALAD

10 oz. pkg. baby spinach, rinsed, drained
2 cups tiny red potatoes, scrubbed, halved, roasted (*NOTE: below)
1 tbsp. dried oregano
2 tbsp. olive oil
1 can (1 lb.) corn kernels
1 small red onion, thinly sliced
1 medium sweet red pepper, seeded, thinly sliced

Honey Mustard Dressing (see page 384)

Prepare Honey Mustard Dressing. Refrigerate dressing until needed. Remove jar from refrigerator 1 hour before serving.

In a large salad bowl, combine and toss: spinach, roasted potatoes, onion, red pepper and corn kernels. Just before serving, drizzle dressing over salad and toss to mix thoroughly. Serves 6.

*NOTE: Place halved tiny potatoes in a bowl. Sprinkle with oregano and olive oil and toss them to coat thoroughly. Spread the potato mix over a cookie sheet and roast them in a preheated oven, at 400° for 20-25 minutes, occasionally stirring them to roast on all sides. Add them to salad, warm, or at room temperature.

GINGER SOY CHICKEN IN WINE

3 boneless, skinless, whole chicken breasts,
    halved and flattened slightly between
    2 sheets waxed paper
$\frac{1}{4}$ cup ginger-soy sauce
    (less-salt variety is available)
1 tsp. peeled gingerroot, minced

$\frac{1}{2}$ cup honey
$\frac{1}{4}$ cup dry sherry
2 tbsp. white wine vinegar
3-4 garlic cloves, minced
salt and black pepper to taste

In a wide dish with a rim, whisk together: ginger-soy sauce, gingerroot, honey, sherry, vinegar, garlic, salt and pepper. Add chicken and let pieces marinate in the soy sauce mix for 30 minutes, turning them a couple of times.

Transfer marinated chicken to the oiled rack of a broiler pan (or grill) and broil or grill the chicken about 6 inches from heat for 5 minutes.

Boil the leftover marinade until it is reduced by half. Brush the chicken with some of the marinade; turn over the pieces and brush with remaining marinade.

Broil or grill chicken for 4-6 minutes longer or until just cooked through. Transfer the chicken pieces to a cutting board and slice them on the diagonal into $\frac{1}{2}$-inch thick slices. Serve over rice or noodles. Serves 6.

SESAME GREEN BEANS
(Wear plastic gloves when working with hot peppers.)

3 cups green beans, cut in small pieces
2 fresh red cayenne peppers, seeded, sliced thin
    (seeding the peppers will create
    a milder taste)
$\frac{1}{4}$ cup sesame seeds (2 tbsp. extra for garnish)
1 tsp. Chinese 5-spice powder

1 tsp. sesame oil
3 tbsp. *lite* soy sauce
3 tbsp. honey
1 garlic clove, minced
2 tbsp. peanut oil

Blend soy sauce, honey, sesame oil and 5-spice powder in a cup. Set aside. Heat peanut oil in large wok or skillet to moderate-high, 320°. Lightly brown garlic for 30 seconds. Add green beans and peppers and stir fry for 2 minutes. Sprinkle sesame seeds as you cook.

Drizzle sauce mix over beans, tossing to coat thoroughly; cook 1 minute longer. Remove wok from heat. Sprinkle with sesame seeds and serve. Serves 6.

POTATO AND APPLE CHEDDAR PANCAKES
(Pancakes may be prepared well in advance and frozen in small stacks,
waxed paper between each pancake.)

2 all-purpose potatoes, pared, grated

1 small onion, freshly chopped

1 Granny Smith apple, pared, finely chopped

1 cup cheddar cheese, shredded

4 cups Bisquick low-fat flour mix

2 cups low-fat or fat-free evaporated milk

$\frac{1}{4}$ tsp. each: ground nutmeg, ground cinnamon, ground cloves

2 eggs, or $\frac{1}{2}$ cup egg substitute, beaten

canola oil for griddle (skillet)

Beat 2 cups milk and 2 beaten eggs into 4 cups Bisquick. Stir in grated potatoes, onion, apple, cheddar and spices. Mix thoroughly. If batter is too thick add a few tablespoons of milk.

Grease griddle or skillet with canola oil and heat to 320°.

Pour $\frac{1}{2}$ cup of batter per pancake. Bake on both sides until light golden brown. Transfer pancakes in stacks of 3 to a warming tray.

Recipe makes about 13-15 pancakes. Cover them with foil to keep warm in a low oven, 200°. Serve with pure maple syrup or honey. Serves 4-6.

PUMPKIN SPICE PANCAKES

4 cups Bisquick low-fat flour mix

1 can (1 lb.) pure pumpkin

2 cups low-fat evaporated milk (fat-free available)

2 eggs, beaten or $\frac{1}{2}$ cup egg substitute

$\frac{1}{4}$ cup brown sugar

1 tsp. ground cinnamon

1 tsp. ground ginger

$\frac{1}{2}$ tsp. ground cloves

Preheat griddle or skillet to 320°. Grease pan with canola oil.

Beat milk and eggs into Bisquick. Add/blend 1 can of pumpkin, brown sugar and the spices. Continue the recipe by following the directions in the previous pancake recipe: Potato and Apple Cheddar Pancakes. Makes about 13-15 pancakes. (Pancakes freeze well. Simply, stack the pancakes, waxed paper between each; wrap stacks in foil and freeze up to a couple of months.)

CHOCOLATE SPICE APPLES

(May be prepared a day or two in advance.)

6 large apples, like Rome beauty or red delicious, washed, cored,
   trim a circle of skin off the tops of apples
½ cup dried cranberries
½ cup walnuts, chopped
¼ cup red-hots (cinnamon candy decors)
1 cup apple juice or apple cider
½ cup dark chocolate cocoa (like Ghiradelli 60% cacao)
½ cup brown sugar
1 tsp. each: ground cinnamon and ginger

Lay 6 cored and trimmed apples in a 9x15-inch heat-resistant casserole dish, pared side on top.

Preheat oven 350°.

In a small bowl make a mix with: dried cranberries, chopped walnuts and red-hots. Stuff each apple cavity with this mix.

In another small bowl make a mix with ½ cup cocoa and ¼ cup apple juice. Set aside.

Stir cinnamon, ginger and brown sugar into the remaining apple juice (¾ cup); carefully, pour the liquid mix over each apple and into the bottom of baking dish. Spoon the chocolate mix over each apple top, equally.

Bake the apples in a preheated oven, 350° for 40-45 minutes, or until cracks begin to form in the skins of the apples, and the apples are tender when pierced with a thin metal skewer. (The quantity of moisture in the apples determines how quickly they soften.) Remove the apples from the oven; spoon chocolate sauce from bottom of baking dish over and into the hot apples. Serve at room temperature or slightly warm. If baked apples have been refrigerated, allow them to come to room temperature before serving. Spoon chocolate sauce over apples just before serving. Serves 6.

More of Cathy and Chip's
new kitchen.

Spring-Summer

The Science of the Art of Cooking
Or Is It?
"The Art of the Science of Cooking"

Humble Cooking is definitely a science; a very distant relative to pharmacology and chemistry. Measuring, mixing, creating tastes, caring for the body. Whether or not you are the one who prepares the food for the welfare of your body (as nourishment to maintain your body's health), the "feeding trough" must be filled. Preferably, with a mix of grains, vegetables and fruits, dairy and animal protein – (the food pyramid).

Our health-conscious modern society guarantees that "our conscience be our guide". We are totally informed; all of our questions are guaranteed educated answers.

All living things must have their "nourishment" in order to help to continue their species. Animals gradually learned through trial, error and experimentation, what was harmful and what was beneficial for their continued existence. Our modern civilization has research scientists and their trials which result in investigative tomes and files of documentation. We are so civilized, we actually perform scientific investigations upon the scientific investigations.

The humble cook receives so much documented assistance, she needs to concentrate only on the art of culinary presentation.

This not-so-humble cook asks:
*   "How many cooks does it take to create a feast?"*

*   If you're in my kitchen – only one!*

Marion cooks on Nana's stove.

175

Spring-Summer

MESCLUN WITH OLIVES AND FIGS
PARMESAN CHEESE DRESSING
CIOPPINO
SALMON MEXICALI
WHITE or BROWN RICE
MINTED LEMON ICE

MESCLUN WITH OLIVES AND FIGS

3-4 cups mesclun salad greens (about 1 lb.), washed, spun dried
8 fresh figs (calimyrna, kadota or brown turkey), gently rinsed, trimmed, quartered
1 cup Kalamata olives, pitted
½ cup Parmesan cheese slivers

Parmesan Cheese Dressing (see page 388)

Prepare Parmesan Cheese Dressing. Refrigerate dressing if not needed within a couple of hours. Remove dressing from refrigerator 1 hour before serving.

Assemble all salad ingredients into a large serving bowl. At serving time, add dressing; toss and serve in individual bowls. Serves 6.

CIOPPINO

1 doz. Little Neck clams, scrubbed with seafood brush,
    soak clams in cold water
1 doz. mussels, soaked and scrubbed in cold water
2 onions, coarsely chopped
2 garlic cloves, finely chopped
2 lg. red peppers and 1 lg. green pepper, washed, seeded,
    sliced into 1-inch strips
2 tbsp. olive oil
1 tbsp. hot red pepper flakes (optional)
2 cups dry white wine
$\frac{1}{2}$ cup dried porcini mushrooms
6 plum tomatoes, coarsely chopped
4 tbsp. tomato paste
$\frac{1}{2}$ cup fresh basil, torn into pieces
1 lb. large shrimp, cleaned
2 cups sea scallops, rinsed in cold water
6 crab claws, cooked
$\frac{1}{2}$ tsp. salt
$\frac{1}{2}$ tsp. freshly ground black pepper

Heat oil in a 4-quart saucepan over moderate heat. Add garlic and onions and cook for 2-3 minutes until onions have softened. Add red and green peppers and pepper flakes (if desired) and continue to cook, stirring occasionally.

Meanwhile, pour $\frac{1}{2}$ cup wine into a small pot and bring to a boil. Remove pot from heat and add the dried mushrooms. Set pot aside to allow mushrooms to plump up.

Stir chopped tomatoes into onions and peppers mix. Stir in remaining white wine (into which you've stirred tomato paste); add basil and blend the mix thoroughly. Simmer the sauce for 10-15 minutes, until all the vegetables are tender.

Stir in mussels and clams; cover pot and simmer the stew for an additional 5 minutes. (Clams and mussels should open as they cook; discard any which do not open.) Add shrimp, scallops and crab claws; cover pot again and continue to cook the stew for 5 minutes longer. Season with salt and pepper to taste. Serves 6.

SALMON MEXICALI

2 lbs. wild salmon fillets, skin removed

MARINADE:
2 tbsp. extra-virgin olive oil
$\frac{1}{2}$ tsp. each: ground cumin, allspice, cinnamon
1 tbsp. honey
salt, black pepper to taste
juice of 2 limes
1 small chopped, seeded chile

Boston lettuce leaves, rinsed, drained
2 lg. beefsteak tomatoes, thickly sliced
$\frac{1}{2}$ doz. scallions, trimmed

Preheat oven to 425°.

In a small bowl, prepare the marinade: combine oil, spices, honey, lime juice, chile, salt and pepper. Lay the fillets in a 9x15-inch non-stick pan. Baste them with the marinade. Roast the salmon in a preheated oven 425° for 18-25 minutes, depending upon the thickness of the salmon. Fish will appear opaque when cooked. Do not overcook.

Meanwhile, prepare beds of lettuce on individual plates; with a spatula, cut and transfer a serving of salmon to each bed of lettuce. Garnish with slices of tomato and scallions. Serves 6.

Serve WHITE RICE or BROWN RICE as an accompaniment.

MINTED LEMON ICE

⅓ cup granulated sugar
1 cup fresh lemon juice
1 cup packed fresh mint leaves, rinsed, spun dry
sprigs of mint for garnish

In a saucepan, combine sugar and lemon juice. Bring mixture to a boil, stirring until sugar is dissolved; let syrup cool. In a blender, or food processor, purée mint with the syrup. Transfer the mix to 2 metal ice cube trays, dividers removed (or a shallow metal pan). Freeze the trays.

Every 30 minutes, stir the mixture in the trays, mashing any obvious lumps with a fork. Do this for 2-3 hours, or until the ice is firm but not solidly frozen. Scrape and fluff up the lemon ice with a fork; spoon the ice into chilled goblets. Garnish with mint sprigs and serve immediately.
Serves 6 (½ cup each).

Spring-Summer

Notes on Preparing and Processing Vegetables

ena Hebner Combs shares fond memories about growing up in Croton, New York. The Hebner family, including the children, not only planted and tended a vegetable garden; they also spent many days of "summer vacation", canning and processing the bountiful harvest. Lena offers us tasty samples of her pickle preserves in the following recipes.

Notes on: "Preparing to Preserve Vegetables and Fruits":

1.   Wash the jars and lids with hot, soapy water; rinse them thoroughly; drain them on a rack. OR: Set the jars and lids on the top shelf of the dishwasher as you would glassware; wash jars and lids and allow them to dry for the full heating cycle. The jars/lids will remain hot for awhile if you do not remove them until needed.

2.   OR: If you're not using a dishwasher to sanitize the jars/lids, set the hand-washed jars/lids in a large pot, to which you've added enough water to cover them. Bring the pot of jars in water to a boil and continue to boil the pot of jars for 15 minutes.

Using tongs, remove jars and lids to a rack; empty the water from the pot and replace the jars and lids to rest in the hot pot as you prepare the vegetables for pickling.

3.   Proceed to prepare the vegetables for pickling.

Spring-Summer

LENA COMBS' RECIPES FOR:

GARLIC DILL PICKLES
CHOW-CHOW
BREAD 'N' BUTTER PICKLES

GARLIC DILL PICKLES

6 pickling cucumbers (about $1\frac{1}{8}$ lbs.)
$1\frac{3}{4}$ cups water
$1\frac{3}{4}$ cups cider vinegar
3 tbsp. Kosher salt
12-18 fresh dill heads
6 whole garlic cloves, peeled

3 pt.-size jars with lids
a plastic knife

Prepare jars as instructed in introductory notes. Thoroughly rinse cucumbers. Remove stems and cut off a thin slice from each end. Prepare brine by combining water, vinegar and salt in a 2-quart pot and bring the liquid to a boil. Cut each cucumber into 4 spears.

Pack cucumber spears into 3 hot, clean, pint-jars with lids, leaving $\frac{1}{2}$-inch head space. Add 2 or 3 dill heads and 2 garlic cloves to each jar. Pour hot brine over cucumbers, leaving $\frac{1}{2}$-inch head space. Remove air bubbles with a plastic knife; wipe the jar rims and adjust the lids.

Process the filled jars for 5 minutes, in a pot containing enough boiling water to cover 2 inches over the tops of the jars; or process the jars for 5 minutes in a water bath as directed for a canning processor. (Start timing after the water starts to boil.)

With a jar-gripper and heat-resistant mitts, remove jars from canning pot. Allow the jars to stand 1 week in a cool place before using. Makes 3 pints of Garlic Dill Pickles.

CHOW-CHOW

(Chow-Chow is a mustard-spiked, pickled mixture of vegetables. This recipe is believed to have been brought to America by Chinese railroad workers.)

3 large onions, chopped

4 medium green tomatoes, cored, chopped into small pieces

4 medium sweet green peppers, cored, chopped into small pieces

2 medium sweet red peppers, cored, chopped into small pieces

2 medium carrots, pared, chopped coarsely

2 cups (about $\frac{3}{4}$ lb.) fresh green beans, cut into $\frac{1}{2}$-inch pieces

2 cups cauliflower, sectioned into tiny florets

$1\frac{1}{2}$ cups frozen corn kernels

$\frac{1}{4}$ cup pickling (Kosher) salt

3 cups granulated sugar

2 cups white vinegar

1 cup water

1 tbsp. mustard seed

2 tsp. grated gingerroot (optional)

$1\frac{1}{2}$ tsp. celery seed

$\frac{3}{4}$ tsp. turmeric

6 pint-size Mason jars with lids

a plastic knife

a very large pot to fit 6 pint-size jars, standing upright

Using a coarse blade of a food processor, grind onions, tomatoes, peppers and carrots. Combine them in a large non-metallic bowl with the green beans, cauliflower and corn. Sprinkle with Kosher salt; let stand in refrigerator overnight.

Next day, rinse the mixture in cold water and drain. Transfer the mix to an 8-10 quart Dutch-oven or kettle. Combine sugar, vinegar, water, mustard seed, celery seed, turmeric and gingerroot (if desired). Pour this liquid mix over the vegetables. Bring mixture to boiling and simmer gently for 5 minutes.

Prepare jars as directed in the introductory note. Ladle hot Chow-Chow into sterilized pint-size jars leaving $\frac{1}{2}$-inch head space. Remove air bubbles with a plastic knife. Wipe jar rims and adjust lids.

Wearing heat-resistant and protective mitts, and/or using a jar gripper, remove pints of Chow-Chow to cool on a rack. Makes 6 pints of Chow-Chow.

BREAD 'N' BUTTER PICKLES

$2\frac{1}{4}$ lbs. medium-size cucumbers, thinly sliced

4 medium-size white onions, thinly sliced

1.5 oz. Kosher salt

3 small garlic cloves, or 3 halves of large garlic cloves

2 cups granulated sugar

$1\frac{1}{2}$ cups cider vinegar

1 tbsp. mustard seed

$\frac{3}{4}$ tsp. turmeric

$\frac{3}{4}$ tsp. celery seed

3 pint-size jars with lids

a plastic knife

cracked ice

In a large bowl, combine cucumbers, onions, garlic and salt. Cover with 2 inches cracked ice. Refrigerate the iced mix for 3 hours.

Meanwhile, prepare jars as instructed in introductory notes.

Then, thoroughly drain the cucumber mix. Remove garlic pieces and discard. In an 8-10 quart Dutch oven or kettle, combine sugar, vinegar, mustard seed, turmeric and celery seed. Add cucumber mixture and bring to a boil. Remove pot from burner.

Pack hot cucumber mixture and liquid into hot, clean, pint-size canning jars, leaving $\frac{1}{2}$-inch head space. Remove air bubbles with a plastic knife; wipe jar rims and screw on lids. Process filled jars by standing them in a large, deep pot or canner with enough boiling water to cover 2 inches over the lids. Cover the pot and boil the jars of pickles for 5 minutes (start timing after water starts to boil). Remove jars with a jar-gripper and wear heat-resistant mitts. Cool the jars on a rack.
Makes 3 pints Bread 'n' Butter Pickles.

Summer-Fall

What Kids Prefer

*E*veryone of us prefers tasty food: "not too dry", "a trifle sweet", "slightly nippy", "wine-rich", "naturally juicy", and the list goes on.

Kids, on the other hand, may accept all of the above with the added: "no additives", (unless it's catsup or grease). By additives we mean: "Don't let me see wiggly veins in that leg of chicken"; "E-ech! that green stuff is gross!"; "Cream of what? I know what IT looks like". "I ate all the fries; what more do you want?"

Kids (like adults) don't necessarily prefer what's good for them. First, adults must learn what's good for THEM; then, they must make a promise to themselves and to their children to insure that everyone eats less fats; no trans fats; less sugary things; fruits; veggies ("green stuff"); perhaps looking good with a little melted cheese over the "stuff"; sliced tomatoes and a little splash of catsup to liven things up; _ and no added salt.

Eventually, kids will prefer that we've placed them on the healthy path of life.

John at St. Pius X church barbeque.

Summer-Fall

AVOCADO AND SPINACH SALAD
RASPBERRY VINAIGRETTE DRESSING
PIZZA RUSTICA (heirloom)
THREE EASY GOURMET PIZZAS
A BACKYARD BARBEQUE
RAINBOW SHERBET WITH RASPBERRIES AND MINT

AVOCADO AND SPINACH SALAD

10 oz. baby spinach, rinsed, drained
1-2 Hass avocados, depending on size, pared and thinly sliced at time of serving
3-4 garlic cloves, chopped
1 small red pepper, seeded, finely sliced
1 poblano pepper, seeded, thinly sliced
½ cup chopped walnuts

Vinaigrette Dressing (see page 389)
(Add ½ cup mashed raspberries.)

Carrot twirls for garnish (use 1 large carrot)

Prepare the dressing and refrigerate it.

Slice the peppers and rinse and drain spinach. Place this mix in a salad bowl. Lightly cover bowl with plastic wrap and refrigerate.

At serving time, add garlic and walnuts to salad. Peel and slice the avocado and add slices to salad bowl. Drizzle salad with a thoroughly mixed Raspberry Vinaigrette Dressing. Toss well to mix. Arrange salad in individual salad bowls and add a few carrot twirls to each salad. Serves 6.

PIZZA RUSTICA

(A traditional Italian meat pie. May be prepared days in advance and refrigerated or frozen.)

2 lbs. ricotta

6 eggs beaten

½ lb. slicing pepperoni, sliced thin

½ lb. Genoa salami, sliced thin

½ lb. pepper ham (prosciuttini), sliced thin

½ lb. mozzarella, shredded

½ lb. sharp provolone, diced

1 cup grated Parmesan cheese

½ lb. Swiss cheese, diced

¼ tsp. black pepper

3 links sweet Italian Sausage, cooked, chilled, sliced into thin rounds

9-inch spring-form pan, greased with olive oil

Preheat oven to 375°.

In a large mixing bowl, beat the ricotta; stir in the beaten eggs, and mix well. Stir in the remaining ingredients and pour into a well-greased 9-inch spring-form pan. Bake for 1 hour or until firm. Cool to room temperature. Run a knife around the edge of the pie before removing the sides. Serve at room temperature. Serves 8-10.

THREE EASY GOURMET PIZZAS

CRUST (makes one, 12-inch round pizza)

1 lb. dough ball, sold fresh or frozen in food stores, bakeries, supermarket

¼ cup grated Parmesan cheese

olive oil for coating bowl, oil to grease pizza pan

1.) If ball of dough was purchased frozen, transfer to oil-coated bowl for 2 or more hours, turning ball a couple of times to coat on all sides. If fresh, refrigerate until needed, up to a day or two; place in oil-coated bowl and turn several times to coat with oil.

2.) Stretch dough to fit over an oiled 12-inch pizza tin or stone pan. Press a round platter on top of dough in pan and allow to rest for 1 hour. Remove plate and sprinkle cheese over dough. Preheat oven to 375°.

3.) Partially bake pizza crust at 375° for 5 minutes. Remove crust from oven and proceed to garnish crust with one of the toppings (see following page). Keep oven temperature at 375° as you prepare toppings. (Continued on next page)

(Continued from page 186)

TOPPINGS:

A.) 1 cup slivered low-fat ham

1-2 ripe Bartlett pears, cored, sliced with skin
   (or use red delicious apples)

½ cup cranberry raisins

1 cup chopped gorgonzola cheese

1 tsp. rosemary

1 tbsp. brown sugar

Arrange sliced pears over partially baked crust. Sprinkle with brown sugar and rosemary. Add slivered ham; sprinkle with cranberry raisins and gorgonzola cheese. Bake at 375° for 15-30 minutes. Serves 6.

B.) 1 cup canned, crushed tomatoes

½ cup slivered sun-dried tomatoes

1 cup slivered Genoese salami

1 cup low-fat ricotta

1 tbsp. oregano

3 garlic cloves, chopped

salt and pepper

olive oil

Spread tomatoes over prepared crust; sprinkle with salt, pepper and oregano; scatter garlic, sun-dried tomatoes and salami. Spoon teaspoons of ricotta over salami. Drizzle olive oil on topping. Bake pizza in preheated oven 375° for 15-20 minutes. Serves 6.

C.) 2 large red bell peppers, seeded, thinly sliced

1-2 large Portobello mushrooms, washed,
   drained, thinly sliced

1 onion, thinly sliced

3-4 garlic cloves, chopped

½ cup pitted, chopped, assorted olives

½ cup smoky mozzarella, chopped

olive oil

Arrange pepper slices, mushroom slices, onion and garlic over par-baked crust. Scatter chopped mozzarella and olives over vegetables. Sprinkle pie with olive oil. Bake in preheated oven 375° for 15-20 minutes. Serves 6.

A BACKYARD BARBEQUE

Have ready: some beef or chicken patties, pork or turkey sausages, beef hot dogs and a selection of whole grain buns. Fire up the grill and cook the meat. (Cook beef to medium; fowl or pork to well-done.) Use a meat thermometer as reference to individual meat doneness.

RAINBOW SHERBET WITH RASPBERRIES AND MINT

1 qt. rainbow sherbet

1 cup raspberries; or raspberries mixed with blueberries

mint sprigs for garnish

6 frappé dessert glasses, half-pint size

Scoop $\frac{1}{2}$ cup of rainbow sherbet into each frappé glass. Sprinkle each bowl with 2 tablespoons of berries and garnish with mint. Serves 6.

College buddies at a picnic in the park.

Summer-Fall

A Backyard Buffet

A backyard party can be quite relaxing in almost every aspect: menu selections; dual cooking areas; less restricted and varied age groups; use of disposable dinnerware (generally speaking); minimal in-home wear and tear.

In my assessment, there are more responsibilities the host must be aware of, especially if your property features a swimming pool or a fish pond. Children need proper and continuous supervision, no matter where a party is held; but outdoors is "limitless", even with property fencing and gate enclosures.

Planning the menu for an outdoor buffet can be fun. But, you have a tendency to over-do in the number of recipe selections and the quantity of those choices. I tend to increase the number of items on my menu because I equate an outdoor gathering as an open-door invitation to the highways and the by-ways. The host (and servers) tally more mileage by party's end _ and beyond (for example: clean-up time).

And by the way, there's that strong possibility of weather-related stress: whether the weather man will forecast outdoor party weather _ or whether, the outdoor party and the host will weather the weather. Renting a tent affords another possibility...........

Summer-Fall

JALAPEÑO CORN BREAD
TUNA AND LENTIL SALAD
HONEY MUSTARD DRESSING
CHICKEN SALAD IN LIME
LIME RICE (See page 165)
VANILLA ICE CREAM AND APPLE CRUNCH

JALAPEÑO CORN BREAD

2 cups cornmeal

1 cup flour

2 tsp. baking powder

1 tsp. baking soda

$\frac{1}{4}$ tsp. salt

1 cup coarsely grated, extra-sharp cheddar cheese

4 tbsp. finely chopped jalapeño peppers
(Wear plastic gloves when
handling hot peppers.)

3 eggs

1 cup buttermilk

$\frac{1}{2}$ cup butter or Smart Balance spread

Preheat oven to 425°.

In a large bowl, whisk together: cornmeal, flour, baking powder, baking soda and salt. Add cheddar and jalapeño and toss to mix thoroughly. In a small bowl, beat eggs with buttermilk. Melt butter in an 8-inch heavy skillet with oven-proof handle.

Add half of the melted butter to the buttermilk mix, whisking as you add. Transfer the skillet with remaining butter to the preheated oven 425° and heat the skillet for 5 minutes. Meanwhile, add buttermilk mixture to cornmeal mixture and blend the batter until it is just combined.

Remove skillet from oven; add batter to skillet, smoothing top of batter, and bake it at 425° for 15-20 minutes, or until top of bread is golden, and an inserted toothpick tests clean. Cut the cornbread into wedges; serve warm or at room temperature, directly from the pan. Serves 6.

TUNA AND LENTIL SALAD

1 lb. fresh tuna (brush with 2 tbsp. olive oil and 1 tbsp. balsamic vinegar; broil or grill
    tuna, about 3-4 minutes on each side); or use 2 cans (6 oz. each) solid tuna

1 lb. dried lentils
3 cups water
1 tbsp. olive oil
1 small red onion, chopped
3 garlic cloves, minced
3 ripe plum tomatoes, diced
1 large celery stalk, chopped
2 tbsp. chopped Italian parsley (and 1 tbsp. extra for garnish)
1 sweet pimiento, seeded, finely chopped
salt, black pepper to taste

Honey Mustard Dressing (see page 384)

    Prepare Honey Mustard Dressing. Store dressing in refrigerator until 1 hour before serving.

    Simmer lentils, onion, garlic and celery in 3 cups water and 1 tablespoon olive oil for 30 minutes.
Taste for tenderness (or cook 5-10 minutes longer, and add a little more water if needed). Drain lentil
mix and pour into a bowl; cool the mix to room temperature.

    Add and mix: diced tomatoes, pimiento, parsley, salt and pepper.

    With 2 forks, flake the grilled tuna (or spoon the canned tuna into a bowl and flake it with 2 forks).
Add the flaked tuna to the bowl; drizzle Honey Mustard Dressing over tuna-lentil mix and toss to mix.
Pour this salad into a serving bowl. Sprinkle parsley over the bowl. Serves 6.

CHICKEN SALAD IN LIME

3 full chicken breasts, boneless, skin removed; simmered in 1 cup water for 20 minutes;
  remove chicken to cutting board; reserve stock for cooking Lime Rice
2 stalks celery with greens, chopped
1 carrot, shredded in curls
¼ cup pitted, chopped, oil-cured olives
2 dozen red seedless grapes

juice of 1 lime
½-1 cup mayonnaise
2 tbsp. Dijon mustard spread
3-4 garlic cloves, chopped
black pepper

bed of mesclun greens, rinsed, drained

In a small bowl, blend mayonnaise, mustard, black pepper, garlic and lime juice. Refrigerate this dressing until needed.

Cut cooked chicken into bite-size cubes and pour chicken into a large serving bowl. Add celery and ⅔ of the carrot curls (save remainder for garnish). Stir in olives and grapes. Spoon dressing over chicken salad, and toss with 2 spoons to mix thoroughly.

Prepare a bed of mesclun on each of 6 salad plates. Spoon chicken salad over mesclun. Garnish with carrot curls. Serves 6.

Serve with a side of LIME RICE. Recipe for LIME RICE (see page 165). Use chicken stock from recipe, above.

VANILLA ICE CREAM AND APPLE CRUNCH

4 Granny Smith apples, pared, cored, cut into narrow slices
$\frac{1}{4}$ cup water
$\frac{1}{2}$ cup dried cranberries
1 tsp. cinnamon
$\frac{1}{2}$ tsp. nutmeg
$\frac{1}{2}$ tsp. powdered cloves
$\frac{1}{4}$ cup brown sugar
1 tbsp. butter or Smart Balance
$\frac{1}{4}$ cup chopped walnuts
$\frac{1}{2}$ cup oatmeal cookies, crumbled
1 qt. vanilla bean ice cream

Combine sliced apples, cinnamon, nutmeg, cloves, dried cranberries, brown sugar, butter and water in a saucepot; cover the pot and simmer the apple mix for 8-10 minutes, or until apples are softened. Remove pot from heat. Set aside to cool for a little while.

Set out six $\frac{1}{2}$ pint dessert bowls. Scoop vanilla ice cream into the center of each bowl. Spoon warm apple mix over ice cream. Sprinkle crumbled cookies and walnuts over apples and ice cream. Apples may be served warm or cooled. Serves 6.

Summer-Fall

"I'm going away for the weekend;
would you mind feeding my husband and kids while I'm gone?"

How could I refuse my dearest friend's request? I was honored she had asked me. Little did I know that my friend, Arline, was to become a breast cancer survivor and I was to walk with her, shoulder-to-shoulder, on the chemo path: hoist her body up the staircase; sanitize the areas her vomit graced; shop with her for a wig; be her advocate when she thought her oncologist had failed her.

However, afterwards, I was there for all of the 20 years of celebrations our families enjoyed - together.

Arline and Dick Scaglione and John.

Summer-Fall

———— ✦ ————

ROMAINE, AVOCADO AND GRAPES
BALSAMIC VINEGAR AND OLIVE OIL DRESSING
PORK LIVER AND BAY LEAVES WRAPPED IN AREZZIO (heirloom)
RISOTTO (See page 66) (heirloom)
'SCAROLA IMBOTTIRE (STUFFED ESCAROLE) (heirloom)
BERRY WHIPPED CREAM PIE

ROMAINE, AVOCADO AND GRAPES

4 cups Romaine lettuce, rinsed, trimmed, cut into small pieces
2 ripe Hass avocados, peeled, cut into small chunks, sprinkled with lemon juice
    to prevent browning
1 small red onion, thinly sliced
1 lg. carrot, pared, shaved into twirls
1 cup red seedless grapes, rinsed, drained

Balsamic Vinegar and Olive Oil Dressing (see page 384)

Prepare dressing. Combine all salad ingredients (except avocado) into a large salad bowl. Refrigerate salad and dressing.

Remove dressing from refrigerator about 1 hour before serving.

Just before serving, peel avocados and cut them into small chunks; sprinkle them with lemon juice and add to the salad. Shake the dressing to mix thoroughly; drizzle over salad; toss salad and serve in individual bowls. Serves 6.

PORK LIVER AND BAY LEAVES WRAPPED IN AREZZIO
(Arezzio is stomach lining of a pig. As you grill the liver, most of the wrap will melt.)

12-15 prepared pieces of pork liver with bay leaves, wrapped in arezzio

(This delicious peasant delicacy may be prepared to order at most Italian gourmet butcher shops or food specialty stores.)

Sprinkle black pepper over wrapped liver pieces; set them to grill 5 inches over heat (or slow broil about 5-6 inches under broiler element). Turn over the liver wraps after broiling for 4-5 minutes; repeat with other side.

Depending upon the thickness of the chunks of liver, the wraps may require slow grilling for a couple of minutes longer on each side. Do not dry out the liver. They are ready to eat just as the juices turn brown and the outside starts to char. (Do not eat bay leaves.) Serve with a side of RISOTTO, (see page 66). Serves 6.

'SCAROLA IMBOTTIRE (STUFFED ESCAROLE)

(In his downtown Brooklyn Bar and Grill, my paternal grandfather served a different luncheon selection every afternoon. This recipe is derived from his customary Friday noon meal. NOTE: cut the cheese into small chunks and remove the string before serving.)

May be prepared day before. Warm in steamer or covered ovenproof platter.

3 small heads escarole (remove outer leaves and
   trim base), soak-wash and drain thoroughly;
several washings may be necessary
$\frac{1}{2}$ cup olive oil
3 garlic cloves, minced
$\frac{1}{2}$ tsp. salt
$\frac{1}{4}$ tsp. black pepper
1 cup Parmesan or provolone cheese, cubed

$\frac{1}{2}$ cup raisins
$\frac{1}{4}$ cup anchovies, chopped

1 cup water for bottom portion of steamer
2 tbsp. olive oil
salt to taste

white string to tie

Thoroughly soak-wash escarole. Discard tough outer leaves and trim the base. Flatten each head so the tender leaves are exposed and the base is sitting on the worktable. Meanwhile, in a small bowl, mix garlic, salt, pepper, raisins, cheese and anchovies. Divide the mix into 3 parts, and pack the stuffing into center of each head. Drizzle a couple of tablespoons of olive oil into each head and tie up the escarole packages with string. Cook them in a large steamer pot with 1 cup water, salt and 2 tablespoons olive oil in bottom layer.

Cover pot and simmer gently for 20-25 minutes, until tender. Transfer to serving platter with slotted spoon. Remove string before serving. If preparing in advance, use ovenproof serving dish with rim. Cover with foil and warm in oven at 200° for 15-20 minutes before serving.

BERRY WHIPPED CREAM PIE

CRUST:
2 cups chocolate wafers, finely crushed
8 tbsp. melted butter or Smart Balance spread
½ cup finely ground almonds

FILLING:
1 pt. heavy cream, whipped to fluffy peaks
1 cup strawberries, rinsed, drained, thinly sliced
1 cup blueberries, rinsed, drained

8-10 strawberries, rinsed, drained, leave whole, for garnish
½ cup chopped almonds, for garnish

Preheat oven 350°.

Thoroughly blend crushed chocolate wafers and ½ cup ground almonds in a large bowl. Stir in melted butter and mix thoroughly. Press crumbs mix into a 9-inch oven-resistant pie dish, firmly pressing the crumb-mix into the base of the dish and up its sides.

Bake crust in preheated oven 350° for 10 minutes. Cool crust thoroughly.

Beat heavy cream in a large bowl to form stiff peaks. Fold in blueberries.

Spoon sliced strawberries into base of cooled crust. Spoon berry cream over sliced strawberries, swirling the cream to form small peaks. Garnish pie with whole strawberries; sprinkle chopped almonds over cream. Refrigerate pie until serving. Serves 6-8.

Summer-Fall

A Sit-Down Dinner

I've hosted at least 1,000 dinner gatherings in my long life as "Cookie Crone". If I count all of the breakfasts, lunches and suppers I've prepared for two or more servings, I'd estimate a total of 40,000 + meals.

Of course, hosting over 20 guests for dinner has always been a challenge. My preference is a sit-down dinner for no more that 8 guests seated at my table of plenty, where all of us participate in lively chatter and delicious and wholesome cuisine.

Arline Scaglione, Jane and Paul Smaldone, Lena Zukowski, Terry and Howie McGuffog
join John at the dining room Table of Plenty.

Summer-Fall

FISH SOUP PROVENÇALE

COD ARRAGANATE

or

CHILEAN SEA BASS ARRAGANATE

GARLIC SPINACH WITH PEANUTS

CURRANT POUND CAKE

FISH SOUP PROVENÇALE

2 tbsp. olive oil

1 lg. onion, finely chopped

1 lg. fennel bulb, trimmed, finely chopped

2-3 leeks, trimmed, finely chopped

1 lg. carrot pared, finely chopped

1 celery stalk, trimmed, chopped

6 garlic cloves, minced

1 can (20 oz.) plum tomatoes in juice,
   puréed in blender

1 cup dry white wine

7 cups water

1 bay leaf

2-3 fresh basil leaves

1 tbsp. dried oregano

1 tsp. fennel seeds

1 tbsp. grated rind from 1 orange

1 tsp. saffron threads

½ tsp. salt

½ tsp. pepper

1 lb. white fish fillets, (suggestions: flounder,
   grey sole, snapper), remove skin,
   slice into narrow strips

Heat oil in a large 4-quart soup pot with cover. Cook onion, leeks, garlic, fennel, carrot and celery in oil for 3-4 minutes, until vegetables soften. Add puréed tomato, wine and water. Stir in bay leaf, basil, oregano, fennel seeds, rind, saffron, salt and pepper.

Cover pot and bring to a boil; reduce heat; cook gently, covered, for 30 minutes, stirring occasionally. Add fish, simmer for an additional 20-30 minutes. Remove bay leaf before serving. Serve with crusty bread. Serves 6.

COD ARRAGANATE

2 thick cod fillets, about 1 lb. each, washed, drained, patted dry with paper towels

2 tbsp. olive oil

$1\frac{1}{2}$ cups unseasoned bread crumbs

$\frac{1}{4}$ cup chopped fresh oregano or 2 tbsp. dried oregano

6 garlic cloves, chopped

$\frac{1}{2}$ tsp. black pepper

$\frac{1}{2}$ tsp. salt

3-4 tbsp. extra-virgin olive oil (plus extra oil at serving)

$\frac{1}{2}$ cup grated Parmesan cheese

$\frac{1}{2}$ cup chopped walnuts

juice of 2 lemons

grated rind of 1 lemon

Preheat oven to 400°.

Lay cod fillets in 9x15-inch nonstick pan, coated with 2 tablespoons olive oil. Sprinkle fish with lemon juice and grated rind.

In a 2-quart bowl, mix thoroughly: crumbs, garlic, oregano, pepper, salt, Parmesan cheese and 3-4 tablespoons olive oil. Sprinkle some water over crumbs if mix is too dry.

Pack one-half of crumb mix on top of one cod fillet; repeat for the other fillet. Sprinkle coated fish with chopped walnuts. You may wish to sprinkle a few drops of olive oil over fish.

Roast fish in preheated oven, 400° for 25 minutes, or until crumbs start to brown and the fish flakes with a fork. Sprinkle with additional olive oil; spoon sauce over fish. Serves 6 portions.

CHILEAN SEA BASS ARRAGANATE

about 2 lbs. Chilean Sea Bass steaks,
    enough for 6 servings; remove skin

1 cup coarse bread crumbs

$\frac{1}{4}$ cup olive oil

juice of 2 lemons

6 garlic cloves, quartered

2 tbsp. dried oregano

$\frac{1}{2}$ tsp. freshly ground pepper

$\frac{1}{2}$ tsp. salt

$\frac{1}{2}$ cup chopped, pitted oil-cured olives

$\frac{1}{4}$ cup grated Asiago cheese

olive oil to coat 9x15-inch ovenproof pan

lemon wedges for garnish

Preheat oven 375°.

Rinse fish in cool water; drain and pat dry with paper towels. Coat a 9x15-inch ovenproof pan with olive oil. Arrange fish steaks side by side in the pan.

In a small bowl, mix bread crumbs, oregano, garlic, pepper, salt, olives and cheese. Stir in olive oil and lemon juice. Add a tablespoon or two of warm water if crumbs are too stiff. Spoon crumb mix over fish in pan. Bake fish, moderate high at 375° for 20-25 minutes, or until crumb mix becomes golden. Sprinkle more olive oil over fish if desired. Garnish with lemon wedges. Serves 6.

GARLIC SPINACH WITH PEANUTS

2 lbs. baby spinach, rinsed, drained

2 tbsp. peanut oil

4 garlic cloves, minced

2 cups bean sprouts

3-4 tbsp. *lite* soy sauce

2 tsp. brown sugar

$\frac{1}{2}$ cup peanuts

Heat peanut oil in wok; stir-fry baby spinach, garlic and bean sprouts for 30 seconds. Remove from heat. Make a dressing by blending 3-4 tablespoons soy sauce and 2 teaspoons brown sugar. Drizzle dressing over spinach; add nuts. Toss to mix. Serves 5-6.

CURRANT POUND CAKE
(Prepare a few days in advance.)

3 cups flour
1 tbsp. baking powder
$\frac{1}{4}$ tsp. salt
1 tbsp. cinnamon
$\frac{2}{3}$ cup butter or Smart Balance spread, cut into small cubes
$\frac{3}{4}$ cup light brown sugar
$\frac{3}{4}$ cup currants
6 tbsp. orange juice
grated rind of 1 orange
6 tbsp. low-fat milk
2 eggs, beaten or $\frac{1}{2}$ cup egg substitute
confectioners' sugar for garnish

Preheat oven 350°.

Grease a 5x7-inch loaf pan. Line bottom of pan with greased brown paper. Sift together: flour with baking powder, cinnamon and salt. Pour flour mix into a large bowl and add the butter, working it into the flour by mixing it with a fork. The mixture should be crumbly.

Stir in sugar, currants and orange rind. Beat in orange juice, milk and eggs. Blend batter thoroughly and spoon the mixture into the prepared pan.

With the back of a tablespoon, make a slight vertical indentation in the middle of the dough mix to assist in an even rise. Bake loaf in center of preheated oven at 350° for 60-70 minutes or until inserted toothpick comes out clean. Cool the cake before removing from pan. Just before serving, sprinkle with confectioners' sugar. Serves 8.

Summer-Fall

"Let's Eat!"
Yom Kippur ____ Break the Fast!
So it is written; so it is done.
Amen ____ "Let's Eat!"

I have had the honor and pleasure of participating in several Yom Kippur__ "Break the Fast" gatherings. I have always been emotionally impressed by the meaningful and inspirational message of contrition and fasting which is the Day of Atonement.

Yom Kippur is the last day of ten days of Penitance. The first two holy days comprise the New Year (Rosh Hashanah). The service of Yom Kippur in the synagogue, continues throughout the day, and is characterized by a recapitulation of the duties of the high priest on the Day of Atonement in the Temple.

It concludes by the blowing of the shofar (ram's horn) at the end of the service, with the community affirming that: "the Lord, He is God". Then, the Book of Jonah is read.

Translated literally, Yom Kippur is interpreted as "affliction of soul".
Leviticus 16: 29, 23-27

Summer-Fall

ROSE FRUCHTMAN'S BORSCHT (heirloom)

FILET MIGNONS WITH ARTICHOKE HEARTS

FRAGRANT RICE (See page 91)

CHOCOLATE HAMANTASHEN

ROSE FRUCHTMAN'S BORSCHT
(May be made several days in advance.)

8-10 medium-size beets, cooked, peeled,
    and finely chopped in a food processor

2 qts. beef broth (low-salt available)

2 tbsp. butter

1 onion, chopped

2-3 garlic cloves, minced

1 tsp. salt

$\frac{1}{2}$ tsp. black pepper

$\frac{1}{4}$ cup lemon juice

1 tsp. sugar

2 bay leaves

2 tbsp. chopped fresh dill

(2 tbsp. additional chopped dill for garnish)

1 cup sour cream (low-fat available)

    Heat butter in 4-quart soup pot, with cover, at moderate heat to soften the onion and garlic. Stir bottom of pot; stir in beef broth, chopped cooked beets, salt, pepper, lemon juice, sugar, bay leaves and dill. Partially cover the pot and simmer soup for 25 minutes.

    Just before serving, discard bay leaves; pour soup into a tureen. Garnish soup with chopped dill and accompany with a bowl of sour cream to be spooned on top of each serving. Serves 6.

FILET MIGNONS WITH ARTICHOKE HEARTS

6 filet mignons, about 1½ inches thick

2 tbsp. olive oil

½ tsp. dried thyme

½ tsp. dried oregano

1 cup pearl onions, peeled

1 cup canned unseasoned artichoke hearts, drained, cut each in half

salt, freshly ground black pepper to taste

Preheat broiler to 500°.

In a small skillet, heat olive oil to moderate-high and cook the onions and artichoke hearts, stirring occasionally for 2-3 minutes, until onions are tender. Sprinkle thyme, oregano, salt and pepper over vegetables. Remove from burner and set aside.

Lay filet mignons on grill, 5-6 inches from heat. Broil them 3-4 minutes on each side. Do not overcook. Check with meat thermometer to medium-rare/medium. Transfer filets to warmed serving platter. Spoon warm onion-artichoke mix over meat. Serve with FRAGRANT RICE (see page 91). Serves 6.

CHOCOLATE HAMANTASHEN

4 eggs or 1 cup egg substitute

1 cup granulated sugar

½ cup canola oil

juice of 1 lemon

grated rind of 1 lemon

1 tsp. vanilla extract

5 cups flour

2 tsp. baking powder

1 cup unsweetened cocoa

4 oz. raspberry preserves

4 oz. apricot preserves

4 oz. prune butter

Grease 3 cookie sheets, 9x15 inches. Preheat oven to 350°.

In a large bowl, beat eggs and sugar. Add oil, lemon juice and rind, vanilla, flour, cocoa and baking powder.

Knead dough thoroughly on a floured board to form a soft dough (use your hands); divide dough into 3 parts.

On the floured board, roll each portion of dough to about ¼-inch thick (cover the unused dough portions in plastic wrap).

Using a round cookie (or biscuit) cutter, cut out 4 or 5-inch circles. Spoon 1 tablespoon preserves in center of dough circles. Shape each circle into a triangle by bringing up right and left sides, leaving the bottom flat, to form a pocket; and by bringing both sides to meet at the center, just above the filling. Bring top flap down to meet the two sides. Pinch edges together. (Moisten your fingers with cold water to pinch edges.) Repeat with remainder of dough portions.

Place cakes on greased cookie sheets 1 inch apart. Bake cakes in preheated oven, 350° for 20-30 minutes, until dough is set and firm, and starts to color. Yields about 20-22 hamantashen.

Cakes may be prepared in advance, and frozen for storage up to a month or two; cool cakes thoroughly before freezing; arrange cakes, side by side, in a 9x12-inch foil tin, waxed paper sheets to separate the layers. Wrap the entire package with foil, plus one layer of plastic wrap (to place in freezer). Defrost cakes at room temperature, uncovered, cakes separated; place them directly on a serving plate.

Summer-Fall

—◆✦◆—

My Favorite Prayer

"Prayer Of St. Francis"

Lord, make me an instrument of your peace.

Where there is hatred, let me sow love;
Where there is injury, pardon;
Where there is doubt, faith;
Where there is despair, hope;
Where there is darkness, light;
Where there is sadness, joy.

O Divine Master, grant that I may seek not so much
to be consoled as to console;
to be understood as to understand;
to be loved as to love;
for it is in giving that we receive;
it is in pardoning that we are pardoned;
and it is in dying that we are born to eternal life. Amen.

Summer-Fall

SALAD OF SPINACH, CORN, TOMATOES AND APRICOTS
HONEY MUSTARD DRESSING
VEAL STEW PAPRIKA
PIGNOLA FRUIT CAKE

SALAD OF SPINACH, CORN, TOMATOES AND APRICOTS

3 cups baby spinach, washed, drained

1 doz. or more, grape tomatoes, rinsed

1 can (1 lb.) corn kernels, rinsed in cold water, drained

4 fresh apricots, washed, pitted, quartered (or use canned apricots, drained)

Honey Mustard Dressing (see page 384)

Prepare Honey Mustard Dressing; if not using dressing within a few hours, refrigerate dressing until 1 hour before serving.

In a large salad bowl, combine spinach, corn kernels, tomatoes and apricots. Shake or stir dressing to blend thoroughly. Pour dressing over salad and toss to coat. Serves 6.

VEAL STEW PAPRIKA

$2\frac{1}{2}$ lbs. boneless veal (from shoulder or leg), cut into small chunks

2 tbsp. olive oil

1 lg. onion, thinly sliced

2 garlic cloves, minced

1 green bell pepper, seeded, chopped

8 small white mushrooms, rinsed, halved

2 ears corn, each cut into 3 pieces

1 cup beef broth, less-salt variety

$\frac{1}{2}$ cup sweet vermouth

1 tbsp. dried rosemary

2 tsp. Hungarian paprika

$\frac{1}{2}$ tsp. black pepper

Coat the bottom of a 4-quart stew pot (with lid) with olive oil. At moderate heat, cook onion, garlic and veal in oil for 4-5 minutes, stirring bottom of pot as stew cooks. Stir in beef broth, bell pepper, mushrooms, corn chunks, rosemary, paprika and black pepper. Cover pot and simmer the stew gently for 25 minutes. Stir in vermouth. Simmer stew for an additional 5 minutes. Serve with crusty Italian bread. Serves 6.

PIGNOLA FRUIT CAKE
(Prepare several days in advance.)

2 cups self-rising flour
4 tbsp. sugar
$\frac{1}{2}$ cup milk
4 tbsp. orange juice
$\frac{2}{3}$ cup olive oil
$\frac{2}{3}$ cup mixed dried fruit, chopped into small pieces
$\frac{1}{4}$ cup pignola (pine nuts)

confectioners' sugar for garnish

Preheat oven 350°.

Grease an 8-inch square cake pan and line bottom with greased brown paper. Sift flour into a large mixing bowl and stir in sugar. Make a well in the center of the dry ingredients and pour in milk and orange juice.

Blend the mix, to create a smooth batter. Pour in olive oil and stir to mix thoroughly. Fold in dried fruit and nuts; then, spoon batter into the prepared pan.

Bake cake in preheated oven 350° for 45 minutes, until cake is golden and firm to the touch. Allow cake to cool in pan for 5 minutes before inverting it onto a serving dish. Dust the cake with confectioners' sugar before serving. Serves 6.

Summer-Fall

What Does My Gardener Eat for Lunch?

Sal and the guys have been a vital part of our garden's life for almost 20 years. The staff of 6 men has pretty much been intact over the years; except for "shrubbery pruning" when Sal adds 2 or 3 additional young fellows.

Tuesday is our garden's assigned sprucing-up day. Many Tuesdays at midday will find the guys sitting (and reclining) on our lush lawn, taking lunch before they cut the grass and perform the other garden-related tasks.

I've asked them about the secrets in their lunch bags. Those of Italian heritage love their heros (salami and cheese, chicken or veal cutlets are faves); the Hispanic staff enjoys a hero (any filling) also; but most of their lunches start with a soft taco or tortilla wrap. They inform me that most times they buy lunch at fast food shops or delis.

On some "special" Tuesdays, I offer the men parts of menus I have been working on that day. They especially love October and November, when they know Cookie Crone starts her massive holiday baking. They enjoy the samples of biscotti and cookies, with or without frosting. They never refuse those tasty morsels.

Summer-Fall

FISH IN SAFFRON SOUP

MEDITERRANEAN SCALLOPS

PEPPERS AND SOY BEAN SALAD

CHOCOLATE MINT/CHOCOLATE/ CHOCOLATE CRUST ICE CREAM PIE

FISH IN SAFFRON SOUP

1 lb. fish fillets, skin removed, cut into small
  chunks (suggestions: cod, haddock, monkfish)

2 tbsp. olive oil

1 lg. onion, chopped

3-4 garlic cloves, chopped

2 carrots, pared, sliced thin

1 lg. celery stalk, trimmed,
  chopped into small chunks

1 small can (1 lb.) plum tomatoes, mashed

2-3 basil leaves, torn

1 bay leaf

1 tbsp. saffron threads

1 tsp. salt

$\frac{1}{2}$ tsp. pepper

5 cups water

1 cup dry white wine

1 cup evaporated milk

Heat oil in a 4-quart pot with lid. Cook onion, garlic and celery in oil at moderate high for a few minutes, until tender. Scrape bottom of pot to loosen food particles. Stir in water. Add tomatoes, carrots, herbs, saffron and other seasonings; stir to mix; cover pot and simmer soup for 30 minutes. During the last 10 minutes, stir in wine, milk and fish. Soup should thicken slightly. Remove and discard bay leaf before serving. Serves 6.

MEDITERRANEAN SCALLOPS

2½ lbs. sea scallops, shucked, washed, drained

2 tbsp. olive oil

5-6 scallions, finely chopped (include greens)

3-4 garlic cloves, finely chopped

1 chile pepper, seeded, chopped fine

½ cup pitted, chopped oil-cured olives

2 tbsp. cilantro, finely chopped

salt, black pepper to taste

juice of 1 lime

1 lemon, 1 lime - each cut into 6 wedges

Heat oil in a large heavy-duty skillet. Cook scallions, garlic and chile in oil for 1-2 minutes on moderate heat, scraping bottom of skillet, frequently. Add drained scallops and olives and cook, turning them often for 3-4 minutes. Transfer scallop mix from skillet into serving platter; sprinkle with lime juice, salt, pepper and cilantro. Serve with wedges of limes and lemons. Serves 6.

PEPPERS AND SOY BEAN SALAD
(May be prepared in advance.)

1 lb. (about 2 cups) cooked soybeans -
    edible variety (*NOTE: below)

1 can (1 lb.) black beans

1 can (1 lb.) corn kernels (less-salt)

1 small red pepper, chopped

1 small poblano, finely chopped

2-3 garlic cloves, minced

2 tbsp. finely chopped red onion

¼ cup sun-dried tomatoes, slivered

1 carrot, pared, shredded

½ cup packaged seasoned croutons (optional)

½ cup fresh cilantro, chopped

¼ cup pitted, chopped black olives

2 tbsp. extra-virgin olive oil

2 tbsp. red wine vinegar

¼ tsp. freshly ground black pepper

dash of cayenne

dash of salt

*NOTE: You will need a couple of pounds of soybeans in shells to fill 2 cups. Cook edible soybeans as follows: Slit open pods, pop out beans into a bowl. Rinse beans in cold water. Drain. Pour them into a pot with a lid. Bring them to a boil; simmer beans for 10-15 minutes until they are tender. Do not add salt to water; at the cooking stage, salt will toughen the beans. Drain beans into a bowl and chill bowl in refrigerator. (Or you may purchase cooked soybeans sold in packages; available in the produce department.)

In a 2-quart bowl, mix cooked soybeans, corn kernels and black beans. Add poblano, red pepper, garlic, onion, carrot, tomatoes, olives, croutons and all but 2 tablespoons of cilantro (save for garnish). Toss to mix in bowl.

In a small bowl or jar, blend oil, vinegar, salt, pepper and cayenne. Shake dressing well and drizzle it over the bean mix. Toss to mix thoroughly. Garnish salad with 2 tablespoons cilantro. Refrigerate bean salad for at least one-half hour before serving. May be prepared a day or two in advance and refrigerated. Serves 6.

CHOCOLATE MINT/CHOCOLATE/ CHOCOLATE CRUST ICE CREAM PIE
(Prepare crust on day before. Complete pie early on the serving day.)

CHOCOLATE CRUST:
$1\frac{1}{4}$ cups chocolate wafers, food processed to crumbs
4 tbsp. melted butter or melted Smart Balance spread
9-inch pie pan, lightly coated with canola oil

FILLING:
1 pt. mint chocolate chip ice cream
1 pt. chocolate ice cream
1 pt. heavy cream for whipping
$\frac{1}{2}$ cup tiny dark chocolate morsels

Grease a 9-inch pie pan. In a 2-quart mixing bowl, combine chocolate crumbs and melted butter. Combine thoroughly and press the crumbs into the oiled pan (use a very small amount of canola oil).

Wrap crust in plastic and set aside in refrigerator until the next day. (Or, proceed as directed.)

Remove ice cream from freezer and allow to sit for a few minutes to soften slightly. Spoon mint chocolate chip ice cream into the crust and gently tamp down ice cream with the back of a large wooden spoon. Flatten top with spatula.

Spoon chocolate ice cream over mint ice cream and proceed as directed for the first layer. Set the pie in the freezer while you whip the cold heavy cream into peaks at high speed.

Spoon whipped cream over ice cream pie; swirl cream with a butter knife (or use whipped cream-filled pastry tube). Scatter tiny chocolate chips over whipped topping. Do not wrap, yet; however, place pie in freezer for several hours. Then, remove pie and cover in plastic wrap. Return it to freezer. (If you wish, this pie may be made in its entirety, and freezer-stored up to a couple of weeks before serving.) Serves 6-8.

Summer-Fall

Guess Who Just Stopped By?

*Y*ou know the old "newlywed stories": the boss comes to dinner; the in-laws arrive unannounced; the entire bowling team shows up for the barbeque.

Today's newlywed (or other-wed) would probably never blink as they order fast food or gourmet cuisine over a cell phone or a laptop.

At first, it may be a little challenging to attempt your own "on the spot" meal preparation. Even a modestly stocked freezer/pantry/fridge can provide you with the necessary courage to meet this challenge. You'll be pleasantly surprised to discover that a package of pasta, some vegetables and cheese can create a delicious entrée in just a few minutes. Add a greens/fruit/nuts salad and some multi-grain rolls and you have a deliciously healthy meal; and don't forget to drizzle one tablespoon of liqueur over the ice cream. That's a fast-food menu with gourmet touches.

You'll be pleasantly surprised to hear the compliments you receive about "YOUR" cooking.

"The boys" of St. Michael's Diocesan H.S. with their girlfriends:
Peter and Eileen Smaldone, Jane and Paul Smaldone,
Gerry and Kay Harms, Marion and John, Ed Mehring (kneeling).

Summer-Fall

ORANGE PUMPKIN SOUP
FILLET OF FISH PICCATA
TROPICAL FRUIT WITH LENTILS
MARION'S VERSION OF TUNNEL OF FUDGE CAKE (LOW-FAT)

ORANGE PUMPKIN SOUP
(Prepare a day or two before.)

2 tbsp. olive oil

3 lbs. canned pumpkin

1 large yellow onion, minced

3 garlic cloves, minced

6 cups boiling less-salt, canned chicken stock

    (OR: refer to page 44 for recipe on "How to Prepare Chicken Stock")

juice of 1 orange

grated rind of 1 orange

1 tbsp. ground ginger

2 tbsp. chopped thyme leaves (extra 1 tbsp. chopped thyme for garnish)

1 can (12 oz.) evaporated milk, fat-free available

salt, black pepper to taste

    Heat oil in 6-quart soup pot. Soften garlic and onion in hot oil but do not brown. Spoon and stir in pumpkin, orange juice and rind, ginger, thyme and milk. Blend thoroughly, scraping bottom of pot.

    Pour in boiling stock water, one cup at a time, stirring to mix. Add salt and pepper to taste. Cover pot and slowly bring soup to a low simmer. Cook for 20 minutes, stirring frequently. Soup will thicken. Sprinkle soup with more fresh thyme at serving. Serves 6. (Soup may be frozen for several weeks. Heat thoroughly before serving.)

FILLET OF FISH PICCATA

6-8 large fish fillets (suggestions: flounder, lemon sole, grey sole, tilapia)

3 eggs, beaten or ¾ cup egg substitute

½ cup flour

½ cup unseasoned bread crumbs

1 tbsp. chopped parsley

salt, black pepper to taste

¼ cup grated Romano cheese

juice of 2 lemons

1 tbsp. olive oil

½ cup sherry

1 onion, chopped

¼ cup (or a little more) canola oil

   Wash the fish fillets; pat them dry with paper towels. Pour flour onto a sheet of waxed paper; pour crumbs on another sheet of waxed paper. Sprinkle pepper and salt on the flour.

   Preheat canola oil in a non-stick skillet to moderate (about 320°). Sauté onions in hot oil until tender. Spoon onions to side of pan. In a small bowl blend sherry, lemon juice and olive oil. Pour eggs into a large flat plate with an edge; beat in parsley and cheese.

   Dip fillets first in flour mix; then dip fillets into egg mix. Coat fish with crumbs mix and sauté them in hot oil (with onions) for 2-3 minutes on each side. Lay cooked fillets to drain on paper towels; transfer cooked fish and onions to a heat-resistant serving platter.

   Pour sherry mix into skillet; while stirring, quickly bring it to a boil. Turn off heat and pour sauce over fish fillets. Serve hot. Serves 6.

TROPICAL FRUIT WITH LENTILS

1 lb. pkg. brown lentils, rinsed in cold water, drained

6 cups water

1 lg. yellow onion, chopped

6 garlic cloves, chopped

2 tbsp. olive oil

1 lg. Granny Smith apple, chopped (with skin)

$\frac{1}{2}$ ripe pineapple, cored, skin removed and chopped into small chunks

2 tomatoes, seeded, diced with skin

salt to taste

cayenne pepper to taste

1 lg. almost ripe banana, cut into small chunks

parsley for garnish

Simmer lentils in 6 cups water, covered, for about 40 minutes until lentils are tender. Do not overcook. Remove lentils from heat.

Meanwhile, heat oil in skillet and sauté onions and garlic until lightly browned. Add apple and continue to cook for 1-2 minutes, until apples are golden. Add pineapple; heat through. Add tomatoes and stir to mix.

Continue to cook stew on medium heat until sauce thickens, about 5 minutes. Drain lentils, reserving 1 cup of cooking liquid. Pour lentils into sauce and stir in reserved liquid. Heat through. Stir in banana chunks and season with salt and cayenne pepper. Pour into serving bowl. Garnish with parsley. Serves 6.

MARION'S VERSION OF TUNNEL OF FUDGE CAKE
(Low in fat; no trans fat.)

The "Tunnel of Fudge" cake grew in popularity after it was developed for a Pillsbury Bake-Off in 1966. The original winner, Ella Rita Helfrich, won $5,000 for her chocolate cake recipe with the sinfully rich tunnel of fudge. Only one problem: very heavy on fats and sugar. My version eliminates the "bad" fats. Results: as devilishly rewarding.

1¾ cups sugar

1¾ cups Smart Balance spread

1½ cups egg substitute

2 cups confectioners' sugar

2¼ cups flour

¾ cup dark unsweetened cocoa (at least 60% cacao)

2 cups walnuts, chopped

Preheat oven to 350°. Grease and flour 10-inch Bundt pan. In a large bowl, combine sugar and Smart Balance; beat until light and fluffy. Add egg substitute, ¼ cup at a time, beating well after each addition. Gradually, add confectioners' sugar and blend thoroughly into the batter. By hand, smoothly blend in flour, cocoa and walnuts. Spoon and evenly spread the batter into prepared pan.

Bake cake in preheated oven, 350° for 45-50 minutes, until top is set and edges begin to pull away from sides of pan. This cake has a soft filling. A doneness test cannot accurately be performed. Cool upright in pan for 1½ hours. Invert cake onto serving plate and cool for at least 2 hours.

GLAZE:

¼ cup brown sugar

¼ cup dark unsweetened cocoa (60% cacao)

4-6 tsp. low-fat or fat-free milk

¼ cup chopped walnuts, for garnish

After the cake has thoroughly cooled, outside of its pan, prepare the frosting. In a bowl, completely blend until smooth: brown sugar and cocoa and enough milk to form a loose icing. Drizzle icing over cake, allowing some of it to run down the sides. Sprinkle chopped walnuts over icing on cake.
Have icing set, before tightly covering the cake, to store in a cool place. Hint: insert 6-8 protruding sandwich picks into top of cake to form a barrier (if using foil and/or plastic wrap to cover the cake). Serves at least 12.

Summer-Fall

Wine and Dine

*Y*ou've seen those titillating scenes on TV shows and cinema flicks. *You know, young, professional male (or female) invites the other young professional female (or male) to the sparse, glamorous, cubby-hole, duplex apartment. He (she) cooks an elegant meal, complete with candles, fireplace, couch (or hearthrug) __ plus the ubiquitous bottle of cabernet, merlot, pinot noir, complete with two extremely long-stemmed wine glasses.*

She (he) spoons some concoction from the Calphalon skillet onto the sparkling dinner plate (Lenox, no doubt); they work their forks; they guzzle the wine between breathy conversation. And you know the rest of the story. The old "wine and dine" seduction.

I must confess, although I never ever partook of such a scene (never had the opportunity), the old wine and dine caper really seduced me, time and time, and time again. Guess I'm a sucker for romantic glitz. Or was it that sizzling skillet – and the wine? ..... Ah, the wine!

Cathy Shea and Chip Celenza
at their wedding table.

Summer-Fall

PUMPKIN SOUP

GRILLED HONEY GINGER SALMON

MASHED SWEET POTATO

GRILLED ASPARAGUS AND APPLE SLICES

HARVEY WALLBANGER CAKE (heirloom)

PUMPKIN SOUP

1 lg. can (20 oz.) pure pumpkin

1 can (20 oz.) dark red kidney beans

1 lg. onion, finely chopped

2-3 garlic cloves, minced

2 tbsp. olive oil

1 lg. carrot, pared, shredded

1 lg. celery stalk, thinly chopped

1 cup tomato purée

6 cups water

$\frac{1}{2}$ cup white rice

1 bay leaf

$\frac{1}{2}$ tsp. each: cumin, chili powder,
    cracked black pepper

1 tsp. each: oregano, thyme, salt

2 tbsp. fresh cilantro, chopped, for garnish

Heat oil in a 4-quart soup pot with lid. Cook onion and garlic on moderate-high heat, stirring bottom of pot to prevent particles from sticking. Add: tomato purée, water, pumpkin, rice, carrot and celery. Cover pot and simmer for 20 minutes. Add and stir to thoroughly blend: herbs (except cilantro) and spices and beans. Cover pot and continue to simmer for 15 minutes. Remove bay leaf and discard. Garnish soup with chopped cilantro. Serves 6-8.

MASHED SWEET POTATO

4-5 med. to lg. sweet potatoes, pared,
    cut into chunks

2 tbsp. butter or Smart Balance spread

black pepper to taste

1 tbsp. brown sugar

Hungarian paprika for garnish

Boil sweet potatoes 10-12 minutes, or until tender. Drain potatoes; pour them into a large bowl. Add butter, pepper and brown sugar. Mash the mix just until lumps are softened. Spoon mashed sweet potatoes into a serving bowl. Sprinkle with paprika. Serves 6.

GRILLED HONEY GINGER SALMON

2 lg. salmon fillets, about 2 lbs. total; remove skin;
    cut portions when serving

1-inch piece gingerroot, peeled, minced

$\frac{1}{2}$ cup honey

juice from 2 limes

$\frac{1}{4}$ cup chopped dill

2 tbsp. balsamic vinegar

2 tbsp. extra-virgin olive oil

$\frac{1}{2}$ tsp. freshly ground pepper

salt to taste

2 limes, quartered, for garnish

Preheat broiler; set grate 5 inches below heat; OR, set grill to high and place grate 5 inches above heat. Brush a large solid metal sheet pan with olive oil.

In a small bowl, blend oil, balsamic vinegar, gingerroot, honey, dill, lime juice, pepper and salt. Brush the marinade on both side of the fillets. Lay the salmon, top side down, on the pan. Grill fish for 4-5 minutes. With a long spatula, turn over the fillets on the pan. Again, brush the fillets on the top side. Broil the other side of the fillets for another 4-5 minutes. Transfer fish to a serving platter. Brush salmon with remaining marinade. Serve with lime wedges. Serves 6.

GRILLED ASPARAGUS AND APPLE SLICES

about 2 dozen asparagus stalks, trimmed

3 Granny Smith apples, washed, cored, sliced into 1-inch rounds (do not pare)

$\frac{1}{4}$ cup olive oil

$\frac{1}{4}$ cup mustard spread

black pepper to taste

juice of 1 lemon

In a small bowl, blend oil, mustard, black pepper and lemon juice. Whisk the mix until smooth and creamy. Grill or broil asparagus and sliced apples on a grill pan, turning apples over to grill both sides, about 3-4 minutes. Cook them at the same time you grill the salmon. As soon as apples and asparagus are prepared, transfer them to a serving platter, and keep them warm. Spoon the mustard sauce over them as you serve. Serves 6.

HARVEY WALLBANGER CAKE
(A cake from the past, from a mix.)

1 pkg. (about 22 oz.) orange cake mix
1 pkg. (3⅝ oz.) instant vanilla pudding
4 eggs or 1 cup egg substitute
½ cup canola oil
4 oz. Galliano liqueur
1 oz. vodka
¼ cup orange juice

GLAZE:
1 oz. Galliano liqueur
1 oz. vodka
1 oz. orange juice

1 cup confectioners' sugar, sifted - for garnish

Preheat oven 350°.

Grease and flour a 10-inch Bundt pan. In a large bowl, combine cake mix and pudding. Blend in eggs, canola oil, Galliano, vodka and orange juice. Beat until smooth. Pour batter into a greased and floured 10-inch Bundt pan.

Bake the cake at 350° for 45 minutes or until an inserted toothpick removes clean. Allow cake to cool for ½ hour. Invert pan onto a serving platter. Remove pan from cake.

Blend ingredients for the glaze; drizzle glaze over cake while cake is still warm. (If preparing cake a day or two in advance, refrigerate the cake when cooled; cover with plastic wrap.) Dust the cake with sifted confectioners' sugar just before serving. Serves 8-10.

Summer-Fall

Before You Write a Cookbook, Hire an Attorney

I hadn't intended to self-publish my first cookbook, MENU LOG: A Collection of Recipes as Coordinated Menus. Barely six months into publication, the publisher I had contracted with, suddenly went bankrupt. My assigned editor was without a job and she offered me (and several other victims) her talents and services, for a fee. She promised to take us through the actual publication of our books.

Immediately, I sought legal assistance from a dear and long-time friend, an attorney. He informed me of the alternatives, and ended his evaluation with, "Go for it!"

Easy for "you", dear lawyer. Notwithstanding, I had wished my book to achieve publication, and I took his advice. I willingly learned about the publishing world and a few of its positives, all of its negatives. The final outcome was worth the sacrifices. I have no regrets. Also I'm not so foolish to believe that I could have done it "alone" - never in a zillion years.

Without the honest, diligent and knowledgeable editor, - without the support of family and friends (especially my son), - without the understanding and helpful professional contacts I would meet, - the doors of publication would never have been unlocked.

Summer-Fall

LENTIL SOUP WITH PASTA
or
SPLIT PEA SOUP
A ROASTED SUCKLING PIG (heirloom)
TRAY OF MELON SLICES

LENTIL SOUP WITH PASTA
(Soup may be prepared several days in advance.)

1 onion, chopped

3 garlic cloves, chopped

1 all-purpose potato, pared,
    chopped into small cubes

1 carrot, pared, chopped

2 celery stalks, trimmed, peeled, chopped

1 cup canned plum tomatoes, mashed

1 chile pepper, seeded, chopped (optional)

1 pkg. (1 lb.) dried brown lentils, picked over,
    rinsed, drained

8 cups water, or ham stock made from a hambone
    (or 2-3 links sweet Italian sausage,
    remove casing, chop into small pieces)

1 tbsp. dried oregano

1 bay leaf

2 tbsp. olive oil

salt and black pepper to taste

1 cup uncooked tiny shells pasta (or tiny elbows)

If using sausage for stock: in a 6-quart soup pot, lightly brown sausage meat, onions and garlic in hot oil. Scrape leavings from bottom of pot; pour 8 cups water into the pot and bring to a boil. OR: If using a ham bone, brown onion and garlic in hot olive oil, in a 6-quart soup pot; scrape leavings from bottom of pot; pour 8 cups water into pot with the ham bone, and bring pot to a boil.

To the boiling water, add celery, potato, carrot, (chile pepper), mashed plum tomatoes, herbs and spices. Return pot to boil and stir in the lentils. Bring soup to simmer; cover the pot.

Stir soup occasionally as it cooks for 45 minutes. Raise the heat under pot. When the soup starts a slow roll, stir in the pasta. Cook the pasta in the soup on a low boil for 8 to 10 minutes longer, stirring frequently. Remove bay leaf before serving. (Remove ham from hambone; cut ham into small pieces. Discard bone.) This soup may be frozen up to several months. Serves 6-8.

SPLIT PEA SOUP
(May be prepared several days in advance; may be frozen.)

Split Pea Soup, with or without pasta, may be prepared by following the same basic recipe as Lentil Soup. These changes should be noted:

1. Substitute 1 pkg. (1 lb.) dried split peas for lentils

2. Substitute 1 tbsp. dried thyme for oregano

Continue as directed on page 224.

AN INTRODUCTION TO A ROASTED SUCKLING PIG

My husband had determined that we should roast A SUCKLING PIG for a late Autumn gathering of friends. He convinced Stan Zukowski, one of our long-time buddies, to be his chief assistant. The suckling pig was ordered and purchased from a butcher shop whose specialty was pork.

The children of the guests gushed over the "cute little piggy". I couldn't believe they would accept a serving of "Porky" at suppertime.

Bags of charcoal had been purchased the day before; and the charcoal fire had been started at ten in the morning of the festivities. The Cooks trussed the dressed pig and they tied it securely to the thick metal spear in the large bowl of the charcoal cooker which had been imbedded into the earth. A three-foot circular clearing gave Porky and the Cooks lots of space.

At noon, the charcoal fire was deemed ready for the trussed pig on the spit. And so, the Challenge of the Roasted Suckling Pig commenced!

Our Chefs turned the pig on its rack - by hand - every 20 minutes. By 6 pm, Porky was looking quite sunburned and crisped. However, a meat thermometer informed the excited crowd that the pork's internal temperature had barely reached 120°.

We hostesses and our hungry guests voted to quarter the pig, and to roast the pig in sections, - in the conventional gas oven, to complete the masterful job. By 7:30 pm, we raised our wine glasses to a delicious roasted suckling pig - and to the bedraggled Cooks!

Recipe for ROASTED SUCKLING PIG, conventional oven method, follows.

A ROASTED SUCKLING PIG
(Conventional oven method.)

1 suckling pig, no larger than 10-12 lbs.

12 cups unseasoned bread crumbs	*cook's string*
1 cup butter or Smart Balance spread	*1 cup dry light red wine, eg.*
1 cup chopped onions	*chianti or sangiovaise*
1 cup chopped celery	*flour for gravy*
1 cup chopped apples with skin, remove pits	*(garland of watercress, parsley, cranberries*
1 tbsp. each: dried sage, thyme, marjoram	*AND a large apple to insert in its mouth -*
2 tsp. salt	*for garnish)*
1 tsp. black pepper	*a small block of wood*
2 cups hot beef broth or hot water	*foil*
several metal skewers	

Preheat oven 350°.

Wash the pig in several changes of cold water. Pat it dry with paper towels.

Pour bread crumbs into a large bowl. In a skillet, at moderate high, melt the butter and sauté onion and celery until tender. Mix in apples and seasonings. Add this mix to crumbs in bowl. Moisten crumb mix with hot broth or hot water.

Cool the stuffing mix. Then, stuff the pig loosely; insert several metal skewers and lace the pig's opening with cook's string. Truss the legs to the body with string. Place a small block of wood in the pig's mouth so it will stay open for the apple garnish. Cover the ears with foil to prevent burning. Place the pig on a rack in a very large roasting pan.

Pour 1 cup wine over the pig. Roast the pig in a preheated oven, 350° and allow 25 minutes per pound. Cover the pig with a foil tent, if browning occurs too quickly. Baste the pig frequently with pan drippings. Use a meat thermometer as directed. When pig is almost cooked, prepare some gravy by using pan drippings, flour and a little more wine.

To serve: lift roasted pig to a large platter. Remove foil from ears (and body); place a crown of watercress on its head; remove the wood block from its mouth and replace it with a large red apple; and strew the platter with cranberries and bunches of parsley. Serves a crowd.

TRAY OF MELON SLICES

1 ripe cantaloupe, cut into 8 wedges

$\frac{1}{4}$ lg. watermelon, cut into 8 or more slices, 1-inch thick

1 ripe honeydew melon, cut into 8 or more $1\frac{1}{2}$-inch wedges

1 lemon, 1 lime, skin washed; each cut into 6 wedges

(Before serving: skin of all fruit, when ripened, should be washed under cool running water; pat dry with paper towels and chill fruit before cutting.)

Have ready: a very large serving tray, about 18 inches in diameter, or 9x15 inches; you may lay paper doilies over the tray. Pare skin from melon slices. Arrange melon slices around the tray: honeydew around the outer edge; cantaloupe following around the inside; and stand-up watermelon sections in the center. Insert wedges of lemon and lime between the slices of melon. Serve chilled. Serves 6-8.

John and the suckling pig.

Summer-Fall

Grasses and Grains

*I*n agriculture, grain is the caryopsis, or dry fruit, of a cereal grass, the seeded fruits of buckwheat and other plants bearing such fruits. Grains, whole, or ground into meal or flour, are the mainstay food of humans and domestic animals. The food content is mostly carbohydrate, but some protein, oil and vitamins are present. Grains are low in water content and can be stored for long periods.

The primary grain crops _ wheat, barley, rice, corn, oats, rye - together occupy about half of total world cropland. Grains - cereal grasses, are the staple foods in most countries.

Bread is the biggest staple made from cereal grasses, leavened or unleavened, and is man's primary food for sustenance. The symbolical definitions of "bread" connote livelihood, food and sustenance for the world, money, the Eucharistic wafer, and life, itself.

Summer-Fall

SEAFOOD AND ESCAROLE SOUP
BAKED FLOUNDER FILLET AND PEPPERS
STEAMED BEETS IN ORANGE
THREE MUFFINS

SEAFOOD AND ESCAROLE SOUP

6 cups water

6-8 jumbo shrimp, remove vein, leave in shell

2 crab claws

1 small head of escarole, trimmed, washed, drained

1 onion, thinly sliced

3-4 garlic cloves

1 lg. carrot, pared, sliced thin

1 lg. celery stalk, chopped

2-3 ripe tomatoes, skin removed, chopped

1 small jalapeño pepper, seeded, chopped

$\frac{1}{4}$ cup fresh cilantro, chopped

1 tbsp. dried oregano

salt, black pepper to taste

2 tbsp. olive oil

Brown garlic and onion in olive oil in a 6-quart soup pot with cover. Scrape bottom of pot to remove onion/garlic particles. Pour 6 cups of water in pot; cover pot and bring to a boil. Add escarole, carrot, celery, tomatoes, jalapeño, herbs, salt and pepper. Cover pot and return it to a slow simmer. Cook for 15 minutes.

Add shrimp in shells and crab claws. Cover and simmer the stew for another 10-15 minutes. Before serving, crack crab claws and remove the flesh with a pick. Return crab meat to pot. Peel shells from shrimp as you enjoy this delicious soup. Serves 4-6. Accompaniment: cornbread squares.

BAKED FLOUNDER FILLET AND PEPPERS

6 med.-lg. slices flounder fillets,
    rinsed, patted dry with paper towels
1 cup cornmeal
black pepper, salt to taste
1 tbsp. chili powder
oil to coat 9x15-inch ovenproof pan

1 lg. red bell pepper
1 lg. orange pepper
1 lg. green bell pepper
1 lg. yellow pepper
1 small cayenne pepper
1 lg. onion, thinly sliced
2 tbsp. olive oil

**All peppers
washed, seeded and
thinly sliced**

Preheat oven to 375°.

Grease an oven-resistant 9x15-inch pan or Pyrex dish, with olive oil.

Blend and spread on a large sheet of waxed paper: cornmeal, pepper, salt, chili powder. Coat fish on both sides with cornmeal mix. Lay fillets adjacent to each other in the oil-coated pan.

Mix all of the sliced peppers and onions in a large bowl; drizzle olive oil over the pepper mix and toss to evenly coat. Spoon the mix over and around the fish in the pan.

Bake casserole in preheated oven, at 375° for 20-25 minutes, or until fish is golden in color. Remove casserole from oven and serve directly from pan with the aid of a spatula. Serves 6.

STEAMED BEETS IN ORANGE

12-15 small-medium beets
juice of 1 orange
1 tbsp. orange rind
1 tbsp. olive oil

1 tbsp. white wine vinegar
1 tsp. dried thyme
1 red onion, finely sliced
salt, black pepper to taste

Steam beets for 15-25 minutes, depending on their size. Halve (or quarter) beets. In a small bowl, blend together: orange juice, rind, olive oil, vinegar, thyme, salt and pepper.

Peel the beets, halve or quarter them and place them in a bowl. Add sliced onion; drizzle the sauce over the beet mix and toss to coat thoroughly. Serve them at room temperature. Serves 6.

THREE MUFFINS

1) LENA'S BLUEBERRY ORANGE MUFFINS

$\frac{1}{4}$ cup butter or Smart Balance spread, melted
1 egg
$\frac{1}{4}$ cup canola oil
$\frac{2}{3}$ cup milk
$\frac{2}{3}$ cup orange juice
grated rind of 1 navel orange

2 cups sifted flour
2 tsp. baking powder
1 tsp. baking soda
$\frac{1}{3}$ cup sugar
$\frac{1}{2}$ cup cornmeal
1 cup blueberries (rinsed, drained),
    tossed with 1 tbsp. flour

TOPPING:
1 tbsp. sugar
$\frac{1}{4}$ tsp. cinnamon

Preheat oven 425°.

In a large bowl, beat egg into cooled, melted butter. Add liquids; blend thoroughly. In a medium bowl, combine all dry ingredients; add dry ingredients to liquid mix, mixing by hand. Gently fold in floured berries.

Grease muffin tin(s). Fill muffin cups with batter, $\frac{3}{4}$ filled. Sprinkle tops of muffins with sugar and cinnamon mix. Bake in preheated oven 425° for 15-20 minutes, or until an inserted toothpick comes out clean. Makes about 12 medium-size muffins.

(Continued on next page)

(Continued from previous page)

2) CRANBERRY PECAN MUFFINS

2½ cups flour
½ cup sugar
¼ cup canola oil
1 tbsp. lemon rind
1 tbsp. lemon juice

1 egg or ¼ cup egg substitute
1 cup low-fat or non-fat milk
2 tsp. baking powder
dash of salt
2 cups fresh cranberries,
    coarsely chopped in food processor
1 cup chopped pecans

confectioners' sugar for sprinkling

Preheat oven 400°.

Grease muffin cups. In a large bowl, thoroughly mix all ingredients except: cranberries, pecans and confectioners' sugar. Fold in cranberries and nuts. Spoon batter into muffin cups, ¾ filled. Bake muffins in a preheated oven at 400° for 15-20 minutes. Cool. Sprinkle muffins with confectioners' sugar just before serving. Yields about 6 medium-size muffins.

---

3) PUMPKIN APPLE-CINNAMON MUFFINS

1⅓ cups wheat flour (or white)
1 cup oat bran uncooked
½ cup honey (or ¼ cup brown sugar)
½ tsp. cinnamon
¼ tsp. nutmeg
2 tsp. baking powder
dash of salt
1 cup low-fat or non-fat milk

1 egg, beaten or ¼ cup egg substitute
3 tbsp. canola oil
1 cup canned pumpkin
½ cup apple, pared, chopped
¼ cup white raisins (optional)

more cinnamon and brown sugar
    to sprinkle tops of muffins

Preheat oven 400°.

Grease cups of muffin tin. Combine all ingredients in a large bowl; blend thoroughly. Spoon batter into greased muffin cups, ¾ filled. Sprinkle with additional cinnamon mixed with brown sugar. Bake muffins at 400° for 15-20 minutes, or until inserted toothpick returns clean. Makes about 6-8 medium-size muffins.

Summer-Fall

"Honey, I've Just Bought 3,000 Shares, Each, of Alcoa & Kimberly-Clark."

A roll of paper towels resides in almost every room in my house, including the 2-car garage (actually, an entire "in-use" case of paper towels takes up the northwest corner of the garage). Correction: make that EVERY room.

And I house tissue boxes (cubes and rectangles) in quaint- ornate- glitzy receptacles to accommodate our more personal hygiene needs.

The pantry stocks assorted packages of cleaning "wipes" for any and all cleaning categories and assignments. We're talking "utility pantry", whose entire 3x6-foot top shelf is a veritable "deli's delight". Categorically arranged, I will find foil wrapping: plain, heavy duty, holiday printed; plastic wrap, plastic bags of all sizes; waxed paper: plain, holiday print; and freezer wrap.

Then, there's bathroom tissue rolls __.

So, now you know the reason for my husband's opening statement.

Summer-Fall

THREE-BEAN SALAD WITH FETA
RED WINE VINEGAR AND OLIVE OIL DRESSING
EGGS AND PEPPERS WITH SHRIMP SAUCE
WATERMELON CHILL

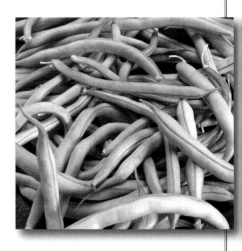

THREE-BEAN SALAD WITH FETA

2 cups green beans, trimmed, cut into small pieces, steamed for 5 minutes

1 small can (1 lb.) red kidney beans, rinsed, drained

1 small can (1 lb.) chick peas (ceci), rinsed, drained

1 small red onion, chopped

1 doz. cherry tomatoes

3-4 tbsp. cilantro, chopped

$\frac{1}{2}$ lb. feta cheese, chopped into small chunks

Red Wine Vinegar and Olive Oil Dressing (see page 384)

    Prepare dressing in advance. Refrigerate dressing until 1 hour before using. In a large salad bowl, mix the three beans. Add onion, cherry tomatoes and feta cheese; sprinkle cilantro over salad. Shake the dressing thoroughly. Add dressing to salad just before serving and toss well to mix. Serves 4-6.

EGGS AND PEPPERS WITH SHRIMP SAUCE
(Eggs in Purgatory in Shrimp Sauce)

1 doz. large eggs

6 Italian frying peppers, seeded, vertically sliced

2 long Italian peppers, seeded, vertically sliced

1 lg. onion, finely sliced

4-6 ripe plum tomatoes, chopped with juice

2 tbsp. olive oil

$\frac{1}{2}$ cup dry white wine

1 tbsp. dried oregano

1 bay leaf

6 fresh basil leaves, torn

$\frac{1}{4}$ tsp. salt (to taste)

$\frac{1}{2}$ tsp. freshly ground black pepper

pinch or two of hot red pepper flakes

6-8 extra large shrimp, shelled, cleaned

$\frac{1}{2}$ cup Parmesan cheese

3 slices cooked bacon, drained, crumbled

Break 1 dozen eggs into a large bowl. Be careful to keep the eggs whole. In a large heavy skillet with cover, lightly brown sliced onions in 2 tablespoons of olive oil at moderate heat.

Add and stir in: peppers; cook for 2-3 minutes, scraping bottom of skillet to prevent sticking. Add plum tomatoes in juice, oregano, basil, black pepper, hot pepper flakes, salt, shrimp and wine. Bring to a slow boil; then cover pot and simmer for 10 minutes. Stir occasionally as sauce cooks.

As sauce is simmering, pour eggs into pan with sauce and pepper mix. Sprinkle cheese over the pan and lay a bay leaf on top. Cover pot and continue to gently simmer sauce and eggs until eggs are just set. DO NOT STIR SAUCE as eggs cook. Remove bay leaf and discard. Garnish with crumbled bacon. Serve from skillet, using a long, wide spatula and serving spoon. Accompaniment: frizelle pepper biscuits or pepper biscotti. Serves 6.

WATERMELON CHILL

6 cups cold watermelon, cubed

1 pt. cold blueberries, rinsed, drained

1 pt. chilled Asti Spumante (more at serving time)

mint sprigs for garnish

(half-straws to sip wine)

Place cubed watermelon into a large bowl. Just before serving, pour 1 pint chilled Asti Spumante over watermelon. Carefully toss watermelon with 2 spoons. Spoon one cup watermelon into glass serving bowls, lined with 2 tablespoons blueberries. Sprinkle more blueberries over the watermelon in bowls. Drizzle one-quarter cup Asti Spumante over fruit in bowls. Garnish with sprigs of mint. Insert small straw into each bowl and serve immediately. Serves 6.

Garlic

Garlic is one of the oldest known cultivated plants. Garlic, as we know it today, is a domesticated crop. It is said to have been in use for over 5,000 years. Garlic probably originated in Central Asia and made its way to ancient Egypt, Greece, India and China. The new world was introduced to "allium longicuspis" through Spain, Portugal and France. We find garlic growing in temperate and tropical regions all over the world, with many different types of cultivars to suit many different climates.

Garlic was used in medicine, as an aphrodisiac, a stimulant. It was thought to ward off evil spirits and the spread of diseases (like smallpox). Upper classes despised garlic because of its strong odor. However, as the centuries changed, so did attitudes. In modern cooking, garlic along with onions, shallots and leeks, ranks in the top scented flavors for cooking. Modern science highly touts this little bulb and bestows many accolades on its miraculous benefits. What would world cuisine do without its garlic?

My own life bas been strongly influenced by this magnificent bulbous herb. Every year in October, I perform the ritual of inserting 2 dozen unpeeled cloves of garlic, point up, into a small section of cultivated garden soil.

By July of the ensuing year, I usually harvest 2 dozen heads of garlic. I wash off the clinging soil and sun-dry the heads before storing. Meanwhile over the maturation months, I cut off a delicate fragrant frond, here and there, to add to my spring salads. Many times, lovely pink or lavender feathery pom-poms (alium) burst forth from the plants to indicate that the harvest is near. My garlic heads are milder than most varieties which are available at the green grocer, probably because my soil imparts its own zonal/area flavors.

P.S. In the "olden days", during seasonal "viral epidemics", my mother would insert a few garlic cloves into a gauzy sack fastened with a long ribbon. She would drape it around her daughter's neck to tuck into her undershirt, to ward off smallpox and influenza viral infections.

Summer-Fall

POTATO AND CECI CURRY CHOWDER

RED SNAPPER WITH CURRY SALSA

TANDOORI LAMB

PEAR AND GINGER CAKE

POTATO AND CECI CURRY CHOWDER
(May be prepared a day before serving; refrigerate chowder in non-metal bowl with cover;
warm thoroughly before serving.)

4-5 all-purpose potatoes, pared,
   chopped into small chunks

1 lg. onion, finely chopped

4-5 garlic cloves, minced

1 carrot, pared, chopped fine

1 lg. can (20 oz.) crushed tomatoes in juice

6 cups water

1 lg. can (20 oz.) chick peas (ceci)

$\frac{1}{2}$ cup frozen peas, softened in refrigerator

1 tsp. each: red curry powder, chopped parsley, salt,
   garam masala (*NOTE: below)

$\frac{1}{4}$ tsp. each: ground turmeric, black pepper

2 tbsp. olive oil

Heat olive oil in a 4-quart soup pot with lid. Cook onion and garlic in oil until tender. Stir bottom of pot as you add potatoes, tomatoes, carrot and water. Add all spices and herbs and stir to mix, thoroughly. Cover pot and simmer for 30 minutes. Add chick peas and peas and continue to simmer for 15 minutes. Serves 6.

*NOTE: "Garam Masala" is a blend of spices, which when mixed, becomes a flavorful part of Indian cooking. A tasty combination of these spices follows.

GARAM MASALA

2 tbsp. cardamom

2 tbsp. ground cloves

2 tbsp. coriander seeds, crushed

2 tbsp. ground cinnamon

2 tbsp. whole peppercorns

2 tbsp. cumin

Blend spices thoroughly to pour into a $\frac{1}{2}$-pint jar with screw-top lid. As with any spice, potency will dissipate over a prolonged time.

RED SNAPPER WITH CURRY SALSA

6-8 fillets red snapper (depends on size), skin removed
coriander sprigs for garnish

SAUCE (CURRY SALSA):
1 lg. onion, chopped fine
2 tbsp. olive oil
1 tbsp. peeled gingerroot, minced
2 garlic cloves, minced
1 green bell pepper, finely chopped
1 red bell pepper, finely chopped
2 tbsp. curry powder
$\frac{1}{4}$ cup flour
2 cups chicken broth (less-salt variety)
1 can (20 oz.) chopped plum tomatoes
2 tbsp. fresh lime juice
1 tbsp. grated lime rind
salt, black pepper to taste

Prepare sauce. In a large pot with lid, cook onion in oil over moderate heat until tender; add garlic and gingerroot, stirring and cooking for 1-2 minutes longer. Add peppers and cook for several minutes until softened. Stir in curry and flour and cook for 2 minutes.

Add the broth and tomatoes, mixing thoroughly, and cook for 5 minutes. Stir in lime juice, rind, salt and pepper. Remove from burner. (Sauce may be prepared a couple of days in advance, covered and refrigerated. Reheat sauce before continuing with recipe.)

Preheat oven to 350°.

Arrange snapper fillets in a 9x15-inch oil-coated oven-proof pan. Ladle about one-half of the salsa over the fillets. Keep remaining sauce covered and warm. Oil a large sheet of foil and place the foil, oil-side down, tightly over the pan of fish/salsa. Bake the snapper at 350° for 45-50 minutes, or until it flakes (depending on thickness of fillets). Garnish with sprigs of coriander. Serve with additional salsa. Serves 6.

TANDOORI LAMB
(Start the recipe on day before.)

6-8 bone-in shoulder lamb chops

1 container (8 oz.) plain fat-free Greek yogurt

$\frac{1}{4}$ tsp. salt

$\frac{1}{2}$ tsp. black pepper

$\frac{1}{4}$ tsp. ground cloves

1 tbsp. freshly grated gingerroot

3 garlic cloves, minced

2 tsp. Hungarian paprika

1 tsp. each: cumin, cinnamon, coriander

a 2-gallon re-sealable plastic bag

In a medium bowl, mix together all of the ingredients except lamb chops. Place the chops in a large 2-gallon re-sealable plastic bag. Pour bowl of yogurt/spices mixture over the chops in the plastic bag. Turn over the bag a few times to coat the chops. Refrigerate the bag of chops in the marinade for 12 to 24 hours; turn bag occasionally.

Preheat oven 350°. Coat broiler pan with olive oil.

Transfer chops from the plastic bag to the rack of the broiler pan, which you've coated with olive oil. Discard the marinade. Bake the chops at 350° for 40-45 minutes or until meat thermometer registers 180°. Then, set oven to broil; broil chops for 3-5 minutes on each side, depending upon thickness of chops. Serves 6.

PEAR AND GINGER CAKE
(Prepare cake several days in advance. Refrigerate.)

1 box (22 oz.) yellow cake mix

1 cup low-fat milk

$\frac{1}{3}$ cup canola oil

3 eggs or $\frac{3}{4}$ cup egg substitute

3 tsp. ground ginger

2-3 Bosc pears, peeled, cored, thinly sliced

1 tbsp. brown sugar

ground ginger for garnish

vanilla ice cream, sprinkled with ground ginger, as an accompaniment

Preheat oven 350°. Grease a deep 8-inch cake pan.

In a large bowl, beat eggs with oil and ginger. Pour cake mix into the bowl, a little at a time, beating batter after each addition. Gradually blend in milk, continuing to beat at medium speed for 2 minutes. Pour batter into prepared pan.

Lay sliced pears in a ring around top of cake. Sprinkle brown sugar and ginger over pears. Bake cake in preheated oven, 350° for 35-40 minutes or until tester returns clean.

Cool cake in pan for 20 minutes. Run a thin knife around the edge of the pan to loosen cake. Invert cake to a plate; then, invert again onto a serving plate (pears side up). Sprinkle ground ginger to garnish. Cover cake and refrigerate at this point, if not serving. When ready to serve, accompany cake with a portion of vanilla ice cream, sprinkled with ginger. Serves 6-8.

Summer-Fall

Statti Zitto e Mangia!

By the time I had celebrated fifteen exciting years, my family included forty-eight first cousins and eighteen second cousins, and counting. Most of my fifteen living aunts and uncles, my parents' sisters and brothers, continued to gather together in family groups, to celebrate life. On both Coasts, we formed Orlando-Capriglione Cousins Clubs.

Every cousin's cousins were part of our Club. I'm certain that the gatherings were noisy, chaotic, boisterous, lovingly disorganized. Yet, not one time could be heard that familiarly assigned Italian admonition, "Statti zitto e mangia!"___not even in English.

Chip and friends celebrate a birthday.

Summer-Fall

STUFFED AVOCADO
EAST-WEST CHOWDER
STUFFED FISH FILLETS WITH CRAB, SHRIMP AND APRICOTS
COFFEE ALMOND STREUSEL CAKE

STUFFED AVOCADO

3 Hass avocados, skin washed, pitted (do not pare); sprinkle flesh with lemon juice
   to prevent discoloration

1 cup sliced banana

1 cup fresh pineapple chunks

1 navel orange, washed, peeled, pith removed,
   cut into small chunks

1 tbsp. extra-virgin olive oil

1 tbsp. cider vinegar

½ cup chopped almonds with skin, for garnish

beds of Boston lettuce, washed, drained

In a large bowl, combine banana, pineapple and orange. In a small bowl, whisk oil with vinegar until mixture is emulsified; add the dressing to the fruit and toss to mix. Lay a bed of Boston lettuce on each of 6 salad plates. Place half of an avocado upon each lettuce bed. Spoon the fruit over halves and sprinkle with almonds. Serves 6.

EAST-WEST CHOWDER

2½ doz. cherrystone clams, scrubbed

4 cups water

2 tbsp. butter or Smart Balance spread

1 lg. onion, finely chopped

1 carrot pared, diced

¼ cup flour

½ cup dry white wine

2-3 medium-large all-purpose potatoes, pared, diced

1 lg. can (1 lb.) corn kernels

1 can (13 oz.) evaporated milk, fat-free available

½ tsp. salt

½ tsp. black pepper

1 tbsp. chopped parsley

Hungarian paprika for garnish

Scrub clams with a seafood brush under cold running water. Put them into a heavy saucepan with a lid. Add about 4 cups water to pan. Cover pan, bring to a boil at medium-high and cook clams for 2-4 minutes, or until clams open. Shake pan occasionally. Remove pan from heat; discard any unopened clams.

Remove cooked clams from shells; strain cooking liquid into a bowl, through a fine mesh sieve. Reserve clams in a small bowl. Discard shells.

Heat butter in a 4-quart pot with a cover. Cook onion and carrot in butter until softened, scraping bottom of pot to remove leavings. Pour clam stock into the pot with onion/carrot; stir to mix. Remove 1 cup clam/vegetable stock to a small bowl and stir in ¼ cup flour until smooth. Return it to the stock pot. Stir in potatoes and cover the pot. Raise heat under pot and bring to a low boil. Then, simmer the chowder for 15 minutes, until potatoes are tender. Stir in milk, salt, pepper, parsley, corn. Chop reserved clams and add to the chowder pot. Stir in wine; cover pot and bring to a boil. Lower heat under pot to simmer for 2-3 minutes.

Taste chowder and add more salt or pepper if needed. Before serving, sprinkle paprika, to taste, over the bowls. Serves 6-8.

STUFFED FISH FILLETS WITH CRAB, SHRIMP AND APRICOTS

6-8 large fish fillets (suggestions: flounder, sole, tilapia)

12-15 jumbo shrimp, cleaned, leave on tail

1 cup crab meat, chopped

$\frac{1}{4}$ cup finely chopped celery

2 tbsp. chopped gingerroot

2 tbsp. finely chopped parsley

2 tbsp. finely chopped onion

$\frac{1}{4}$ cup fine breadcrumbs

a few dashes Tabasco

salt, black pepper to taste

ground cayenne pepper, to taste

4-6 ripe apricots (or use canned whole apricots in water, drained), pitted, quartered

$\frac{1}{4}$ cup *lite* ginger soy sauce

2 tbsp. olive oil

a few tablespoons water, as needed, to dampen stuffing

6-8 metal skewers

Preheat oven 400°. Brush 2 tablespoons olive oil on bottom of non-stick 9x15-inch baking pan.

In a bowl, combine chopped crab, celery, onion, parsley, crumbs, Tabasco, gingerroot, salt and black pepper. Add 1 or 2 tablespoons of water to the mix to form a crab stuffing which will hold together.

Lay fish fillets on a sheet of waxed paper. With your hands, pat down one portion (about 2-3 tablespoons) of crab stuffing over each fillet. Carefully roll up fillets and fasten with metal skewers. Lay the fillets on the prepared 9x15-inch oiled pan.

Combine shrimp and apricots into a large bowl; pour ginger soy sauce over this mix and toss to coat thoroughly. Arrange coated shrimp/apricots around the fillets in the pan. Lightly sprinkle the fillets with cayenne pepper (to taste).

Bake the seafood and fruit in a preheated oven at 400° for 20 minutes or until the stuffing starts to brown. Remove pan from oven; baste fillets with shrimp/apricot sauce from bottom of pan. Serve immediately. Serves 6.

COFFEE ALMOND STREUSEL CAKE
(May be prepared a few days in advance.)

$1\frac{1}{4}$ cups flour

1 tbsp. baking powder

$\frac{1}{3}$ cup sugar

$\frac{2}{3}$ cup milk

2 eggs or $\frac{1}{2}$ cup egg substitute

$\frac{1}{2}$ cup canola oil

2 tbsp. instant coffee blended with 1 tbsp. boiling water

$\frac{1}{3}$ cup chopped almonds

confectioners' sugar for dusting cake

TOPPING:

$\frac{1}{2}$ cup flour

$\frac{1}{3}$ cup sugar

2 tsp. apple pie spice

1 tbsp. water

2 tbsp. butter or Smart Balance spread, cut into tiny cubes

Preheat oven 375°. Grease a 9-inch spring-form cake pan.

Sift together: flour and baking powder into a large bowl. Stir in sugar and nuts. Beat eggs, oil and milk in a small bowl; add coffee and blend thoroughly. Pour the wet mixture into the dry mix and blend. Spoon batter into the prepared pan.

Prepare the topping. Combine flour and sugar in a bowl. With a fork, mix in butter bits to form a crumbly mix. Sprinkle pie spice and water into the mixture, working with a fork to form crumbs. Sprinkle the crumbs over the cake batter in the pan.

Bake the cake in the center of a preheated oven 375° for 50-60 minutes. Loosely cover the top of the cake with foil, if the topping begins to brown too quickly. Cake is baked when an inserted toothpick removes clean. Allow the cake to cool in the pan; then, run a knife around the spring-form edge to loosen the cake. Remove sides of the pan and let the cake cool completely. Do NOT remove cake from bottom of pan. Place cake on serving platter. Dust with confectioners' sugar just before serving. Serves 8.

Summer-Fall

At what age did you discover that there are at least 2 Other Ways to Make a Peanut Butter Sandwich?

By the time I was eleven, life had dealt me a near-fatal twist of the peanut butter spreader. I realized that my favorite snack of nutty peanut butter (the kind you had to stir) and strawberry jam on grainy whole wheat was NOT the recipe of note.

Creamy, homogenized peanut butter and grape jelly on mushy white square sandwich bread was "the one". How could my Mother allow this lie to persist? Not only that! Have you tried nutty peanut butter AND sliced banana, stuffed into a croissant? And how about creamy peanut butter on white toast, dressed with two strips of crisp bacon, two thin slices of beefsteak tomato, lettuce and MAYO???

P B & J - any way you spread it! M-m-m-m! Yum!

Santa Chip with children at St. Pius X religious ed.

Summer-Fall

SALAD OF SPINACH, SHRIMP, RED ONION AND PINEAPPLE (See page 14)
BLEU CHEESE DRESSING (See page 386)
HONEY WINGS AND SESAME RIBS
CORN, TOMATOES AND MUSHROOMS
SUNDAY MORNING ZEPPOLE (heirloom)
HUSH PUPPIES (heirloom)

SALAD OF SPINACH, SHRIMP, RED ONION AND PINEAPPLE (See page 14)
with BLEU CHEESE DRESSING (See page 386)

HONEY WINGS
(May be prepared in advance and frozen. Serve hot.)

$2\frac{1}{2}$ dozen chicken wings, tips removed, rinsed in cold water, patted dry with paper towels

MARINADE:

$\frac{1}{4}$ cup *lite* soy sauce	$\frac{1}{4}$ cup orange juice
$\frac{1}{4}$ cup hoisin sauce	grated zest of 1 orange
1 tsp. chili powder	2 tbsp. honey
1 tsp. ground ginger	2 tbsp. finely chopped peanuts
	(2 tbsp. canola oil for skillet)

Combine all ingredients for marinade. Brush wings with marinade and lay them in a shallow dish. Refrigerate wings for a couple of hours. Reserve leftover marinade in refrigerator.

Heat canola oil to 320° in a wok or a large skillet. Brush wings with reserved marinade. Fry wings 5 or 6 at a time, about 3 to 4 minutes on each side. Drain wings on paper towels. OR: You may bake the prepared wings on a oiled metal tray in a preheated oven, 450° about 12 minutes on each side. Serves 6.

SESAME RIBS
(May be prepared in advance and frozen. Heat thoroughly to serve.)

3 lbs. pork spare ribs (or baby back pork ribs); separate ribs

MARINADE:

3 tbsp. *lite* ginger soy sauce	1 tsp. chopped coriander
3 tbsp. hoisin sauce	3 garlic cloves, minced
$\frac{1}{2}$ tsp. Chinese 5-spice powder	2 tbsp. catsup
3 tsp. brown sugar	$\frac{1}{4}$ cup creamy peanut butter
$\frac{1}{4}$ cup sesame seeds	4 tbsp. sherry

In a small bowl, thoroughly blend all marinade ingredients. Place ribs in a shallow dish. Baste ribs with marinade, turning them several times to coat thoroughly. Refrigerate ribs for 1 hour, turning them over in marinade a couple of times.

Preheat oven 375°.

Remove ribs from marinade and arrange them on a wire rack, placed over a roasting pan filled with 1-inch hot water. Brush ribs with marinade; reserve remainder of marinade. Bake ribs in preheated oven, 375°, 12-15 minutes on each side (or grill them, 4-5 inches from heat for 8 to 10 minutes on each side; less time for baby back ribs). Brush marinade on both sides of ribs.

Do not overcook the ribs; add more water to pan if necessary. The hot water steam aids in cooking the ribs. Transfer ribs to a warmed platter and serve hot. Serves 6.

CORN, TOMATOES AND MUSHROOMS

1 lg. can (1 lb.) corn kernels

4-5 plum tomatoes, coarsely chopped

1 green bell pepper, seeded, chopped

1 red bell pepper, seeded, chopped

1 small red onion, finely sliced

6 porcini mushrooms, washed, thinly sliced

1 small jalapeño pepper, seeded, chopped
(optional, to taste)

$\frac{1}{4}$ cup fresh cilantro, chopped

salt, freshly ground black pepper, to taste

2 tbsp. olive oil

Heat olive oil in a 2-quart sauce pan. Cook onion in oil at moderate-high for 2 minutes, until light golden brown. Stir in peppers and mushrooms and cook 2 minutes longer. Stir in corn kernels. Remove pot from burner; sprinkle and stir in salt, pepper and 2 tablespoons cilantro. Transfer stew to serving bowl. Add chopped tomatoes; toss to mix. Garnish with remainder of cilantro. Serves 6.

SUNDAY MORNING ZEPPOLE

1½ cups flour

pinch of salt

3 tsp. baking powder

¼ cup granulated sugar

½ cup milk (low-fat)

2 eggs, beaten

confectioners' sugar for dusting

canola oil for frying (about 1 inch
    in bottom of skillet)

You will need a deep-fryer or a large heavy skillet. Add oil to pot and preheat to moderate-high 340°.

In a large bowl, sift together: flour, salt, baking powder and sugar. Combine beaten eggs and milk and blend them into dry ingredients. Dip a serving spoon into cold water; shake off water from spoon. Scoop about 2 tablespoons batter into the spoon and use a spatula to scrape the batter off the spoon into the hot oil.

Fry zeppoles until light brown, turning them over to cook all sides. Drain them on paper towels. Sprinkle them with confectioners' sugar and serve immediately. Makes 8-10 zeppoles.

HUSH PUPPIES

1½ cups yellow cornmeal

1 tbsp. baking powder

¼ tsp. salt

2 eggs, beaten

1 sm. onion, chopped fine

canola oil for deep-frying

¼ cup flour

½ tsp. baking soda

⅛ tsp. black pepper

¾ cup buttermilk

In a deep-fryer or large skillet, heat at least a couple of inches oil to 340°. In a medium bowl, combine cornmeal, flour, baking powder, baking soda, salt and pepper. In a small bowl, beat eggs and buttermilk. Add to dry ingredients. Stir in onion; blend thoroughly.

Drop batter by heaping tablespoonfuls, a few at a time, into hot oil; fry fritters on all sides for 3-4 minutes or until golden brown and cooked through. Drain fritters on paper towels. Repeat procedure until batter is finished. Keep fritters warm, in a low oven, 200°.

Makes about 2 dozen hush puppies. (These are too good to be tossed to the barking dog. Although, he'll love you for 'em.)

Summer-Fall

Olive Oil

The olive tree is the symbol of abundance, glory and peace. The leaves and branches were used to "adorn"; the oil of the fruit was used to "anoint". In many religions, in many countries, sacramental oils are still used to anoint, to bless and purify. Olive tree symbols were found in Egypt's Tutankhamen's tomb. His body was probably anointed in holy oils.

The olive tree has ancient roots dating as far back as 20 million years ago, although actual cultivation probably did not occur until 5,000 B.C. Olive cultivation spread from Crete to Syria, Palestine and Israel; then to Turkey, Cyprus and Egypt; and finally to southern Italy, North Africa and Southern France. Pliny, in the first century A.D. wrote that Italy "had excellent olive oil at reasonable prices".

It was believed that olive oil conferred strength and youth. Today, it is not so far-fetched to believe that ingesting olive oil and massaging it into your skin creates a younger, more supple-skinned "You". Lots of our cosmetics contain purified olive oil.

Extra-virgin olive oil is said to be the most digestible of the edible fats. Climate, soil, variety of tree and time of harvest account for the different properties in different oils. Certain extra-virgin olive oils are blends of varieties of olives; others are made from one cultivar.

A virgin olive oil is the liquid of the first pressing (later pressings require more pressure which releases stronger tastes from olive skins and seeds). "Cold pressed" means that almost no heat was used to extract the oil.

Use the virgin olive oils (more costly oils) for salads; try the darker, heartier, more fruity olive oils when cooking and preparing sauces, soups, meats (they truly taste of olives).

Olive oil helps to assimilate vitamins A, D, and K; it contains essential acids which cannot be produced by our own bodies; it slows down the aging process; it helps bile, liver and intestinal function _ and adding it to our menu helps to make foods taste better, smell better and look better.

Summer-Fall

PENNE WITH SALSA PUTTANESCA (heirloom)
GRILLED SURF/TURF AND ACCOMPANIMENTS
GINGER-PEACHY BROCCOLI
COFFEE MOUSSE

PENNE WITH SALSA PUTTANESCA
(Whore's Sauce)

Salsa Puttanesca (see page 300)
1-1½ lbs. penne rigati

grated Asiago cheese for topping

Prepare Salsa Puttanesca in advance. Heat sauce thoroughly when needed. You will need 4 cups of sauce for 6 people. Any leftover sauce may be frozen for several weeks.

Prepare penne pasta according to directions on package. Drain pasta and pour into a large serving bowl. Pour 2 cups hot sauce over pasta; toss to coat thoroughly. Pour another cup of sauce over top of bowl and generously sprinkle cheese over sauce. Serve remainder of sauce and cheese in individual bowls. Serves 6.

GRILLED SURF/TURF AND ACCOMPANIMENTS

1 dozen lg. prawns, washed, butterflied with shells on
3 sirloin strip steaks, $\frac{1}{2}$-inch thick, about $\frac{3}{4}$ lb. each

2 medium-size slender purple eggplants, skin peeled, $\frac{1}{2}$-inch thick slices
3 lg. California, white potatoes, scrubbed, $\frac{1}{2}$-inch thick slices (with skin)
3 firm beefsteak tomatoes, sliced into $\frac{1}{2}$-inch rounds

MARINADE FOR STEAK AND PRAWNS:
$\frac{1}{4}$ cup olive oil
2 tbsp. A-1 sauce
$\frac{1}{4}$ tsp. black pepper
$\frac{1}{8}$ tsp. cayenne pepper
dash of salt

DRESSING FOR VEGETABLES:
2 tbsp. olive oil
1 tbsp. balsamic vinegar
black pepper to taste

Prepare marinade and dressing in separate small bowls.

Lightly brush two 9x15-inch narrow open-grated grill trays with olive oil. Brush one solid metal sheet pan with olive oil.

Prepare vegetables first. Set broiler or grill to moderate-high, 450°. Grill sliced potatoes on oiled solid metal sheet pan for 2-3 minutes; add eggplant slices and brush the vegetables with a light coating of dressing. Cook for several minutes on all sides of vegetables. Transfer to heat-resistant serving platter and keep vegetables warm.

Lay the tomato slices on the same pan; brush them with the dressing and grill them for 1 minute. Add the tomatoes to the vegetable platter (they will be soft).

Next, prepare the shrimp and beef. Brush shrimp on both sides with marinade. On one of the open grill trays, lay the butterflied shrimp one side down; grill shrimp for 2 minutes on this side; turn them over and baste the other side; grill for another 2 minutes. Remove grill (with shrimp) and lay butterflied grilled shrimp on one-half of a heat-resistant platter, flesh-side up. (Cover shrimp lightly with foil and keep them warm.)

Lastly, lay the steaks on the second open grill; brush both sides of steaks with marinade and grill them for 2-3 minutes on each side on high heat (for medium-rare). Transfer meat to the other half of the serving platter (with the shrimp). Cut the steaks in 2-3 pieces each. Serve shrimp and steak with a side of grilled vegetables. Serves 6.

GINGER-PEACHY BROCCOLI

2 tbsp. peanut oil

4 cups broccoli florets, washed, trimmed

1 can (6 oz.) sliced water chestnuts

2 garlic cloves, chopped

1 red bell pepper, seeded, sliced thin

2 fresh peaches, skin peeled,
   sliced into narrow wedges

2 tbsp. grated gingerroot

2 tbsp. *lite* soy sauce

2 tsp. brown sugar

$\frac{1}{2}$ cup water

Blend soy sauce and brown sugar into $\frac{1}{2}$ cup water. Set aside. Heat peanut oil in a large wok or skillet to moderate high, 320°. Stir-fry garlic and broccoli for 2 minutes. Add and stir in: sliced red pepper and water chestnuts to the wok. Cook for 1 minute. Stir in gingerroot and peaches and cook for 1 minute longer. Drizzle soy mix over wok, tossing broccoli mix to coat thoroughly. After 1 minute, remove wok from heat. Serves 6.

COFFEE MOUSSE

$1\frac{1}{2}$ tsp. unflavored gelatin

6 tbsp. water

$1\frac{1}{2}$ cups sweetened condensed milk

3 tsp. instant caffé espresso powder

$1\frac{1}{2}$ tsp. almond extract

2 cups cold heavy cream

In a small sauce pot sprinkle gelatin over the water and let it soften for 2 minutes. Add milk and espresso powder and heat the mixture over moderate heat, whisking constantly, until powder is dissolved.

Remove pan from heat; stir in almond extract and set the pan in a bowl of cold water with ice.

Stir the mix frequently, until it is thick and cold. In a small bowl, beat cream until it forms stiff peaks and gently and thoroughly fold the coffee mixture into it. Spoon the mousse into chilled goblets and refrigerate them until ready to serve. Serves 6.

Summer-Fall

M(N)IX the Butter with the Eggs

Since the early 1980's, I have undertaken a personal crusade to ingest a minimum of potentially harmful fats. My dedication to offer alternatives in cooking, inspired my third and final revision of MENU LOG, my first cookbook.

Many recipes instruct us to "mix the butter with the eggs". Well, I simply "nixed" the butter with the eggs. Yes, I still include the traditional butter and eggs in my recipes; I also offer alternatives: canola oil, olive oil, Smart Balance, nuts, egg whites, egg substitutes, other vegetable alternatives. Healthier options; less "stuff" to clog the arteries.

Summer-Fall

CHICORY WITH ORANGES AND KALAMATA OLIVES
RED WINE VINEGAR AND OLIVE OIL DRESSING
SHREDDED PORK WITH SHRIMP
WALNUT RICE PILAF
WALNUT CAKE WITH ORANGE GLAZE

CHICORY WITH ORANGES AND KALAMATA OLIVES

4-6 cups chicory, trimmed, washed and drained
2 navel oranges, rind and pith removed and the flesh, sectioned
1 medium-size red onion, sliced very thin
1½ doz. pitted Kalamata olives

Red Wine Vinegar and Oil Dressing (see page 384)

Prepare Red Wine Vinegar and Oil Dressing in a small jar.

Tear the chicory into small pieces and place the greens in a large salad bowl. Add orange sections, onions and olives; toss to combine. Just before serving this salad, drizzle the dressing over the bowl; toss the salad to mix. Serves 6.

SHREDDED PORK WITH SHRIMP

1½ dozen jumbo shrimp, shelled, cleaned, leave on tail

3 pork tenderloin, ½-inch thick, thinly sliced

    (HINT: if meat is frozen, thinly slice before pork softens)

4 garlic cloves, chopped

3-4 scallions, chopped (including greens)

2-3 leeks, trimmed, thinly sliced

1 red pepper, seeded, thinly sliced

2 cups snow peas, ends pinched

2-3 fresh peaches (with skin), cut 6 sections per peach

2 tbsp. peanut oil

SAUCE:

1 cup water

¼ cup sherry

2 tbsp. *lite* soy sauce

2 tbsp. Asian plum sauce

3 tbsp. cornstarch stirred into ½ cup water to form a smooth paste

black pepper to taste

1 tbsp. gingerroot, chopped

    Heat peanut oil in a large wok or skillet. Sauté shrimp for 3-4 minutes until opaque. Or use ready-cooked shrimp: sauté cooked shrimp for 1-2 minutes. Transfer shrimp to ovenproof platter and keep them warm in oven. Add garlic, scallions, leeks and shredded pork to skillet and cook for 4-5 minutes, stirring and scraping bottom of the wok (or skillet) with spatula.

    Add snow peas, peaches and peppers and stir-fry for another couple of minutes. Return shrimp to wok and remove wok from heat.

    Meanwhile, in a 1-quart bowl make a smooth paste with cornstarch and water; stir in 1 cup water, gingerroot, sherry, soy sauce, plum sauce and a little black pepper. Pour the liquid over the vegetable/pork/shrimp mix and toss with 2 spoons to coat thoroughly. Raise the heat under the pot to simmer and cook for 5 minutes until sauce thickens and contents are heated through. Serve from wok. Serves 6.

WALNUT RICE PILAF

½ cup brown rice

½ cup wild rice (soak rice in 1 cup hot water for 1 hour)

1 small onion, chopped

1 carrot, pared, chopped

1 lg. celery stalk, chopped

½ green pepper, seeded, chopped

1 tbsp. olive oil

salt and pepper to taste

2½ cups chicken broth, less-sodium variety

½ cup dried cranberries

½ cup chopped walnuts

In a 2-quart sauce pan, heat oil and lightly brown onion and celery for 5 minutes. Scrape bottom of pot and add brown and wild rice, broth, green pepper, carrot, cranberries and walnuts, salt and pepper to taste. Stir to mix. Simmer stew, covered, for 40-45 minutes until liquid is almost absorbed. Serves 6.

WALNUT CAKE WITH ORANGE GLAZE
(May be prepared several days in advance. Glaze the cake on serving day.)

2 cups flour

1½ tsp. each: cinnamon powder, allspice, nutmeg powder

1 tsp. each: baking soda, baking powder

½ tsp. salt

1 cup butter or Smart Balance spread, softened

1 cup sugar

3 large eggs, separated

1 tsp. vanilla extract

1 cup walnuts, chopped fine

1¼ cups sour cream (fat-free available)

GLAZE:

1 cup confectioners' sugar

2 tbsp. orange juice

Preheat oven 350°.

Grease a 3-quart, deep Bundt cake pan. Into a bowl, sift together: flour, cinnamon, nutmeg, allspice, baking soda, baking powder and salt.

In a large mixing bowl of electric mixer, cream together: butter and sugar until light and fluffy; beat in egg yolks (1 at a time), beating well after each addition. Beat in vanilla. Beat in flour mix alternately with sour cream in 3 batches, beginning and ending with flour mixture. Wash and dry the electric beaters thoroughly. In another bowl, with the electric mixer, beat the egg whites to form stiff peaks; fold them and the walnuts into the batter. Spoon the batter into the greased pan, smoothing the surface of the batter.

Bake the cake in a preheated oven at 350° for 45-50 minutes, or until a toothpick tests clean.

Transfer cake to a rack for 15 minutes; then, invert it on the rack to cool completely. Transfer cake to decorative serving dish.

GLAZE:

In a small bowl whisk together: sugar and orange juice until smooth. Slowly pour the glaze though a narrow funnel over the cake to create circular designs across the surface of the cake. Serves 8-10 slices. (If you prepare the cake a day or two in advance, when thoroughly cooled, wrap the cake in plastic wrap and store in a cool place. Glaze the cake on the serving day.)

Summer-Fall

Set a Place for Your Dog

*O*ur family's Labrador Retrievers love to eat. Anyone's cooking, any nation's specialties, fast-food, gourmet cuisine, cooked or raw. They sniff the bacon before it begins to sizzle in the pan.

And boy! Do these pups chow-down fast. Their portions of "lean dog cuisine" are devoured as soon as the food touches the bowl. Our Labs are trained to observe the "Home Rules". They do not feed at or from the dinner table.

Patiently, they allow us two-legged beasts all of the time in the world, to dine and chat and linger around our trough. But as soon as our chairs are pushed away from the table, and the folks commence the melt-down, up they go, into the kitchen. They're ready to share in the feast: our meager scraps become a veritable canine feast.

Summer-Fall

SEAFOOD COCKTAIL

GRILLED T-BONE STEAK WITH VIDALIA ONIONS AND MIXED PEPPERS

BABY LIMA BEANS AND PLUM TOMATOES

MACADAMIA CUPCAKES WITH ORANGE ICING

SEAFOOD COCKTAIL

1 lb. jumbo shrimp, shelled, cleaned

1 lb. sea scallops

1 lb. thinly sliced squid (plus tentacles)

2 cups water

1 lg. avocado, sliced

juice of 1 lime

large leaves of Boston lettuce

SAUCE:

1 cup catsup

¼ cup chili sauce

½ tsp. cumin

salt, black pepper to taste

2 shakes of Tabasco (to taste)

juice of 2 limes

½ cup chopped fresh cilantro (for garnish)

8 oz. tortilla chips in a basket

Simmer seafood in 2 cups of water for 2-3 minutes. Bring seafood to room temperature in liquid. Meanwhile, prepare sauce by blending catsup, chili sauce, cumin, Tabasco, salt and pepper and juice of 2 limes.

Drain seafood. (Save seafood stock in a jar and refrigerate up to a day or two to use as base for seafood tomato sauce or soup.)

Arrange lettuce leaves on bottoms of 4-6 glass salad plates. Divide seafood onto each plate. Spoon sauce over seafood; add avocado slices around one side of each plate. Sprinkle avocado slices with juice of 1 lime to prevent discoloration. Garnish plates with chopped cilantro, and serve with a basket of tortilla chips. Serves 6.

GRILLED T-BONE STEAK WITH VIDALIA ONIONS AND MIXED PEPPERS

3 lbs. T-bone steaks, 1-inch thick (for 6 portions)

2-3 Vidalia onions, thinly sliced

1 red bell pepper, cored, thinly sliced

2 green bell peppers, cored, thinly sliced

1 yellow pepper, cored, thinly sliced

MARINADE FOR VEGETABLES:

2 tbsp. olive oil

1 tbsp. red wine vinegar

black pepper, salt to taste

1 tbsp. oregano

Heat the grill or broiler to moderate-high, about 400°- 450°.

Prepare the vegetables marinade by blending oil, wine vinegar, pepper, salt and oregano in a small bowl. Place vegetables in a large bowl. Drizzle dressing over the vegetables and toss to coat thoroughly. Spread the onions and peppers over an oiled solid metal sheet pan. Grill or roast them, for 4-5 minutes, scraping the pan frequently. Keep vegetables warm while you grill steaks.

Raise the heat in grill or broiler to 500°. Lay the whole steaks on the grill grate, 5 inches away from heat and cook steaks 4-5 minutes on each side for medium-rare. Dress the meat with a little salt and freshly ground black pepper, if desired. Form portions after grilling. Serve with warm grilled peppers and onions. Serves 6.

BABY LIMA BEANS AND PLUM TOMATOES

1 pkg. (1 lb.) frozen baby lima beans,
    cook as directed on package

4-6 plum tomatoes, quartered

3-4 garlic cloves, chopped

2 tbsp. olive oil

$\frac{1}{4}$ tsp. salt

$\frac{1}{4}$ tsp. freshly ground black pepper

3-4 basil leaves, chopped

Pour cooked beans into serving bowl. Add tomatoes, garlic, oil, salt , pepper and basil and toss gently to mix. Serves 6.

MACADAMIA CUPCAKES WITH ORANGE ICING

CAKE:

1 cup flour

½ cup Macadamia nuts, coarsely chopped in food processor

1¼ tsp. baking powder

pinch of salt

⅓ cup canola oil

½ cup sugar

1 large egg or ¼ cup egg substitute

½ tsp. almond extract

⅓ cup water

Preheat oven 350°.

Line a 12-cup muffin pan (½-cup each portion) with paper liners. In a bowl, whisk together: flour, baking powder, pinch of salt and nuts.

With electric mixer, cream together in a large bowl: sugar and oil; beat in egg and extract. Alternately, beat flour mixture and the water into the egg mixture, beating well after each addition.

Spoon batter into 12 paper-lined cups in a muffin tin. Bake muffins in preheated oven 350° for 15-20 minutes, or until toothpick tests clean. Turn cupcakes out onto a rack to cool completely.

ICING:

1¼ cups confectioners' sugar

1½ tbsp. butter or Smart Balance spread, softened

1 tbsp. grated orange rind

1 tbsp. orange juice

3 slices orange sugar candy, chopped into wedges, for garnish

In another bowl, beat together: confectioners' sugar, softened butter, orange rind and juice, beating until icing is blended and fluffy. Spread icing over tops of cooled cupcakes. Cut each orange slice candy into 4 tiny wedges. Garnish each cupcake with a candy wedge. Makes 12 medium cupcakes. (Peel off cupcake paper before eating cake.)

Summer-Fall

Wine

Grape cultivation and wine imbibing probably commenced about 4000 BC – 6000 BC. Artifacts from tombs in ancient Egypt prove that wine was in use around 3000 BC. Archeological digs have unearthed sunken jars which housed wine. Priests and royalty were using wine; beer was drunk by the working class. The Egyptians are credited with developing the first arbors and pruning methods.

For centuries, wine had been thought to evolve through "spontaneous generation". In 1857, Louis Pasteur proved that wine is made by microscopic organisms, yeasts. This scientific find ultimately has led to the world-wide wine industry as we know it today.

Wine is made by fermentation of the juice of the grape. Wines are distinguished by color, flavor, aroma (bouquet) and alcoholic content; they may be red (when the whole crushed grape is used), white (using the juice only), or rosé (when skins are removed after fermentation has commenced). Wines are classified as dry (when grape sugar ferments completely), or sweet (when some sugar remains).

Basically, there are three main types of wine: natural (still), fortified and sparkling. The alcoholic content of "natural" wine comes from fermentation. Fortified wine (e.g. sherry, port, Madeira) has brandy or other spirits added. Sparkling wine (Champagne, for example), is fermented a second time after bottling.

Wine is differentiated by variety of grape, climate, location and soil of the vineyard and treatment of the grapes before and during wine-making. Fermentation commences when wine yeasts on the ripe grape skins come in contact with the grape juice (called "must"). Run-off into barrels (the "new wine"), then undergoes chemical processes: oxidation, precipitation of proteins and fermentation of chemical compounds. This process creates the "bouquet". After timed aging and clarification in barrels, the wine is ready to be bottled.

Our modern world's leaders in wine production are France – Bordeaux, Burgundy, Loire and Rhone Valleys, Alsace; Italy, Spain, Germany and the United States (California). (Continued on page 266)

Summer-Fall

PANZANELLA (heirloom)
PICKLED VEGETABLE STEW
ELSIE'S CHICKEN FRICASSEE (heirloom)
RICE OR NOODLES
ALMOND GINGER BISCOTTI

PANZANELLA

2-day old crusty artisan-style bread, multi-grain,
    cut into 1-inch cubes
6-8 plum tomatoes, trimmed,
    each sliced into 4 wedges

1 slender cucumber, pared, sliced very thin
$\frac{1}{4}$ cup extra-virgin olive oil
$\frac{1}{4}$ cup red wine vinegar
6 basil leaves, torn into small pieces

In a large serving bowl, thoroughly toss and combine all of the ingredients. Serves 6.

PICKLED VEGETABLE STEW

2 tbsp. olive oil
1 onion, thinly sliced
4 garlic cloves, thinly sliced
3-4 carrots, pared, sliced into thin rounds
2 Italian fryer peppers, cored, sliced into strips
1 chile, seeded, minced (wear plastic gloves)
1 celery stalk, trimmed, cut into small chunks
1 small red pepper, seeded, sliced into thin strips

1 small cauliflower, rinsed, broken into small florets
1 tsp. dried oregano
1 bay leaf
$\frac{1}{4}$ tsp. ground cumin
$\frac{1}{2}$ cup cider vinegar
$\frac{1}{4}$-$\frac{1}{2}$ cup water
salt, black pepper to taste

    Heat oil in skillet; sauté onion, garlic, celery, peppers, carrots, cauliflower for 1-2 minutes. Add oregano, bay leaf, cumin, pepper, salt, vinegar and just enough water to barely cover the vegetables. Cook the stew for 5-7 minutes or long enough for vegetables to be tender but firm. Remove pot from heat; leave to cool. Remove and discard bay leaf. Serve stew as a side. Serves 6. (This recipe will keep up to one week, covered and refrigerated.)

ELSIE'S CHICKEN FRICASSEE

4 chicken legs	3 lg. carrots, pared, cut into 1-inch chunks
2 split chicken breasts (4 pieces)	1 cup milk
4 chicken thighs	$\frac{1}{4}$ cup flour
4 chicken wings	$\frac{1}{4}$ cup chopped parsley
2 lg. onions, quartered	salt, black pepper to taste
2 lg. celery ribs with greens, cut into thick chunks	2-3 tbsp. olive oil

Wash chicken; pat dry with paper towels. Heat oil in a large Dutch oven. Brown chicken on all sides in oil. Transfer chicken pieces to a large plate as you brown them. Add a small amount of water to the pot (about $\frac{1}{4}$ cup), scraping the bottom of the pot to loosen any chicken particles. Return chicken pieces to the pot and add just enough water to cover the chicken. Add onion quarters, celery and carrot chunks. Stir in parsley; add salt and pepper to taste.

Bring water in the pot to a boil, removing the froth from top of pot as the water boils, about 10 minutes. Cover pot and reduce heat. Simmer chicken for about 45 minutes to 1 hour, depending on thickness of chicken pieces. Transfer chicken to a large oven-proof platter and keep it warm. Drain the broth into a bowl, saving the vegetables in another bowl. Return the broth to the Dutch oven and cook the liquid to simmer.

In a small jar with a lid, blend 1 cup milk with $\frac{1}{4}$ cup flour. Fasten lid on jar and shake contents vigorously, until milk and flour are blended. Slowly stir this mix into the simmering broth, stirring constantly as broth thickens. (Stir more flour into the liquid if you prefer a thicker gravy.)

Add vegetables to the chicken platter. Pour some gravy over chicken and vegetables. Serve remainder of gravy in a bowl, and ladle it over rice or noodles, to accompany the chicken fricassee. Serves 6-8.

WHITE OR BROWN RICE   or   WIDE NOODLES
...make a nice accompaniment.

ALMOND GINGER BISCOTTI
(Prepare well in advance.)

$^3/_4$ cup whole almonds with skins, coarsely chopped
$^1/_2$ cup candied ginger, finely chopped
1 cup flour
$^1/_2$ cup sugar
$1^1/_2$ tsp. powdered ginger
$^1/_4$ tsp. salt
$^1/_2$ tsp. baking soda
1 lg. egg or $^1/_4$ cup egg substitute
egg white from 1 lg. egg
$^1/_2$ tsp. almond extract

Preheat oven 300°.

Grease a 5x7x3-inch loaf pan with butter or Smart Balance spread. Line the bottom of the pan with waxed paper.

Sift together into a bowl: flour, sugar, powdered ginger, salt and baking soda. In another bowl, with electric mixer, beat together: egg, egg white and almond extract. Stir in flour mix and beat until blended. Stir in chopped almonds and chopped ginger.

Press dough into the prepared 5x7-inch loaf pan and bake dough in the middle of the oven at 300° for 45 minutes until pale golden. Do not turn off oven.

Invert loaf onto a rack to cool for 10 minutes. Transfer loaf to cutting board and with a serrated-edged knife, cut loaf in half, horizontally. Slice each half into 20 vertical slices, $^1/_4$-inch thick.

Arrange biscotti on one or two baking sheets and bake them in the middle of the oven at 300° until crisp, around 8-10 minutes. Cool biscotti thoroughly before storing them in an airtight container at a cool temperature for 2 weeks (or freeze in layers, waxed paper between layers). Makes about 40 slender biscotti. Serve with espresso.

Summer-Fall

Wine

(Continued from page 262)

*Y*ou ask: What wine with what food?

If you're serving multiple styles of wine for tasting, it makes a big difference to try them in the proper order: 1) sparkling before still; 2) white before red;   3) lighter to full-body;   4) low to high alcohol percentage;   5) dry to sweet;   6) younger to older.
Most oenologists will agree the only sensible "rule of thumb" is to do whatever you find enjoyable. Who's to say you should not enjoy red wine with fish? Be adventurous; explore the vineyard. And have you read recent medical journals? "Wine, drunk in moderation, is beneficial to your health."

"SLAINTE"   "CHOC-TEE"   "KAMPAI"   "YUNG SING"
"ZUM WOHL"   "KIPPIS"   "SALUTE"

"CHEERS"!!!!

Summer-Fall

GREEK VEGETABLE BEAN SOUP

LAMB AND PORTOBELLOS WITH APRICOTS

WHITE or BROWN RICE

ZABAGLIONE WITH STRAWBERRIES (heirloom)

GREEK VEGETABLE BEAN SOUP
(Prepare several days in advance.)

2 tbsp. olive oil

1 onion, chopped

3 garlic cloves

2 carrots, pared, sliced into thin rounds

2 celery stalks, trimmed, chopped

2 baby eggplant, diced

6 canned artichoke hearts, quartered

1 can (1 lb.) plum tomatoes, mashed

6 cups water

1 can (1 lb.) cannellini beans, rinsed, drained

juice and zest of 1 lemon

1 tbsp. oregano

1 bay leaf

1 tsp. salt

½ tsp. black pepper

¼ cup chopped mint leaves, for garnish

Heat oil in a 4-quart pot with lid. Simmer onion and garlic in oil until tender. Scrape bottom of pot to prevent sticking as you add carrots, celery, eggplant and artichokes to the mix. Add tomatoes and stir to blend. Pour water into the pot; add and stir in: herbs (except mint) and spices. Cover pot and cook soup for 30 minutes. During last 5 minutes, stir in beans, lemon juice and zest. Remove and discard bay leaf before serving. Garnish with mint. Serves 6.

LAMB AND PORTOBELLOS WITH APRICOTS

1 tbsp. olive oil

6-8 baby loin lamb chops, 1-inch thick
   (at least 1 chop per serving)

1 tbsp. rosemary

4-6 slender carrots, pared, par-boiled

3 lg. Portobello mushrooms, washed, drained;
   section each into $\frac{1}{2}$-inch slices

6 garlic cloves, peeled, leave whole

3-4 leek bulbs, trimmed, chopped

6 apricots, quartered (If using canned apricots,
   drain thoroughly)

MARINADE:

$\frac{1}{4}$ cup gingerroot, chopped

$\frac{1}{4}$ cup chopped roasted peanuts

$\frac{1}{4}$ cup *lite* soy sauce

2 tbsp. rice wine vinegar

1 tbsp. honey

Parboil carrots for 4-5 minutes. Preheat broiler to 500°.

In a small bowl, blend soy sauce, rice wine vinegar, honey, gingerroot and chopped peanuts. Grease a grill pan with tray with olive oil. On the grill pan, lay: lamb chops, sprinkled with rosemary. Brush chops with sauce, and broil them for 4-5 minutes on EACH SIDE, basting both sides with sauce. Add mushrooms, par-boiled carrots, leeks and garlic to the grill pan after the first 5 minutes. Add apricots during the last couple of minutes. Baste lamb and accompaniments with sauce as they cook. Use all of the basting sauce; do not overcook the chops. Meat thermometer will register 180° for doneness. Serve lamb and fruit/vegetable mix over WHITE RICE or BROWN RICE. Serves 6.

ZABAGLIONE WITH STRAWBERRIES

4 cups strawberries, hulled and
   quartered, lengthwise

8 eggs, separated

1 cup confectioners' sugar

dash of salt

$\frac{1}{2}$ cup marsala wine

AND

(another $\frac{1}{2}$ cup marsala wine at serving time)

Beat egg whites and salt until very stiff peaks are formed. In a separate bowl, with clean beaters, beat yolks and sugar until light and fluffy. Place yolks mix in top-half of double boiler (over boiling water). DO NOT ALLOW TOP POT WITH CUSTARD TO TOUCH WATER IN BOTTOM POT. With electric mixer, beat custard constantly over the hot water. When mix is foamy, add $\frac{1}{2}$ cup wine. Beat custard until thick. Remove pot from heat and water and fold yolks mix into the egg white mix.

Set up 6 dessert bowls; spoon $\frac{1}{2}$ cup strawberries into each bowl; sprinkle 1 tablespoon marsala over berries in each dessert bowl. Spoon 2-3 tablespoons custard over berries. Garnish with a few slices of strawberries. Serves 6.

Summer-Fall

This is the Table with Two Desserts

My Mother's younger brother, Albert (real name: Umberto, in recognition of King Umberto of Italy), labeled our home "the table with two desserts". Actually, Mama always served seasonal fruit to conclude our supper meals. (Fruits had seasons in those days.) Fruits were a necessary part of our menu in order to **"sciacquare"** (cleanse) our taste buds from the varied spices, oils and tangs of the delicious dinner she had served. And then, we'd have **"real"** dessert: cakes, puddings, gelatins, pies, ice cream, pastries.

Although Apple Pie contained apples, it wasn't considered the fruit which sufficiently cleansed our palates. In later years, Mama adjusted her first course: a salad of greens and vegetables, plus fruit: orange segments, apple chunks, blueberries, grapes. In the minds of her family, this translated into: **"DESSERT"**.

There would be meals which served fruit with salads; fruit before the dessert course; AND fruit in the dessert course.

A veritable Garden of Eden.

Summer-Fall

ZUCCHINI, TOMATOES AND CORN RELISH
GRILLED TUNA STEAK WITH OLIVE SAUCE
STEAMED ORANGE CAULIFLOWER AND BROCCOLI
APPLE AND CRANBERRY CRISP

ZUCCHINI, TOMATOES AND CORN RELISH

1 can (1 lb.) corn kernels, rinsed, drained

3-4 small zucchini, scrubbed, sliced into rounds

1 small can (1 lb.) chopped tomatoes

2 garlic cloves, chopped

2 Italian fryer peppers, seeded, sliced into rounds

1 small chile, seeded, chopped (wear plastic gloves)

2 tbsp. olive oil

1 tbsp. red wine vinegar

$\frac{1}{2}$ tsp. chili powder

$\frac{1}{2}$ tsp. cumin powder

salt, black pepper to taste

pinch of sugar

Heat oil in a large non-stick skillet. Sauté zucchini rounds at moderate-high (320°), using spatula to toss vegetables. Add fryers, chile pepper and garlic; sauté for 1-2 minutes longer. Lower heat and add tomatoes and corn. Stir in vinegar, chili powder, cumin, salt, pepper and sugar. Cook stew for 3-4 minutes longer. Serve warm with corn tortillas or crusty bread chips. Serves 4-6.

John at bat with
a zucchini.

GRILLED TUNA STEAK WITH OLIVE SAUCE

6 portions fresh tuna steaks, 1-inch thick, remove skin
1 lg. red bell pepper, cored, thinly sliced
1 lg. green bell pepper, cored, thinly sliced
2 onions, thinly sliced
1 cup assorted pitted olives, chopped
2 tbsp. butter or Smart Balance spread, melted
2 tbsp. olive oil (a little more to coat pan)
1 tbsp. balsamic vinegar
juice of 1 lemon
zest of 1 lemon
$\frac{1}{2}$ cup white wine vinegar
$\frac{1}{2}$ tsp. cracked black pepper
salt to taste

Preheat broiler to 500°.

Set broiler grate 5 inches below heat; or set the grill grate 5 inches above heat and preheat to high. Coat a solid metal sheet pan with olive oil.

In a large bowl, place sliced red peppers and green peppers, sliced onions and olives. In a small bowl, blend melted butter, olive oil, balsamic vinegar, lemon juice and rind, white wine vinegar, black pepper and salt. Generously brush both sides of tuna steaks with this marinade.

Lay tuna on oiled sheet pan and set the pan on the grill or in the broiler at high heat. Meanwhile, pour $\frac{1}{4}$ cup marinade over the sliced vegetables. Toss vegetables with 2 spoons to coat thoroughly.

Grill the fish, about 3-4 minutes on each side for medium-rare. Pour the vegetables on and around the tuna steaks after you turn over the tuna to roast the other side. Stir vegetables with metal spatula. Remove only tuna to a large heat-resistant platter. (Keep fish warm in low oven.) Cook the vegetables for a few minutes longer. Transfer grilled pepper mix over the tuna on the platter. Serve immediately. Serves 6.

STEAMED ORANGE CAULIFLOWER AND BROCCOLI

1 lg. orange cauliflower, trimmed

2 tbsp. extra-virgin olive oil

salt, freshly ground black pepper

¼ cup chopped parsley

1-2 bunches broccoli

    (or 6-8 large florets), trimmed

2 tbsp. extra-virgin olive oil

salt, freshly ground black pepper

2-3 chopped garlic cloves

In separate steamers, cook cauliflower and broccoli until just tender. Prepare the dressings ahead of time and save in separate small bowls or cups. When vegetables are cooked, remove them, each to serving platters, and cover them lightly with waxed paper; keep them at room temperature. At serving time, separate both vegetables into florets; drizzle their respective dressings over them and serve. Serves 6.

APPLE AND CRANBERRY CRISP

1 cup dried cranberries

1 cup water

⅔ cup flour

1 tsp. powdered cinnamon

dash of salt

⅔ cup brown sugar, firmly packed

6 tbsp. butter or Smart Balance spread,

    chopped into bits

9-10 Granny Smith apples, peeled,

    cored, sliced thin

2 tbsp. lemon juice

a little more butter for the glass pan

a 9x13-inch heat-resistant glass pan (Pyrex)

Preheat oven 400°.

In a small sauce pot, simmer dried cranberries in water for 10 minutes. Drain them and set aside. In a small bowl, blend flour, brown sugar, salt, butter and cinnamon, until the mixture resembles coarse meal. Toss the mix well.

Butter a 9x13-inch heat-resistant glass pan. Place the sliced apples in the buttered pan; sprinkle them with lemon juice, and toss them together with the cranberries. Sprinkle brown sugar mixture over the apples mix. Bake the apples mix in preheated oven at 400° for 25 minutes, or until apples are tender and topping is golden in color. Serve warm, with or without vanilla ice cream. Serves 6.

Summer-Fall

Bite Your Tongue! Use Your Brain!

*T*he 19th and 20th centuries in the United States, witnessed an expansive development of cultures complete with their unique traditions. The foods which were grown, raised, marketed and eaten boldly confirmed our country's reputation as a "melting pot".

Volumes can be documented when it came to entrées prepared with animal parts and fish. None of the animal's body parts was overlooked. Our ancestors believed in "waste not, want not"_ from the skin pelts to the entrails; ten different cultures: ten and more exciting recipes for oxtail, sweetbreads, giblets, cod fish, roe, pâté de foie gras.

SWEETBREADS: Sweetbreads from a young calf seemed to be those most favored. "Take 2 pairs of calf's sweetbreads; soak them in cold water for 2 hours. Sauté several onions, sliced, in a little fat (suet or oil); drain the water from the sweetbreads and broil them all over; sprinkle with pepper and salt and cover them in the sautéed onions." That's how Mrs. Maresca prepared this recipe.

Mrs. Fudge was an Irish immigrant who occasionally made traditional dishes like Kidney Stew, which she said, contained lamb's kidneys, onions, mushrooms and - Jamison Whiskey. Her daughter, Helen, said her mother made Oxtail Soup with cut-up tails of an ox. Helen said the soup contained vegetables such as celery, carrots and potatoes. I don't believe my girlfriend ever tasted the soup. (I'm not certain if she had tried the kidney stew.) As an avid reader, I had read about Kidney Pie and Kidney Stew in Jane Austen and Charles Dickens. These dishes are still quite a treat in the British Isles.

My Aunt Susie's wide-ranged culinary repertoire included what I shall call Braised Tongue. I believe it was a lamb's (or cow's) tongue she had used. I remember she soaked the tongues in cold water. Then, she sautéed them with onions as a preface to laying them in a heavy pot. She poured white vinegar and some water at the bottom of the pot and simmered the tongue and onions for a while.

Of course, along this path she prepared sautéed fowl livers, hearts, gizzards and kidneys; her turkey stuffing always included giblets. A note about these edible viscera: they have a very short "shelf life" and tend to spoil quickly.

My mother frequently cooked a delicious calves (or beef) liver with onions and bacon. She cooked the bacon in a skillet; drained "most" of the bacon fat from the pan and sautéed lots of sliced onions with the calves liver. Always included in the recipe: bay leaves and black pepper; sometimes a sprinkling of capers, when available. And Mom always cooked the liver "just a trifle pink", the juices sizzling in the pan.

Intermittently, throughout FROM THE TABLE OF PLENTY, I have included complete family recipes of foods not often served in our nation's modern homes; but foods which were a part of our families' heritage.

Summer-Fall

ARUGULA, POTATO AND TOMATO SALAD
HONEY MUSTARD DRESSING
MINESTRA DE PIEDE PORCO (heirloom)
or
MINESTRA AND SAUSAGES
TRIPA A LA CREOLE (heirloom)
SUFRITO (heirloom)
BANANA AND STRAWBERRY PUDDING

ARUGULA, POTATO AND TOMATO SALAD

6 small red bliss potatoes, scrubbed, halved or quartered,
    boiled until tender, about 5 minutes
6 plum tomatoes, each quartered
4 cups arugula, trimmed, rinsed, drained

Honey Mustard Dressing (see page 384)

Prepare Honey Mustard Dressing in advance. If not using dressing within a few hours, refrigerate dressing until 1 hour before serving.

In a large salad bowl, combine potatoes, tomatoes and arugula. At serving time, drizzle dressing over salad; toss to mix. Serves 6.

MINESTRA DE PIEDE PORCO
(Greens Soup with Pigs' Feet)

12 pieces pigs' feet and knuckles, pre-cleaned (*NOTE: at end of recipe)
    may be purchased at food specialty shops
6 cups water
1 large onion, chopped
3-4 garlic cloves, chopped
2 tbsp. olive oil
1 head escarole, discard tough outer leaves, center part rinsed in cold water
    several times, drained
1 small bunch kale (about 1 lb.), trimmed, rinsed in cold water, drained,
    chopped into small pieces
8 oz. Swiss chard, trimmed, rinsed in cold water, drained
2 medium all-purpose potatoes, pared, cut into chunks
1 cup dried cannellini beans (soak beans in hot water overnight; to cook beans, follow
    directions on package); or use 1 lg. can (20 oz.) cannellini beans
1 tbsp. dried oregano
1 tsp. salt
$\frac{1}{2}$ tsp. black pepper
hot pepper flakes (to taste)

    Bring a large pot with 6 cups water to boil; add prepared pigs' feet and knuckles and simmer
for 30 minutes.
    Lightly brown onions and garlic in olive oil in a small skillet. Scrape bottom of skillet for
any leavings.
    Remove 1 cup of stock from the pigs' feet and pour it into the browned onion mix. Stir up the onion
mix and return this liquid to the stock pot.
    With tongs, transfer pigs' feet and knuckles to a platter. Place the greens and potatoes in the stock
pot; cover pot and bring to a boil; cook greens and potatoes at low boil for 20-25 minutes.
    Return pigs' feet and knuckles to pot and stir in: oregano, salt and black and hot pepper and cooked
beans. Cover pot, bring to a boil; then, simmer for 10-15 minutes longer. Serves 6-8.

    *NOTE: Purchase pigs' feet which are "ready-to-cook". Have butcher chop the pigs' feet in half.
In the "olden" days, pigs' feet would be cleansed of grit and dirt in a couple of boiling water baths for a
couple of hours prior to using them in a recipe.

OR: TRY THE FOLLOWING RECIPE AS A MODERN SUBSTITUTE.

MINESTRA AND SAUSAGES

You may substitute 8 links sweet and hot Italian sausages (for the pigs' feet and knuckles). The remainder of ingredients remain as is (see page 275), except: omit hot pepper flakes.

In a large skillet, heat oil to moderate-high and lightly brown onion, garlic and sausages (on all sides). In a large 6-quart soup pot bring 6 cups water to boil; place the potatoes and greens to cook in the pot; cover pot and low-boil greens mix for 20-25 minutes. Spoon sausage and onion mix into the soup pot, scraping the bottom of the skillet to remove any leavings. Add oregano, salt, pepper and cooked beans. Combine to mix thoroughly. Cover pot; bring to a boil. Then, simmer for 10-15 minutes longer. Serves 6-8.

TRIPA A LA CREOLE

$1\frac{1}{2}$ *lbs. honeycomb tripe, cut into strips*
   (2 cups salted water)
2 onions, finely sliced
3-4 garlic cloves, chopped
$\frac{1}{4}$ cup olive oil
1 lg. can (20 oz.) plum tomatoes,
   mashed with liquid

1 Italian spicy pepper, seeded, chopped coarsely
1 tsp. salt
$\frac{1}{2}$ tsp. black pepper
2-3 bay leaves
$\frac{1}{4}$ cup torn basil leaves
2 eggs, beaten
$\frac{1}{4}$ cup grated Parmesan cheese

Simmer tripe in 2 cups salted water, for 1 hour. Drain tripe; discard water. In a large skillet at moderate heat, sauté the tripe, onions and garlic in olive oil for 4-5 minutes. Stir in tomatoes, pepper, herbs and spices; cover pot and simmer for 15 minutes. Stir in beaten eggs and cheese to make the sauce creamy. Remove and discard bay leaves before serving. Serve hot. Serves 4-6.

SUFRITO

(This is known as "Depression Food". Sufrito is related to Scotland's Haggis which is a mix of sheep's, or calf's, heart, liver, lungs, minced with suet, onions and oatmeal. Then, the mix is sewn up in the stomach of the animal and boiled in a large pot. Haggis is served with great fanfare – blaring bagpipes, kilts, Glengarrys and Balmorals.)

1-1½ lbs. sheep hearts, cut into bite-size

2 lbs. sheep liver, cut into bite-size

1-1½ lbs. sheep lungs, cut into bite-size

1 large onion, thinly sliced

6 garlic cloves

1 can (1 lb.) tomato sauce with pulp, mashed

1 long Italian pepper, seeded, chopped

3 large all-purpose potatoes, pared, cut into chunks

¼ cup olive oil

1 cup water

1 tbsp. dried oregano

6 fresh basil leaves, chopped

salt, black pepper to taste

In a large skillet, heat oil and sauté onions and garlic for 2 minutes; add livers, hearts and lungs (in pieces) and sauté them in batches until cooked. Transfer each batch to a large bowl.

While you cook the meat mix, boil the chunks of potatoes in 1 cup water in a 4-quart pot and cook for 5 minutes. Add tomatoes, fresh chopped pepper, herbs, salt and pepper; raise heat under pot; cover and simmer the tomato sauce mix for 10 minutes. Add and stir in the meat mix. Cover the pot and cook the stew for another 15 minutes to blend the flavors. Serve with chunks of artisan bread and a hearty Burgundy wine. Serves 6.

BANANA AND STRAWBERRY PUDDING

2 cups strawberries, hulled, rinsed, drained, sliced (set aside)

1¼ cups sugar

½ cup flour

6 eggs or 1½ cups egg substitute

2 cups evaporated milk (fat-free available)

¼ tsp. salt

3 large bananas, cut into ½-inch slices

¼ cup butter or Smart Balance spread, cut into bits

1 tbsp. vanilla extract

Preheat oven 400°.

In a blender, combine 1 cup of sugar (reserve ¼ cup for later in recipe), flour, eggs, milk, vanilla and salt and blend until mixture is smooth.

Arrange banana slices in one layer in a buttered 9x15-inch ovenproof, flame-proof pan. Pour pudding over bananas and bake pudding in the middle of the oven at 400° for 20 minutes, or until top is puffed and springy to the touch.

Sprinkle top with remaining ¼ cup sugar; dot with butter and broil the pudding under a preheated broiler (about 3 inches from heat) for 1-2 minutes or until lightly browned. Spoon pudding over sliced strawberries in dessert bowls. Serves 6.

Summer-Fall

Thanksgiving Day with Linda and Alan

*I*t's become a tradition. Yes, we know Thanksgiving Day is an American family tradition. I mean, it's become a tradition for our family to celebrate this great feast with chefs Alan and Linda. Alan makes THE BEST roasted turkey. He whets your holiday appetite by performing his culinary artistry right before your eyes (if you arrive at their home early in the day).

Complete instructions to follow.

Linda and Alan with the Big Bird.

Summer-Fall

"A SPECIAL MENU"
PUMPKIN SOUP (See page 220)
or
ORANGE PUMPKIN SOUP (See page 215)
ICEBERG LETTUCE WEDGES WITH CAPERS (See page 27)
VINAIGRETTE DRESSING (See page 389)
MANDEL BREAD
ALAN'S THANKSGIVING TURKEY WITH STUFFING
WHOLE CRANBERRY ORANGE SAUCE
ONE HUNDRED VEGETABLES (See page 71)
SAUSAGE STUFFED MUSHROOMS A LA PARMESANA
BRUSSELS SPROUTS WITH TOMATOES AND WALNUTS
PECAN PUMPKIN PIE

WHOLE CRANBERRY ORANGE SAUCE
(Prepare in advance; keep refrigerated.)

12 oz. fresh cranberries, rinsed, drained
1 cup granulated sugar
1 cup orange juice with pulp
$\frac{1}{4}$ cup chopped walnuts

In a medium sauce pot with a lid, dissolve sugar into orange juice; bring to a boil and add cranberries. Return to a boil; reduce heat and simmer for 10 minutes, stirring occasionally. Remove pot from heat; stir in walnuts. Cool sauce completely at room temperature. Then, pour sauce into a container with screw cap or tight lid. Refrigerate sauce up to 1 month. Serves 8-10.

MRS. PHILLIPS' MANDEL BREAD
(As interpreted by Alan Schwartz)

Mandel Bread is a twice-baked biscotti-type sweet dessert bread. Of German heritage, Mandelbrot may contain dried fruits, nuts or chocolate morsels.

$\frac{1}{4}$ cup margarine (butter)

$\frac{3}{4}$ cup sugar

3 eggs

1 tsp. vanilla extract

$2\frac{1}{2}$ cups all purpose flour

$1\frac{1}{2}$ tsp. baking powder

$\frac{1}{2}$ cup chopped walnuts or $\frac{1}{2}$ cup chocolate morsels - optional

(or $\frac{1}{4}$ cup chopped walnuts and $\frac{1}{4}$ cup chocolate morsels)

Preheat oven to 350°. Have ready: 1 greased baking sheet.

Melt margarine in a small pot. Blend and beat melted margarine with sugar in a bowl until light and creamy. Add eggs, one at a time, beating well after each addition. Stir in vanilla. Combine flour with baking powder and gradually add them to the butter and egg mixture by hand. Batter will be thick.

Stir in walnuts and/or chocolate morsels. Shape the dough into 2 small round flattened loaves and place them on a greased baking sheet. Bake loaves in a preheated oven at 350° for 20-25 minutes. Remove tray to a cutting board, but do not turn off oven.

Cut each warm loaf in place, into slices, about $\frac{3}{4}$-inch thick. Using a spatula, transfer each sliced loaf, as a loaf, to the baking sheet and return the tray to the oven to lightly brown the loaves (3-5 minutes). Makes 2 small loaves.

ALAN'S THANKSGIVING TURKEY WITH STUFFING
(Alan uses a frozen turkey, not self-basting. You may prepare a fresh turkey in much the same manner, by-passing its thawing period.)

one 18 lb. frozen turkey (thaw the turkey in its packing in the refrigerator)

4 tbsp. margarine or butter	poultry pins
turkey giblets, chopped fine	poultry cradle
3 cups water	12x18x4-inch heavy-duty roasting pan with rack
1 tsp. garlic powder	aluminum foil
$\frac{1}{2}$ tsp. dried thyme	
1 chicken bouillon cube, mashed and mixed into $\frac{1}{4}$ cup warm water	
1-2 tbsp. flour or cornstarch (for gravy)	

Prepare the stuffing; refrigerate the stuffing while your prepare the turkey. (Use half of this recipe for stuffing the turkey; and the other half for a casserole dish.)

STUFFING:

2 bags (16 oz. each) cornbread stuffing	2 cups chopped onion
4 cups water	1 tsp. each: dried sage, dried thyme
2 sticks ($\frac{1}{2}$ lb.) margarine or butter	$\frac{1}{2}$ tsp. each: garlic powder, poultry seasoning
2 cups chopped celery	salt, black pepper to taste
1 lb. pan-fried Italian sausage (casing removed and sausage meat crumbled)	(Reminder: stuffing mix contains salt.)

Bring water and butter to a boil. Pour cornbread stuffing mix into a large mixing bowl. Add celery, onion, cooked sausage meat, herbs and seasonings. Stir in hot water, butter mix and toss to mix thoroughly. Set stuffing aside in refrigerator while you prepare the turkey.

Preheat oven to 325°.

Carefully read the directions on the turkey packaging. Remove the turkey from its packing. Remove the packages of giblets and turkey parts from the cavities of the bird. Rinse giblets under cold running water; set aside to drain in a small bowl. Thoroughly wash the outside and inside of the turkey under cold running water. Place the turkey into a large bowl to drain from its cavities. Dry the turkey with paper towels.

(Continued on next page)

ALAN'S THANKSGIVING TURKEY WITH STUFFING

(Continued from previous page)

Stuff the turkey with the prepared and blended cornbread-sausage mix. Stuff the turkey fully, but loosely. Use half of the stuffing for the cavity of the bird; spoon the rest of the stuffing into a greased 2-quart casserole dish and set the bowl into the refrigerator until the turkey has been roasted.

Use poultry pins to "nail" the wings and legs to the turkey's body. Place the turkey on a poultry cradle before laying it into the roasting pan. Lay the stuffed turkey in a 12x18x4-inch heavy roasting pan. In a 2-quart bowl, pour 3 cups water; add and stir in 1 teaspoon garlic powder, $\frac{1}{2}$ teaspoon dried thyme and mashed chicken bouillon; add the drained giblets. Pour this liquid mix and giblets into the bottom of the roasting pan with the turkey. (You will use this liquid and giblets as a base for the gravy, once the turkey has been roasted.)

Rub 3-4 tablespoons margarine (or butter) on the surface of the turkey. Cut a sheet of aluminum foil, large enough to form a tent over the turkey. Roast the prepared turkey with its loose foil tent in the middle of a large oven, preheated to 325°. Roast the turkey, 20 minutes per pound, until its surface is golden brown. Insert a poultry thermometer into the thickest part of a leg; the turkey should be cooked when the thermometer registers 190°. Remove the foil tent in the last 20 minutes of roasting; baste the turkey every half-hour with its own juices from the bottom of the pan. You may have to add a little more water due to evaporation.

Remove the pan to the counter and allow the turkey to rest while you prepare the gravy and bake the casserole of stuffing. (Bake extra stuffing at 325° for 30 minutes.)

Carefully remove the turkey to the carving board. Prepare GRAVY by straining the liquid from the bottom of the roasting pan into a sauce pot. Discard the residue of giblets from the strainer. Transfer $\frac{1}{4}$ cup of the liquid to a small bowl; add and whisk 1-2 tablespoons flour or cornstarch into the liquid to form a smooth paste. Bring the liquid in the sauce pot to a low simmer and gently stir in the small bowl of flour-thickened pan juices. Stir in pepper, salt, more garlic powder and thyme and poultry seasoning, as desired. Stir the gravy constantly as it simmers and thickens. Strain again, into a gravy bowl. Serve hot, to accompany a perfectly carved turkey with its trimmings. Feeds a hungry crowd.

SAUSAGE STUFFED MUSHROOMS A LA PARMESANA

1 doz. lg. stuffing mushrooms (remove stems; chop for stuffing); trim, rinse, drain

STUFFING:

1 cup unseasoned bread crumbs

3 links sweet fennel sausage, casing removed; crumble sausage meat
    and lightly sauté with 1 tbsp. finely chopped onion

$\frac{1}{4}$ cup fresh parsley, chopped

2 garlic cloves, minced

$\frac{1}{4}$ tsp. black pepper

dash of salt

$\frac{1}{4}$ cup olive oil

SAUCE:

2 cups prepared tomato sauce

1 cup mozzarella, diced

$\frac{1}{2}$ cup Parmesan cheese, grated

Preheat oven 375°. Have ready: 9x15-inch heat-resistant casserole dish, rubbed with olive oil.

In a large bowl, combine crumbs, mushroom stems, cooked and crumbled sausage meat with onion, parsley, garlic, pepper and salt. Stir in and blend olive oil and mix thoroughly. (Add a tablespoon or two of hot water if stuffing is too stiff.)

Divide the stuffing among the mushrooms (pack a heaping tablespoonful of stuffing per mushroom). Arrange the stuffed mushrooms in the greased casserole dish, to fit, side-by-side.

In a medium-size bowl, combine tomato sauce, chopped mozzarella and grated Parmesan. Spoon the sauce mixture over the stuffed mushrooms in the casserole dish. Bake the mushrooms in a preheated oven at 375° for 20-25 minutes. Cheese will melt; crumbs will appear lightly browned. (May be prepared the day before, up to baking; cover casserole with plastic wrap and refrigerate. When needed, proceed to bake, uncovered, before serving, very warm.) Serves 6-8.

BRUSSELS SPROUTS WITH TOMATOES AND WALNUTS

1-1½ lbs. Brussels sprouts, stem end trimmed
   (Soak sprouts in a large bowl of cold, salted water for 10 minutes.)

1 cup chopped walnuts

1 tsp. olive oil

2 garlic cloves, minced

12-15 grape or cherry tomatoes, rinsed, drained

salt, black pepper to taste

a little more olive oil

   Drain sprouts. Steam them in a steamer basket for 10-12 minutes, or pressure cook. Do not overcook. Meanwhile, coat walnuts in oil; spread the nuts over a 5x7-inch metal pan and roast them at 475° for a couple of minutes. Drain cooked sprouts and pour them into a serving bowl. Add tomatoes, minced garlic and toasted walnuts; sprinkle 1-2 tablespoons olive oil over the bowl and add salt and pepper to taste. Gently toss the mix to coat thoroughly. Serves 6-8.

PECAN PUMPKIN PIE
(May be prepared a few days in advance; cover and refrigerate.)

CRUST:

2 cups flour

4 tbsp. canola oil (or butter or
   Smart Balance spread)

¼ cup granulated sugar

¼ tsp. salt

1 tbsp. grated lemon zest

¼ cup puréed pecans

½ cup water (add a tablespoon or
   two more, if needed)

   Have ready: 1 10-inch metal pie pan

   Pour flour into a large bowl. Make a well in center of flour and add rest of ingredients. Add water a little at a time, as needed. Turn the dough onto a floured board and knead the dough until smooth and pliable, about 5-6 minutes. Cut the dough in half.

   Form each portion of dough into a large, flat circle by rolling the dough between 2 sheets of waxed paper. Roll the dough thin and large enough to hang 1 inch over the 10-inch pan. Drape the dough over the pie pan; first: unpeel the top sheet of waxed paper. Carefully settle the circle of dough into the pie pan, pressing the dough to fit into the pan. Cover the pan in plastic wrap and refrigerate the uncooked crust, if not using immediately.

   Prepare the top crust in the same way; set it aside, between 2 sheets of waxed paper.

   Prepare the filling.

(Continued on next page)

PECAN PUMPKIN PIE

(Continued from previous page)

FILLING:

1 can (1 lb.) solid pumpkin

2 eggs or $\frac{1}{2}$ cup egg substitute, beaten

1 cup evaporated milk

$\frac{1}{2}$ cup brown sugar

$\frac{1}{4}$ cup granulated sugar

2-3 tbsp. mixed: cinnamon, ginger, nutmeg, cloves

$\frac{1}{4}$ tsp. salt

1 cup pecan halves for garnish

Beat together: all pumpkin filling ingredients.

ASSEMBLING THE PIE: Preheat oven to 425°.

Remove pie crust pan from refrigerator. Form the crust's edge to stand $\frac{1}{2}$-inch above the metal pan. Pour the pumpkin filling into the pie shell.

Remove top layer of waxed paper from top crust. Lay the top crust on the board and cut 1-inch wide strips from the second crust. Form a wide lattice design across the top of the pumpkin pie, pinching both upper and lower crusts along the entire edge of the pie. (The pumpkin mixture will "grow" as it cooks.) Arrange and press pecan halves around the inside edge of the top lattice crust.

Bake the pie in a preheated oven at 425° for 10 minutes. Lower the temperature to 350° and continue to bake the pie for an additional 30 minutes. Pie is cooked when inserted toothpick removes clean; crust is light golden brown. Serves 6-8.

Honey Bows, page 38

Baked Eggplant Parmagiano, page 29, with Red Pepper Sauce, page 402

Pignola Cookies, page 67

Pineapple in Rum, page 4

Pizza Rustica, page 186

Roasted Potatoes and Mushrooms, page 124

Chicken Francese, page 110

Chocolate Hamantaschen, page 206

A Peachy Melba, page 342

Stuffed Meatloaf, page 15

Pastiera di Grano, pages 144-145

Black and White Cookies, page 87

Warm Key West Vegetable Salad, page 305

Italian Flag Salad, page 100
Stuffed Shells, page 101, in Meatball/Sausage Sauce, page 399

A Devil of a Chocolate Cake, page 97

Brussels Sprouts with Bacon and Pignola, page 46

Strawberry Crostata, page 304

Pasta

Pasta

Food for the Gods

I've often mused: why haven't the Italians canonized Marco Polo? After all, his 13th century travels from Venice to China introduced Italians to our glorious food for the gods __ pasta. (Or so they say.)

Actually, Marco Polo's authority on the subject of pasta has been long debunked. Believe it, gods (like Vulcan), were thought to be involved. Apicus, a Roman writer of the first century A. D. described a pasta-type dough which resembled lasagna (laganon). The prepared dish included layering of the pasta with spices, meats and fish.

Some say Arab invaders of Sicily introduced them to pasta. The Sicilian word macaruni means dough by force. There is documented knowledge that Thomas Jefferson brought the first macaroni maker to the U.S.A. in 1789 from France. His pasta in our country was first produced by a Frenchman in Brooklyn.

Pasta (paste) is the word which describes the dough.

Homemade fresh pasta dough can be made with a floured board, a rolling pin and a sharp knife, like **tagliatelle** (thin cuts) or **linguine** (little tongues). Cut the strips a little wider and we have **lasagna**. Run spoonfuls of a filling every few inches over the strands of lasagna; top with another strand of lasagna noodles; cut into measured filled sections; crimp on all sides. Voila! We have **ravioli** (little pillows) or other stuffed pasta like **tortalini** (little twists). Many tube-like macaroni originally were made by arranging pasta dough around knitting needles. Commercially made **macaroni** (maccheroni) are made with pasta machines.

Pasta was, and still is a preparation of semolina or farina wheat flour and water; oftentimes mixed with eggs or egg solids. It's what the Italians did with these basic recipes that has made culinary history.

In 1860, when Naples was liberated by one thousand volunteer "red shirts", their leader, the patriot, Giuseppe Garibaldi stated:

"It will be maccheroni, I swear to you, that will unite Italy".

Perhaps, Giuseppe, pasta has united the whole world to Italy!

Pasta

FENNEL AND OLIVE SALAD
WINE VINEGAR AND OLIVE OIL DRESSING
CHICKEN AND MUSHROOM LASAGNA
TANGERINE-ORANGE SHERBET

FENNEL AND OLIVE SALAD

2 medium-large fennel bulbs, trimmed, rinsed, sliced into $\frac{1}{2}$-inch rounds

1 doz. pitted green Sicilian olives

1 doz. pitted black Greek olives

6 basil leaves, shredded

2 garlic cloves, chopped

1 small red onion, sliced thin

1 tbsp. dried oregano

Wine Vinegar and Olive Oil Dressing (see page 384)

Prepare Wine Vinegar and Olive Oil Dressing in advance. Refrigerate dressing until one hour prior to serving. In a glass salad bowl, combine sliced fennel, pitted olives, basil, red onion and garlic. Sprinkle oregano over the salad. Refrigerate salad until serving. Dress salad with Vinegar and Olive Oil Dressing just before serving; toss to mix. Serves 6.

CHICKEN AND MUSHROOM LASAGNA
(May be frozen for 2 weeks.)

$1\frac{1}{2}$ lbs. curly-edge lasagna
   (about 3 dozen lasagna sheets)
1 tbsp. olive oil
1 tsp. salt

SAUCE:
$1\frac{1}{2}$ lbs. chicken sausage, sliced into narrow rounds
   (*NOTE: below)
2 tbsp. olive oil
1 yellow onion, chopped
3 garlic cloves, chopped
8 oz. small white mushrooms,
   trimmed, rinsed, chopped
1 Italian fryer pepper, seeded, chopped
3-4 basil leaves, torn
1 lg. can (about 3 cups) tomato purée
$\frac{1}{4}$ tsp. black pepper
1 tsp. salt
$\frac{1}{2}$ cup red table wine
   (like a Barolo or a Barbaresco)

FILLING:
2 lbs. low-fat ricotta
1 egg, beaten or $\frac{1}{4}$ cup egg substitute
1 tbsp. chopped parsley
black pepper, salt to taste
$\frac{1}{2}$ cup grated Asiago or Parmesan cheese,
   plus $\frac{1}{2}$ cup cheese at serving
2 cups (1 lb.) fresh mozzarella,
   chopped into small chunks

*NOTE: Partially frozen sausages are easier to slice.

STEP 1) Heat 2 tablespoons olive oil in a 2-quart saucepan with cover. Lightly brown onion, garlic and pepper. Scrape bottom of pan to remove leavings. At medium heat, 300°, brown sausage rounds and mushrooms, scraping bottom of pan as they cook. Add and stir in tomato purée, salt, pepper and basil. Cover pot and bring to a slow simmer; cook sauce for 15 minutes with lid askew. Lower heat and pour in wine; stir to mix. Continue to simmer sauce for 5 more minutes, stirring occasionally. Remove pot from burner. Remove 2 cups of sauce (only) to a small pot; reserve this sauce.

STEP 2) In a 2-quart bowl, combine ricotta, parsley, salt, pepper, beaten egg and $\frac{1}{2}$ cup cheese (reserve another $\frac{1}{2}$ cup grated cheese); set bowl aside.

STEP 3) Meanwhile, set a 6-quart pot with enough water to boil the lasagna. Add 1 teaspoon salt and 1 tablespoon olive oil (to prevent pasta pieces from sticking together).
Cover pot and bring it to a rolling boil. Carefully, add lasagna sheets, a few at a time, to the boiling water, crisscrossing them as you layer them in the pot. Parboil pasta, uncovered, as directed on package, usually about 7-8 minutes. Have a large colander ready to drain the pasta. Run cool water into the pasta pot to stop the cooking process. Drain and return pasta to the large pot; add cool water to cover the pasta.

(Continued on next page)

(Continued from previous page)

STEP 4) Oil bottom of a 14x18x4-inch lasagna pan. Spread 2 cups sauce over bottom of pan. Vertically line bottom of pan with 14 lasagna sheets, 7 on one side; 7 on the opposite side; each draping over the vertical sides, and meeting at the bottom of the pan. (You are forming an "envelope" to enclose the filling.) Preheat oven to 350°.

STEP 5) Spoon sausage and mushroom sauce over the lasagna at bottom of pan. Horizontally, lay 18 lasagna sheets over the filling, 9 on one side; 9 on the opposite side; each draping over the horizontal sides and meeting in the middle of the casserole. Evenly spoon ricotta mix over this layer of pasta. Carefully close the "envelope" with the lasagna which overhangs the pan. You've created a neat package.

STEP 6) Remember the reserved sauce? Spread 2 cups reserved sauce over lasagna package. Sprinkle with remaining Parmesan; spread with chopped mozzarella. Bake the lasagna casserole in preheated oven, 350° for 45-50 minutes. You may wish to lay a foil tent over the lasagna during the last 10 minutes to prevent burning. Serve hot, with remaining sauce and the additional cheese. Serves 6-8.

TANGERINE-ORANGE SHERBET

5-6 large tangerines, wash skin, pat dry with paper towels; peel and
    section them; remove pits; place tangerine segments in a bowl
$\frac{1}{4}$ cup Grand Marnier (or other orange liqueur)
1 qt. orange sherbet or orange sherbet/vanilla ice cream combo

Pour orange liqueur over tangerines in bowl; gently toss fruit to mix. Refrigerate fruit until needed. Set out 6 large dessert glasses with stems (1 pint-size). At serving time, place a large portion of sherbet (and ice cream) into each glass; spoon tangerine-liqueur mix over each glass. Serve immediately. Serves 6.

Pasta

❖❖❖

SALAD OF SPINACH AND FIGS
BALSAMIC VINEGAR AND OLIVE OIL DRESSING
HOT AND SWEET FENNEL SAUSAGE WITH ANGEL HAIR PASTA
PINEAPPLE WITH GRAPES
UNCLE CLEM'S ALMOND BRITTLE (CROCCANTE) (heirloom)

SALAD OF SPINACH AND FIGS

6 cups baby spinach, rinsed, drained
1 small red onion, thinly sliced
4 garlic cloves, minced
8 fresh figs, gently rinsed, trimmed, quartered
½ cup sharp provolone cheese, shredded
1 lg. carrot, pared, shredded
1 cup coarsely chopped walnuts

Balsamic Vinegar and Olive Oil Dressing (see page 384)

Prepare dressing in advance; refrigerate dressing until one hour prior to using. In a large salad bowl, combine spinach, onion, garlic, figs, provolone, walnuts and shredded carrot. At serving time, add dressing to salad and toss to mix. Serves 6.

HOT AND SWEET FENNEL SAUSAGE WITH ANGEL HAIR PASTA

3-4 links hot Italian fennel sausages,
    sliced into $\frac{1}{2}$-inch rounds (*NOTE: below)
3-4 links sweet Italian fennel sausage,
    sliced into $\frac{1}{2}$-inch rounds
1 cup chopped long green Italian peppers, seeded
1 medium-size onion, chopped
4 garlic cloves, chopped
2 tbsp. olive oil
1 can (1 lb.) chopped tomatoes

1 lg. can (29 oz.) tomato purée
$\frac{1}{2}$ cup chopped parsley
3-4 basil leaves, chopped
1 tbsp. dried oregano
$\frac{1}{4}$ tsp. black pepper
$\frac{1}{4}$ tsp. salt, to taste
$\frac{1}{2}$ cup grated Romano cheese
    (additional cheese for garnish)

2 packages (9 oz. each) angel hair pasta

*NOTE: Sausages will slice evenly if they have been frozen and are only slightly softened.

Brown onion and garlic in olive oil at moderate heat in a 4-quart sauce pan with lid. Scrape bottom of pan; add sliced sausages and green peppers; lightly brown sausages.

Stir in chopped tomatoes, purée, parsley, basil, oregano and seasonings. Bring pot to a slow simmer; reduce heat; cover pot and simmer sauce for about 1 hour. Stir in cheese.

This sauce may be cooked and frozen up to several weeks. When needed, soften in refrigerator for 2 days before heating thoroughly.

Cook pasta according to directions on package. Drain. Pour pasta into serving bowl; ladle 1-2 cups hot sauce into pasta and toss to mix. Add more sauce and garnish with additional cheese for each serving portion. Serves 6.

PINEAPPLE WITH GRAPES

1 large chilled, ripe, aromatic pineapple; run cold water over pineapple to rinse
    just before cutting; pat dry with paper towels
6 small bunches red seedless grapes
sprigs of fresh mint

Cut off bottom end of pineapple. With a large sharp knife cut pineapple in half, lengthwise; then, cut each half into 3 vertical sections, keeping the spiny foliage intact for each section. With a serrated-edged paring knife, carefully cut off the vertical hard core of the pineapple which runs in center of the fruit.

Place each slice on its own dessert plate. Run a knife between the skin and the fruit to dislodge the pulp; however, sit the fruit on its skin. Make horizontal bite-size cuts, across the slice, careful to keep the chunks in place. Garnish each plate with a small bunch of red seedless grapes and a sprig of mint. Serves 6.

UNCLE CLEM'S ALMOND BRITTLE (CROCCANTE)
(Prepare a week in advance.)

4 cups whole almonds with skin

3 cups granulated sugar

1 tsp. almond extract

$\frac{1}{4}$ cup water

2 tbsp. colored nonpareils

5x7-inch Teflon pan (spray inside of pan lightly
    with oil, wipe with paper towel)

In a 1-quart sauce pot, combine sugar, water and extract. Cook the sugar mix over medium-high heat until sugar is melted. Try not to stir the mix.

Cook the sugar mix until it turns brown, about 15-20 minutes. Do not burn the sugar; do not overcook. Remove the pot from heat. Fold in almonds to quickly incorporate into the sugar mix.

Immediately pour the sugar/almond mix into the prepared 5x7-inch Teflon-coated pan, spreading the candy mix evenly, about $\frac{1}{2}$-inch thick. Quickly sprinkle the surface of the candy with nonpareils.

Cool the candy completely. With a spatula, transfer the 5x7-inch candied nut tray to a cutting board. Use a very sharp serrated-edged knife to gently saw through the candy. Wet the knife and wipe it clean each time you cut a 1-inch slice. Cut 7 horizontal slices; then, halve each slice. Makes 14 bars of almond brittle. Store in an airtight container. As with any hard candy and nut confection, caution must be observed when biting into the brittle, not to damage your teeth.

Pasta

Salt

We were educated about the powers of salt in the Bible. Lot, Abraham's nephew was fore-warned about the destruction of the cities of Sodom and Gomorrah. He fled with his family; however his wife, disobeying God's orders, looked back at the destruction, and was turned into a pillar of ___ salt.   Gen. 19: 11-14

Sodium - we can't live with too much of it; we can't live without it. Sodium is necessary for our bodies to maintain the proper fluid balance to regulate blood pressure. Sodium is responsible for the body's transmission of nerve impulses. It also helps muscles (including the heart) to relax. Too little or too much sodium in our blood can lead to confusion or coma. It is interesting to note that drinking fluids gets rid of some salt through bodily functions such as urination and perspiration.

Most raw vegetables naturally contain some minute amounts of sodium: celeriac, artichokes, celery, turnips and beets contain the most sodium. Sodium is almost negligible in fruits: avocado, grapefruit, tomato, some melons have the most sodium. Canned and packaged foods contain tremendous amounts of salt to aid in their preservation.

There is no official daily recommendation for sodium intake. We are told to limit our daily sodium intake to 2400 mg. for "healthy" individuals. Consider: there are 2325 mg. in 1 teaspoon of table salt.

The recipes in my cookbooks reflect my policy of "no added salt" or at least, a bare minimum use of added salt.

So called "salt-substitutes" are created to taste like table salt (mostly sodium chloride). However, they contain mostly potassium chloride which, when consumed, increases our potassium intake. Excessive potassium intake can cause potentially fatal hyperkalemia.

The "Salt Spice" recipe, printed on page 297, can be home made by anyone, kept in an airtight jar and used to augment and bolster flavors in meats, fish and vegetables. As long as one isn't allergic to any of the ingredients, the spice mix makes a flavorful salt-substitute.

When all is said and done, salt is the first and only all-natural substitute that tastes like ___ salt.

Pasta

BROCCOLI LINGUINE
FRICANDELS OF VEAL (heirloom)
MELON BALLS IN ASTI SPUMANTE

BROCCOLI LINGUINE

1 bunch broccoli, cut into florets
1-1½ lbs. linguine

1 cup sour cream
1 egg, beaten or ½ cup egg substitute
½ tsp. freshly ground pepper, salt to taste
1 tsp. dried thyme
1 tsp. dried oregano

1 cup grated Romano cheese for garnish
2 tbsp. extra-virgin olive oil

In a small bowl, smoothly blend sour cream, egg substitute, pepper (salt) and herbs. Set in refrigerator until needed.

Cook linguine in a large pot of boiling water, as directed on package. Boil 1-inch water in a large steamer pot; add broccoli florets and cook for 4-5 minutes, until broccoli is barely softened.

Drain linguine and broccoli and enjoin them in a large serving bowl. Spoon olive oil and sour cream dressing over the pasta mix; toss gently to coat thoroughly. Garnish with Romano cheese. Serves 6.

FRICANDELS OF VEAL

3 lbs. loin of veal, finely ground
   (or you may use finely ground chicken)
1 cup coarse bread crumbs
$\frac{1}{2}$ cup milk
3 eggs, beaten or $\frac{3}{4}$ cup egg substitute

$\frac{1}{4}$ tsp. salt (*NOTE: at end of recipe)
$\frac{1}{2}$ tsp. black pepper
$\frac{1}{4}$ cup chopped parsley

1 egg, beaten
1 cup fine bread crumbs for coating
$\frac{1}{4}$ cup canola oil
1 cup boiling water

Soften coarse crumbs in milk; combine with eggs. Stir in ground meat, salt, pepper and parsley. With your hands, shape $\frac{1}{2}$ cup of the mixture at a time into small ovals (egg-shaped). Roll the fricandels in beaten egg, then, into fine crumbs. Fry them in hot oil until light golden brown.

Pour off any fat from skillet but allow fricandels to sit in skillet. Then, pour boiling water over them; cover the pan and simmer them for 30 minutes. Spoon pan juices over fricandels. Serves 6.

*NOTE: You may wish to try the flavorful "No-Salt"- Salt Spice Mix (see below) in recipes such as: Fricandels of Veal, meatball and meatloaf recipes, crumb coated chicken/meat cutlet recipes. Simply exchange any recipe-designated amounts of salt/pepper with 1 teaspoon to 1 tablespoon of "No-Salt"- Salt Spice Mix.

"NO-SALT" - SALT SPICE MIX

1 tbsp each: garlic powder, mustard powder

2 tsp. each: dried thyme leaves, onion powder, paprika, celery leaves

1 tsp. each: white pepper, black pepper, oregano

2 tbsp. grated dried lemon peel

Blend ingredients in a small bowl. Place a small funnel with a $\frac{1}{2}$-inch tube opening into a half-cup jar (with a screw-on lid). Spoon, and force the herbs through the funnel tube into the jar. Screw the lid securely. This mix stays quite potent for several months in a cool dark pantry.
(Also, the spices and herbs provide a delicious scent.)

MELON BALLS IN ASTI SPUMANTE

2 small cantaloupes, rinse and paper towel-dry melon skin before you cut into the
    melons; halve the melons and discard seeds

$\frac{1}{8}$-section watermelon

1 small honeydew melon; wash exterior of melon, paper towel-dry;
    halve melon and discard seeds

2 cups Asti Spumante

mint sprigs for garnish

    Set out a large bowl. With a round tablespoon or a melon baller, form melon balls from the melons; combine the balls in the large bowl; refrigerate bowl until serving.

    When needed, pour 2 cups Asti Spumante over melon balls and toss the mix with 2 spoons. Carefully, ladle melons in wine into tall water glasses or tall dessert glasses. Insert mint sprigs to garnish. Serves 6-8.

Cousin Ruth Sanson Bastien's family at their Table of Plenty.

Pasta

CANNELLINI WITH TUNA SALAD
LEMON-OIL DRESSING
SALSA PUTTANESCA WITH PASTA (heirloom)
AUNT LOUISA'S CHERRY COOKIES TO DIE FOR

CANNELLINI WITH TUNA SALAD

1 lg. can (20 oz.) cannellini beans
black pepper and salt to taste
3 cups red leaf lettuce, washed, drained
1 small yellow onion, chopped
1 tbsp. olive oil
6 plum tomatoes, halved
2 cans (8 oz. each), Italian tuna fish in olive oil
$\frac{1}{2}$ cup pitted chopped Kalamata olives

Lemon-Oil Dressing (see page 385)

Prepare dressing and refrigerate until needed.

On a large glass platter with an edge, lay a bed of red leaf lettuce. Brown onion in olive oil in a small saucepot. Add beans, pepper and salt and stir to blend. Simmer the mix for 1-2 minutes.

Pour warm bean mix over the bed of red leaf lettuce. With a fork, flake the tuna in a bowl. Spoon equal portions of tuna over bean mix. Garnish with tomato wedges and olives. Shake jar of dressing to thoroughly blend. Drizzle Lemon-Oil Dressing over salad. Serve warm. Serves 6.

SALSA PUTTANESCA WITH PASTA

1-1½ lbs. spaghetti or perciatelli

1 lg. can (20 oz.) plum tomatoes
    (or 1 lg. can crushed tomatoes)

6 ripe plum tomatoes

1 large yellow onion, sliced thin

6 garlic cloves, chopped

2 tbsp. olive oil

1 tbsp. butter or Smart Balance spread

½ cup chopped oil-cured olives, pitted

6 anchovy fillets, coarsely chopped

1 tbsp. capers

6 basil leaves, torn into pieces

⅛ tsp. salt

hot red chile pepper flakes (optional)

¼ tsp. freshly ground black pepper

1 tsp. dried oregano

Drop 6 ripe plum tomatoes into boiling water for 1 minute. Remove tomatoes from pot; peel off skin with your fingers. Coarsely chop tomatoes and set aside in a 2-quart bowl.

Meanwhile, strain 1 large can plum tomatoes through a colander or through a food mill which separates seeds from pulp. Add pulp to chopped tomatoes in bowl. (Or add 1 can crushed tomatoes to bowl.)

In a 2-quart sauce pan with lid, lightly brown onion and garlic in a mix of olive oil and butter. Do not burn. Scrape bottom of pot. Pour tomatoes into this saucepot; add black pepper, salt, chili flakes, anchovies, capers, olives, oregano and basil leaves and stir to mix.

With lid askew, simmer sauce for 30 minutes. Turn off heat under pot. Remove basil leaves and discard. Serve over 1 to 1½ pounds of spaghetti or perciatelli pasta. Serves 6.

AUNT LOUISA'S CHERRY COOKIES TO DIE FOR

1 cup butter or Smart Balance spread, softened	1 egg
6 oz. cream cheese, softened	2 tbsp. milk
1 cup granulated sugar	2 cups flour
$\frac{1}{4}$ tsp. salt	$\frac{1}{4}$ cup candied cherries, minced
1 tsp. almond extract	confectioners' sugar

In a 2-quart mixing bowl, cream together: butter, cream cheese, sugar, salt and almond extract. Beat in egg and milk. Stir in minced candied cherries; add flour, $\frac{1}{2}$ cup at a time, blending thoroughly.

Form dough into a ball; wrap dough in waxed paper and refrigerate dough for one hour.

Preheat oven to 325°.

Remove dough from refrigerator and cut dough into 4 sections. (Cover unused dough until needed.) On a lightly floured board roll each section of dough into ropes, about $1\frac{1}{2}$ inches in diameter. Cut ropes into 1-inch pieces. Roll each piece of dough between your hands to form small balls.

Lay the cherry balls on 3 ungreased cookie sheets, 9x15 inches (about 20 per tray).

Bake cookies in center of preheated oven, at 325° for 12-15 minutes or until just set and firm and slightly tanned on bottoms. Remove trays from oven and allow to cool. When cookies are cooled, roll them in a small bowl of sifted confectioners' sugar.

Layer them in a large tin or foil-lined box with cover, waxed paper between layers. Store box in a cool place up to 1 month; or freeze until needed (within 4-6 weeks). Makes about 5 dozen cherry balls.

Aunt Louisa on her
90th Birthday.

Pasta

GRILLED PORTOBELLO AND TOMATO
SPAGHETTI AGLIO OLIO (heirloom)
JOANNE'S STRAWBERRY CROSTATA

GRILLED PORTOBELLO AND TOMATO

1 lb. Portobello mushroom caps, rinsed, drained, sliced into $\frac{1}{2}$-inch thick pieces

1 large onion, thinly sliced

2 beefsteak tomatoes, ripe but firm, $\frac{1}{2}$-inch slices

3-4 bay leaves

6 garlic cloves, chopped

$\frac{1}{4}$ cup balsamic vinegar

$\frac{1}{4}$ cup olive oil

freshly ground black pepper

$\frac{1}{4}$ cup grated Parmesan cheese

Lightly coat a 9x15-inch solid metal grill pan. Preheat broiler.

Pat dry mushroom slices with paper towels. In a small bowl blend oil and vinegar. Brush this mix over both sides of sliced mushrooms. Lay mushrooms, side by side, on the grill pan. Arrange tomato slices and sliced onion over the mushrooms. Sprinkle with garlic, cheese and black pepper. Lay bay leaves upon various areas of the vegetable mix.

Broil vegetables 5 inches below heat for 3-5 minutes or until cheese melts and is light golden brown. Turn off broiler. Allow tray to sit in oven for another minute. Remove bay leaves and discard. Serve hot; use a spatula to assist in the serving. Serves 6.

SPAGHETTI AGLIO OLIO

1 to 1½ lbs. spaghetti
1 small onion, chopped
6 garlic cloves, leave whole
¼ cup olive oil
6 large basil leaves
3-4 sun-dried tomatoes, sliced thin
salt, freshly ground black pepper to taste
½ cup Romano cheese, grated (additional cheese at serving)
few grains hot red pepper flakes (optional)

Heat oil in a small skillet. Lightly brown onion and garlic in hot oil for 1 minute; stir in sun-dried tomatoes and basil and cook for 1 minute longer. Remove skillet from heat and set aside.

Meanwhile, cook the spaghetti as directed on package. Drain spaghetti and save ½ cup hot pasta liquid.

Return skillet to burner and reheat the oil mix. Stir the pasta liquid into the skillet with the garlic and onion mix, scraping the bottom of the pan to remove leavings. Stir in: salt, black pepper and a few grains of hot red pepper flakes.

Pour spaghetti into a large serving bowl; sprinkle spaghetti with ½ cup of grated Romano cheese. Remove basil leaves from oil mix in skillet and pour the hot sauce over the bowl of spaghetti. Toss pasta with sauce to mix thoroughly. Grate more cheese over the pasta and serve. Serves 6.

JOANNE'S STRAWBERRY CROSTATA

3 cups flour

$\frac{3}{4}$ cup sugar

dash of salt

3 tsp. baking powder

1 cup butter or Smart Balance spread

2 slightly beaten eggs or $\frac{1}{2}$ cup egg substitute

$\frac{1}{4}$ cup milk

2 tsp. vanilla extract

1 jar (32 oz.) strawberry preserves

1 cup slivered blanched almonds

confectioners' sugar for sprinkling

Have ready: one $10\frac{1}{2}$x$15\frac{1}{2}$x1-inch baking pan. Preheat oven 400°.

In a large bowl combine flour, sugar, baking powder and salt. Cut in butter and work it with 2 forks to create coarse crumbs.

Combine eggs, milk and vanilla and add to dry ingredients; mix thoroughly. Gently knead dough on a floured board until smooth and elastic. Cut off $\frac{1}{3}$ portion of the dough; wrap it in plastic and set aside for lattice crust.

On floured board, roll remaining dough into a 15x10-inch rectangle. Unroll dough onto the ungreased baking pan. Spread strawberry preserves over the dough in the pan. Sprinkle slivered almonds over preserves. Set aside.

Roll remaining dough to form a 10x12-inch rectangle. Cut the dough into $\frac{1}{2}$-inch wide strips. Carefully, lay strips diagonally across crostata to form a lattice design. Bake crostata in the center of a preheated oven 400° for 20-25 minutes. Cool thoroughly; sift confectioners' sugar over entire crostata just before cutting into portions. Makes 20-40 servings, depending on size.

Pasta

WARM KEY WEST VEGETABLE SALAD
RAVIOLI IN RED PEPPER VODKA SAUCE (heirloom)
LEMON MACAROON BARS

WARM KEY WEST VEGETABLE SALAD

1 can (1 lb.) black beans, rinsed, drained
1 can (1 lb.) corn kernels, rinsed, drained
2 cups baby bella mushrooms, washed, sliced (about 1 dozen)
1 medium red bell pepper, cored, thinly sliced
1 medium poblano (pepper), cored, thinly sliced
¼ cup chopped Vidalia onion
½ lb. fresh mozzarella, cut into small cubes
2 tbsp. chopped parsley
1 tbsp. dried oregano
½ tsp. freshly ground black pepper
2 tbsp. extra-virgin olive oil
2 tbsp. balsamic vinegar
2 tbsp. fresh chopped cilantro for garnish

Blend oil, vinegar, black pepper and oregano in a small bowl or cup; set aside. In a large bowl mix black beans, corn, sliced mushrooms, sliced peppers, onion and mozzarella cubes. Sprinkle parsley over the vegetables and toss to combine.

Stir and drizzle the dressing over the vegetables and gently toss them with two spoons. Pour the vegetable salad into a 9x13-inch oven-proof casserole dish. Garnish with freshly chopped cilantro. At this point, you may wish to refrigerate the casserole, covered with plastic wrap.

Before serving, preheat oven to 300°; remove plastic wrap from dish and replace it with a sheet of foil. Bake the vegetable salad for 15-20 minutes. Cheese should soften; onions and peppers should have a slightly crisp texture. Serve warm; serves 6.

RAVIOLI IN RED PEPPER VODKA SAUCE

(If you prefer, freshly made ravioli and other pastas may be purchased at many Italian food shops and bakeries.)

(Prepare Ravioli as directed; do not cook them until ready to serve. Lay them side by side in metal pans, waxed paper between layers of Ravioli; cover tins with plastic wrap. Raviolis may be prepared in advance and frozen up to 2 weeks.)

DOUGH:

5 eggs

$\frac{1}{4}$ cup cold water

$\frac{1}{2}$ tsp. salt

$3\frac{1}{2}$ cups sifted flour (plus a little extra if needed)

Red Pepper Vodka Sauce (see page 402)

FILLING:

12 oz. ricotta cheese

1 egg yolk

2 tbsp. chopped parsley

$\frac{1}{8}$ tsp. nutmeg

$\frac{1}{2}$ tsp. salt

$\frac{1}{4}$ tsp. black pepper

$\frac{1}{2}$ cup grated Parmesan cheese

$\frac{1}{2}$ cup finely chopped mozzarella cheese

Prepare Red Pepper Vodka Sauce in advance.

PREPARE THE DOUGH: In a large mixing bowl, beat eggs; add salt and water and beat again. Stir in flour with a wooden spoon, mixing until a soft dough forms. Turn dough onto a well-floured board and knead with your hands for 10 minutes, until dough becomes soft and pliable. Add a little more flour (up to $\frac{1}{2}$ cup) if dough feels too sticky.

Place dough in a bowl and cover for 20 minutes. Then, divide the dough into 4 parts. Cover the rest of the dough and roll out one-fourth of the dough as thinly as possible. Cut 3-inch squares or circles and spoon 1 tablespoon of the filling in center of each square. Cover each with another piece of dough of equal size and press the edges of the sandwich with a pastry wheel or tines of a fork, making certain the edges are tightly sealed. Lay clean paper towels on a large table surface and place the ravioli atop the paper. It would be a good idea to sprinkle some semolina or fine meal over the paper first.

In the 20 minutes rest period above, prepare the FILLING by blending one egg yolk, ricotta, cheeses and spices. Place 1 tablespoon of this cheese mix in the center of each square (or circle) of dough and proceed as directed above. Let the formed ravioli rest on the table for 4 to 5 hours to dry. Then, either pack them in a foil pan in layers with waxed paper in between and thoroughly plastic wrapped (to refrigerate or to freeze); OR, cook them in 6 quarts of rapidly boiling water (add a dash of salt) for 8-10 minutes. Remove cooked pasta with a slotted spoon to a wide, large pasta dish. Serve with Red Pepper Vodka Sauce and extra grated Parmesan cheese. Makes about 40 Ravioli.

LEMON MACAROON BARS

1 pkg. (18½ oz.) lemon cake mix
⅓ cup butter or Smart Balance spread, softened
2 lg. eggs or ½ cup egg substitute
1 can (14 oz.) sweetened condensed milk (DO NOT USE EVAPORATED MILK.)
2 tbsp. lemon juice
1 tbsp. grated lemon rind
2½ cups (7 oz. pkg.) flaked sweetened coconut, divided

Preheat oven to 350°. (*NOTE: at end of recipe)

Grease bottom only, of 9x13-inch metal baking pan.

In a large bowl, pour the cake mix; add softened butter and 1 egg. Beat for 2 minutes with electric mixer at low speed. Press the mix into bottom of the prepared pan.

In a medium bowl, whisk condensed milk, the remaining egg, lemon juice and rind until thoroughly blended. Stir in 1⅓ cups coconut. Spread the coconut mix evenly over the dough base in pan. Sprinkle filled pan with remaining coconut; lightly press coconut into the condensed milk layer, using a wide spatula.

Bake cake on rack in center of oven for 28-30 minutes or until center of cake is almost set. Pastry will firm, out of the oven, as the pan stands. Transfer pan to a rack to cool completely. Cut cake into bars with sharp knife. Makes about 26 bars.

*NOTE: If using dark-coated metal pan, preheat oven to 325°.

Pasta

Everyone Has An Angel

I just know my Father watches over me; is always there for me. Daddy is not only my parent; my Dad is my Guardian Angel, always with his guiding hand on my shoulder, his comforting and encouraging words in my heart. Sometimes he sends his love for me through messengers: his only grandson, his grandson's new family, Daddy's nieces and nephews, my bosom buddies, religious confidentes and our family's Labs.

This brilliant gentleman patiently helped me to solve the challenging theorems in my young life. With his quiet and humble demeanor, he repeatedly aided the blind to see the light, the hearing-impaired to listen to the wisdom of others.

No more may I shower him with grateful and welcoming hugs: as the loving child who patiently had waited by a bus stop for her Dad to end his day at the job; or the grad student who breathed a sigh of relief to see her Father's slight but protective figure standing at the other end of the "Double R" subway tunnel; and especially as a mid-life matron who thankfully greeted the white-haired old man when he returned from the dead, not once, but twice.

No matter. Always, my angel is with me.

Daddy (Dominick Orlando) and Marion.

Pasta

ICEBERG LETTUCE AND TOMATO WITH SPICY SALAD DRESSING
BROCCOLI RABE WITH SAUSAGES AND FARFALLE (heirloom)
or
BROCCOLI RABE, WHOLE WHEAT PENNE AND CANNELLINI
FRUIT AND CHEESE TRAY

ICEBERG LETTUCE AND TOMATO WITH SPICY SALAD DRESSING

1 lg. head iceberg lettuce, trimmed, rinsed, drained
2 large tomatoes, ripe but firm, thinly sliced

Spicy Salad Dressing (see page 387)

Set out 6 salad plates. Prepare dressing in advance and refrigerate it until needed.

Using a long knife, with a sharp serrated edge, cut the lettuce into 6 wedges (you may need 2 medium heads of iceberg lettuce to accomplish the portions). Arrange sliced tomatoes, evenly distributed among the 6 plates. Just before serving, drizzle dressing over lettuce and tomatoes. Serves 6.

BROCCOLI RABE WITH SAUSAGES AND FARFALLE
(Broccoli Rabe should show lots of flower clusters.)

6-8 links sweet fennel sausage

1½ lbs. broccoli rabe (rapini), trimmed, washed, drained, parboiled for 5 minutes

1-1½ lbs. farfalle pasta

4 tbsp. olive oil (in 2 parts)

8 garlic cloves, peeled, leave whole

½ cup grated Parmesan cheese (more grated Parmesan for garnish)

½ cup coarsely chopped Parmesan cheese

freshly ground black pepper, salt to taste

a few grain hot red pepper flakes

Lightly brown sausages at moderate-high, on all sides in a large skillet. Transfer sausages from skillet to a heat-resistant platter. Cover sausages with foil and keep them warm.

Drain parboiled broccoli rabe; pour the rapini into the skillet with garlic cloves and sauté at moderate-high, stirring frequently, for 5 minutes.

At the same time, set pasta pot to boil. Follow cooking directions on farfalle package. Drain pasta and pour into a large serving platter.

Spoon broccoli rabe and garlic onto same platter; add remainder of oil, grated and chopped Parmesan, black pepper, salt and red pepper flakes. Toss rapini mix with 2 serving spoons to mix thoroughly in oil-spice mix. Arrange warm sausages on top of pasta/greens. Add more grated Parmesan over the platter and serve. Serves 6.

BROCCOLI RABE, WHOLE WHEAT PENNE AND CANNELLINI

2 lbs. broccoli rabe (rapini),
   trimmed, rinsed, drained

12 oz. whole wheat penne rigati pasta

1 can (1 lb.) cannellini beans, rinsed, drained

6 garlic cloves, leave whole

$\frac{1}{2}$ cup slivered sun-dried tomatoes

$\frac{1}{4}$ cup extra-virgin olive oil

$\frac{1}{4}$ tsp. black pepper

$\frac{1}{4}$ tsp. salt

a sprinkling of dried hot red pepper

1 tsp. dried oregano

$\frac{1}{4}$ cup Asiago cheese, grated

You will need a 4-quart steamer pot. Pour 2 cups water at bottom of steamer. Insert the basket and spread uncooked pasta over the bottom.

In a large bowl, mix the rapini with slivered sun-dried tomatoes and garlic. Lay this mix over the pasta. Cover the steamer, with vent closed.

Turn the burner on high. When the water rapidly boils, lower heat to medium and steam the pasta-rapini mix for 12 minutes. Turn off burner; remove lid from steamer and spread cannellini beans over the top. Replace the lid and let pot rest for 1 more minute.

Remove steamer from burner. Drain off all but 1 cup of liquid from steamer. Pour the pasta and vegetables with the liquid into a very large platter with an edge. Over the platter, sprinkle salt, peppers and oregano. Drizzle olive oil over the platter. Sprinkle grated cheese over all. Serve immediately with crusty Italian bread as an accompaniment. Serves 6.

FRUIT AND CHEESE TRAY

Have ready: one 9x15-inch tray (or a 15-inch diameter tray).

Select 3 or 4 different fruits: melon slices, pineapple spears, apple or pear slices, strawberries, kiwi slices and peach slices. Arrange fruit in sections on the tray; for dividers, use cubes or slices of firm cheese: Swiss, cheddar, provolone, Edam.

Serve a bowl or biscuit tray with plain crackers to accompany the fruit and cheese – plus an after-dinner dessert wine such as Asti Spumante, Marsala, Recioto di Soave.

Pasta

---◆◆◆---

'SCAROLA IMBOTTIRE (STUFFED ESCAROLE) *(See page 196) (heirloom)*
MANICOTTI IN RAGOUT *(heirloom)*
CHOCOLATE, CHOCOLATE COVERED PEANUTS BISCOTTI
MARBLED ANISE BISCOTTI *(heirloom)*

'SCAROLA IMBOTTIRE, (STUFFED ESCAROLE) (See page 196)

MANICOTTI IN RAGOUT

(Make your own Manicotti shells. They're simple to prepare. As directed in the recipe, prepare the shells a day in advance, and fill them on the serving day. Once you've tasted homemade Manicotti shells, you'll realize 30 minutes of your time and talent was worth it. Arrange the meat in the ragout on a separate platter and serve along with the Manicotti. Delicioso!)

(Prepare Manicotti shells a day before. Stack with waxed paper between each and refrigerate. Prepare sauce a day or two in advance and refrigerate. Heat sauce thoroughly before serving. Complete Manicotti early on the serving day and arrange in casserole dish. Bake as directed. Or prepare completely, without sauce on pasta, and freeze up to two weeks.)

MANICOTTI SHELLS:
$1\frac{1}{4}$ *cups water*
5 eggs
$1\frac{1}{4}$ *cups flour*
$\frac{1}{4}$ *tsp. salt*

FILLING:
2 lbs. ricotta
8 oz. mozzarella cheese, chopped fine
$\frac{1}{2}$ *cup grated Parmesan cheese*
2 eggs beaten or egg substitute
$\frac{1}{2}$ *tsp. salt*
$\frac{1}{4}$ *tsp. black pepper*
1 tbsp. chopped parsley

$\frac{1}{2}$ *cup grated Parmesan cheese at serving time*
$\frac{1}{2}$ *cup olive oil - enough to continuously coat pan*

(Continued on next page)

(Continued from previous page)

Ragout Sauce (see page 400). *Set aside in refrigerator.*

    SHELLS: *In a 2-quart mixing bowl, beat eggs, flour, water and salt until smooth (use electric mixer). Pour ½ cup light olive oil in a small bowl. Gently dip wad of paper toweling into oil and wipe the bottom of a 5-inch Teflon or non-stick pan. Wipe the pan with oil before each pouring of batter. Pour 2 tbsp. batter into pan, turning pan quickly to spread batter evenly over bottom of pan. Cook over medium heat until top of shell is dry, but bottom is not brown (a minute may do it). Turn shells out onto a wire rack to cool and keep them separate. Continue making shells until all the batter is used. As shells cool, waxed paper should be used to separate them, as you form stacks.*

    FILLING: *In a 2-quart bowl, combine all filling ingredients and mix until blended. Spoon about ¼ cup of this filling into center of each shell and roll up. Spoon some sauce onto bottom of a 9x15x2-inch Pyrex or heat-resistant pan, which has been coated with olive oil. Arrange manicotti on Pyrex pan, seam-side down, in a single layer. At this point you may wish to wrap the pan in plastic and freeze; or refrigerate with plastic wrap until needed (within 2 days).*

    AT BAKING TIME: *Preheat oven to 350° and bake casserole uncovered, for 30 minutes. Meanwhile, the sauce should be heated thoroughly and spooned over manicotti at serving time, along with more cheese. Serves 6-8.*

CHOCOLATE, CHOCOLATE COVERED PEANUTS BISCOTTI

1 cup granulated sugar
1 cup brown sugar
1 cup melted butter or $\frac{3}{4}$ cup canola oil
$\frac{1}{4}$ cup anise seeds, crushed
3 tbsp. amaretto liqueur
5 eggs or 2 whole eggs plus $\frac{3}{4}$ cup egg substitute
1 tbsp. baking powder

$5\frac{1}{2}$ cups all purpose flour
$\frac{1}{4}$ cup anisette
2 envelopes Redi-bake chocolate
1 tbsp. cinnamon
1 cup unsalted peanuts
1 cup chocolate covered peanuts,
    coarsely chopped in chunks

In a large bowl, cream melted butter with sugars. Stir in anisette, amaretto, anise seed, Redi-bake chocolate, cinnamon and eggs. Add flour mixed with baking powder, a cupful at a time, mixing thoroughly. Work in the nuts; knead by hand on a floured board, forming a large round circle, about 2 inches thick. Wrap the dough in plastic and refrigerate it for 2-3 hours.

Preheat the oven to 375°. Grease three 9x15-inch baking tins.

Lay the dough on a floured board and divide it into 6 wedges. Cover the rest of the dough as you work. Form each wedge into a flat, long loaf, 2x12x$\frac{1}{2}$ inches. Form each loaf manually, with the aid of a rolling pin.

With 2 long spatulas to assist you, gently lay down 2 loaves per greased pan. Bake the loaves, one pan at a time, in the center of a preheated oven at 375° for 20 minutes, or until underside of the loaves appears lightly tanned.

Remove pans from oven and allow to slightly cool. With the aid of the thin spatulas, lift the loaves, one at a time, to the board and slice each loaf into pieces, $\frac{3}{4}$-inch thick; cut on a diagonal.

Return biscuits to pan; stand them with spaces between each. Bake them again at 375° for 5 minutes longer. Remove trays from oven to cool thoroughly. Frost the tops of the biscuits as directed below.

FROSTING:
2 cups confectioners' sugar
1 envelope Redi-bake chocolate
5-6 tbsp. amaretto liqueur

Combine frosting ingredients into a bowl, stirring in the liqueur one teaspoon at a time. Frosting should be thick. Use a frosting spatula or a flat knife to spread a thin layer of frosting on top of each biscotti.

Frosting will firm faster if you place the trays of frosted biscotti in the refrigerator for 30 minutes. Package the biscotti in layers in large lasagna foil pans; lay sheets of waxed paper between the layers. Wrap the filled tin in foil and store in a cool place for several weeks; or freeze biscotti for several months. Makes about 6 dozen biscotti.

MARBLED ANISE BISCOTTI

4 eggs (do not use egg substitute in this recipe)
1⅓ cups granulated sugar
2½ cups flour
4 tsp. anise seeds, crushed
6 oz. semisweet chocolate morsels, melted
4 tsp. anise extract

Preheat oven to 375°.

Grease and flour four 5x7-inch loaf pans. Lightly grease 2 cookie sheets, 9x15 inches.

Melt chocolate morsels over a pot of hot water. Keep pot of melted chocolate over hot water.

In a large bowl of the electric mixer, beat eggs with sugar at medium speed for 5 minutes, until thick and lemon-colored. At medium speed, gradually beat in flour for 2-3 minutes, until batter is smooth.

Add and beat in anise seeds and anise extract to the batter. Evenly distribute the batter to four greased and floured 5x7-inch loaf pans. Drizzle the melted chocolate over each pan. With a knife, cut the melted chocolate into the batter to make a marbleized effect.

Bake the loaves in a preheated oven at 375° for 25 minutes. Place 2 pans at a time to bake, on one rack in the oven; place the rack in the center of the oven. Loaves are baked when the tops are a light golden tan.

Remove the tins from the oven; cool cakes slightly. Remove cakes from tins onto a clean board. Slice the loaves ½-inch thick, diagonally across the short side (5-inch). Stand the biscuits cut-side down and re-bake biscuits for 5 minutes on each side. Remove biscuits from oven to cool thoroughly.

Store biscotti when completely cooled, in a lasagna aluminum foil pan, in layers, with waxed paper between layers. Wrap tins in aluminum foil and store in a cool place for several weeks; or freeze for several months. Makes about 24-28 biscotti.

TURKEY-BARLEY CHOWDER SALAD
SPAGHETTI WITH POMIDORO ARRABBIATA
LOUISE'S PIE CRUST COOKIES

TURKEY-BARLEY CHOWDER SALAD

3 cups water

1 wing, 1 leg: turkey

½ lb. fresh turkey cutlets, sliced in strips

½ cup barley, added to 2 cups water and simmered for 30 minutes; drain

4-6 small white mushrooms, rinsed, chopped

2 lg. celery stalks, trimmed, finely chopped

2 lg. carrots, pared, thinly sliced in rounds

3-4 fresh sage leaves, chopped or 1 tsp. dried sage

1 tbsp. fresh chopped parsley (additional 1 tbsp. chopped parsley for garnish)

½ tsp. ground turmeric

½ tsp. freshly ground black pepper

½ tsp. salt

2 tbsp. olive oil

Cook turkey parts in 3 cups boiling water, in covered 4-quart pot for 30 minutes; add turkey strips and continue to simmer 15 minutes longer. Remove turkey parts and strips to a bowl.

Bring turkey stock to a slow boil; add barley, celery, carrots and mushrooms. Cover pot and simmer gently for 5 minutes.

Meanwhile, discard skin and remove meat from bones of turkey wing and leg. Chop all turkey meat into bite-size pieces. Drain vegetables and save broth in a small pot.

In a serving bowl combine cooked vegetables and turkey, herbs and spices. Sprinkle 2 tablespoons olive oil over mix. Toss to blend; sprinkle with additional parsley. Serve warm and accompany salad with cups of reserved hot turkey broth (salt and pepper to taste). Serves 6.

SPAGHETTI WITH POMIDORO ARRABBIATA

1½ lbs. spaghetti #8

sprigs of basil for garnish

½ cup Asiago cheese, additional cheese for garnish

Pomidoro Arrabbiata Sauce (see recipe below)

Prepare sauce in advance. If sauce has been frozen place it in refrigerator for 2 days. When needed, simmer until heated thoroughly.

Prepare spaghetti as directed on package. Drain; transfer to a large serving bowl. Ladle 2 cups of sauce and ¼ cup cheese over pasta and toss to mix. Ladle another cup of sauce over top of bowl; sprinkle with cheese. Garnish with sprigs of basil. Serve remainder of cheese in a separate bowl. Serves 6.

POMIDORO ARRABBIATA

1 lg. can (20 oz.) plum tomatoes
    (or 1 lg. can crushed tomatoes)
6 ripe plum tomatoes, peel skin, coarsely chop
6 large basil leaves (½ cup), torn
1 small yellow onion, chopped
4-6 whole garlic cloves

1 tsp. salt
¼ tsp. freshly ground black pepper
pinch of hot red pepper flakes (to taste)
¼ cup Chianti wine (a light red wine)
2 tbsp. olive oil

Drop ripe plum tomatoes in boiling water to cover. Remove tomatoes after 60 seconds and peel off skin with fingers. Coarsely chop tomatoes in 2-quart bowl.

Strain canned tomatoes (or use a food mill) to separate pulp from seeds. Pour pulp into bowl with fresh chopped tomatoes; set aside.

Lightly brown onion and garlic cloves in oil in a 2-quart sauce pan with lid. Scrape bottom of pot to loosen onion and garlic particles. Pour tomatoes into sauce pan and add salt, peppers and torn basil. Stir to mix on low heat, bringing sauce to a gentle simmer. Cook with lid askew for 30 minutes. Remove pot from burner and stir in wine.

LOUISE'S PIE CRUST COOKIES
(An easy cookie to make and bake with help from young children.)

Use your favorite pie crust recipe; or package of pie crust mix
$\frac{1}{2}$ cup granulated sugar
2 tbsp. cinnamon

Have ready: two 9x15-inch cookie-sheets and two cutting boards.

Preheat oven to 400°.

Prepare pie crust dough; roll dough on floured board to $\frac{1}{4}$-inch thick.

Combine sugar and cinnamon in a small bowl. Sprinkle half of the sugar mix over the clean board. Gently roll the prepared dough around the rolling pin and transfer it onto the sugared board. Sprinkle some of the sugar mix over the top side of the rolled dough.

Cut dough into strips, 1-inch wide; cut strips into 1x4-inch rectangles. Twist each rectangle in middle, to form a bow. Place bows on ungreased cookie sheet.

Follow these instructions until all the dough is used. (You may have to replenish sugar-cinnamon mix.)

Bake cookies in center of oven, one cookie sheet at a time at 400° for 8 to 10 minutes. When thoroughly cooled, drizzle lemon icing over cookies. Makes about 3 dozen bows.

LEMON ICING:
1 cup confectioners' sugar
1-2 tablespoons fresh lemon juice

Stir juice into sugar to blend into a loose icing. Add a little more juice if needed. Drizzle over cookies.

Pasta

MESCLUN, RADISHES AND OLIVES
AIOLI DRESSING
FARFALLE WITH ARTICHOKES IN RED PEPPER SAUCE
CLAFOUTI

MESCLUN, RADISHES AND OLIVES

6 cups mesclun greens, rinsed, drained
1 cup radishes, rinsed, trimmed, finely sliced
1 cup sliced Sicilian pitted olives

Aioli Dressing (see page 389)

   Prepare dressing in advance. Refrigerate until one hour before needed. In a large salad bowl, combine mesclun, radishes and olives. Just before serving, add dressing to salad. Toss to mix thoroughly. Serves 6.

FARFALLE WITH ARTICHOKES IN RED PEPPER SAUCE
(Red Pepper Sauce may be prepared in advance.)

6-8 links spicy Italian sausages
2 tbsp. olive oil

Red Pepper Sauce (see page 402)

1-1½ lbs. whole wheat farfalle (Follow cooking directions on package.)
1 can (1 lb.) artichoke hearts, unseasoned
2 tbsp. olive oil
1 tbsp. balsamic vinegar
1 tsp. dried oregano
2 garlic cloves, minced
black pepper, salt to taste
½ cup grated Romano cheese

Re-heat Red Pepper Sauce if made in advance. Brown sausages in oil in a large skillet with lid. Drain sausages on a paper towel-lined platter. Add cooked sausages to Red Pepper Sauce. Keep sauce warm on low simmer.

In a small skillet, heat oil on moderate-high; cook garlic and artichokes in hot oil for 2 minutes, stirring to prevent particles from sticking to bottom of skillet.

Remove artichokes from burner; stir in vinegar, oregano, pepper and salt.

Meanwhile, set pasta pot to boil. Follow directions on package. Drain pasta and transfer to serving bowl.

Remove sausages from sauce to a serving platter. Ladle 1 cup Red Pepper Sauce into pasta; toss to mix thoroughly. Spoon another cup of sauce over pasta. Add artichoke mix to top of pasta in sauce. Sprinkle with grated Romano. Serve pasta immediately, with a side of sausages. Serves 6-8.

CLAFOUTI

$\frac{2}{3}$ cup sugar

8 tbsp. butter or Smart Balance spread

4 eggs or 1 cup egg substitute

$\frac{3}{4}$ cup evaporated milk (fat-free available)

2 tbsp. Cherry Heering liqueur

$1\frac{1}{2}$ tsp. vanilla extract

1 cup flour

$\frac{1}{4}$ tsp. ground nutmeg

2 cups fresh Bing cherries, pitted (or use thawed, frozen cherries or canned cherries, thoroughly drained)

confectioners' sugar for garnish

Heat oven to 375°.

Lightly butter a 9-inch cake or pie pan. In a large bowl, beat sugar and butter until light and fluffy. Add and beat in eggs, one at a time.

In a small bowl, blend milk with liqueur and vanilla. In another bowl combine flour with nutmeg.

To the egg/butter mix, alternately add flour mix with the liquid mix. Fold in the cherries.

Pour batter into prepared pan and bake in preheated oven at 375° for 40-50 minutes or until inserted toothpick removes clean.

Cool cake on rack. Invert cake into a serving plate when thoroughly cooled. Dust cake with confectioners' sugar just before serving. Serves 6.

Pasta

ROMAINE, CRANBERRIES AND ORANGES
HONEY MUSTARD DRESSING
PASTA E SARDE (heirloom)
COFFEE KALHUA SUNDAE

ROMAINE, CRANBERRIES AND ORANGES

1-2 heads romaine lettuce, trimmed, rinsed, drained, torn (about 5-6 cups)
2 navel oranges, washed, peeled, pith removed, separated into sections
1 cup dried cranberries

Honey Mustard Dressing (see page 384)

    Prepare dressing in a small jar with a lid. Refrigerate until 1 hour before serving. In a large salad bowl combine romaine lettuce, navel orange segments and cranberries. Just before serving, pour dressing over salad; toss to mix thoroughly. Serves 6.

Ready – Set – "Jet"!

PASTA E SARDE
(Prepare Marinara Sauce a day or two in advance.)

1- 1½ lbs. linguine
1 small can (2 oz.) flat anchovy fillets
2 tbsp. olive oil
½ cup pitted, chopped, green Sicilian olives
1 long Italian pepper, seeded, chopped
2 fennel bulbs with fennel grass, trimmed, finely chopped
½ cup pine nuts (pignola)
Marinara Sauce (see pages 398-9)

Prepare Marinara Sauce in advance. On the day, in a small pot at moderate high, cook pignola, pepper, fennel and anchovies in olive oil for 2 minutes, until fennel softens. Add chopped olives to fennel mix; then stir the mix into the pot of Marinara Sauce. Place on burner; cover and heat at low-medium until sauce begins to slowly bubble. Reduce heat to low-simmer and cook for 15 minutes.

Meanwhile, cook linguine in a large pot of boiling salted water as directed on pasta package. Drain pasta completely and transfer the linguine into a large serving bowl.

Ladle 2 cupfuls hot sauce into pasta; toss with 2 spoons to mix and coat thoroughly. Ladle another cupful or two of sauce over bowl. Serve immediately. Serves 6.

COFFEE KALHUA SUNDAE

1 quart coffee ice cream
½ cup Kalhua liqueur
6 Savoyard biscuits (packaged)
6 paper half straws (or dark chocolate straws for an added treat)

6 glass dessert bowls with stems (each 1 cup)

Set out glass bowls, liqueur bottle, biscuits and straws before serving. When serving, scoop one large ball coffee ice cream into center of dessert glasses. Drizzle 2 teaspoons Kalhua over ice cream; lay one biscuit next to each ball of ice cream and insert straw into side of ice cream (to sip liqueur). Serves 6.

Pasta

Great Stuff! - Tomatoes

Every summer since my birth, I (or my parents) have grown tomato plants. My son, a geneticist, grows a variety of heirloom tomatoes (from seeds) in large pots on their sunny deck.

Up to a few years ago, my 2 dozen and more assorted tomato plants resided in the fertile earth. My first rule as a home garden farmer is an annual attempt to rotate the crops. It's not easy, space-wise - and physically. Turning over grasses to prepare "growing" soil is tiring work. The luscious tomatoes the plants have produced were well worth the labor.

However, for many years, I've grown about 1 dozen Roma plum tomato plants in large planter pots with drainage holes, which measure at least 14x15 inches and which are lined one-half inches high with small pebbles (to assist in proper drainage).

Each Spring, I prepare my pots by decanting one-third or more of the used soil, replacing the growing medium with nutrient-laden potting soil which provides a great mulch; then I work in a dose of Miracle Grow fertilizer. Most importantly, the plants are watered on a daily schedule, to provide each plant with about 1-inch of water per week.

Once the plants are established, I add another dose of fertilizer and never allow the soil to become dry. The plants are placed in full sun and receive about 1 gallon of water evenly divided over 7 days. I insert six-foot stakes into each pot and tie-up the plants as they grow.

This system has been working well for me. I supply many folks with homegrown tomatoes and homemade marinara sauce each year. Or, as my daughter-in-law prefers to label the finished product: Marionara Sauce.

Cousin Tina Mazza Miller.

Pasta

STUFFED TOMATOES
LASAGNA WITH WALNUT PESTO SAUCE
A POLYPHENOL DELIGHT

STUFFED TOMATOES

6-8 tomatoes, ripe but firm
4 garlic cloves, minced
1 small onion, chopped
$\frac{1}{4}$ cup extra-virgin olive oil
$\frac{1}{4}$ cup chopped, pitted oil-cured olives
6 anchovy fillets
$\frac{1}{4}$ cup parsley, chopped
$\frac{1}{4}$ cup capers, drained
2 cups unseasoned Italian bread crumbs
2 tbsp. oregano
$\frac{1}{4}$ tsp. black pepper
pitted olives for garnish

Core the tomatoes with a sharp knife. Remove seeds with teaspoon; do not cut the skin. Place tomatoes on a plate to drain, core-side down.

Preheat oven 350°.

In a small skillet, sauté garlic and onion in olive oil until golden. Stir in olives and anchovies. In a small bowl, combine crumbs, parsley, oregano, capers and black pepper.

Spoon onion-anchovy mix into crumb mix and blend thoroughly. Spoon this stuffing mixture into the tomato cavities. Garnish each tomato with an olive. Place stuffed tomatoes in a baking pan with $\frac{1}{4}$ cup of water, mixed with 1 tablespoon olive oil and bake them, uncovered, at 350° for 20 minutes. Serves 6-8.

LASAGNA WITH WALNUT PESTO SAUCE
(Pesto may be prepared in advance and frozen.)

2 lbs. curly-edge lasagna
1 cup Pecorino Romano cheese, grated
$\frac{1}{4}$ cup chopped fresh parsley
1 pt. low-fat ricotta
1 egg or $\frac{1}{4}$ cup egg substitute, beaten
$\frac{1}{2}$ tsp. freshly ground black pepper
1 tsp. salt

WALNUT PESTO SAUCE:
2 cups fresh basil leaves, washed, drained
6 garlic cloves
$\frac{1}{4}$ cup chopped walnuts
$\frac{1}{2}$ cup grated Parmesan cheese
$\frac{1}{2}$ cup olive oil
salt, freshly ground pepper to taste
(a few tablespoons of water)

Prepare the WALNUT PESTO SAUCE.

Combine all ingredients with a few tablespoons of water in a food processor. Purée for 30 seconds or until basil leaves are creamed.

Serve immediately or pour into a 1-pint plastic container and freeze until needed. (If frozen, transfer pesto to refrigerator early on the day needed; then, warm the container, lid removed, over a pot of hot water. Stir the sauce in the container occasionally, while warming.)

Preheat oven to 350°.

In a 2-quart bowl, add and thoroughly blend: 1 pint ricotta, $\frac{1}{4}$ cup Romano cheese, parsley, salt, pepper and beaten egg. Set aside.

Cook lasagna in a very large pasta pot with lots of water, 1 tablespoon olive oil and 1 teaspoon of salt. Follow directions on pasta package for par-boil. For example: if the pasta is cooked in 8-10 minutes, rinse pasta in cold water and drain, after 7 minutes of cooking.

Return noodles to pot to which you've added enough cool water to cover.

Oil a 9x15-inch heat-resistant deep dish or Pyrex casserole. Line the dish vertically with noodles; spread $\frac{1}{2}$ cup warm walnut pesto sauce over noodles; sprinkle 2 tablespoons Romano cheese over the sauce. (Keep sauce warm, over pot of hot water.)

Form another layer of noodles horizontally across dish; spread the reserved ricotta mix over the noodles, to cover.

Vertically, cover with a final layer of noodles (use all of the lasagna noodles). Sprinkle with remaining Romano cheese.

Bake lasagna in center of oven at 350°. Allow to sit for 5 minutes after removing tray from oven. Cut into 6-8 wedges. Serve with spatula; top with a serving of warm Walnut Pesto Sauce.

A POLYPHENOL DELIGHT

2 cups red seedless grapes

1 cup raspberries

1 cup blueberries

½ cup dried cranberries

½ cup shaved almonds, with skins

½-¾ cup dark chocolate, coarsely chopped (*NOTE: in recipe)

½ cup dessert wine: Marsala, Moscato or Asti Spumante

(Wash and drain all fruits; handle raspberries very gently.)

(*NOTE: Dark chocolate contains high amounts of polyphenol antioxidants. Be sure to select a brand of chocolate with the highest cacao percentage.)

Have ready six 1-pint glass dessert bowls. Chill the glasses in the refrigerator for 1 hour.

Apportion one layer of grapes at the bottom of each glass; sprinkle 1 teaspoon of chopped dark chocolate over the grapes. Add a layer of dried cranberries and a layer of blueberries over the grapes-chocolate; sprinkle another teaspoon of chocolate over the cranberry-blueberry mix. Add a layer of raspberries and shaved almonds; then, sprinkle the third teaspoon of dark chocolate over the top of the almonds. (This totals 1 tablespoon of dark chocolate per dessert bowl.)

Drizzle 1 tablespoon of wine over each delightfully filled dessert bowl. (The cook may enjoy the reward of the leftover wine.) Serve immediately. Serves 6.

Pasta

RADICCHIO, ROMAINE IN PARMESAN
PARMESAN CHEESE DRESSING
SPAGHETTI WITH CRABS (heirloom)

or

LINGUINE WITH RED CLAM SAUCE (heirloom)
STRAWBERRY ALMOND CREAM

RADICCHIO, ROMAINE IN PARMESAN

2 cups radicchio, trimmed, rinsed, drained, cut into wide strips

1 lg. head romaine, about 3-4 cups, trimmed, rinsed, drained, cut into pieces

1 red onion, finely sliced

2 cups croutons

$\frac{1}{4}$ cup tiny chips Parmesan cheese

$\frac{1}{2}$ cup pitted oil-cured olives

Parmesan Cheese Dressing (see page 388)

Prepare dressing in advance and refrigerate it until 1 hour before serving.

In a large salad bowl, combine radicchio, romaine, croutons, onion, olives and Parmesan chips. Just before serving, add Parmesan Cheese Dressing and toss salad to mix thoroughly. Serves 6.

SPAGHETTI WITH CRABS

1-1½ lbs. spaghetti #8; prepare al dente
    just before serving
6-8 hard shell crabs
4 cups canned plum tomatoes, strained
¼ cup tomato paste
3 garlic cloves, minced

½ tsp. salt
1 onion, chopped
3 tbsp. olive oil
1 tbsp. chopped basil
1 tsp. oregano
1 hot chile pepper, chopped (use to taste)

Wash crabs after removing sacs. Remove the sac by pulling the 2 parts of the shell apart at back end and cutting out sac. Discard bottom darker shell. In a large 6-quart pot with cover, preheat oil to 300° to brown onion and garlic in olive oil. Add strained tomatoes, paste, herbs, and spices. Cover and simmer for 30 minutes. Sauce will be of a loose consistency. Add crabs and continue to simmer for another 10 minutes.

Meanwhile, cook spaghetti al dente in a large pot, according to directions on package. Drain spaghetti and pour into a large serving bowl. Ladle hot sauce over spaghetti and toss to mix with 2 spoons.

Remove crabs from sauce and serve them on a separate platter, accompanied with nutcrackers, picks and bibs. Serves 6.

LINGUINE WITH RED CLAM SAUCE

1-1½ lbs. linguine;
    prepare al dente just before serving
3 dozen Little Neck clams,
    scrubbed, keep them cold
recipe for Marinara Sauce (see pages 398-9)

½ cup dry white wine
⅛ tsp. hot red pepper flakes, to taste
½ cup chopped parsley
½ tsp. black pepper
¼ tsp. salt (to taste)

Prepare Marinara Sauce.

In last minutes of cooking the sauce, as sauce simmers, stir in wine, parsley, black pepper, salt, hot pepper flakes and clams. Cook clams in sauce for 5 minutes or until they open (discard any clams which do not open).

At the same time, bring a 6-quart pasta pot, three-quarters filled with water, to a boil. Add linguine and cook according to directions on pasta package. Drain.

Pour pasta into large serving bowl. Ladle 2 cups sauce only (no clams) over pasta and toss to coat pasta thoroughly. Now, ladle clams with some sauce over top of pasta. Serve immediately. Serves 6. (Provide separate bowls for discarding shells.)

STRAWBERRY ALMOND CREAM

2 lbs. fresh strawberries, gently rinsed and drained; slice all but 1 cupful of berries
1 cup chopped almonds with skin
2 pts. heavy whipping cream, whipped into peaks
½ cup Chambord liqueur (strawberry liqueur)

    With a fork, coarsely mash 1 cup strawberries in a 2-quart bowl. Fold in chopped almonds. Spoon and fold this mix into the whipped cream.

    Divide sliced strawberries into 6 large dessert bowls. Drizzle Chambord over each bowl of berries. Spoon strawberry-almond cream over each bowl of sliced strawberries. Serve immediately. Serves 6.

Pasta

SPICY BEAN SALAD
SPICY SALAD DRESSING
TORTELLINI WITH CREAM SAUCE
FRESH FIG CRUMB CAKE

SPICY BEAN SALAD

2 cups green beans, trimmed, washed, drained, cut into 2-inch segments,
    blanched (Blanching: add cut green beans to 1 cup boiling water; simmer for 2 minutes; drain.)
1 small can (1 lb.) red kidney beans, rinsed in cold water, drained
1 small can (1 lb.) ceci (chick peas), rinsed in cold water, drained
2 red peppers, washed, seeded, cored, finely sliced
2-3 garlic cloves, minced
1 small onion, chopped
¼ cup chopped parsley
4-5 lg. basil leaves, torn into small pieces

Spicy Salad Dressing (see page 387)

    Prepare dressing in advance and refrigerate it until 1 hour prior to serving.

    On a large platter with a rim (about 15 inches in diameter, or 9x15 inches), arrange green beans, ceci, red kidney beans and red peppers, separately. Scatter garlic and onion, parsley and basil over the beans and peppers.

    At serving time, drizzle the dressing over the salad. Serves 6.

TORTELLINI WITH CREAM SAUCE

two 9 oz. pkgs. fresh tortellini
  (meat or cheese filled)
1/4 cup olive oil
4 garlic cloves, minced

2 tbsp. fresh basil, minced
1/2 cup parsley, minced
1/2 cup grated Parmesan cheese
1/4 cup anchovy fillets, minced
1 cup heavy cream (or fat-free evaporated milk)

Cook tortellini two minutes less then directions on package. Drain them and return them to pot.

In a small skillet, heat oil and lightly brown garlic. Add basil, parsley, cheese and anchovies. Stir in cream. Add sauce to tortellini, mixing thoroughly; simmer for 2-3 minutes before serving. Serves 6.

FRESH FIG CRUMB CAKE
(May be prepared a day or two in advance.)

TOPPING:

1 cup flour
1/2 cup firmly packed brown sugar
6 tbsp. butter or Smart Balance spread, softened
3/4 tsp. cinnamon

CAKE:

1/2 cup butter or Smart Balance spread, softened
2 large eggs or 1/2 cup egg substitute
3/4 tsp. baking powder
1 doz. fresh figs (Kadota, Brown Turkey or
  Calimyrna), rinsed, drained,
  trimmed, quartered

2/3 cup sugar
1 cup flour
1/2 tsp. salt

Prepare an 8-inch square or round baking pan: butter and flour the pan. Preheat oven to 350°.
First, prepare the topping: combine flour, brown sugar, butter and cinnamon with 2 forks to make a crumbly and well-blended mix. Set aside.
Prepare the cake batter. With an electric mixer in a bowl, cream together: butter and sugar until mixture is light and fluffy; add eggs, 1 at a time, beating thoroughly after each addition. Sift in flour, baking powder and salt. Beat the batter until just combined.
Spread the batter evenly in the prepared pan. Arrange fig quarters in rows over the batter; sprinkle the topping over the figs. Bake the cake in center of the oven at 350° for 50 minutes to 1 hour, or until inserted toothpick tests clean. Serve the cake from the pan, warm or at room temperature. Serves 6.

Pasta

CHICORY, DANDELIONS AND RED GRAPES

BLEU CHEESE DRESSING

FETTUCCINE ALFREDO

CHOCOLATE FRUIT CAKE

CHICORY, DANDELIONS AND RED GRAPES

3 cups chicory, trimmed, rinsed, drained

3 cups dandelions, trimmed, rinsed, drained

    (tear or cut up greens into bite-size pieces)

2 cups red seedless grapes, rinsed, drained

8-10 cherry tomatoes, stems removed

1 lg. carrot, pared, shredded

Bleu Cheese Dressing (see page 386)

Prepare dressing in advance. Refrigerate dressing until serving.

In a large salad bowl combine greens, tomatoes and grapes. Shred carrot and reserve in a small plastic bag until serving. Refrigerate greens mix and grapes until serving time.

Then, spoon about $\frac{1}{2}$ cup dressing over salad bowl and toss to coat tomatoes, greens and grapes thoroughly. Spread shredded carrot over top of salad and spoon $\frac{1}{4}$ cup dressing over carrots. Serve remainder of dressing individually when you serve the salad. For 6 servings.

FETTUCCINE ALFREDO

two 9 oz. pkg. fettuccine
1½ cups heavy cream (or fat-free evaporated milk)
1 cup butter or Smart Balance spread
½ tsp. freshly ground black pepper
1 tsp. nutmeg
salt to taste
1 cup grated Romano cheese

Cook pasta as directed on package. While fettuccine cooks, combine 1 cup cream, butter, pepper, nutmeg, (salt) in a pot, large enough to accommodate the pasta, and cook over low heat until mixture thickens.

Drain fettuccine and add the pasta to the large sauce pot, tossing to coat thoroughly. Add remaining cream and ¾ cup of the cheese. Toss again and serve with remaining cheese sprinkled on top. Serves 6.

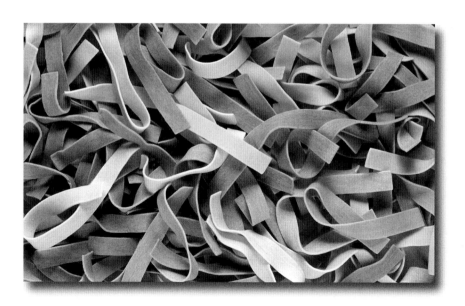

CHOCOLATE FRUIT CAKE
(Best prepared several weeks before serving.)

1 lb. mixed candied fruits
    (sold in plastic containers)

$\frac{1}{2}$ cup light raisins

$\frac{1}{2}$ cup dark raisins

$\frac{1}{4}$ cup chopped dates

$\frac{1}{4}$ cup chopped apricots

$\frac{1}{4}$ cup pitted prunes, chopped

$\frac{1}{4}$ cup each: chopped walnuts, almonds, pecans

$1\frac{1}{2}$ cups flour (in 2 parts)

$\frac{1}{4}$ tsp. each: baking soda, allspice, cinnamon

3 eggs, beaten or $\frac{3}{4}$ cup egg substitute

3 tbsp. dark rum
    (1-2 tbsp. rum for moistening
    cake after baking)

3 tbsp. applesauce

$\frac{1}{2}$ tsp. almond extract

$\frac{1}{4}$ cup canola oil

$\frac{1}{2}$ cup granulated sugar

$\frac{1}{2}$ cup brown sugar

$\frac{1}{2}$ cup unsweetened dark cocoa

$\frac{1}{2}$ cup finely chopped dark chocolate

Grease and flour one 9x5x3-inch baking pan. Use butter or Smart Balance spread. Dust the pan with flour. Set aside.

Preheat oven to 275°.

In a large 6-quart bowl, combine candied fruits, raisins, apricots, prunes, dates and nuts and toss with $\frac{1}{2}$ cup flour.

In a small bowl, combine 1 cup flour, baking soda, allspice and cinnamon. Set aside.

In a 2-quart bowl, beat eggs, sugars, cocoa and oil until light and fluffy; beat in rum, applesauce and almond extract.

To the bowl with eggs/sugars, add and mix the bowl of flour, baking soda, spices.

With a wooden spoon, mix fruits and nuts thoroughly into the batter. Stir in chocolate pieces. Turn batter into prepared pan, pressing the batter firmly into the pan (batter will be stiff).

Bake cake in preheated oven at 275° for 2-2½ hours or until tester removes clean. Remove cake from oven and sprinkle 1-2 tablespoon dark rum over hot cake. Let cake cool completely. Remove from tin.

Wrap cooled cake in one layer of foil and one layer of plastic wrap (plastic first). Store and age cake in a cool, dry place for several weeks. Serves 10-12 slices.

Pasta

ESCAROLE, TOMATO AND FETA
ITALIAN DRESSING
GREEK PASTITSIO
STRAWBERRY MERINGUES

ESCAROLE, TOMATO AND FETA

1 lg. bunch tender escarole, trimmed, tough outer leaves discarded, rinsed thoroughly,
 drained, cut into bite-size pieces (about 5-6 cups)
1 cup pitted Kalamata olives
12-15 cherry tomatoes, rinsed, drained
1 small onion, finely sliced
1 slender cucumber, sliced thin, in rounds
1 cup feta cheese, crumbled into small chunks

Italian Dressing (see page 384)

 Prepare dressing in advance and refrigerate it until 1 hour before serving.

 In a large salad bowl, combine escarole, tomatoes, onion, cucumber, olives and cheese; toss to mix.

 Just before serving, drizzle dressing over salad and mix to thoroughly coat. Serves 6.

GREEK PASTITSIO

1 lb. rotelle pasta

2 tbsp. olive oil

1 onion, chopped

1½ lbs. ground beef round, crumbled

1 can (12 oz.) tomato purée

¼ tsp. each: cinnamon, nutmeg

1 tsp. dried oregano

½ tsp. salt

¼ tsp. freshly ground pepper

¼ cup butter or Smart Balance spread, melted

¼ cup flour

3 cups milk

¾ cup heavy cream   OR substitute:

    3¾ cups fat-free evaporated milk for milk AND cream

3 egg yolks, lightly beaten, or ¾ cup egg substitute

1 cup Romano cheese, grated

Preheat oven to 375°.

Cook pasta accordingly to directions on package. Drain, rinse and set aside.

In a skillet, heat oil and sauté onion at moderate heat, until onion softens. Stir in meat and sauté until brown. Add purée, herbs and seasonings. Simmer five minutes.

In a saucepan, stir flour into melted butter; add milk; cook and stir until thickened.

Blend together: cream with egg yolks and stir into the white sauce. Heat the mixture; do not boil (mixture will curdle).

Place half of the cooked rotelle in a 9x13-inch baking dish. Cover with half of the tomato mix. Repeat the layers.

Then, pour cream sauce over all and sprinkle with cheese. Bake pasta for 45 minutes at 375°. Cool slightly; serve by cutting into large squares. Serves 6-8.

STRAWBERRY MERINGUES
(Start on day before.)

MERINGUES:

canola oil to lightly coat 9x15-inch cookie sheet

whites from 2 large eggs

$\frac{1}{8}$ tsp. cream of tartar

$\frac{2}{3}$ cup plus 3 tbsp. granulated sugar

Preheat oven 350°. (Preheat oven at this temperature for a couple of hours before baking.) Lightly brush a 9x15-inch cookie sheet with canola oil.

In a medium-size bowl with electric mixer at high speed, beat egg whites and cream of tartar until foamy. Gradually beat in sugar, 2 tablespoons at a time, until mix forms stiff and glossy peaks.

Spoon 2 tablespoons of meringue for each serving into rounds on the prepared cookie sheet. Form 6 rounds and depress the centers with a large spoon, to form a well. Set meringues in preheated oven 350°, door closed, oven OFF, for at least 3-4 hours or overnight.

FILLING:

8 oz. softened cream cheese

3 tbsp. sour cream

3 tbsp. sugar

1 tsp. vanilla extract

2 cups heavy cream for whipping, beaten into stiff peaks

TOPPING:

2 cups sliced fresh strawberries

Several hours before serving, in a medium bowl, beat softened cream cheese and 3 tablespoons of sugar at high speed, until light and fluffy. Beat in sour cream and vanilla. Fold in whipped cream. Refrigerate this mix for 1 hour.

Prepare strawberries and set aside in a bowl in the refrigerator.

Carefully remove meringue shells from baking sheet onto a doily-lined serving tray. At serving time, spoon cheese mix evenly distributed among and into the 6 shells. Spoon the strawberries over the cheese mix in the meringue shells. Serve immediately. Serves 6.

Pasta

CARROTS, TOMATOES AND STUFFED CELERY
RUSSIAN DRESSING
SPINACH LINGUINE WITH WHITE CLAM SAUCE
FRITTATAS (heirloom)
A PEACHY MELBA

CARROTS, TOMATOES AND STUFFED CELERY

4-5 celery stalks, trimmed, rinsed, drained, cut into 4-inch sections (to stuff)

4-6 medium carrots, pared, trimmed, cut into thick sticks

$1\frac{1}{2}$ dozen cherry or grape tomatoes

Russian Dressing (see page 386)

Olive-Pepper Cream Cheese Stuffing

Prepare Russian Dressing in advance. Refrigerate dressing until serving time.

Prepare Olive-Pepper Cream Cheese Stuffing and refrigerate if not using immediately.

OLIVE-PEPPER CREAM CHEESE STUFFING:

8 oz. cream cheese (low-fat available)

1 tbsp. finely chopped, pitted olives

1 tbsp. finely chopped red pepper

Smoothly blend stuffing ingredients: cream cheese, olives and red pepper. Stuff each celery cavity with 1 tablespoon of cream cheese mix. Refrigerate celery covered in plastic wrap, if not using within 1 hour.

Arrange carrot sticks and tomatoes on a large sectional plate, leaving center section for dressing and 1-2 sections for stuffed celery.

Just before serving, spoon Russian Dressing into bowl in center of plate. Serves 6.

SPINACH LINGUINE WITH WHITE CLAM SAUCE

6 garlic cloves, minced
1 onion, chopped fine
1 green Italian fryer pepper, seeded, chopped
$\frac{1}{4}$ cup olive oil
1 cup dry white wine
$\frac{1}{2}$ tsp. black pepper
$\frac{1}{4}$ tsp. salt
$\frac{1}{4}$ tsp. hot red pepper flakes (optional)
$\frac{1}{2}$ cup packed basil leaves, torn

2 doz. Little Neck or cherrystone clams in shell, scrubbed, keep cold

two 9 oz. pkgs. spinach linguine

In a 4-quart sauce pot at moderate high, heat oil and lightly brown garlic, onion and pepper. Stir in wine, pepper, salt, hot pepper, basil and clams, stirring to mix.

Cook the mix about 5 minutes or until clams open. (Discard any unopened clams.)

Meanwhile, cook pasta as directed on package in a large pasta pot, three-quarters filled with water. Drain linguine, saving about $\frac{1}{2}$ cupful pasta liquid to add to sauce.

Pour pasta into a large serving bowl. Add clams and sauce and toss to mix. Distribute pasta and clam sauce among individual serving bowls. Serves 6.

FRITTATAS
(For best results, use 9-inch Teflon or non-stick skillets with lids.)

1 tsp. olive oil

6-8 large eggs or 1½-2 cups egg substitute, for each frittata

¼ tsp. salt

⅛ tsp. black pepper

1 tbsp. chopped basil

1 tsp. oregano

Select from the following list of ingredients and prepare in advance:

Mushrooms and Onions
    4 chopped mushrooms and 1 chopped onion.
    Sauté 4 chopped mushrooms in 1 tbsp. olive oil. Add 1 chopped onion.
    Toss to cook.
    After 2 to 3 minutes transfer to bowl.

Peppers
    4 seeded and sliced frying peppers, sautéed al dente.
    Sauté 4 green fryers in 1 tbsp. olive oil until tender, tossing occasionally.
    Transfer to bowl.

Asparagus
    6 stalks asparagus, trimmed, cut in 2-inch pieces, sautéed al dente.
    Sauté asparagus pieces in 3 tbsp. olive oil for 3-4 minutes, tossing occasionally.
    Transfer to bowl.

Ham and Olives
    ½ cup cubed ham, ¼ cup chopped pimiento olives.
    Chop ham into small cubes; add chopped pimiento.

Zucchini
    2 small zucchini thinly sliced in rounds; sauté al dente.
    Scrub zucchini, slice thin rounds (do not pare); sauté in 1 tbsp. olive oil,
    for 4-5 minutes. Transfer to bowl.

Potato
    1 large pared, cooked, sliced potato, 1 small onion, chopped.
    Boil potato in jacket for 20 minutes. Peel off skin and slice into rounds. Sauté
    potato slices and 1 chopped onion in 2 tbsp. oil for 3-4 minutes. Transfer to bowl.

Italian Cheeses
    ½ cup each: grated Parmesan cheese, cubed mozzarella.

(Continued on the following page)

(Continued from the previous page)

Preheat lightly oiled skillet at 300°. Beat 6-8 eggs with $\frac{1}{8}$ tsp. black pepper, $\frac{1}{4}$ tsp. salt, basil and oregano until thick and foamy. Pour the egg mixture into hot oiled skillet. When the eggs start to set, add the prepared frittata ingredients of your choice from previous page. Cover with lid. When omelet is set and firm, loosen with spatula and invert it onto a larger platter and then back to the skillet to cook the other side of the frittata, about 2 minutes longer. Slide from skillet to serving platter. Serve warm.

For variety try:

(1) Add 1 cup cooked halved shrimp, to the egg mix. Use a 5-inch skillet and cook up a batch of shrimp omelets. Stack them in groups of threes. Between each frittata, ladle Curry Sauce (see page 393). This makes an excellent Egg Foo Yung.

OR

(2) Add 1 cup spicy sausage rounds to egg mix. First, cook sausage rounds in skillet; then pour egg mix over them and cook to set. Prep two different cheese omelets (e.g. Provolone, Asiago, Mozzarella or Gruyere) and alternate cheese/sausage/cheese omelets in a stack. Serve with Marinara Sauce (see pages 398-9).

A PEACHY MELBA

3 large fresh, ripe freestone peaches, washed, each peach cut into 6 slices, pit removed

1 qt. raspberry sherbet

1 pt. raspberries, gently rinsed, drained

$\frac{1}{4}$ cup cherry liqueur or Chambord (strawberry liqueur)

1 pt. heavy cream for whipping, beaten into stiff peaks (refrigerate until serving)

Assemble this dessert at time to serve.

Arrange 3 slices of peaches on each of 6 dessert dishes to form a flower. Using a round tablespoon, form sherbet balls and set 2 rounded tablespoons of sherbet into the center of each peach flower.

Apportion raspberries over the fruit and sherbet in the dishes; sprinkle 2 teaspoons of liqueur over the sherbet. Add a dollop of whipped cream over each ball of sherbet and serve immediately. Serves 6.

Pasta

❖━◆━❖

BABY ROMAINE, CHEDDAR AND BLUEBERRIES
VINAIGRETTE DRESSING
PENNE PALERMO
ARTICHOKES STUFFED WITH SAUSAGE AND MUSHROOMS
PINE CONES IN THE SNOW

BABY ROMAINE, CHEDDAR AND BLUEBERRIES

6 cups baby romaine greens, rinsed, drained
1 cup cheddar cheese, cut into small chunks
½ pt. blueberries, gently rinsed, drained
1 dozen cherry tomatoes, rinsed, drained

Vinaigrette Dressing (see page 389)

Prepare dressing in advance. Refrigerate it until 1 hour before using.

In a large salad bowl, combine baby romaine, cheddar, blueberries and tomatoes. Add dressing and toss salad to mix thoroughly. Serves 6.

PENNE PALERMO

1 can (22 oz.) plum tomatoes, mashed

1 small can (6 oz.) tomato paste

1 oz. pignola (pine nuts); spread on metal tray and toast under broiler for 2 minutes until nuts are golden

½ cup raisins, soaked in a bowl of warm water for 20 minutes, drained

2 tbsp. olive oil

4 garlic cloves, chopped

½ cup chopped Sicilian olives

1 small tin (2 oz.) anchovy

black pepper, salt to taste, sprinkling of hot pepper flakes

1½ lbs. penne pasta

Lightly brown garlic in oil in a 4-quart sauce pot. Pour in tomatoes; stir in tomato paste.

Simmer sauce for 20 minutes. Stir in toasted pine nuts, soft raisins, anchovy, salt (to taste), pepper, hot pepper flakes. Cook for 10 minutes longer. Stir in olives and cook a few minutes longer.

Meanwhile, prepare pasta according to directions on package. Drain the pasta. Pour it into a large pasta serving bowl. Ladle sauce over pasta and toss to coat thoroughly. Serve immediately. Serves 6.

ARTICHOKES STUFFED WITH SAUSAGE AND MUSHROOMS
(May be prepared in advance.)

6 medium-large globe artichokes

$1\frac{1}{2}$ cups water

1 tbsp. olive oil, set aside (extra olive oil at serving)

1 tsp. salt (extra salt and black pepper to taste)

STUFFING:

3 small white mushrooms, scrubbed, trimmed, minced

2 links Italian fennel sausage, casing removed; crumble sausage and sauté in 1 tbsp. olive oil; set aside

3 garlic cloves, minced

$\frac{1}{2}$ cup unseasoned bread crumbs

1 tbsp. fresh parsley, chopped

$\frac{1}{4}$ cup Parmesan cheese, finely chopped

black pepper to taste

2-3 tbsp. olive oil

1-2 tbsp. warm water

    Trim artichokes by cutting off bottom stem close to base. Cut off tips, an inch or more. Carefully, spread open each artichoke (fresh, tender artichokes may crack if handled roughly). Snip off pinchy inner leaves with vegetable shears. Wash the inside and outer leaves of the artichokes in cool running water. Set them to drain, bottom-side up.

    Prepare stuffing in a 2-quart bowl by mixing crumbs, sautéed crumbled sausage, minced mushrooms and garlic and cheese. Add parsley, black pepper and 2-3 tablespoons olive oil and mix thoroughly. If stuffing is too dry and stiff, add a little warm water, 1 tablespoon at a time (no more than 2 tablespoonfuls).

    Pack each trimmed artichoke with 2-3 tablespoons stuffing mix. Arrange the artichokes, stuffing side up, in a 6-quart pot with lid, to which you've added $1\frac{1}{2}$ cups water mixed with 1 tablespoon olive oil and 1 teaspoon salt. Sprinkle artichokes with additional salt and pepper to taste. Cover pot and set pot to cook on burner at moderate-high. After the liquid starts to boil, lower heat under artichokes to simmer them for 45-50 minutes, until tender. (Pull out an outer leaf and taste the soft tip for tenderness.) Remove pot from burner. Transfer artichokes to a large oven-proof serving dish, 9x15x2 inches. Spoon the cooking liquid over each artichoke.

    If you cook the artichokes a day or two before, cover the casserole dish with plastic wrap and refrigerate the artichokes. Before serving, remove plastic; lay a foil tent over the artichokes and warm them in a preheated oven at 300° for 20 minutes, basting them with the cooking liquid in the casserole dish. Drizzle a little olive oil over the artichokes at serving. Serves 6.

PINE CONES IN THE SNOW

1 pt. blackberries, gently rinsed, drained
1 qt. vanilla bean ice cream
1 pt. heavy whipping cream, beaten into stiff peaks

    Rinse berries prior to serving. Drain thoroughly and refrigerate until needed. Whip cream to peaks and refrigerate until needed.

    At serving time, lay a large ball of vanilla ice cream in center of each of 6 dessert bowls (1 cup each). With your hands gently press blackberries over the surface of the ice cream ball. Spoon whipped cream in a circle around bottom edge of ice cream (or use pastry tube). Serve immediately. Serves 6.

Banshee with prizes.

Pasta

The Hand Who Fed Me

*M*y mother was my inspiration. She would read stories to me and sing the latest tunes on the "Hit Parade" (she had a fine, on-key voice). She taught me printing and script before I turned 4 years old. Together, we prepared sandwiches; crimped raviolis; and rolled potato gnocchi off the tines of a fork (when I was five). When I turned six, she invited me to grow my own little vegetable patch of radishes and string beans. I even planted sweet potato vines in waxed cardboard milk cartons. Mama never refused my requests to invite a girlfriend or two for an overnight when my girlfriends and I would bake the latest Betty Crocker cakes.

My mother cleaned our home from top to bottom; washed windows, standing on a ladder; rotary mowed the lawns; painted window frames, doors and fences.

She and her Singer sewing machine turned out gorgeous outfits for me and her and my girl cousins. She crocheted tablecloths, bedspreads, doilies and knitted sweaters, hats and scarves; she embroidered, tatted and designed needle-point.

And she could re-wire lamps and vacuum cleaner sockets with the best electricians (not to mention her expertise in unclogging sinks!).

The "hand who fed me". Wow!!

Mama (Josephine Capriglione Orlando)
and Marion.

Pasta

SPINACH, CARROT AND GRAPES SALAD
PARMESAN CHEESE DRESSING
POTATO GNOCCHI (heirloom)
or
POTATO CURRY GNOCCHI
BEEF TENDERLOIN IN A NUT CRUST
PECAN PIE

SPINACH, CARROT AND GRAPES SALAD

10 oz. baby spinach, rinsed, drained

1 large carrot, pared, shredded

2 cups red seedless grapes

3 garlic cloves, finely chopped

$\frac{1}{2}$ cup Parmesan or Asiago cheese, coarsely grated

1 cup packaged garlic croutons

Parmesan Cheese Dressing (see page 388)

Prepare Parmesan Cheese dressing and refrigerate until 1 hour prior to use.

In a large salad bowl assemble spinach, grapes, chopped garlic, croutons and shredded carrot. Sprinkle salad with grated cheese. Drizzle dressing over salad and toss it to mix thoroughly. Serves 6.

POTATO GNOCCHI

(A gourmet's touch! Use HOT riced potatoes. I roll the gnocchi off the pebbly side of the cheese grater. My mother preferred rolling them off the concave tines of a fork. Make them in advance and freeze. Spread them on a baking sheet to freeze; then, gather bunches of gnocchi into plastic bags and return to freezer.)

3 lbs. all-purpose potatoes, boiled in jackets

$1\frac{1}{2}$ cups flour

$\frac{1}{2}$ tsp. salt

dash of black pepper

3 eggs, beaten

Marinara Sauce (see pages 398-9)
Parmesan cheese for garnish, grated

(If you prefer, some specialty food stores carry freshly made or frozen gnocchi.)

Boil potatoes in jackets until tender, about 20-30 minutes. While hot, peel off skin from potatoes and press potatoes through a ricer. Add flour, seasonings and eggs. Add more flour if dough is not firm enough (up to a cupful) to hold together. Mix the ingredients thoroughly. Break off small pieces of dough and roll into a ball the size of a cherry. Roll gnocchi off the tines of a fork or use the pebbly side of a cheese grater. (*NOTE: at end of recipe.)

Fill a 6-quart pot with salted water. Bring to a boil. Drop the gnocchi into the boiling water a bunch at a time until they float to top of pot (within minutes). Skim them off the pot with a large slotted spoon into a serving bowl. Pour Marinara Sauce over the gnocchi and serve with grated Parmesan cheese.

*NOTE: Roll gnocchi off the tines of a fork or use the pebbly side of a cheese grater. At this point you may spread formed gnocchi onto a baking sheet and freeze them, uncovered, for 2 or 3 hours. First, sprinkle fine semolina over the baking sheets to prevent gnocchi from sticking to baking sheet. When frozen, divide gnocchi into several small plastic bags and quickly refreeze, up to 2 weeks. When needed, proceed as in above instructions.

POTATO CURRY GNOCCHI
(May be prepared without the sauce and frozen up to 2 weeks.)

3 lbs. all-purpose potatoes, boiled in jackets

1½ cups flour

¼ tsp. salt

¼ tsp. black pepper

1 tsp. curry powder

¼ cup finely chopped parsley

1 sm. onion, finely chopped

3 beaten eggs

semolina for sprinkling surface of baking sheets

Curry Sauce (see page 393)

Prepare Curry Sauce early on the serving day. Boil potatoes in jackets until tender, from 20-30 minutes, depending on size of potatoes. After potatoes are cooked, while still hot, peel off skin; press hot potatoes through a ricer.

Add and combine: onion, flour, seasonings, parsley and beaten eggs. Mix the ingredients thoroughly. Add a little more flour if dough is not firm enough to hold together (up to 1 cupful).

Break off dough, 1 teaspoon at a time, the size of a cherry. Roll the pieces into balls and lay them on a lightly floured board. Roll the gnocchi off the concave tines of a fork; or, roll them off the pebbly side of a cheese grater.

At this point, you may wish to spread the formed gnocchi onto a cookie sheet, lightly sprinkled with semolina to prevent them from sticking to the pan. And freeze the tray(s), uncovered, for several hours. When frozen, divide gnocchi into several 8x10 plastic bags and quickly return them to the freezer (up to 2 weeks).

Before serving, fill a six-quart pot with enough water and 1 teaspoon salt; bring the pot to boil; drop frozen (or fresh) gnocchi into the boiling water, a bunch at a time. Remove them with a slotted spoon as they float to the top of the pot (within a few minutes). Transfer them to a serving bowl. Pour prepared and thoroughly heated Curry Sauce over the gnocchi and serve immediately. Serves 6.

BEEF TENDERLOIN IN A NUT CRUST

a 3 lb. trimmed beef tenderloin roast, center-cut

1 cup filberts, finely ground

1 cup dried cranberries, finely chopped

3 garlic cloves, minced

$\frac{1}{2}$ cup sun-dried tomatoes, finely chopped

$\frac{1}{4}$ cup Parmesan cheese, finely grated

1 tsp. coarsely ground black pepper

$\frac{1}{4}$ cup olive oil

Preheat oven to 425°.

In a small bowl, combine ground filberts, dried cranberries, garlic, sun-dried tomatoes, cheese, black pepper and oil. Spread this mix on a sheet of waxed paper.

Roll the roast in the nut mix; coat entire surface of roast.

Insert a meat thermometer into the thickest part of the beef roast. Place the coated roast on the rack of a shallow roasting pan. Roast the beef, uncovered, in a preheated oven at 425°.
Roast time: 30-40 minutes for medium-rare; 45-50 minutes for medium. The roast is ready when an inserted meat thermometer registers 135° for medium-rare; 150° for medium.

Remove roast to carving board. Allow it to rest for 10 minutes. (Cover roast lightly with foil as it sits.) Carve the roast into slices. Serves 6.

PECAN PIE
(Prepare in advance.)

CRUST: (a single crust to fit into a 9-inch pie pan)
1 pkg. (3 oz.) cream cheese, softened
$\frac{1}{4}$ lb. butter or Smart Balance spread, softened
1 cup flour, plus flour for the board

$\frac{1}{2}$ cup pecan halves to garnish edge of pie

FILLING:
1 cup pecans, chopped
$\frac{3}{4}$ cup dark brown sugar, packed
1 tbsp. butter or Smart Balance spread, melted
3 eggs, beaten or $\frac{3}{4}$ cup egg substitute
1 tbsp. rum or 1 tsp. vanilla extract
pinch of salt

In a bowl, cream softened butter and cream cheese together. Blend in flour and form into a ball. Refrigerate the dough, wrapped in foil, for 12 hours, or overnight.

When ready to bake the pie, add and mix all filling ingredients together. Remove dough from refrigerator and preheat oven to 375°. Lay a sheet of waxed paper on a pastry board and sprinkle waxed paper with flour. Lay dough on the floured paper; flour the rolling pin and roll out a 9 to 10-inch circle of dough, $\frac{1}{8}$-inch thick. Sprinkle rolled pastry with flour.

Gently lift the sheet of waxed paper with the pie crust on it and carefully reverse the crust into the 9-inch pie pan. Peel off the waxed paper and discard it. Gently press the crust to fit into the pan. Flute the edge of the crust, forming it just slightly higher than the edge of the pan.

Pour the filling ingredients into the pie crust, smoothing the top to pack evenly into the pan. Garnish the edge of the pie with pecan halves. Place pie in center of preheated oven and bake it at 375° for 40-50 minutes, or until a thin knife inserted into the center of the pie, removes clean. Serve PECAN PIE, warm or cool or at room temperature. Serves 6-8.

Pasta

PAGLIA E FIENO (STRAW AND HAY)
UNCLE JOE RAINONE'S CRAZY SPAGHETTI
BROCCOLI RABE AND GRILLED SCALLOPS
STRAWBERRY-BANANA RICE PUDDING
HOT COCOA CHOCOLATE SUNDAE

PAGLIA E FIENO (STRAW AND HAY)

1 pkg. (9 oz.) spinach fettuccine
1 pkg. (9 oz.) egg fettuccine
4 tbsp. olive oil, divided
1 lg. onion, finely chopped
4-5 garlic cloves, minced
1 cup sliced white mushrooms

2 cups fresh peas (or use frozen peas, thawed)
1 cup prosciutto, sliced thin into strips
2 cups heavy cream (or fat-free evaporated milk)
$\frac{1}{2}$ tsp. freshly ground black pepper
salt to taste
$\frac{1}{2}$ cup or more, grated Romano cheese

Cook fettuccine al dente (or slightly undercooked) according to directions on package. Drain and keep pasta warm.

Meanwhile, in a skillet, heat 2 tablespoons olive oil on moderate high; sauté onion and garlic in oil until softened. Add mushrooms and sauté until tender. Add peas and prosciutto and sauté another 2 minutes.

Remove skillet from heat; spoon onion mix over fettuccine tossing to coat pasta thoroughly. Cover; keep pasta warm.

In a medium sauce pot, heat cream; stir in remaining oil, pepper and salt until mixture is very warm. Pour over fettuccine mix; sprinkle with cheese and toss to combine. Pour into serving bowl. Serves 6.

Uncle Joe Rainone's
CRAZY SPAGHETTI
(A Version of Paglia e Fieno)

The Barbarottos and their extended families invite us to share in their Uncle Joe's pasta celebration which "hits the spot!". Warning: don't wear a new blouse or shirt.

9 oz. linguine

9 oz. spinach linguine

$\frac{1}{2}$-$\frac{3}{4}$ cup olive oil

1 slice ($\frac{1}{4}$-inch thick) prosciutto, cut into small cubes

1 slice ($\frac{1}{4}$-inch thick) ham, cut into small cubes

1 small garlic HEAD (at least 4-5 cloves, peeled, finely chopped)

4-5 medium-large white mushrooms, washed, sliced

$\frac{1}{2}$ cup black olives, pitted, sliced

1 large Italian green pepper, seeded, chopped

1 qt. low-salt prepared chicken broth

$\frac{1}{4}$ cup marsala wine

(hot red pepper flakes, to taste - optional)

1 cup grated Parmesan cheese

Have ready: a very large pasta serving bowl with rim.

Commence to boil at least 3 quarts salted water for the pasta. Heat olive oil in a 5-quart pot and sauté prosciutto and ham for 3-4 minutes; remove meat with perforated spatula/spoon to a 1-quart bowl. Sauté olives and peppers for a few minutes and remove to same bowl. Sauté mushrooms and garlic for 2-3 minutes. Return meat/olives/peppers mix to the oil/mushroom/garlic pot. Pour and stir in chicken stock. Stir in wine and gently simmer the pot, uncovered, for 30 minutes. Add a sprinkling (to taste) of hot red pepper flakes (optional). Keep pot on very warm burner.

Boil water for linguine and spinach linguine; cook pasta al dente, according to directions on packages. Drain. Pour 1 cup hot broth/vegetable mix into the bottom of a very large serving bowl with a rim. Pour the pasta into the serving bowl and add another cupful of broth mix. Gently toss the pasta with the broth mix.

At serving time, prepare individual pasta portions; ladle $\frac{1}{2}$ cup broth/vegetables over each portion and sprinkle with a generous serving of Parmesan. Serves 8.

BROCCOLI RABE AND GRILLED SCALLOPS

2 lbs. sea scallops, rinsed and drained

1 lb. broccoli rabe, trimmed, washed and drained

2 tbsp. olive oil

3-4 garlic cloves, minced

$\frac{1}{4}$ cup chopped sun-dried tomatoes

$\frac{1}{4}$ cup fresh lemon juice

1 tbsp. grated lemon rind

salt, freshly ground black pepper

a sprinkling hot red pepper flakes (optional)

$\frac{1}{2}$ cup grated Romano cheese

    Parboil broccoli rabe for 5 minutes. Drain. Heat olive oil in large skillet to moderate-high. Stir fry the parboiled broccoli, tomatoes, garlic, lemon juice, rind, salt, pepper and hot pepper flakes for 2-3 minutes.

    Add scallops to skillet and sauté them in the broccoli mix for 2 minutes on each side, or until they are cooked through.

    Spoon the contents of the skillet to a large warmed serving platter. Sprinkle with Romano cheese. Serve hot. Serves 6.

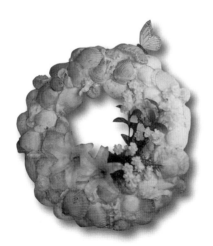

STRAWBERRY-BANANA RICE PUDDING
(Prepare a day in advance.)

1½ cups milk (or fat-free evaporated milk),
    heat until warm

1 cup cooked white rice, drained

2 tbsp. sugar

2 eggs, separated

¼ tsp. nutmeg

1 tsp. lemon rind, grated

1 tsp. vanilla extract

½ cup thinly sliced bananas

½ cup sliced strawberries

(extra banana slices and whole strawberries
    for garnish)

(extra nutmeg for garnish)

Preheat oven 400°.

Coat a 2-quart casserole glass (Pyrex) heat-resistant bowl with butter or Smart Balance spread.

In a large bowl blend 1 cup cooked rice with beaten egg yolks and 1½ cups heated milk. Stir in and blend thoroughly: rind, vanilla, nutmeg and sugar. Stir in bananas and strawberries. Beat egg whites until they hold stiff peaks. Fold them into rice mix.

Pour pudding into a greased heat-resistant glass bowl. Place the bowl to sit in a pan of hot water, and bake the pudding in a preheated oven 400° for 40-45 minutes. Top of pudding will be light-brown and an inserted toothpick will test clean. Sprinkle with nutmeg and garnish with banana slices and whole strawberries. Serve warm or chilled. Serves 6.

HOT COCOA CHOCOLATE SUNDAE
(The following recipe is measured for a single 8 oz. serving.)

3 tbsp. cocoa – select a quality cocoa, like Ghirardelli or Droste

4 oz. water

4 oz. low-fat or fat-free milk

1 heaping tbsp. vanilla or chocolate ice cream

1 chocolate swizzle stick

Add water and milk in a teapot with a removable lid. Stir in cocoa. Heat the cocoa mix on moderate-high, stirring occasionally, until liquid is very hot, but not simmering, and all of the cocoa has been incorporated. Spoon a small ball of ice cream into a 12 ounce mug; insert a chocolate swizzle stick into the ice cream; slowly pour hot cocoa into the cup. M-m-m.

Pasta

CICORIA AND AVOCADO SALAD
LEMON-OIL DRESSING
SEA SHELLS (MARUZZELLE), SHRIMP AND BROCCOLI IN RED PEPPER SAUCE
MARY LOU'S APPLE-PUMPKIN PECAN BREAD
CANTALOUPE SUNDAE

CICORIA AND AVOCADO SALAD

1-2 bunches chicory (or frisée) – about 5 cups, trimmed, rinsed, drained, cut bite-size
2 medium-size ripe avocadoes, peeled, cubed, sprinkled with lemon juice
6 plum tomatoes, rinsed, cut into $\frac{1}{2}$-inch rounds

Lemon-Oil Dressing (see page 385)

Prepare dressing and refrigerate it until 1 hour before serving.

In a large salad bowl, combine cicoria, avocadoes and tomatoes. Just before serving, add the dressing. Toss salad to combine thoroughly. Serves 6.

SEA SHELLS (MARUZZELLE), SHRIMP AND BROCCOLI IN RED PEPPER SAUCE
(Prepare Red Pepper Sauce in advance.)

1-1½ lbs. maruzzelle pasta (large shells)
1 lb. ex. large uncooked shrimp in shells;
    rinse shrimp under cold water, cut out vein, drain, do not peel
3 cups broccoli florets
1 tbsp. finely chopped onion
1 garlic clove, finely chopped
1 tbsp. olive oil for each skillet

Red Pepper Sauce (see page 402)

Prepare Red Pepper Sauce a day or two in advance. When needed, reheat the sauce thoroughly, on low-simmer. Set water to boil pasta in a large pot.

Heat oil in a large skillet, at medium-high and lightly brown onion and garlic scraping bottom of pan to loosen food particles.

Add broccoli florets and stir fry them for a few minutes.

Heat oil in another skillet, and sauté shrimp in shells for a few minutes on both sides, until shells are opaque.

Pour the cooked shrimp and broccoli mix into the simmering sauce; cook the mix for another 2 minutes to blend the flavors. Keep the sauce very warm.

Meanwhile cook pasta as directed on package. Drain maruzzelle thoroughly and pour the pasta into a large serving bowl. Ladle the shrimp-broccoli-red pepper sauce into the cooked pasta; toss with 2 spoons to mix thoroughly. Ladle more sauce with shrimp and broccoli over top of bowl. Serve immediately. Peel the shrimp as you eat them. Provide small saucers to discard the shells. Serves 6.

MARY LOU'S APPLE-PUMPKIN PECAN BREAD

1 cup sugar

1 tsp. baking soda

$\frac{1}{4}$ tsp. baking powder

$\frac{1}{2}$ tsp. cinnamon

$\frac{1}{4}$ tsp. each: ginger, ground cloves, nutmeg

$\frac{1}{2}$ tsp. salt

$1\frac{2}{3}$ cups unsifted flour

$\frac{1}{2}$ cup canola oil

1 cup cooked pumpkin
    (or use canned pure pumpkin)

2 Macintosh apples, cored, pared, cubed

$\frac{1}{2}$ cup chopped pecans

$\frac{1}{2}$ cup dried cranberry raisins

2 eggs, unbeaten

Preheat oven to 325°.

Grease a 5x7-inch loaf pan.

Combine dry ingredients in a large bowl (sugar, baking powder, baking soda, spices and flour). Add oil, pumpkin, cubed apples and eggs and stir until just mixed. Stir in nuts and cranberry raisins. Pour batter into prepared, greased 5x7-inch loaf pan. Bake bread for 1 hour and 15 minutes, or until a tested toothpick removes clean. Allow bread to cool thoroughly before removing from pan. Serves 6-8.

CANTALOUPE SUNDAE

1 lg. or 2 small ripe cantaloupe melons, skin washed, cut into 6-8 circles, 1-inch thick

1 cup blackberries (or blueberries) rinsed, drained

1 cup cherries, rinsed and drained

6-8 portions vanilla bean ice cream ($\frac{1}{2}$ cup each)

sprigs of mint for garnish

Have ready: 6-8 dessert plates. Pare the skin from melon rounds. Lay one thick melon circle on each plate.

Prepare berries and cherries; rinse and drain mint sprigs. At serving, add a portion ($\frac{1}{2}$ cup) of ice cream in the center of each melon circle. Sprinkle each plate with berries and cherries; add a sprig of mint for garnish. Serves 6-8.

Pasta

RAW VEGETABLES WITH LEMON AND OLIVE OIL
LEMON-OIL DRESSING
FETTUCCINE CARBONARA
ALMOND CHERRY CAKE

RAW VEGETABLES WITH LEMON AND OLIVE OIL

1 bunch broccoli (about 3 cups florets), trimmed, rinsed, drained
1 small head orange cauliflower (about 3 cups florets), trimmed, rinsed, drained
about 1 dozen very slender carrots with greens, pared, rinsed, leave a little greens at ends of carrots
1 dozen grape tomatoes, rinsed, drained

Lemon-Oil Dressing (see page 385)

Prepare dressing in advance. Refrigerate until one hour prior to using.

Arrange broccoli florets, cauliflower florets, carrots and tomatoes in sections, around a large sectioned serving dish. Refrigerate platter with a layer of plastic wrap over the plate, if preparing more then one hour before serving. Leave center section empty; use for dressing.

Before serving, pour dressing into a bowl and place in center section of round sectioned vegetable plate. Serves 6-8.

FETTUCCINE CARBONARA

two 9 oz. packages fettuccine, cooked according to directions on package

6-8 slices prosciutto, shredded

1 tbsp. olive oil

$\frac{1}{2}$ cup chopped scallions (include some tender green tops)

$\frac{1}{2}$ cup Chablis or dry white wine

$1\frac{1}{2}$ cups heavy cream or fat-free evaporated milk

1 cup mixed: Romano, Asiago, Parmesan cheeses

$\frac{3}{4}$ cup egg substitute

$\frac{1}{4}$ cup chopped parsley

$\frac{1}{2}$ tsp. freshly grated black pepper

(salt to taste)

While pasta cooks, sauté prosciutto and scallions in oil until light brown. Pour off all but $\frac{1}{4}$ cup of fat and stir in wine. Simmer mix for 5 minutes.

Add 1 cup cream and cheese mix and cook while stirring, until mix starts to bubble and sauce begins to thicken.

Combine remaining $\frac{1}{2}$ cup cream with egg substitute, parsley and pepper (and salt). Stir into sauce; remove from heat and pour sauce into fettuccine. Toss to mix thoroughly. Serves 6.

ALMOND CHERRY CAKE

3 cups canned sour cherries, drained and pitted; reserve the juice

½ cup blanched almonds, finely ground in food processor

1 cup plus 2 tbsp. flour

1 tsp. baking powder

¼ tsp. salt

¾ cup butter or Smart Balance spread, softened

½ cup plus 1 tbsp. sugar

3 lg. eggs, separated

1 tsp. vanilla extract

½ tsp. almond extract

confectioners' sugar

½ cup fresh cherries for garnish

Preheat oven 375°.

Butter a 9x12-inch pan; then line the pan with buttered waxed paper and dust with flour.

In a medium bowl, thoroughly blend flour, baking powder, ground almonds and salt.

In a bowl with electric mixer, cream butter with ½ cup sugar until mixture is light and fluffy. Add egg yolks, 1 at a time, beating well after each addition; stir in the flour mix, vanilla and almond extracts and reserved cherry juice.

In another clean bowl with electric mixer and clean beaters, beat egg whites until they hold stiff peaks. Stir one-fourth of the beaten whites into the yellow batter and gently fold in the remaining whites.

Turn the batter into the prepared pan, smoothing the top of the pan. Arrange cherries evenly on top of batter, slightly pressing them into the batter. Sprinkle cherries with the remaining 1 tablespoon granulated sugar.

Bake the cake in the center of oven at 375° for 30-35 minutes, or until tester returns clean. Cool cake in pan for 10 minutes on rack. Invert cake onto a large plate; place a second plate over the inverted cake; then, return the cake upright onto the second plate. (Cherries on top.)

Dust the cake with confectioners' sugar at serving time and garnish with fresh cherries. Serve the cake warm or at room temperature. Serves 6-8.

Pasta

A Delicious Remembrance from Filomena Ramaglia, Our "Kitchen Bouquet"

(submitted by the Ramaglia Sisters: Rose, Evelyn and Joan)

Filomena Ramaglia.

In the days before our parents had a telephone, it was not unusual for relatives and friends to drop by our home, unannounced, around 4 p.m. and still be there at dinner time. Our mom, Filomena Ramaglia, our "Kitchen Bouquet", generated an aroma of her fine cooking and baking which made our house, a home.

We never saw our mother panic about what she would feed everyone. Never perplexed, she would create mouth-watering menus around such staples as eggs, potatoes, onions, fried peppers, eggplant marinara, tomato sauce, mixed salads, and a loaf of Italian bread. She could always cook a peasant dish out of cauliflower, broccoli or escarole – and some pasta. We all know "Italians LOVE you with their food". Everyone ate.

The following menu has been created around just a few of her many recipes. Buon Appetito!

Rose Ramaglia Barbarotto
Evelyn Ramaglia Paladino
Joan Ramaglia Romano

Joan Romano, Evelyn Paladino and Rose Barbarotto.

Pasta

'SCAROLA E MARUZZELLE (ESCAROLE AND SHELLS)
STUFFED GREEN FRYING PEPPERS
EGGPLANT CROQUETTES MARINARA
WALNUTS

'SCAROLA E MARUZZELLE (ESCAROLE AND SHELLS)

1 lb. large shells pasta, cooked as directed on package, drained
lg. head escarole, trimmed, washed, drained, torn into small pieces
    (discard tough outer leaves)
2 medium-size potatoes, peeled, cubed
2 tbsp. extra-virgin olive oil
2 fresh ripe plum tomatoes, diced
1 onion, diced
2 large garlic cloves, minced
1 tbsp. fresh parsley leaves, chopped
$1\frac{1}{2}$ cups reserved water from cooking escarole and potatoes
1 cup chicken broth, homemade (or use less-salt prepared variety)
a few leaves fresh basil (or 1 tbsp. dried basil)
salt, black pepper to taste
$\frac{1}{2}$ cup grated Parmesan cheese

Eva Rose (Great-granddaughter of
Catherine and Al Shea and
Rose and Buzz Barbarotto.)

    In a large 4-quart pot, bring 3 cups water to a boil; add escarole and potatoes. Cover the pot and simmer vegetables for 12-15 minutes, until fork tender; drain and reserve 2 cups of the vegetable stock in a bowl. Leave escarole in pot and set aside.
    In a large skillet, heat oil; add and sauté onion and garlic. Add diced tomatoes, parsley, basil, salt and pepper. Stir in reserved water and chicken broth. Cook tomato mix on medium heat, uncovered, for 15 minutes or until tomatoes soften. Transfer tomato stew to pot with escarole. Add the cooked shells and gently stir to mix. Serve very warm in a large bowl. Generously sprinkle with grated cheese.
Serves 6.

STUFFED GREEN FRYING PEPPERS

6 large Italian frying peppers

(Select large fryers with stems attached. Rinse peppers and wipe dry. Cut off tops of peppers with stems still attached. You will need these stemmed tops to cap the stuffed peppers. REMOVE SEEDS WITHOUT BREAKING PEPPERS.)

2 oz. (1 can) flat anchovy in oil, finely chopped (reserve oil)

5 slices white bread; wet bread in water and squeeze bread to remove excess water;

then, crumb the bread, (set bowl of wet crumbs aside)

1 medium-size ripe red tomato; skinned and diced; include juice (* NOTE: below)

1 large garlic clove, minced

$\frac{1}{4}$ cup grated Pecorino Romano cheese

1 tsp. dried parsley

black pepper to taste

oil for drizzling

*NOTE: HOW TO SKIN A TOMATO
1. wash tomato
2. immerse tomato in boiling water for 1 minute
3. remove tomato from boiling water and plunge it into cold water
4. peel off skin with fingers

Preheat oven to 350°.

In a medium-size bowl, combine wet, squeezed bread which you've crumbled, diced tomato, garlic, chopped anchovy in a little oil, cheese, parsley and black pepper. If mixture is too dry, add a little water (not runny); if mixture is too wet, add a small amount of crumbled bread.

Stuff peppers with anchovy-bread mix, leaving just enough room to press caps into the tops of peppers to hold stuffing in place.

Lay stuffed peppers in an oiled baking pan, 9x12 inches. Drizzle peppers with a little olive oil and bake them in a preheated oven at 350° for 30 minutes, or until peppers are lightly browned on top.

Our family enjoyed these peppers best at room temperature. If cooked a day or two before, remove peppers from refrigerator at least 3 hours before serving them at room temperature. (Or serve when first prepared.) Serves 6.

EGGPLANT CROQUETTES MARINARA

3 medium-size eggplants (about 1 lb. each), skinned, cubed
3 slices soft white or wheat bread, finely crumbled
2 garlic cloves, minced
2 large eggs, beaten
$\frac{1}{2}$ cup grated Romano cheese
2 tbsp. olive oil
2 cups prepared Marinara Sauce
$\frac{1}{2}$ cup water
1 cup unseasoned Italian bread crumbs
1 tbsp. fresh parsley, minced
salt, black pepper to taste
fresh basil leaves

Heat oil in skillet and sauté cubed eggplant and garlic at low-medium for about 10 minutes. Gradually add and stir in the water as you cook the eggplant. Remove skillet from burner and set aside.

In a medium-size bowl, combine finely crumbled bread, beaten eggs, cheese, parsley, salt and pepper. Stir in cooked eggplant mix and thoroughly blend. With the aid of a tablespoon, scoop up portions of the mix to form 2-inch balls or croquettes.

Pour 1 cup unseasoned Italian bread crumbs on a sheet of waxed pepper. Coat the croquettes with crumbs.

In the same skillet used to sauté the eggplant, warm the oil (you may have to add a little more oil); fry the croquettes on all sides until light golden brown. Drain on paper towels.

Scrape the bottom of the skillet and stir in prepared Marinara Sauce. Drop the eggplant balls into the sauce and simmer on low heat for 7-10 minutes. Add fresh basil leaves at serving. Serves 6.

WALNUTS

(This Italian-style cookie is typical of the sweets, "Dolci", you would serve at a wedding party. The bride and groom would visit guests at their tables and they'd wheel a cart, laden with the "guantiera", a serving tray, and its "Dolci".)

$1\frac{1}{2}$ cups butter or Smart Balance spread

$1\frac{1}{2}$ cups confectioners' sugar

3 cups flour (in this recipe try using 2 cups enriched all-purpose flour mixed
    with 1 cup whole wheat flour)

pinch of salt

2 tsp. almond or walnut extract

$1\frac{1}{2}$ cups ground walnuts

$\frac{1}{2}$ tsp. nutmeg

1 tsp. cinnamon

$\frac{1}{4}$ tsp. ground cloves

3 ungreased 9x15-inch cookie pans

2 cups confectioners' sugar for coating

Beat and cream confectioners' sugar with butter in a large mixing bowl. Add and stir in: salt, spices and extract. Mix flour, one cup at a time, into the butter mix; add and mix in ground nuts.

Knead the dough until smooth and form into a ball. Wrap the dough ball in plastic and refrigerate it for 1 hour. Preheat oven to 350°.

Break off pieces of the dough, one tablespoon at a time; roll the pieces between your hands to form walnut-size balls. Lay the "walnuts" on 3 ungreased cookie pans, about 20 cookies per pan and bake them, one pan at a time, in the center of a preheated oven, at 350° for 12-13 minutes. Cookies should appear lightly tanned on their bottoms.

Transfer the cookies to a clean tray; when they are thoroughly cooled, dredge them into a bowl of confectioners' sugar. May be stored in foil lasagna pans, in layers, separated by waxed paper; wrap the pans in aluminum foil. Store Walnuts in a cool place for 1 month, or freeze for several months. Makes about 60 Walnuts.

Pasta

PLUM TOMATO SAILBOATS
PASTA PRIMAVERA
CHOCOLATE PEANUT BUTTER CUPCAKES

PLUM TOMATO SAILBOATS

1 doz. plum tomatoes, rinsed, drained

1 doz. 1-inch mozzarella balls in water, drained

$1\frac{1}{2}$ doz. large basil leaves, rinsed, patted dry with paper towels

12 wood sandwich picks

6-8 large leaves, Boston lettuce, rinsed, drained

$\frac{1}{4}$ cup extra-virgin olive oil, a sprinkling of dried oregano, freshly ground pepper

Prepare a 15-inch platter by laying a bed of lettuce leaves over the platter.

Cut out a 1-inch triangle across the length of one side of each plum tomato (save the tomato triangles in a small bowl and set aside). With a teaspoon, scoop out seeds from the tomatoes. Fit 1 mozzarella ball into each triangle and arrange the filled tomatoes on the bed of lettuce, leaving a small space in the center of the platter to fit the small bowl of tomato triangles.

Knit a toothpick into a large basil leaf, and insert the "sail" into one of the mozzarella balls, sitting in a plum tomato. Repeat this process with the basil leaves and picks until each tomato boat has its sail. Chop the remaining 6 basil leaves and combine them with the tomato triangles in the small bowl. Set the bowl in the center of the platter.

Drizzle all of the sailboats with olive oil; sprinkle oregano; grind black pepper over the entire platter. Serve with small chunks of crusty Italian bread. Serves 6-8.

PASTA PRIMAVERA

$1\frac{1}{2}$ cups broccoli, chopped into small pieces

$1\frac{1}{2}$ cups tiny frozen peas, thawed

1 cup sliced zucchini; scrape the skin; rinse

8-10 asparagus stalks; or slice 6 thick stalks, lengthwise

1 red pepper, seeded, thinly sliced

4 tbsp. olive oil

3 plum tomatoes, chopped

4 garlic cloves, minced

$\frac{1}{4}$ cup parsley, chopped

$\frac{1}{2}$ tsp. salt

$\frac{1}{2}$ tsp. freshly ground black pepper

$\frac{1}{3}$ cup pignola (pine nuts)

1 cup white mushrooms, thinly sliced

two 9 oz. pkg. linguine

1 cup heavy cream or fat-free evaporated milk

$\frac{1}{2}$ cup grated Romano cheese

$\frac{1}{4}$ cup torn basil leaves

In a large bowl, pour boiling water over a mix of broccoli, peas, zucchini, asparagus and red pepper. Let stand for 5 minutes. Rinse vegetables under cold water and drain. Set aside.

Heat 4 tablespoons olive oil in a large skillet and sauté tomatoes, garlic, nuts, parsley, salt and pepper for a few minutes; add mushrooms and blanched vegetables and stir-fry the mix for several minutes, until asparagus are barely tender.

Boil 6 quarts water and cook linguine according to directions on package. Drain the pasta and pour it into a large serving bowl. Add cream, cheese and basil and toss to coat pasta evenly; spoon vegetables over the pasta and toss again to mix. Serves 6.

CHOCOLATE PEANUT BUTTER CUPCAKES

1 cup flour

$1\frac{1}{2}$ tsp. baking powder

$\frac{1}{8}$ tsp. salt

$\frac{1}{2}$ cup firmly packed dark brown sugar

$\frac{1}{4}$ cup chunky peanut butter

3 tbsp. butter or Smart Balance spread, softened

1 large egg or $\frac{1}{4}$ cup egg substitute

$\frac{1}{2}$ tsp. almond extract

$\frac{1}{2}$ cup evaporated milk (fat-free available)

1 cup semisweet chocolate morsels

ICING:

$\frac{1}{4}$ cup evaporated milk (fat-free available)

$\frac{3}{4}$ cup semisweet chocolate morsels

Preheat oven 350°.

Prepare $\frac{1}{2}$-cup muffin tins, enough for 12 muffins, medium-size. Line muffin cups with paper liners. In a small bowl, combine flour, baking powder and salt. In another bowl, with electric mixer, cream together: brown sugar, peanut butter and butter; beat in the egg and almond extract. Beat in the flour mix, alternating with $\frac{1}{2}$ cup evaporated milk, beating thoroughly after each addition; stir in 1 cup chocolate morsels.

Divide the batter among the prepared muffin cups and bake them in the center of preheated oven, 350° for 20-25 minutes, or until a toothpick removes clean. Allow the cupcakes to cool completely.

Prepare the ICING. In a small saucepan, combine $\frac{3}{4}$ cup of chocolate morsels and $\frac{1}{4}$ cup evaporated milk. Heat the pan over water until chocolate morsels soften. Whisk this mixture until smooth. Cool icing completely; then, whisk it until light and fluffy. Spread the icing on tops of cupcakes. Makes 1 dozen cupcakes.

Pasta

CATHERINE'S ORIENTAL CHICKEN SALAD
ZITI AL FORNO (heirloom)
GRACE GAMMONE'S RAINBOW PETIT-FOURS (VENETIANS)

CATHERINE'S ORIENTAL CHICKEN SALAD

14 oz. packaged fresh baby spinach, rinsed, drained

1 can (11 oz.) mandarin oranges, drained

1 small red onion, thinly sliced in rings

4 medium skinless, boneless, thin-sliced chicken breasts,
     rinse, dry with paper towels

1 red pepper, seeded, thinly sliced in strips

$\frac{1}{4}$ cup roasted sesame seeds (*NOTE: in instructions)

MARINADE:

$\frac{1}{4}$ cup soy sauce (*lite* variety available)

1 tbsp. canola oil

1 tbsp. honey

1 tsp. 5-spice powder

2 garlic cloves, minced

$\frac{1}{4}$ tsp. powdered ginger

DRESSING:

$\frac{1}{4}$ cup rice wine vinegar

1 tbsp. soy sauce (*lite* variety)

3 garlic cloves, minced

$\frac{1}{4}$ cup olive oil

Combine all marinade ingredients in a wide bowl. Add chicken to cover. Place chicken in marinade into refrigerator for 20 minutes. (Discard marinade before proceeding with the recipe instructions.)

Preheat grill to moderate. Lay marinated chicken on grill and cook until chicken juices run clear, turning chicken over several times to cook on both sides. Remove chicken to glass board to cool.

Meanwhile prepare the dressing in a small bowl or jar. Combine and whisk dressing ingredients. Set aside.

In a large salad bowl, combine washed and drained spinach, oranges, onion, pepper.

Slice the cooled chicken into narrow strips and add to salad bowl.

*NOTE: Scatter sesame seeds into a small skillet and toast them lightly in a preheated oven at 250° (just for a few minutes). Sprinkle toasted sesame seeds over salad mix in bowl. Drizzle all of the dressing over the salad and toss to mix thoroughly. Serves 6.

ZITI AL FORNO

(Prepare several days in advance, up to baking, and freeze or refrigerate. Shred and add the mozzarella cheese before baking. Prepare sauce several days in advance and either refrigerate or freeze.)

$1\frac{1}{2}$ to 2 lbs. ziti, cooked al dente, drained

1 lb. ricotta
1 tbsp. chopped parsley
1 cup grated Parmesan cheese

4-6 cups Chopped Beef Sauce (see page 397)
1 lb. mozzarella, cubed
more Parmesan cheese, grated (about 1 cup)

Prepare the Chopped Beef Sauce. Set aside.

Cook the ziti pasta; drain. Pour the cooked pasta into a 6-quart bowl. Add 1 cup sauce, 1 cup Parmesan, ricotta, parsley. Mix thoroughly. Turn into a 9x15x4 baking pan. Top with 2 cups sauce, more Parmesan and the mozzarella cubes.

When ready to bake, preheat oven to 350° and cook for 30 minutes or until sauce bubbles and cheese melts. Serve with remaining sauce, thoroughly heated. Serves 8.

GRACE GAMMONE'S RAINBOW PETIT-FOURS (VENETIANS)
(Prepare several days in advance of serving date.)

(Grace and Danny, her husband of 60 years, have been dear friends who have shared our dedication and devotion to the New York Islanders hockey team, NHL. For many Christmases, we also shared our baking treats with each other.)

1 can (12$\frac{1}{2}$ oz.) almond filling

1 cup (2 sticks) butter, softened at room temperature

1 cup granulated sugar

4 large egg yolks

4 large egg whites

2 cups sifted flour

20 drops red food coloring

12 drops green food coloring

$\frac{1}{4}$ cup seedless red raspberry jam

$\frac{1}{4}$ cup apricot preserves

1 pkg. (6 oz.) semisweet chocolate chips

3 pans, 6$\frac{1}{2}$ x10$\frac{1}{2}$ inches (Grease the pans and line them with waxed paper to fit.
     Then, lightly grease the waxed paper.)

Preheat oven to 350°.

In a large bowl, mix almond filling, butter, sugar and egg yolks; beat with electric mixer until fluffy. With a wooden spoon, beat flour into butter mix.

In another bowl, whip egg whites with clean beaters of an electric mixer until the whites form stiff peaks. Fold egg whites into butter-egg yolk mixture.

Separate this batter into three bowls, about 1$\frac{1}{2}$ cups each. Into one bowl, add 20 drops of red food color and mix thoroughly; into second bowl add 12 drops green food color and mix thoroughly; the third bowl of batter remains uncolored.

Bake the prepared pans at 350° for 12 minutes.

(Continued on next page)

(Continued from previous page)

Remove pans to cutting board and cool the layers. *When layers are thoroughly cooled, gently peel off the waxed paper before spreading the toppings on each of the layers.*

Invert the green layer onto a large plate (which will fit in refrigerator); spread raspberry jam over the top. Cover this green layer with the uncolored layer; spread apricot preserves over the uncolored layer. Top both layers with the red layer.

Wrap the formed rainbow cake in plastic wrap and refrigerate it overnight.

Next day, melt chocolate chips in the top pot of a small double boiler; pour 1 cup water into bottom pot. Bring the water to a low simmer and melt the chocolate in the top pot, stirring the chocolate occasionally.

When the chocolate is melted, spread it over the top of the rainbow cake. Cool the cake thoroughly; cut it into squares, about 2x2 inches. Gently, with a thin spatula, remove the petit-fours to an attractive serving plate (lined with a paper doily). Store loosely, covered in plastic, at room temperature. Makes about 45 petit-fours.

Pasta

SANTA FE SARDINE SALAD

HONEY MUSTARD DRESSING

BROCCOLI RABE, GNOCCHI AND SALMON

MACADAMIA CUPCAKES WITH ORANGE ICING (See page 261)

TRAY OF MELON SLICES (See page 227)

SANTA FE SARDINE SALAD

(Prepare dressing ahead of time.)

6 cups baby spinach, washed, drained

1 can (1 lb.) black beans, rinsed in cold water, drained

1 lg. avocado, peeled, sliced (discard stone)

1 tin ($4\frac{1}{2}$ oz.) sardines in water, no-salt added, drained

1 large carrot, pared, shredded

3 plum tomatoes (each cut into 4 wedges)

Hungarian paprika

1 lemon, cut into 6 wedges for garnish

Honey Mustard Dressing (see page 384)

Prepare dressing in advance and refrigerate dressing until 1 hour before serving.

Lay a bed of spinach on each of 6 large salad plates (preferably glass). If you have time, chill plates in fridge $\frac{1}{2}$ hour prior to assembling salad.

Divide and pour beans over spinach on each plate. Sprinkle beans with paprika to taste. Decorate the edge of each plate with avocado slices, tomato wedges and sardines; strew shredded carrot over the salads. Vigorously shake dressing and sprinkle generously over salads. Add a lemon wedge to each plate for garnish. Corn bread with rye seeds makes a tasty addition. Serves 6.

BROCCOLI RABE, GNOCCHI AND SALMON

$1\frac{1}{2}$ lbs. wild salmon fillet, skin removed; brush with olive oil/balsamic vinegar

$1\frac{1}{2}$ lbs. broccoli rabe (rapini), trimmed, washed, drained

1-2 large roasting red peppers (see page 148 for directions: "How to Roast Peppers")

6 garlic cloves, peeled

1 lb. potato gnocchi, homemade (see page 349); or packaged

4 tbsp. olive oil

$\frac{1}{4}$ tsp. black pepper

$\frac{1}{2}$ tsp. salt

sprinkling of hot red pepper flakes (to taste)

$\frac{1}{2}$ cup grated Asiago cheese

Have ready: large flat platter; preheat oven 400°.

Roast coated salmon at 400° for 25-30 minutes. Cover salmon lightly with foil and keep in warming oven.

Roast red pepper(s) according to directions on page 148. Peel skin off peppers; slice them in strips and set aside. Grate cheese; set aside. Steam trimmed and cleaned broccoli rabe and garlic cloves in 1 cup boiling water for 12-15 minutes. Halfway through steaming the rapini, cook the gnocchi in a 6-quart pot of rapidly boiling water. Transfer gnocchi with slotted spoon, to the center of the platter as they rise to top of pasta pot. Transfer warm salmon to serving plate around the gnocchi; drain rapini/garlic and transfer to the serving platter to surround the salmon. Sprinkle the platter with salt, pepper, hot pepper flakes, grated cheese and olive oil. Garnish with strips of red pepper. Serve while hot. Serves 6.

For DESSERT:

MACADAMIA CUPCAKES WITH ORANGE ICING (See page 261)

TRAY OF MELON SLICES (See page 227)

Pasta

CARROT SALAD
APPLE CIDER DRESSING
WHOLE WHEAT PENNE WITH WALNUTS
CHOCOLATE CUPCAKES WITH BUTTERSCOTCH ICING

CARROT SALAD

6 medium-size carrots, pared, shredded

1 small red onion, finely sliced

1 tbsp. fresh parsley, chopped

$\frac{1}{2}$ cup dried cranberries

1 head romaine lettuce, trimmed, rinsed, drained

Apple Cider Dressing (see page 390)

Prepare dressing in advance and refrigerate until 1 hour before serving.

Line sides of deep salad bowl with romaine lettuce, root side at bottom of bowl.

In a mixing bowl, combine shredded carrots, onion, parsley and cranberries. Pour $\frac{1}{2}$ cup of Apple Cider Dressing over salad. Toss salad to mix thoroughly; carefully pour the salad mix into the lettuce lined salad bowl. Drizzle a little more dressing over salad. Serves 6.

WHOLE WHEAT PENNE WITH WALNUTS

1 lb. whole wheat penne rigati pasta

6 small baby bella mushrooms, scrubbed, sliced thin

1 small onion, chopped

3-4 garlic cloves, chopped

1 long Italian spicy green pepper, seeded, thinly sliced into rounds

1 cup chopped walnuts

5-6 torn basil leaves

2 tbsp. olive oil

$\frac{1}{4}$ cup dry white wine

$\frac{1}{2}$ cup grated Parmesan cheese

salt, freshly ground black pepper to taste

    In a 2-quart sauce pot with cover, at moderate heat, cook onion and garlic in oil; stir in pepper and cook for 1 minute; stir in sliced mushrooms and walnuts and cook for 1 minute longer. Stir in basil leaves, salt, pepper and wine. Cook for 2 minutes. Set aside.

    Prepare pasta according to package directions. Drain and pour pasta into a large serving bowl. Retain about $\frac{1}{2}$ cupful of pasta water with the pasta. Pour walnuts/wine sauce over the cooked penne. Toss well to mix. Sprinkle with cheese. Serves 6.

CHOCOLATE CUPCAKES WITH BUTTERSCOTCH ICING

$\frac{1}{3}$ cup cocoa
$\frac{1}{2}$ cup boiling water
1 cup flour
$\frac{1}{2}$ tsp. baking soda
$\frac{1}{8}$ tsp. salt
6 tbsp. butter or Smart Balance spread, softened
$\frac{1}{2}$ cup sugar
2 large eggs or $\frac{1}{2}$ cup egg substitute

ICING:
$\frac{3}{4}$ cup butterscotch morsels
$\frac{1}{4}$ cup evaporated milk (fat-free available)

Preheat oven to 350°.

Line 12 muffins cups ($\frac{1}{2}$ cup size) with paper liners.

In a small bowl stir and whisk together until well dissolved: cocoa and boiling water. Bring to room temperature.

In a bowl, combine flour, baking soda, salt.

In another bowl with electric mixer, cream together butter and sugar; beat in eggs, until mix is combined. Beat in cocoa mixture alternately with flour mix, beating well after each addition.

Divide batter among 12 lined muffin cups. Bake in center of preheated oven 350° for 25-30 minutes, or until toothpick tests clean. Cool muffins completely.

Prepare the ICING.

In a small saucepot, combine butterscotch chips and evaporated milk. Heat over hot water until chips start to melt and milk is hot. Whisk mixture until smooth. Cool icing completely; then, whisk icing until it is fluffy. Spread icing over each cupcake. Makes 12 cupcakes.

Pasta

BEET AND CHICORY SALAD
FETTUCCINE WITH SPINACH WALNUT PESTO SAUCE
APPLE CRUMB CAKE

BEET AND CHICORY SALAD

15-18 small-medium fresh beets, trimmed, scrubbed, steamed, peeled and sliced

    Beets should be uniform in size. If steaming, be certain to use a large enough pot surface to spread beets in one or two layers. Water in bottom pot should reach at least half-way up the side of pot. Steamed beets will cook between 30-40 minutes depending on size. (Small-medium size: 25-30 minutes.) Or you may pressure cook beets: 12 minutes (small) to 18 minutes (large). Or, you may use 4 cups sliced canned or jarred unseasoned beets in water. Drain water.

1 lg. onion, sliced thin
$\frac{1}{2}$ cup orange juice
1 tbsp. grated orange rind
1 tbsp. chopped parsley
2 tbsp. extra-virgin olive oil
2 tbsp. red wine vinegar
$\frac{1}{4}$ tsp. black pepper, salt to taste

1 bunch chicory, trimmed, rinsed, drained

    Chill cleaned chicory in a bowl in refrigerator for 1 hour. Line 6 individual salad plates with chicory. In a large bowl thoroughly combine sliced beets, onion, parsley, orange juice, rind, olive oil, vinegar, pepper and salt. Spoon $\frac{1}{2}$ cupful onto each prepared salad plate. Serves 6.

FETTUCCINE WITH SPINACH WALNUT PESTO SAUCE

two 9 oz. pkg. spinach fettuccine; follow cooking directions on package

SPINACH WALNUT PESTO SAUCE:
8-10 garlic cloves
1 cup walnuts, shelled
3 cups spinach leaves, packed (no stems)
1 cup parsley (no stems)
$\frac{1}{4}$ cup basil leaves, packed
$\frac{1}{2}$ tsp. black pepper
$\frac{1}{4}$ tsp. salt
$\frac{1}{2}$ cup sun-dried tomatoes, cut into strips
1 cup olive oil
1 cup grated Romano cheese
($\frac{1}{4}$ cup of warm water to thin sauce, if needed)

In a 2-quart food processor bowl, combine the first seven of the spinach-walnut pesto sauce ingredients, one ingredient at a time (from garlic to salt). Turn machine on and off until mixture combines. Add the oil slowly in a thin stream.

Add cheese, blending until mixture has a uniform consistency. Add about $\frac{1}{4}$ cup warm water to pesto to thin the sauce, slightly. Stir in sun-dried tomato strips. Spoon over pasta; toss to mix. Serves 6.

APPLE CRUMB CAKE

(May be prepared a day or two in advance. Refrigerate.)

$\frac{1}{2}$ cup butter or Smart Balance spread, softened

$\frac{2}{3}$ cup sugar

2 large eggs or $\frac{1}{2}$ cup egg substitute

1 cup flour

$\frac{3}{4}$ tsp. baking powder

$\frac{1}{2}$ tsp. salt

4 lg. Granny Smith apples, pared, cored, sliced thin

TOPPING:

1 cup flour

$\frac{1}{2}$ cup firmly packed brown sugar

6 tbsp. butter or Smart Balance spread, softened

$\frac{3}{4}$ tsp. cinnamon

$\frac{1}{2}$ cup chopped pecans

$\frac{1}{2}$ cup dried cranberries

6 oz. semisweet chocolate morsels

Prepare an 8-inch square or round baking pan: butter and flour the pan.

Preheat oven 350°.

First make the TOPPING: combine flour, brown sugar, butter and cinnamon and work the dough with 2 forks to make a crumbly and well combined mix. Melt the chocolate morsels in top pot of a small double boiler. Add 1 cup water to bottom pot. Bring the pot to simmer. Stir chocolate occasionally. Turn off heat under pot and allow pot of chocolate to keep warm. Stir in nuts and cranberries. Set aside.

In a bowl with an electric mixer, cream together: butter and sugar until mixture is light and fluffy; add eggs, 1 at a time, beating well after each addition. Sift in flour, baking powder and salt. Beat the batter until just combined.

Spread batter evenly in prepared pan. Arrange apple slices in slightly overlapping rows over the batter; sprinkle the topping over the apples. Bake the cake in the center of the preheated oven at 350° for 50 minutes to 1 hour, or until inserted toothpick tests clean. Drizzle chocolate icing mix over cake while cake is still warm. Serve the cake from the pan, warm or at room temperature. Serves 6.

Pecan-Pepper Crusted Pork Tenderloin, page 28

Citrus Chicken, page 148

Lentil Soup, page 224

Summer Pasta Salad, page 127

Stuffed Mushrooms a la Parmesana, page 284

Pecan Pumpkin Pie, page 285

Walnut-Pepper Crusted Salmon, page 128

Battered Seafood with Fruit, page 90

Apple Crumb Cake, page 382

Chocolate Spice Apples, page 174

Pesto Preparation, page 396

Fresh Fig Crumb Cake, page 332

Preparing and Cooking Marinara Sauce, pages 398-399

Tangy Lemon Cake, page 121

Risotto Milanese, page 66

Almond Ginger Biscotti, page 265

Accompaniments

Dressings, Sauces, Gravies

ITALIAN DRESSING (OLIVE OIL AND RED WINE VINEGAR DRESSING)

$\frac{1}{2}$ cup olive oil
2 tbsp. red wine vinegar
2 garlic cloves, crushed
$\frac{1}{4}$ tsp. salt
$\frac{1}{8}$ tsp. black pepper
1 tbsp. chopped basil
$\frac{1}{4}$ tsp. oregano
a few flakes hot red pepper

Combine and mix all ingredients into a 1-pint jar with a tight lid. Shake dressing thoroughly before serving. Keeps in refrigerator for 2 weeks.

BALSAMIC OLIVE OIL DRESSING

$\frac{1}{2}$ cup olive oil
$\frac{1}{4}$ cup balsamic vinegar
1 tbsp. mixed: dried oregano, basil, rosemary, marjoram
1 bay leaf
2 garlic cloves, minced
1 tsp. honey
1 tsp. prepared Dijon-style mustard
a few grains hot red pepper flakes

Thoroughly combine all ingredients in a 1-pint jar with a tight cap. Shake dressing before using. Keeps for about 2 weeks in refrigerator.

HONEY MUSTARD DRESSING

$\frac{1}{2}$ cup olive oil
$\frac{1}{4}$ cup red wine vinegar (for sweeter taste, try cider vinegar)
1 tsp. honey
1 tsp. dry mustard
$\frac{1}{4}$ tsp. cracked black pepper, salt to taste
1 tsp. lemon juice
$\frac{1}{4}$ tsp. dill weed

Combine all ingredients in a 1-pint jar with a tight cover. Shake dressing thoroughly to combine. Refrigerate. Shake well to mix before serving. Keeps in refrigerator for 2 weeks.

HONEY ORANGE DRESSING

$\frac{1}{4}$ cup extra-virgin olive oil
$\frac{1}{4}$ cup orange juice
1 tbsp. honey
1 small red chile pepper, seeded, chopped
1 tsp. dried oregano

Combine dressing ingredients in a small bowl or a jar with a screw-on lid. When handling hot pepper varieties, wear plastic gloves. Wash your hands thoroughly; avoid touching face and eyes.
Shake jar of dressing to blend thoroughly. Refrigerate dressing until needed, up to 1 week. Remove dressing from refrigerator 1 hour prior to using. Shake dressing to blend. Drizzle dressing over salad when serving.

FRENCH DRESSING

1 cup mayonnaise
1 tbsp. white vinegar
1 tsp. dry mustard
$\frac{1}{2}$ tsp. Worcestershire sauce
$\frac{1}{4}$ tsp. salt, dash of black pepper
1 tsp. confectioners' sugar
$\frac{1}{2}$ tsp. paprika
$\frac{1}{4}$ tsp. garlic powder

Combine all ingredients in a small bowl. Beat with electric mixer for 2 minutes. Pour into 1-pint jar with a secure cover. Refrigerate until serving. Stir thoroughly to mix. Keeps in refrigerator for 1 week.

LEMON-OIL DRESSING

$\frac{1}{2}$ cup extra-virgin olive oil
$\frac{1}{4}$ tsp. salt, dash of black pepper
1 garlic clove, crushed
juice of 2 lemons, strained

Combine all ingredients in a 1-pint jar with a tight cover and shake dressing thoroughly. Refrigerate dressing until serving. Use over greens salads; vegetables such as broccoli, asparagus, spinach or green beans. Keeps in refrigerator for 2 weeks.

RUSSIAN DRESSING

1 cup mayonnaise
$\frac{1}{2}$ cup chili sauce
$\frac{1}{2}$ cup pickle relish
1 tsp. confectioners' sugar
1 tbsp. black caviar, optional

Combine all ingredients into a 1-pint jar with a tight lid. Stir to mix. Refrigerate until using. Keeps in refrigerator for 1 week.

BLEU CHEESE DRESSING

$\frac{1}{2}$ cup extra-virgin olive oil
$\frac{1}{4}$ cup white vinegar
$\frac{1}{4}$ tsp. salt, $\frac{1}{8}$ tsp. cracked black pepper
1 tsp. onion powder
$\frac{1}{2}$ cup crumbled bleu cheese (or Roquefort or gorgonzola)

Combine and beat all ingredients in a small bowl. Pour into a 1-pint jar with a wide mouth. When ready to serve, stir thoroughly and spoon over salad. Keeps in refrigerator for 1 week.

CAESAR DRESSING

$\frac{1}{2}$ cup extra-virgin olive oil
2 garlic cloves, minced
$\frac{1}{4}$ cup egg substitute
$\frac{1}{2}$ cup grated Parmesan cheese
$\frac{1}{4}$ tsp. salt, $\frac{1}{8}$ tsp. cracked black pepper
$\frac{1}{4}$ tsp. dry mustard
juice of 1 lemon, strained
3-4 chopped anchovy, optional
2 strips cooked bacon, crumbled
1 cup toasted cubes French bread (or prepared croutons)

Let minced garlic sit in olive oil for 1 hour. In a small bowl, beat the egg substitute, cheese, salt, pepper, dry mustard and lemon juice. Add oil mix. Beat with electric mixer for 30 seconds. Stir in anchovy. Refrigerate. When needed, shake dressing thoroughly. Add croutons and crumbled bacon to salad mix and pour dressing over the salad. Toss to coat thoroughly. Serve immediately.

SPICY SALAD DRESSING

1 cup Miracle Whip dressing
$\frac{1}{4}$ cup chili sauce
$\frac{1}{4}$ tsp. salt
$\frac{1}{8}$ tsp. black pepper
$\frac{1}{4}$ tsp. dill weed
1 tbsp. chopped dill pickle
1 tbsp. extra-virgin olive oil
1 tbsp. Worcestershire sauce
dash of red cayenne pepper

    Beat all ingredients in a small bowl. Store in a tightly covered jar in refrigerator until needed. Use within 1 week. Shake dressing thoroughly before serving.

MAYONNAISE

$\frac{1}{2}$ cup egg substitute
2 tbsp. lemon juice (1 tbsp. white wine vinegar, if necessary)
1 tbsp. mild mustard
$1\frac{1}{4}$ cups extra-virgin olive oil
dash of salt, dash of white pepper

    In a small bowl, whisk together: egg substitute, dash of salt and white pepper. Add 1 tablespoon of lemon juice and the mustard. Beat until thick (about a minute or two). Add the oil, a teaspoon at a time, whisking constantly. After you've added 2 tablespoons of oil, the mixture should be thick. Add the remaining oil more quickly, a tablespoon at time, whisking constantly. Taste, and if desired, stir in the rest of the lemon juice (and 1 tablespoon of white vinegar); add more salt and pepper, if necessary. Refrigerate dressing in a covered jar. Use within 1 week.

ASIAN DRESSING I

¼ cup extra-virgin olive oil
2 tbsp. sesame oil
2 tbsp. rice wine vinegar
1 tbsp. grated gingerroot
2 tbsp. *lite* soy sauce
2 tbsp. lemon juice
1 tbsp. grated lemon rind
¼ tsp. salt
1 garlic clove, minced
2 tbsp. peanuts, chopped fine

Combine all ingredients in a jar with a lid. Refrigerate until needed. Shake dressing thoroughly before serving.

ASIAN DRESSING II

¼ cup sherry
2 tbsp. *lite* soy sauce
2 tbsp. hoisin sauce
Chinese 5-spice powder, to taste

Combine all ingredients in a jar with a lid. Refrigerate until needed. Shake dressing thoroughly before serving.

PARMESAN CHEESE DRESSING

½ cup extra-virgin olive oil
¼ cup white wine vinegar
2 tbsp. lemon juice
¼ tsp. black pepper
½ tsp. salt
1 tbsp. oregano
1 bay leaf
½ cup grated Parmesan cheese

Combine all ingredients in 1-pint jar with lid. Refrigerate until needed. Shake dressing before serving.

VINAIGRETTE

$\frac{1}{2}$ cup extra-virgin olive oil
2 tbsp. red wine vinegar
1 tbsp. lemon juice
1 tsp. prepared mustard (or Worcestershire sauce)
$\frac{1}{2}$ tsp. salt
1 tsp. dried basil
$\frac{1}{4}$ tsp. black pepper
1 garlic clove, minced
($\frac{1}{4}$ cup sour cream for creamy style) optional

   Mix all ingredients in a 1-pint jar with lid. Refrigerate. Shake well at serving.

AIOLI (GARLIC SAUCE)

$\frac{1}{2}$ cup mayonnaise
4 garlic cloves, minced
$\frac{1}{4}$ cup extra-virgin olive oil
$\frac{1}{4}$ tsp. black pepper
1 tbsp. lemon juice
dash of salt

   Mix ingredients thoroughly in a small bowl. Seal with plastic and refrigerate until needed. Stir dressing before using. Use within 1 week.

COLE SLAW DRESSING

$\frac{1}{2}$ cup Miracle Whip dressing
$\frac{1}{4}$ cup cider vinegar
juice of 1 lemon
$\frac{1}{4}$ tsp. black pepper
1 tsp. sugar
$\frac{1}{2}$ tsp. celery seed

   Mix all ingredients in a small jar with lid. Refrigerate. Use within 1 week. Shake dressing thoroughly before using.

APPLE CIDER DRESSING

$\frac{1}{2}$ cup apple cider
$\frac{1}{4}$ cup extra-virgin olive oil
1 tbsp. brown sugar
$\frac{1}{4}$ tsp. each: ground cinnamon, nutmeg, cloves
dash of pepper, dash of salt, dash of cumin
1 tbsp. lemon juice
1 tbsp. sherry wine

Mix all ingredients in a small jar with lid. Shake dressing vigorously before serving. Keeps in refrigerator for several weeks.

MARINADE (FOR PORK, CHICKEN, AND FISH)

$\frac{1}{4}$ cup extra-virgin olive oil
3 tbsp. chopped parsley
$\frac{1}{4}$ tsp. cracked black pepper
$\frac{1}{4}$ tsp. salt
1 tbsp. honey
2 tbsp. prepared mustard
juice of 1 lemon, strained

Combine all ingredients in a small bowl. Refrigerate dressing until needed. Brush marinade on both sides of meat, chicken, fish prior to their cooking, and occasionally, during their cooking. Do not save or re-use leftover marinade.

MORNAY SAUCE

4 tbsp. olive oil or butter
4 tbsp. flour
1 cup evaporated milk
$\frac{1}{2}$ tsp. salt
$\frac{1}{4}$ tsp. black pepper
4 oz. grated Swiss cheese (or cheddar or Parmesan)
cayenne pepper to taste

Over medium heat, in a small saucepan, melt butter (or heat oil) and stir in flour to make a smooth blend. Stir in milk, pepper and salt. Blend in grated cheese, stirring constantly to make a smooth sauce. Sprinkle cayenne pepper. Proceed as directed in your recipe.

BÉARNAISE SAUCE

1 small onion, chopped fine
1 tbsp. dried tarragon, crushed
1 tbsp. chopped chervil (or parsley)
$\frac{1}{4}$ cup dry white wine
2 tbsp. white wine vinegar
$\frac{1}{4}$ cup olive oil or melted butter
$\frac{1}{2}$ cup egg substitute
1 tbsp. cold water
$\frac{1}{2}$ tsp. salt
$\frac{1}{4}$ tsp. black pepper

    In top half of 1-quart size double boiler over hot water, whisk egg substitute. Add cold water, herbs, onion, wine and wine vinegar, steadily whipping. Add the oil or butter a little bit at a time; continue to whisk until sauce is thickened and creamy. Season with salt and pepper. Should the sauce curdle, add another tablespoon of cold water. Remove sauce from heat and whip vigorously. Use as directed in recipe.

BARBEQUE SAUCE

1 cup catsup
1 tbsp. white vinegar
$\frac{1}{4}$ cup orange juice
$\frac{1}{4}$ tsp. salt
$\frac{1}{8}$ tsp. Tabasco
1 tbsp. Worcestershire sauce
$\frac{1}{4}$ cup dark molasses
$\frac{1}{4}$ tsp. whole cloves
$\frac{1}{4}$ tsp. garlic powder
$\frac{1}{2}$ tsp. dry mustard
1 tbsp. olive oil
dash of black pepper

    Simmer all ingredients in a small saucepan for 5 minutes. Use as directed in recipe.

CHEESE SAUCE

3 tbsp. olive oil
$\frac{1}{4}$ cup flour
$1\frac{1}{2}$ cups whole milk or evaporated milk
1 cup grated sharp cheddar cheese or other cheese of choice
$\frac{1}{2}$ tsp. salt
$\frac{1}{4}$ tsp. black pepper
$\frac{1}{2}$ tsp. dry mustard
1 tsp. onion powder
1 tsp. Worcestershire sauce
few drops Tabasco

Heat oil over low temperature and stir in flour. Add milk and rest of ingredients. Stir constantly over low heat until mix is creamy and starts to thicken. Serve hot as directed in recipe.

BASIC CURRY SAUCE

3 tbsp. olive oil
3 tbsp. flour
$\frac{1}{2}$ tsp. salt
$\frac{1}{4}$ tsp. black pepper
$\frac{1}{4}$ tsp. each: cardamom, cumin, curry powder, mace
a few whole cloves
$\frac{1}{2}$ tsp. ground ginger
1 cup whole milk or evaporated milk (fat-free available)
1 onion, minced
$\frac{1}{2}$ cup chopped celery
$\frac{1}{2}$ cup apple, chopped, leave skin
1 cup homemade stock (or use bouillon cubes)
1 tsp. grated lemon rind
$\frac{1}{2}$ cup sherry

In a 1-quart saucepan, warm oil over low heat. Stir in flour, salt, seasonings, spices and herbs. Stir to thoroughly mix, over low heat. Gradually add milk, stirring continuously until creamy. Add onion, celery, apple, lemon rind and stock. Stir to mix. Cook until sauce starts to simmer, and thickens. Add sherry. Stir to blend. Pour over cooked chicken, lamb or seafood (from which you have gotten the stock). Stir to combine and continue as in recipe.

CURRY SALSA

1 lg. onion, chopped fine
2 tbsp. olive oil
1 tbsp. peeled gingerroot, minced
2 garlic cloves, minced
1 green bell pepper, finely chopped
1 red bell pepper, finely chopped
2 tbsp. curry powder
$\frac{1}{4}$ cup flour
2 cups chicken broth (less-salt variety)
1 can (20 oz.) chopped plum tomatoes
2 tbsp. fresh lime juice
1 tbsp. grated lime zest
salt, black pepper to taste

In a 2-quart saucepan with lid, cook onion in oil over moderate heat until tender; add garlic and gingerroot, stirring and cooking for 1-2 minutes longer. Add peppers and cook for several minutes until softened. Stir in curry and flour and cook for 2 minutes.

Add broth and tomatoes, mixing thoroughly, and cook for 5 minutes. Stir in lime juice, rind, salt and pepper. Remove from burner.

Curry Salsa may be prepared a couple of days in advance, covered and refrigerated. Reheat sauce when needed. For seafood, chicken, lamb. Serves 6 portions.

CHILI SAUCE

$1\frac{1}{2}$ cups prepared tomato sauce
1 cup prepared beef gravy (or 1 beef bouillon cube dissolved in 1 cup hot water, mixed
    with 2 tbsp. flour dissolved in $\frac{1}{4}$ cup cold water)
$\frac{1}{2}$ cup chili sauce
1 small onion, chopped
1 tbsp. olive oil

Combine and mix all ingredients in a 1-quart saucepan. Simmer for 10 minutes. Serve with meat, fish, poultry or vegetables.

HOLLANDAISE SAUCE

$\frac{1}{2}$ cup olive oil
3 beaten eggs or $\frac{3}{4}$ cup egg substitute
1 tbsp. lemon juice
1 tsp. sherry
a few grains of red cayenne pepper

In top of a double boiler, heat olive oil and slowly stir in beaten eggs. Add lemon juice, sherry and cayenne. Stir constantly.

Do not allow water to boil in lower pot; just keep it warm. You may prepare sauce in advance. Upon removing it from refrigerator, simply warm the sauce over hot, not boiling, water, stirring constantly. Use within 1 week.

HAWAIIAN SWEET AND SOUR SAUCE

$\frac{1}{2}$ cup meat, poultry, or seafood stock
1 tsp. mustard powder
$\frac{1}{4}$ tsp. black pepper
$\frac{1}{2}$ cup dark corn syrup
1 tbsp. brown sugar
1 tbsp. *lite* soy sauce
1 tsp. cornstarch stirred into 2 tbsp. cold water
1 cup pineapple chunks
1 cup pineapple juice (or peach nectar)
$\frac{1}{2}$ cup green pepper, seeded, sliced
6 maraschino cherries, crushed

Combine all sauce ingredients in a small bowl. Pour over meat, poultry or seafood which is cooking and continue to simmer for 10 to 15 minutes longer. Or, to saucepan, add some stock made from $\frac{1}{2}$ cup hot water and chicken bouillon or cooked seafood liquid. (Or prepare a stock by stirring 1 tablespoon Gravy Master into $\frac{1}{2}$ cup water; add to sauce to simmer for 15 minutes as directed above.)

CHINESE BARBEQUE SAUCE
(For pork, beef, shrimp, ribs or chicken.)

3 tbsp. olive oil
1 tbsp. peanut oil
3 scallions, chopped
2 garlic cloves, minced
1 small onion, chopped
1 tbsp. cornstarch stirred into $\frac{1}{4}$ cup cold water
1 cup stock (if none is available, use 1 tbsp. Gravy Master dissolved in 1 cup water)
1 tbsp. *lite* soy sauce
1 tbsp. hoisin sauce (*NOTE: below)
$\frac{1}{4}$ cup plum sauce (*NOTE: below)
$\frac{1}{2}$ cup catsup
1 tsp. grated gingerroot
$\frac{1}{4}$ cup honey
3 tbsp. creamy peanut butter
1 tbsp. rice vinegar

Heat oils in 1-quart saucepan; sauté garlic and onion and scallions. Stir in cornstarch mixed with water. Add remaining ingredients and stir over low heat until peanut butter is melted. Use to baste and/or as a barbeque sauce in Chinese recipes.
*NOTE: Hoisin and plum sauces may be purchased at supermarkets in Asian food sections.

MUSHROOM SAUCE

3 tbsp. olive oil
3 tbsp. flour
$\frac{1}{2}$ tsp. salt
$\frac{1}{4}$ tsp. black pepper
1 cup whole milk or evaporated milk
5-6 small white mushrooms, rinsed, chopped
$\frac{1}{2}$ cup water
($\frac{1}{2}$ cup mushroom stock) (*NOTE: see directions)
1 tbsp. chopped onion
1 tbsp. Worcestershire sauce
1 cup mushrooms, scrubbed, sliced

*NOTE: Make stock. Simmer mushrooms in $\frac{1}{2}$ cup water for 1 minute. Drain mushrooms; reserve $\frac{1}{2}$ cup stock and set aside.
In 1-quart saucepan, heat oil and stir in flour until smooth. Add milk and stock water and seasonings, onion and Worcestershire sauce. Stir constantly over low heat until smooth.
Add mushrooms and stir to blend. Cook for another minute. Keep sauce warm over a pan of hot water until ready to serve.

PESTO SAUCE

2 cups fresh basil leaves, washed, drained
6 garlic cloves
1 oz. pignola (pine nuts)
½ cup grated Parmesan cheese
½ cup olive oil
salt, black pepper to taste

   Combine all ingredients in food processor. Purée for 30 seconds or until basil leaves are creamed. Serve immediately, or pour into a 1-pint plastic container and freeze until needed. If frozen, transfer to refrigerator early on the day and when needed, warm container, lid removed, over a pan of hot water. Stir the sauce occasionally while warming. Serve over pasta or rice. Toss to coat.

BASIC BROWN GRAVY
(For meat and poultry; about 2 cups.)

2-3 tbsp. olive oil
2-3 tbsp. flour, ¼ cup cold water
½ cup prepared tomato sauce
1 tsp. Gravy Master
¼ tsp. salt
¼ tsp. black pepper
1 onion, finely chopped
meat or fowl drippings plus water to make 1 cup stock (*NOTE: in directions)
dash of red cayenne pepper
2 tbsp. marsala wine or sweet vermouth (optional)

   Brown onion in heated olive oil. In a small bowl, stir flour into cold water and add stock, tomato sauce, Gravy Master, salt, pepper and cayenne. Whisk stock mix into the oil/onion mix. Cook and stir gravy over low heat until it thickens. Stir in 2 tablespoons wine (or water) into gravy as it thickens. Keep sauce warm over a pan of hot water.

   *NOTE: If no drippings are available, use 2 beef or chicken bouillon cubes dissolved into 1 cup hot water.

MUSHROOM TOMATO SAUCE
(May be prepared 2 to 3 days in advance and refrigerated; or frozen for several weeks.)

1 lb. mushrooms, scrubbed, thinly sliced
3 cups tomato purée
$\frac{1}{2}$ tsp. salt
$\frac{1}{4}$ tsp. black pepper
1 garlic clove, minced
1 small onion, chopped
3 tbsp. olive oil
$\frac{1}{4}$ tsp each: fresh basil, fresh parsley, dried thyme

    In a 2-quart saucepot, sauté onion, garlic and mushrooms in olive oil over medium heat. When very lightly browned (about 2 minutes), add purée, spices and herbs. Simmer gently for 30 minutes. Serve over pasta or rice or use to accompany beef or fowl.

CHOPPED BEEF TOMATO SAUCE
(May be prepared and refrigerated for several days; or frozen for several weeks.)

3 tbsp. olive oil
2 lbs. lean chopped beef
2 garlic cloves, minced
1 onion, chopped
3 cups tomato purée
$\frac{1}{4}$ cup water
$\frac{1}{2}$ tsp. salt
$\frac{1}{4}$ tsp. black pepper
$\frac{1}{2}$ tsp. each: fresh basil, oregano, thyme, rosemary
$\frac{1}{2}$ cup Parmesan cheese, grated
$\frac{1}{2}$ cup red table wine
a few grains hot red pepper flakes

    Brown onion, garlic and chopped beef in hot oil, stirring occasionally to maintain beef in small chunks. Add remaining ingredients; stir to combine; slowly simmer with lid loosely covering pot of sauce. Simmer gently for $\frac{1}{2}$ hour. Serve over pasta or rice.

MARINARA SAUCE
METHOD I

(Sauce may be prepared and refrigerated up to 3 days or frozen in a plastic container for several weeks.)

4-5 lbs. fresh ripe plum tomatoes
1 can (6 oz.) tomato paste
   (if sauce needs to be thickened)
3 tbsp. olive oil
½ tsp. salt, ¼ tsp. black pepper
1 tbsp. mixed: oregano, thyme, rosemary

1 tbsp. fresh chopped basil
1 green pepper, seeded, chopped
½ cup grated Parmesan cheese
2 garlic cloves, minced
1 small onion, chopped
a few grains hot red pepper flakes

In a 4-quart saucepot, heat oil; brown garlic and onion. Set aside. Wash tomatoes and place in a 6-quart pot (with lid). Add ¼ cup water; cover and bring to a boil. Simmer for about 5 minutes, until tomatoes are very soft. Drain and strain the tomatoes and liquid through a colander or sieve with a large, deep bowl underneath to catch the puréed tomatoes. Or use a food mill which separates the pulp from the skin and seeds.

When using colander, use your hands to push the tomatoes through. Discard the squeezed skins and seeds. Transfer the puréed sauce to the pot with the browned garlic and onion. Add the remaining ingredients and stir to mix. Simmer gently for 1½ hours with lid askew. (Stir in tomato paste as needed, if sauce is too loose.)

MARINARA SAUCE
METHOD II

2 lbs. canned plum tomatoes
1 green pepper, seeded, chopped
6 oz. can tomato paste
1 small onion, chopped
2 garlic cloves, minced
3 tbsp. olive oil

½ tsp. salt, ¼ tsp. black pepper
½ cup grated Parmesan cheese
2-3 basil leaves
1 tbsp. mixed: oregano, rosemary, thyme
a few flakes hot red pepper

Strain plum tomatoes through a colander as in Method I or use blender. Brown garlic and onion in hot oil in a 2-quart saucepan with lid. Add puréed tomatoes, paste and the remaining ingredients. Loosely cover the sauce pot; simmer gently, for 1½ hours, stirring occasionally.

MARINARA SAUCE
METHOD III

3 cups canned tomato purée
3 tbsp. olive oil
½ tsp. salt, ¼ tsp. black pepper
1 small green pepper, seeded, chopped
½ cup grated Parmesan cheese

2 garlic cloves, minced
1 small onion, chopped
1 tbsp. mixed: oregano, rosemary, thyme
a few grains hot red pepper flakes
a few leaves fresh basil

Brown onion and garlic in hot oil in 2-quart saucepot with cover. Add tomato purée and remaining ingredients. Stir to mix and gently simmer, lightly covered, for 1 hour.

SAUSAGE AND MEATBALL TOMATO SAUCE
(May be prepared and refrigerated up to 3 days, or frozen in a plastic container for several weeks.)

MEAT:

3 links sweet Italian sausage
3 links hot Italian sausage
2 lbs. chopped beef for meatballs:
    add ½ cup bread crumbs, 1 tbsp.
    chopped parsley, ½ tsp. salt, ¼ tsp.
    black pepper and 1 beaten egg
    (or egg substitute)

3 tbsp. olive oil
3 garlic cloves, minced
1 small onion, chopped

In a skillet, brown sausages, onion and garlic in olive oil (300°) until sausages are cooked. Remove meat to platter. In a 2-quart bowl, combine meatball ingredients and form 3-inch meatballs. Brown them in same skillet on all sides. Remove meatballs to platter. Scrape bottom of skillet to loosen leavings. In a large bowl, combine the following sauce ingredients:

SAUCE:

4 cups Italian plum tomatoes,
    strained or put through blender
½ cup tomato paste
½ tsp. salt
¼ tsp. black pepper

2-3 fresh basil leaves
1 tbsp. mixed: oregano, rosemary,
    thyme, marjoram
½ cup red table wine
½ cup Parmesan cheese

Combine all meat and leavings in a 4-quart saucepan with cover. Add sauce ingredients and mix thoroughly. Simmer with lid askew for 1½ hours, stirring occasionally. Serve sauce over pasta or rice. Serve meat as an accompaniment.

RAGOUT

(May be prepared up to 3 days in advance and refrigerated, covered, or may be frozen in a plastic container for several weeks.)

SAUCE:

large can plum tomatoes (about 3 cups), strained through colander

6 oz. can tomato paste

2 garlic cloves, minced

1 small onion, chopped

3 tbsp. olive oil

$\frac{1}{2}$ tsp. salt

$\frac{1}{4}$ tsp. black pepper

1 tbsp. mixed: oregano, thyme, marjoram, rosemary

2-3 fresh basil leaves

$\frac{1}{2}$ cup red table wine

$\frac{1}{2}$ cup grated Parmesan cheese (or Pecorino Romano)

a few flakes hot red pepper

MEATS:

2 links sweet Italian sausage

2 links hot Italian sausage

$\frac{1}{2}$ lb. lean pork for gravy

1 lb. lean chopped beef (ADD and MIX: 1 beaten egg, $\frac{1}{2}$ cup fine bread crumbs, salt, pepper, 1 tbsp. chopped parsley; optional: $\frac{1}{4}$ cup raisins.)

1 thin slice top round for braciola (Meat should be pounded thin. SPRINKLE OVER TOP ROUND: 1 tsp. chopped parsley, $\frac{1}{4}$ cup raisins and pignola, mixed; salt and pepper to taste.)

1) Preheat oil in 4-quart sauce pot to 300°. Brown sausages and pork with onion and garlic. Cook thoroughly. Remove from pot, set aside.

2) Form meatballs by combining chopped beef, beaten egg, crumbs, salt, pepper and parsley. Form into 2-inch balls. Brown these in same skillet as sausages and pork. Set aside.

3) Place thinly pounded top round on a sheet of waxed paper. Over it, sprinkle salt, pepper, parsley, raisins and pignola. Roll up and tie with white string or knit with a thin metal skewer to form braciola. Brown the braciola on all sides in skillet. Also brown onion and garlic. Scrape the bottom of the skillet to loosen leavings (which you add to meats).

4) Replace all meats to saucepan and add all of the sauce ingredients. Stir to combine thoroughly. Bring the pan to simmer; cover loosely, and cook the ragout for 1 hour. Serve the sauce over pasta or rice, with the meats as an accompaniment.

SEAFOOD TOMATO SAUCE
(May be prepared a day or two in advance and refrigerated.)

3 cups Italian plum tomatoes, strained or put through blender
2 tbsp. tomato paste
2 garlic cloves, minced
1 small onion, chopped
1 tbsp. chopped basil (or fresh mint)
1 tbsp. mixed: oregano, thyme, marjoram
1 bay leaf
$\frac{1}{2}$ tsp. salt
$\frac{1}{4}$ tsp. black pepper
$\frac{1}{2}$ cup dry white wine
3 tbsp. olive oil
2 cups raw, cleaned seafood (clams, crabs, lobsters, mussels, shrimp, squid,
    - any of these) (*NOTE: below)
a few grains hot red pepper flakes

    In a 4-quart saucepan with cover, sauté garlic and onion in oil (300°) until lightly browned. Add other sauce ingredients, except seafood. Stir and simmer, covered, for 1 hour. Add cleaned seafood and simmer for an additional 10 minutes. Remove bay leaf and discard. Serve over spaghetti, linguini or rice.

*NOTE:
CLAMS: Use 1 cup chopped clams, plus the liquid which you should strain through a
    piece of cheesecloth or fine strainer.
CRABS OR LOBSTERS: Use 6 small crabs or 1 whole lobster or 4 lobster claws.
MUSSELS: Scrub thoroughly. Add 1 dozen mussels in shell to sauce.
SHRIMP: Clean, leave whole, about 1 lb.
SQUID: Clean, cut into rounds. Use 2 cups.

RED PEPPER SAUCE
(May be prepared several days in advance and refrigerated; may be frozen.)

4 large red bell peppers
4 garlic cloves, peeled
1 cup tomato purée, unseasoned
1 small onion, chopped
1 hot chile pepper, chopped (careful handling)
$\frac{1}{4}$ cup olive oil
2 tbsp. balsamic vinegar
$\frac{1}{2}$ tsp. salt
$\frac{1}{4}$ tsp. black pepper
1 tsp. each: oregano, basil, rosemary
1-2 bay leaves, whole
$\frac{1}{2}$ cup grated Parmesan cheese

Wash peppers; remove the core and seeds. Cut the peppers into chunks and purée them in a food processor for a minute or so. Add the garlic and pulse for half a minute. In a medium saucepan with lid, add olive oil and brown the chopped onion and chile pepper (seeded and chopped). Cool slightly and add the puréed red pepper and garlic. Add the tomato sauce, balsamic vinegar, and all of the spices. Stir to mix. Return the pan with cover to the stove and simmer for 30 minutes, stirring occasionally. Remove bay leaf and discard. Stir in the grated cheese. Serve over pasta of your choice. Add more cheese if desired.

RED PEPPER VODKA SAUCE

Use recipe for RED PEPPER SAUCE, see above.

To the INGREDIENTS, add:
1 cup creamy ricotta
$\frac{1}{2}$ cup vodka

Add and stir in ricotta and vodka to prepared Red Pepper Sauce during last 5 minutes of cooking the sauce. Stir in Parmesan cheese and serve over pasta. Add more Parmesan cheese if desired.

HAWAIIAN TOMATO SAUCE
(May be prepared a day in advance.)

1 cup prepared tomato sauce
1 tbsp. Gravy Master
½ cup pineapple juice
2 tbsp. brown sugar
1 tbsp. prepared mustard
½ cup pineapple chunks
½ cup green pepper, seeded, chopped
½ tsp. salt
¼ tsp. black pepper
1 tbsp. cornstarch stirred into ¼ cup cold water
1 tbsp. wine vinegar
few dashes Tabasco

Combine all ingredients in a 1-quart saucepan. Simmer for 5 minutes. Serve hot over rice.

SEASONED DIPPING OILS

(1)	(2)	(3)
½ cup extra-virgin olive oil	½ cup extra-virgin olive oil	½ cup extra-virgin olive oil
2 tbsp. balsamic vinegar	2 tbsp. pitted, chopped	juice of 1 lemon, strained
1 tbsp. chopped, sun-dried	Sicilian olives	1 tsp. grated lemon peel
tomatoes	2 garlic cloves, minced	2 garlic cloves, minced
1 tbsp. crushed, dried rosemary	1 tsp. black peppercorns	1 tsp. black peppercorns
2 garlic cloves, minced	1 tsp. each: dried oregano,	1 tsp. capers
½ tsp. coarsely ground	chopped fresh basil	1 tsp. dried oregano
black pepper	1 bay leaf (whole)	

Store each recipe of seasoned dipping oils in separate glass 1-pint jars with screw-top lids. Shake well. Set aside. At serving time, shake the oils to blend thoroughly; pour each mix into separate serving bowls and set them around a large serving tray. Serve with small chunks of crusty artisan bread, arranged in a basket in center of serving tray. (If not using within a few hours, refrigerate Dipping Oils. Use within 1 week.)

Bibliography and Credits

CULTURE ONLINE (KEW). www.plantculture.org. Garlic History. U.K.: 2005-2006.

ENCYCLOPEDIA OF THE BIBLE (THE LION). Pat Alexander, B.A. (organizational ed). published by THE READER'S DIGEST ASS'N INC. with permission of LION PUBLISHING CORP. 1987.

GLOBAL GOURMET. www.globalgourmet.com. Olive Oil History. 2006.

HOEVER, REV. HUGO, S.O. Cist. PhD. Lives of the Saints. New York: Catholic Book Publishing Co.,1974-1955.

THE JERUSALEM BIBLE. Alexander Jones, General Editor. Darton, Longman and Todd, Ltd. and Doubleday and Co. Inc., Garden City, New York, 1966.

JOHNSON, HUGH. Vintage: The Story of Wine. New York: Simon and Shuster, 1989.

LEVEY, JUDITH S. and GREENHALL, AGNES, Editors. The Concise Columbia Encyclopedia. New York: Columbia University Press, 1983.

O'CONNELL, REV. JOHN P., Editor. The Holy Bible. Chicago, Illinois: The Catholic Press Inc., 1954.

WWW.PANTONE.com.Flag History.

PARRINDER, GEOFFREY, Editor. World Religions. U.K. : Hamlyn Publishing Group, Ltd., 1971.

PEPPERCORN, DAVID and COOPER, BRIAN and BLACKER, ELWYN. Drinking Wine. New York: A Harbor House Book, (Louis J. Martin and Assoc.), 1979.

READER'S DIGEST ILLUSTRATED. Dictionary of Bible Life and Times. New York: 1997.

A TEACHER'S GUIDE TO THE EVERETT CHILDREN'S ADVENTURE GARDEN.The New York Botanical Garden. The Visual Dictionary of Plants. New York: DK Publishing, 1992.

WALKER, MARGARET E. The Sensuous Fig. In Mama's Kitchen.com (www.inmamaskitchen.com), 2007.

WINE 101: WINE HISTORY. (www.winepros.org/wine101/history.htm-46k). Design/Content- Jim La Mar, (1999-2005).

Daddy and baby Chip, Ralph Sanson, Ruthie, John, Ruth Sanson, Mama, Aunt Helen and Grandma Ines.

Food for the Body, Nourishment for the Soul

Sharing in the menus FROM THE TABLE OF PLENTY is an assurance of good, healthy, well-prepared food for the body, and a guarantee of nourishment for the soul.

Our table is set for six; however, one may easily convert the portions to serve fewer or more place-settings. You will select fresh ingredients. Perhaps, you grow a vegetable garden with a variety of vegetables and herbs.

With planning, you can eliminate trans fats; opt to cook with oils which can benefit your heart. You are able to create delicious meals without additional salt, utilizing the myriad of available herbs and spices. You select the options for less fat (or fat-free); you choose desserts from a selection of fruits which are available practically all-year round. You dare to be different by combining tastes of grains and nuts, greens and berries.

And you happily, lovingly, share these menus FROM THE TABLE OF PLENTY with those whom you love, hope to love, grow to love or wish you could love. Thankfully, humankind has been sharing his food since the beginning of time. ***"Sharing is our food for the soul."***

Shea Family Celebration: At Linda and Alan's 25th Anniversary.

INDEX

A

Aglio Olio Spaghetti 303
Aioli (Garlic Sauce) 389
Almond Biscotti 96
Almond Brittle (Croccante) 294
Almond-Cherry Cake 362
Almond Chicken/Pears, Gorgonzola 137
Almond Ginger Biscotti 265
Almond Strawberry Cream 330
Anchovy and Mushrooms 136
Anchovy and Pasta (Pasta e Sarde) 323
Angel Hair Pasta, Fennel Sausage 293
Anguilla (Eel, Marinated) 9
Anise Biscotti, Marbled 315

APPETIZERS:

Artichokes/Sausage, Mushroom 345
Avocado, Stuffed 241
Bread and Butter Pickles 183
Charoseth (Haroset) 141
Chow-Chow 182
Clams on the Barbeque 132
Garlic Dill Pickles 181
Marinated Eel 9
Marinated Shrimp/Guacamole 167
Mozzarella in Carozza 23
Mushrooms and Anchovy 136
Mussels in Beer 82
Panzanella 263
Pizza Rustica 186
Pizzas, Three Easy Gourmet 186-7
Plum Tomato Sailboats 368
Portobellos, Grilled/Tomatoes 302
Prosciutto and Ceci 2
Provolone, Pepper Salad/Croutons 6
Seafood Cocktail 259
Shrimp, Marinated/ Guacamole 167
Shrimp with Cashews 155
Vegetable Fritto Misto 164
Vegetables, Raw/Lemon/Olive Oil 360

Apple and Cranberry Crisp 272
Apple Cider Dressing 390

Apple Cinnamon Pumpkin Muffins 232
Apple Crumb Cake 382
Apple Crunch, Vanilla Ice Cream 193
Apple-Pumpkin Pecan Bread 359
Apple Sauce 33
Apple Slices, Asparagus, Grilled 221
Apples, Chocolate Spice Sauce 174
Apricot-Blueberry Cobbler 134
Arancine (Rice Balls) 67
Artichokes/Farfalle, Red Pepper Sauce 320
Artichokes/Sausage, Mushroom 345
Arugula, Potato and Tomato Salad 274
Arugula, Wild /Shrimp Vinaigrette 141
Arugula with Prosciutto and Figs 104
Asian Dressing I 388
Asian Dressing II 157, 388
Asparagus, Apple Slices, Grilled 221
Asparagus Frittata 341-2
Asparagus, Mushrooms, Almonds 143
Asparagus, Steamed 138, 96
Avocado and Cicoria Salad 357
Avocado and Spinach Salad 185
Avocado, Stuffed 241

B

Baccala, Frito (Fried Salted Cod) 10
Baccala, Salsa Piccante (Salted Cod) 10
Baked Eggplant Parma/Pepper Sauce 29
Baked Flounder Fillet and Peppers 230
Balsamic Vinegar-Olive Oil 384
Banana and Strawberry Pudding 278
Banana Fruit Cake 21
Banana-Strawberry Rice Pudding 356
Barbeque Sauce 391
Battered Seafood with Fruit 90
Bean, Black and Sausage Chili 89
Bean Salad, Spicy 331
Bean (Three) Salad with Feta 234
Beans and Sausages 57
Béarnaise Sauce 391

BEEF

Beef, (Roast) with Gravy 94
Beef Tea 34
Beef Tenderloin in a Nut Crust 351
Braciole 105
Chopped Beef Tomato Sauce 397
Filet Mignons/Artichoke Hearts 205
Greek Beef Stew 37
Grilled T-Bone /Onion, Peppers 260
Pot Roast, A Home Style 6
Stuffed Cabbage 86
Surf-Turf, Vegetables, Grilled 251

Beef (Roast) with Gravy 94
Beef Stew, Greek 37
Beef Tea 34
Beef Tenderloin in a Nut Crust 351
Beet and Chicory Salad 380
Beets in Orange, Steamed 230
Berries and Orange in Lime 157
Berry Whipped Cream Pie 197

BEVERAGES

Beef Tea 34
Cocoa (Hot) Chocolate Sundae 356
Egg Nog 34
Fennel Water 34
Honey and Lemon Tea 33

Black and White Drop Cookies 87
Black Bean and Sausage Chili 89
Blackberry Compote, Warm 107
Bleu Cheese Dressing 386
Blueberry Crumb Cake 129
Blueberry Orange Muffins 231
Borscht 204
Boston Brown Bread 20
Braciole 105

BREAD

Apple-Pumpkin Pecan Bread 359
Boston Brown Bread 20
Bruschetta di Pomidoro 168
Corn Bread, Jalapeño 190
Golden Crescent Rolls 160
Irish Soda Bread 120
Mandel Bread 281
Panzanella 263

Pizza Rustica 186
Pizzas, Three Easy Gourmet 186-7
Potato , Apple Cheddar Pancakes 173
Pumpkin Spice Pancakes 173
Toast, Buttered 32

Bread, Boston Brown 20
Bread, Mandel 281
Bread 'n Butter Pickles 183
Bread Pudding 79
Brittle, Almond (Croccante) 294
Broccoli and Cauliflower, Steamed 272
Broccoli, Ginger-Peachy 252
Broccoli Linguine 296
Broccoli Rabe and Grilled Scallops 355
Broccoli Rabe, Gnocchi, Salmon 376
Broccoli Rabe / Sausages, Farfalle 310
Broccoli Rabe, Penne, Cannellini 311
Broccoli Soup, Cream of 64
Broccoli, Steamed 149
Broth, Homemade Chicken 44
Brown Gravy 396
Brownie Fruit and Nut Roll 7
Bruschetta di Pomidoro 168
Brussels Sprouts, Tomato, Walnuts 285
Brussels Sprouts/Bacon, Pignola 46

BUFFET SELECTIONS
(also refer to SALADS)

Almond Biscotti 96
Almond Chicken/Pear, Gorgonzola 137
Almond Ginger Biscotti 265
Asparagus, Mushrooms, Almonds 143
Asparagus, Steamed 96, 138
Beef Stew, Greek 37
Beets in Orange, Steamed 230
Black and White Drop Cookies 87
Black Bean and Sausage Chili 89
Blueberry Crumb Cake 129
Braciole 105
Bread Pudding 79
Broccoli, Ginger-Peachy 252
Brussels Sprouts, Tomato, Walnuts 285
Butterflies, (Muffins) 58
Cherry Cookies to Die For 301
Chicken and Mushroom Lasagna 290
Chicken Breasts, Stuffed in a Wrap 114
Chicken Francese 110
Chicken Salad in Lime 192

Chinese Chicken Salad 159
Chocolate Covered Peanut Biscotti 314
Chocolate (Double) Fudge Cake 83
Chocolate Meringues, Raspberries 153
Clams on the Barbeque 132
Compote of Pineapple in Rum 4
Corn, Tomatoes and Mushrooms 247
Eggplant Croquettes Marinara 366
Eggplant Parmagiano/Red Pepper Sauce 29
Fish Fillets/Crab, Shrimp, Apricots 243
Ginger Soy Chicken in Wine 172
Greek Salad 36
Green Beans, Sesame 172
Hamantaschen, Chocolate 206
Honey Wings, Sesame Ribs 246-7
Italian Pudding 125
Lamb Meatballs 49
Lamb Stew 12
Lamb Stew, Greek 37
Lasagna with Walnut Pesto 326
Lemon Macaroon Bars 307
Lemon Squares 91
Macadamia (Orange) Cupcakes 261
Manicotti in Ragout 312
Marbleized Anise Biscotti 315
Meatballs, Spicy-Sweet 61
Melon Balls in Asti Spumante 298
Melon Slices, Tray 227
Muffins, Three 231-2
Mushrooms au Gratin 95
Mussels in Beer 82
Pear Crunch 17
Peppers and Soy Bean Salad 212
Peppers, Red Stuffed/Risotto 53
Pignola Cookies 67
Pineapple with Grapes 294
Pizza Rustica 186
Pizzas, 3 Easy Gourmet 186-7
Polenta with Shrimp, Sausage 70
Pork/Apricots/Almonds/Prosciutto 124
Pork, Shredded with Shrimp 255
Pork Stew, Boneless 20
Potato, Apple Cheddar Pancakes 173
Potato Gnocchi 349
Potato Salad 115
Potato Salad, German 78
Potatoes and Mushrooms 124
Potatoes, Roasted Red Bliss 95
Pumpkin Spice Pancakes 173
Ratatouille Sweet and Sour 106
Ravioli in Red Pepper Vodka 306

Rice Balls (Arancine) 67
Rice, Fragrant 91
Rice, Lime 165
Rice Pilaf, Walnuts 256
Risotto 66
Risotto Milanese 66
Salmon, Honey Ginger 221
Salmon, Walnut-Pepper-Crusted 128
Sausage, Eggplant Parmagiano 133
Sausage Mushrooms Parmesana 284
Sausages and Beans 57
Scallops in Ginger Sauce 163
Shrimp with Cashews 155
Stew, Country Style 41
Stew, Rustic 42
Strawberries, Cherries /Chocolate 161
Strawberry Crostata 304
Stuffed Shells 101
Sweet Potato, Mashed 220
Tandoori Lamb 239
Three-Bean Salad 234
Tuna and Lentil Salad 191
Veal Cutlet Parma/Sauce Crust 102
Veal Stew Paprika 208
Vegetable Croquettes 4
Vegetable Fritto Misto 164
Vegetable Stew, Pickled 263
Walnuts 367
Watermelon Chill 235
Ziti al Forno 372

Butterflies (Muffins) 58
Butterscotch Icing 379

C

Cabbage, Stuffed 86
Caesar Dressing 386

CAKES, PIES, PASTRIES

Almond-Cherry Cake 362
Apple Cinnamon Pumpkin Muffins 232
Apple Cranberry Crisp 272
Apple Crumb Cake 382
Apricot-Blueberry Cobbler 134
Banana Fruit Cake 21
Blueberry Crumb Cake 129

Blueberry Orange Muffins   231
Brownie Fruit and Nut Roll   7
Butterflies, (Cupcakes)   58
Chocolate Cake, A Devil of a   97
Chocolate Cherry Sponge Cake   46
Chocolate Cream Filling   58
Chocolate Cupcakes/Butterscotch   379
Chocolate (Double)Fudge Cake   83
Chocolate Fruit Cake   335
Chocolate Meringues, Raspberries 153
Chocolate Peanut Butter Cupcakes 370
Chocolate Stucco 2-Story Cake   30
Chocolate Torte with Almonds   111
Clafouti   321
Coffee Almond Streusel Cake   244
Cranberry Pecan Muffins   232
Currant Pound Cake   202
Devil of a Chocolate Cake, A   97
Fig, Fresh, Crumb Cake   332
Fruit and Nut Brownie Roll   7
Fruit Tart   50
Harvey Wallbanger Cake   222
Hush Puppies   248
Lemon Cake, Tangy   121
Macadamia Cupcakes/Icing   261
Marion's Tunnel of Fudge Cake   218
Meringues, Strawberry   338
Neapolitan Lemon, Orange Cake   149
Orange Chiffon Cake   116
Pastiera di Grano (Easter Pie)   144-5
Peanut Butter Chocolate Cupcakes   370
Pear and Ginger Cake   239
Pecan Pie   352
Pecan Pumpkin Pie   285
Petit-Fours (Rainbow)   373
Pignola Fruit Cake   209
Potato Pie   16
Pumpkin Apple/Cinnamon Muffin   232
Pumpkin Pecan Pie   285
Rainbow Petit Fours   373
Southwestern Fruit Cake   62
Strawberry Crostata   304
Three Muffins   231-2
Torta with Pine Nuts, Almonds   54
Walnut Cake/ Orange Glaze   257
Zeppole, Sunday Morning   248

Cake, Walnut with Orange Glaze   257
Cannellini, Wheat Penne, Broccoli Rabe   311
Cannellini with Tuna Salad   299

Cantaloupe Sundae   359
Caprese Salad   151
Capuzzelle di Agnelli(Sheep Heads)   142
Caramel Icing   30
Carbonara, Fettuccine   361
Carrot Salad   377
Carrots, Tomatoes, Stuffed Celery   339
Cauliflower, Broccoli Steamed   272
Ceci and Prosciutto   2
Celery, Stuffed   339
Charoseth (Haroset)   141

CHEESE

Almond Chicken/Pears, Gorgonzola   137
Caprese Salad   151
Cheese Sauce   392
Cheesy Vegetable Chowder   57
Frittata, Cheeses   341-2
Fruit and Cheese Tray   311
Provolone, Pepper Salad/Croutons   6
Romaine, Cheddar, Blueberry Salad   343
Spinach, Arugula, Carrots, Mozzarella   109
Three Bean Salad with Feta   234
Tossed Salad with Ricotta Salata   93
Zucchini Flowers, Stuffed   161

Cheese Sauce   392
Cheesy Vegetable Chowder   57
Cherries, Strawberries /Chocolate   161
Cherry, Almond Cake   362
Cherry Cookies to Die For   301

CHICKEN

Almond Chicken/Pears, Gorgonzola   137
Chicken and Egg Soup   48
Chicken and Mushroom Lasagna   290
Chicken Breasts Stuffed, Wrap   114
Chicken Broth, Homemade   44
Chicken Francese   110
Chicken Fricassee   264
Chicken Salad, Chinese   159
Chicken Salad in Lime   192
Chicken Soup (Stracciatella)   33
Chicken Vegetable Soup   52
Chinese Chicken Salad   159
Citrus Chicken   148
Cornish Hens Roasted, Lime Juice   45
Ginger Soy Chicken in Wine   172

Honey Wings 246
Oriental Chicken Salad 371

Chicken, Almond, Pears/Gorgonzola 137
Chicken and Egg Soup 48
Chicken and Mushroom Lasagna 290
Chicken Breasts, Stuffed in a Wrap 114
Chicken Broth, Homemade 44
Chicken, Citrus 148
Chicken Francese 110
Chicken Fricassee 264
Chicken, Ginger Soy Sauce in Wine 172
Chicken Salad, Chinese 159
Chicken Salad, Oriental 371
Chicken Salad in Lime 192
Chicken Soup (Stracciatella) 33
Chicken Vegetable Soup 52
Chicken Wings, Honey 246
Chicory and Avocado Salad 357
Chicory, Beet Salad 380
Chicory, Dandelion, Grapes Salad 333
Chicory Orange and Olives Salad 254
Chilean Sea Bass Arraganate 201
Chili, Bean and Sausage 89
Chili Sauce 393
Chinese Barbeque Sauce 395
Chinese Chicken Salad 159
Chinese Fried Vegetables 157
Chocolate Cake, A Devil of a 97
Chocolate Cherry Sponge Cake 46
Chocolate Chip Meringues, Raspberries 153
Chocolate Covered Peanut Biscotti 314
Chocolate Cream Filling 58
Chocolate Cupcakes/Butterscotch Icing 379
Chocolate Double Fudge Sheet Cake 83
Chocolate Frosting 98
Chocolate Fruit Cake 335
Chocolate Hamantashen 206
Chocolate Mint Ice Cream Pie 213
Chocolate Peanut Butter Cupcakes 370
Chocolate Spice Apples 174
Chocolate Stucco 2-Story Cake 30
Chocolate Torte with Almonds 111
Chopped Beef Tomato Sauce 397

CHOWDERS

Black Bean and Sausage Chili 89
Cheesy Vegetable Chowder 57
Corn and Spinach Chowder 60

East-West Chowder 242
Potato and Ceci Curry Chowder 237
Santa Fe Minestrone 123
Tuna Curry Chowder 81
Turkey-Barley Chowder Salad 316

Chowder, Cheesy Vegetable 57
Chowder, East-West 242
Chowder, Tuna Curry 81
Chow-Chow 182
Cicoria, Avocado Salad 357
Cicoria with Yellow Tomatoes 40
Cioppino 177
Citrus Chicken 148
Clafouti 321
Clam Sauce, Red 329
Clam Sauce, Red with Linguine 329
Clam Sauce, White 340
Clam Sauce, White with Linguine 340
Clams on the Barbeque 132
Cocoa (Hot) Chocolate Sundae 356
Cod Arraganate 200
Cod, Dried Salted, Fried (Baccala) 10
Cod, Dried Salted, Spicy (Baccala) 10
Coffee Almond Streusel Cake 244
Coffee Kalhua Sundae 323
Coffee Mousse 252
Cole Slaw Dressing 389
Coniglio Cacciatora (Rabbit Stew) 11

COOKIES

Almond Biscotti 96
Almond Ginger Biscotti 265
Anise Biscotti, Marbled 315
Black and White Drop Cookies 87
Cherry Cookies to Die for 301
Chocolate Chip Meringues/ Raspberries 153
Chocolate Covered Peanut Biscotti 314
Hamantashen, Chocolate 206
Honey Balls and Taralli 72-4
Honey Balls (Struffoli) 72-4, 139
Honey Bows 38
Lemon Macaroon Bars 307
Lemon Squares 91
Mostacciolli 25
Pie Crust Cookies 318
Pignola 67
Rainbow Petit-Fours (Venetians) 373
Struffoli (Honey Balls) 139

Taralli   75
Taralli and Honey Balls   72-4
Walnuts   367

Corn and Spinach Chowder   60
Corn Bread, Jalapeño   190
Corn Bread/ Mushroom Stuffing   3
Corn, Tomatoes and Mushrooms   247
Cornish Hens, Roasted , Lime Juice   45
Country Style Stew   41
Crabs with Spaghetti   329
Cranberry Pecan Muffins   232
Cranberry (Whole) Orange Sauce   280
Cream of Broccoli Soup   64
Creamed Tomato Soup   85
Crème de Menthe and Ice Cream   42
Crescent Rolls   160
Croquettes, Vegetable   4
Crostata, Strawberry   304
Crumb Cake Topping   332
Currant Pound Cake   202
Curry Chowder, Tuna   81
Curry Salsa   238, 393
Curry Sauce   392

D

Dandelion Greens /Yellow Tomatoes   40
Dandelions, Chicory, Red Grapes   333

DESSERTS

Almond Biscotti   96
Almond Brittle (Croccante)   294
Almond-Cherry Cake   362
Almond Ginger Biscotti   265
Anise Biscotti, Marbled   315
Apple and Cranberry Crisp   272
Apple Crumb Cake   382
Apple Crunch, Vanilla Ice Cream   193
Apple-Pumpkin Pecan Bread   359
Apricot and Blueberry Cobbler   134
Banana and Strawberry Pudding   278
Banana Fruit Cake   21
Berry Whipped Cream Pie   197
Black and White Drop Cookies   87
Blackberry Compote, Warm   107
Blueberry Crumb Cake   129

Bread Pudding   79
Butterflies (Muffins)   58
Cantaloupe Sundae   359
Charoseth (Haroset)   141
Cherry Almond Cake   362
Cherry Cookies to Die For   301
Chocolate Cake, A Devil of a   97
Chocolate Cherry Sponge Cake   46
Chocolate Chip Meringues, Raspberries   153
Chocolate Covered Peanut Biscotti   314
Chocolate Cupcakes/Butterscotch Icing   379
Chocolate Fruit Cake   335
Chocolate Fudge Sheet Cake   83
Chocolate Mint Ice Cream Pie   213
Chocolate Peanut Butter Cupcakes 370
Chocolate Spice Apples   174
Chocolate Stucco 2-Story Cake   30
Chocolate Torte with Almonds   111
Clafouti   321
Cocoa (Hot) Chocolate Sundae   356
Coffee Almond Streusel Cake   244
Coffee Kalhua Sundae   323
Coffee Mousse   252
Compote of Pineapple in Rum   4
Crème de Menthe and Ice Cream   42
Currant Pound Cake   202
Fig, Fresh Crumb Cake   332
Fruit and Cheese Tray   311
Fruit, Nut Brownie Roll   7
Fruit Tart   50
Hamantaschen, Chocolate   206
Harvey Wallbanger Cake   222
Honey Balls (Struffoli)   72-4, 139
Honey Bows   38
Hot Chocolate Cocoa Sundae   356
Hush Puppies   248
Ice Cream and Crème de Menthe   42
Italian Pudding   125
Lemon Cake, Tangy   121
Lemon Macaroon Bars   307
Lemon Mousse   165
Lemon Squares   91
Macadamia Cupcakes/Orange Icing   261
Melon Balls in Asti-Spumante   298
Melon Slices, Tray   227
Meringues, ChocoChip/Raspberries   153
Meringues, Strawberry   338
Minted Lemon Ice   179
Mocha Mousse   169
Mostaccioli   25
Mousse, Lemon   165

Mousse, Mocha 169
Muffins, Three 232-3
Neapolitan Lemon, Orange Almond Cake 149
Orange Chiffon Cake 116
Orange-Tangerine Sherbet 291
Oranges and Berries in Lime 157
Pastiera Di Grano 144-5
Peachy, Melba, A 342
Peanut Butter Chocolate Cupcakes 370
Pear and Ginger Cake 239
Pear Crunch 17
Pecan Pie 352
Pecan Pumpkin Pie 285
Pignola Cookies 67
Pignola Fruit Cake 209
Pineapple with Grapes 294
Pine Cones in the Snow 346
Polyphenol Delight, A 327
Pudding, Bread 79
Pudding, Italian 125
Pudding, Strawberry and Banana 278
Pudding, Zabaglione 268
Pumpkin Pecan Pie 285
Rainbow Petit-Fours 373
Rainbow Sherbet/Raspberries, Mint 188
Southwestern Fruit Cake 62
Strawberries, Banana Pudding 278
Strawberries, Cherries/Chocolate Sauce 161
Strawberry Almond Cream 330
Strawberry-Banana Rice Pudding 356
Strawberry Crostata 304
Strawberry Meringues 338
Struffoli (Honey Balls) 139
Tangerine-Orange Sherbet 291
Taralli 75
Taralli and Honey Balls 72-4
Three Muffins 231-2
Torta with Pine Nuts and Almonds 54
Tunnel of Fudge (Marion's Version) 218
Vanilla Ice Cream, Apple Crunch 193
Vanilla Ice Cream/Assorted Liqueurs 102
Walnut Cake with Orange Glaze 257
Walnuts 367
Watermelon Chill 235
Zabaglione with Strawberries 268
Zeppole, Sunday Morning 248

Dill Pickles, Garlic 180

DRESSINGS, SAUCES, GRAVIES

Aioli (Garlic Sauce) 389
Apple Cider Dressing 390
Asian Dressing I 388
Asian Dressing II 157, 388
Balsamic Olive Oil Dressing 384
Barbeque Sauce 391
Béarnaise Sauce 391
Bleu Cheese Dressing 386
Brown Gravy 396
Caesar Dressing 386
Cheese Sauce 392
Chili Sauce 393
Chinese Barbeque Sauce 395
Chopped Beef Tomato Sauce 397
Cole Slaw Dressing 389
Cranberry Sauce 280
Curry Salsa 238, 393
Curry Sauce 392
French Dressing 385
Garam Masala 237
Ginger Sauce 163
Guacamole 167
Hawaiian Sweet and Sour Sauce 394
Hawaiian Tomato Sauce 403
Hollandaise Sauce 394
Honey Mustard Dressing 384
Honey Orange Dressing 104, 385
Italian Dressing (Oil/Vinegar) 384
Lemon-Oil Dressing 385
Marinade for Pork, Chicken, Fish 390
Marinara Sauce 398-9
Mayonnaise 387
Mornay Sauce 390
Mushroom Sauce 395
Mushroom Tomato Sauce 397
Oils (Seasoned Dipping) 403
Olive Oil and Vinegar 384
Parmesan Cheese Dressing 388
Pesto Sauce 396
Pesto, Walnut Sauce 326
Ragout Sauce 400
Red Pepper Sauce 402
Red Pepper Vodka Sauce 402
Red Wine and Vinegar (Italian) 384
Russian Dressing 386
Salsa 132
Salt (No) Salt Spice Mix 297
Sausage and Meatball Sauce 399
Seafood Cocktail Sauce 259

Seafood Tomato Sauce 401
Spicy Salad Dressing 387
Spinach Walnut Pesto 381
Vinaigrette Dressing 389
Vinegar and Olive Oil 384
Walnut Pesto 326

Ɛ

East-West Chowder 242
Easter Pie (Pastiera di Grano) 144-5
Eel, Marinated (Anguilla) 9
Egg Foo Yung (Chinese Omelets) 156, 342
Egg Nog 34
Eggs (Frittatas) 341-2
Eggs, Peppers with Shrimp Sauce 235
Eggplant and Sausage Parmagiano 133
Eggplant Croquettes Marinara 366
Eggplant Parmagiano (Baked), Pepper Sauce 29
Eggplant Stew (Ratatouille) 106
Escarole and Shells (Maruzzelle) 364
Escarole, Seafood Soup 229
Escarole, Stuffed ('Scarola Imbottire) 196
Escarole, Tomato and Feta Salad 336

ℱ

Farfalle, Broccoli Rabe & Sausages 310
Farfalle /Artichokes, Red Pepper Sauce 320
Fennel and Olive Salad 289
Fennel, Cucumber, Egg Citrus Salad 147
Fennel, Pork Chops with 53
Fennel Water 34
Fettuccine Alfredo 334
Fettuccine Carbonara 361
Fettuccine Spinach Walnut Pesto 381
Fig (Fresh) Crumb Cake 332
Figs and Spinach Salad 292
Figs with Arugula and Prosciutto 104
Filet Mignons/Artichoke Hearts 205
Fillet of Fish Piccata 216
Fillet of Flounder, Baked/Peppers 230

FISH

Baccala Fritto (Fried, Salted Cod) 10
Baccala in Salsa Piccante (Spicy) 10

Broccoli Rabe, Gnocchi, Salmon 376
Chilean Sea Bass Arraganate 201
Cod Arraganate 200
Fillet of Fish Piccata 216
Fish Fillet Stuffed/Crab, Shrimp, Apricots 243
Fish in Saffron Soup 211
Fish Soup Provençale 199
Flounder Fillet, Baked /Peppers 230
Pasta e Sarde 323
Red Snapper with Curry Salsa 238
Salmon, Honey Ginger, Grilled 221
Salmon Mexicali 178
Salmon, Walnut-Pepper Crusted 128
Swordfish, Baked Mediterranean 167
Tuna Curry Chowder 81
Tuna Steak, Grilled /Olive Sauce 271
Walnut-Pepper Crusted Salmon 128

Fish Fillets Stuffed/Crab, Shrimp, Apricots 243
Fish in Saffron Soup 211
Fish Soup Provençale 199
Flounder Fillet, Baked with Peppers 230

FOWL (also refer to CHICKEN)

Game Hens, Roasted in Lime Juice 45
Turkey Barley Chowder Salad 316
Turkey with Stuffing 282 ff

Fragrant Rice 91
French Dressing 385
Fricandels of Veal 297
Frittatas 341-2
Fritto Misto, Vegetable 164

FRUIT

Almond Chicken/Pear in Gorgonzola 137
Apple Sauce 33
Apple Slices, Asparagus, Grilled 221
Apples, Chocolate Spice 174
Arugula with Prosciutto and Figs 104
Avocado, Stuffed 241
Banana Fruit Cake 21
Berries and Oranges in Lime 157
Blackberry Compote, Warm 107
Cantaloupe Sundae 359
Chicory, Dandelions and Grapes 333
Compote of Pineapple in Rum 4
Cranberries, Oranges, Romaine 322

Fig, Fresh, Crumb Cake   332
Figs and Spinach Salad   292
Fruit and Cheese Tray   311
Fruit and Nut Brownie Roll   7
Fruit Tart   50
Fruits, Tropical with Lentils   217
Melon Balls in Asti-Spumante   298
Melon Slices, Tray of   227
Mesclun with Olives and Figs   176
Oranges and Berries in Lime   157
Peachy Melba, A   342
Pear and Ginger Cake   239
Pear Crunch   17
Pineapple with Grapes   294
Pine Cones in the Snow   346
Polyphenol Delight, A   327
Rainbow Sherbet/ Raspberries, Mint   188
Roulade of Pork with Apricots   3
Seafood, Battered with Fruit   90
Southwestern Fruit Cake   62
Spinach, Carrots and Blueberries   19
Spinach, Carrots, Grapes Salad   348
Strawberries and Banana Pudding   278
Strawberries, Cherries/Chocolate   161
Strawberries, Fresh, Whole   98
Strawberry Almond Cream   330
Strawberry Banana Rice Pudding   356
Strawberry Meringues   338
Strawberry Zabaglione   268
Tangerine-Orange Sherbet   291
Watermelon Chill   235

Fruit and Cheese Tray   311
Fruit and Nut Brownie Roll   7
Fruit Cake, Chocolate   335
Fruit Cake, Pignola   209
Fruit Cake, Southwestern   62
Fruit Tart   50
Fruits (Tropical) with Lentils   217
Fudge Cake (Marion's Tunnel Cake)   218

G

Game Hens, Cornish   45
Garam Masala (Indian Spices)   237
Garlic Dill Pickles   181
Garlic Spinach with Peanuts   201
German Potato Salad   78

Ginger-Peachy Broccoli   252
Ginger Sauce   163
Ginger Soy Chicken in Wine   172
Gnocchi, Potato   349
Gnocchi, Potato Curry   350
Grain Pie (Pastiera de Grano)   144-5

GRAVIES AND SAUCES

Aioli   389
Apple Sauce   33
Barbeque Sauce   391
Béarnaise   391
Beef (Chopped) Tomato   397
Brown Gravy   396
Cheese Sauce   392
Chili Sauce   393
Chinese Barbeque Sauce   395
Cranberry Sauce   280
Curry Sauce   392
Ginger Sauce   163
Guacamole   167
Hawaiian Sweet and Sour Sauce   394
Hawaiian Tomato Sauce   403
Hollandaise Sauce   394
Marinade (Chicken)   246
Marinade (Ribs)   247
Marinade (Steak and Prawns)   251
Marinara Sauce   398-9
Meatball, Sausage Sauce   399
Mornay Sauce   390
Mushroom Gravy   395
Mushroom Tomato Sauce   397
Pesto   396
Pomidoro Arrabbiata   317
Puttanesca Salsa   300
Ragout   400
Red Clam Sauce   329
Red Pepper Sauce   402
Red Pepper-Vodka Sauce   402
Salsa   132
Salsa Puttanesca   300
Salsa (Relish)-Zucchini, Tomato, Corn   270
Salt (No) Salt Spice Mix   297
Sausage, Meatball Tomato Sauce   399
Seafood Cocktail Sauce   259
Seafood Tomato Sauce   401
Spinach Walnut Pesto   381
Walnut Pesto   326
White Clam Sauce   340

Greek Beef Stew   37
Greek Lamb Stew   37
Greek Pastitsio   337
Greek Salad   36
Greek Vegetable Bean Soup   267
Green Beans, Sesame   172
Green Frying Peppers, Stuffed   365
Greens Salad, Tuscan   131
Grilled Asparagus, Apple Slices   221
Grilled Honey Ginger Salmon   221
Grilled Portobello and Tomato   302
Grilled T-Bone/Onions, Peppers   360
Grilled Tuna / Olive Sauce   271
Grilled Vegetable Mélange   152
Guacamole   167

H

Ham and Olives Frittata   341-2
Hamantashen, Chocolate   206
Harvey Wallbanger Cake   222
Hawaiian Sweet and Sour Sauce   394
Hawaiian Tomato Sauce   403

HEIRLOOM RECIPES

Almond Brittle (Croccante)   294
Apple Sauce   33
Baccala Fritto   10
Baccala in Salsa   10
Beef Tea   34
Borscht   204
Broccoli Rabe/Sausage and Farfalle   310
Butterflies   58
Capuzzelle di Agnelli (Sheep Heads)   142
Charoseth   141
Chicken Fricassee   264
Coniglio Cacciatora (Rabbit Stew)   11
Egg Nog   34
Fennel Water   34
Fricandels of Veal   297
Frittatas (Omelets)   341-2
Fritto Misto   164
Gnocchi, Potato   349
Harvey Wallbanger Cake   222
Honey Bows   38
Honey Lemon Tea   33
Hush Puppies   248

Linguine with Red Clam Sauce   329
Manicotti in Ragout   312
Marbled Anise Biscotti   315
Marinated Eel (Anguilla)   9
Minestra de Piede Porco (Pigs Feet)   275
Mostaccioli   25
Mozzarella in Carozza   23
Osso Bucco   24
Panzanella   263
Pasta e Sarde   323
Pastiera di Grano   144-5
Pastina and Stracciattella   32-3
Pizza Rustica   186
Polenta with Shrimp and Sausage   70
Pork Livers, Bay Leaves/Arezzio   196
Potato Gnocchi   349
Puttanesca Salsa with Pasta   300
Ravioli in Red Pepper Vodka Sauce   306
Risotto Milanese   66
Roasted Suckling Pig   225-6
Salsa Puttanesca with Pasta   300
Sausage and Eggplant Parmagiano   133
'Scarola Imbottite (Stuffed Escarole)   196
Seasoned Dipping Oils   403
Spaghetti Aglio Olio   303
Spaghetti with Crabs   329
Struffoli   139
Sufrito   277
Taralli   75
Tripa a la Creole   276
Veal Saltimbocca   65
Venison Stew   41
Zabaglione with Strawberries   268
Zeppole   248

Hollandaise Sauce   394
Honey and Lemon Tea   33
Honey Balls   72-4
Honey Balls (Struffoli)   139
Honey Bows   38
Honey Ginger Salmon, Grilled   221
Honey Mustard Dressing   384
Honey Orange Dressing   104, 385
Hot Cocoa Chocolate Sundae   356
How to Roast Peppers   148
How to Skin a Tomato   365
Hush Puppies   248

I

Iceberg Lettuce, Tomato/Spicy Dressing 309
Iceberg Lettuce Wedges/Capers 27

ICE CREAM

Cantaloupe Sundae 359
Chocolate Mint Ice Cream Pie 213
Cocoa (Hot) Chocolate Sundae 356
Coffee Kalhua Sundae 323
Ice Cream and Crème de Menthe 42
Minted Lemon Ice 179
Pine Cones in the Snow 346
Rainbow Sherbet/ Raspberries/Mint 188
Tangerine-Orange Sherbet 291
Vanilla Bean Ice Cream/ Liqueurs 102
Vanilla Ice Cream and Apple Crunch 193

Ice Cream and Crème de Menthe 42

ICINGS, FROSTINGS, FILLINGS

Caramel Icing 30
Chocolate Cream Filling 58
Chocolate Frosting 98
Lemon Icing 318
Orange Icing 261
Butterscotch Icing 379

Irish Soda Bread 120
Italian Cheeses Frittata 341-2
Italian Dressing (Red Wine Vinegar/Oil) 384
Italian Flag Salad 100
Italian Pudding 125

J

Jalapeño Corn Bread 190

L

LAMB

Capuzzelle di Agnelli (Sheep Heads) 141
Lamb and Portobellos with Apricots 268
Lamb Chops in Tomato Prune Sauce 143
Lamb Meatballs 49
Lamb Stew 12
Lamb Stew, Greek 37
Tandoori Lamb 239

Lamb and Portobellos with Apricots 268
Lamb Chops in Tomato Prune Sauce 143
Lamb Meatballs 49
Lamb Stew 12
Lamb Stew, Greek 37
Lamb Tandoori 239
Lasagna Chicken and Mushrooms 290
Lasagna with Walnut Pesto 326
Lemon Cake, Tangy 121
Lemon Ice, Minted 179
Lemon Macaroon Bars 307
Lemon Mousse 165
Lemon-Oil Dressing 385
Lemon Squares 91
Lentil Soup with Pasta 224
Lentils and Tuna Salad 191
Lettuce, Tomato/Spicy Salad Dressing 309
Lettuce Wedges (Iceberg) with Capers 27
Lima Beans, Baby and Plum Tomatoes 260
Lime Rice 165
Linguine, Broccoli 296
Linguine with Red Clam Sauce 329
Linguine with White Clam Sauce 340

M

Macadamia Cupcakes/Orange Icing 261
Macaroon (Lemon) Bars 307
Mandel Bread 281
Manicotti in Ragout 312
Marinade, Chicken 246
Marinade: Pork, Chicken, Fish 390
Marinade, Ribs 247
Marinade: Steak, Prawns 251
Marinara Sauce 398-9
Marinated Eel (Anguilla) 9
Marion's Version of Tunnel Cake 218
Maruzzelle,Shrimp,Broccoli/PepperSauce 358
Mashed Sweet Potatoes 220
Mayonnaise 387

MEAT (also refer to: BEEF, LAMB,
PORK, VEAL)

Beef Roast, Old Fashioned, /Gravy 94
Beef Stew, Greek 37
Braciole 105
Capuzzelle di Agnelli (Sheep Heads) 142
Coniglio alla Cacciatora (Rabbit Stew) 11
Country-Style Stew 41
Fricandels of Veal 297
Filet Mignon with Artichoke Hearts 205
Lamb and Portobellos with Apricots 268
Lamb Chops in Tomato Prune Sauce 143
Lamb Meatballs 49
Lamb Stew 12
Lamb Stew, Greek 37
Meatball, Sausage Sauce 399
Meatballs, Spicy-Sweet 61
Meatloaf, Stuffed 15
Pecan Crusted Pork Tenderloin 137
Pecan-Pepper Crusted Pork Tenderloin 28
Pig, Suckling Roasted 225-6
Polenta with Shrimp, Sausage 70
Pork Chops with Fennel 53
Pork Fillets/Apricots,Almonds,Prosciutto 124
Pork Liver, Bay Leaves in Arezzio 196
Pork, Shredded, with Shrimp 255
Pot Roast, A Home-style 6
Roast Beef with Gravy 94
Roulade of Pork with Apricots 3
Rustic Stew 42
Sausage and Beans 57
Sausage, Eggplant Parmagiano 133
Sausages, Farfalle/ Broccoli Rabe 310
Sesame Ribs 247
Steak, T-Bone Grilled/Onions, Peppers 260
Stuffed Cabbage 86
Stuffed Meatloaf 15
Sufrito 277
Surf & Turf, Accompaniments, Grilled 251
Tandoori Lamb 239
Veal and Mushroom Soup 77
Veal Cutlet Parmagiano 102
Veal Fricandels 297
Veal Saltimbocca 65
Veal Schnitzel/ Arugula, Spinach 78
Veal Stew Paprika 208
Venison Stew 41

Meatballs, Lamb 49
Meatballs, Spicy-Sweet 61

Meatloaf, Stuffed 15
Mediterranean Scallops 212
Melon Balls in Asti Spumante 298
Melon Slices, Tray 227
Meringues 338
Meringues, Chocolate Chip, Raspberries 153
Meringues, Strawberry 338
Mesclun, Radishes and Olives 319
Mesclun with Olives and Figs 176
Minestra de Piede Porco (Soup/Pigs Feet) 275
Minestra and Sausages 276
Minestrone, Santa Fe 123
Minted Lemon Ice 179
Mocha Mousse 169
Mornay Sauce 390
Mostacciolli 25
Mousse, Coffee 252
Mousse, Lemon 165
Mousse, Mocha 169
Mozzarella in Carozza 23

MUFFINS (CUPCAKES)

Blueberry Orange Muffins 231
Butterflies 58
Cranberry Pecan Muffins 232
Pumpkin Apple-Cinnamon 232
Three Muffins 231-2

Mushroom Gravy 395
Mushroom Sauce 395
Mushroom Tomato Sauce 397
Mushroom, Veal Soup 77
Mushrooms and Anchovy 136
Mushrooms and Onion Frittata 341-2
Mushrooms and Roasted Potatoes 124
Mushrooms, Asparagus and Almonds 143
Mushrooms, Artichokes, Sausages 345
Mushrooms Au Gratin 95
Mushrooms (Portobello) and Tomato 302
Mushrooms (Stuffed) a la Parmesana 284
Mussels in Beer 82

𝒩

Neapolitan Lemon, Orange Almond Cake 149
No-Salt-Salt Spice Mix 297

NUTS

Asparagus, Mushrooms, Almonds 143
Beef Tenderloin in a Nut Crust 351
Brussels Sprouts/Bacon and Pignola 46
Brussels Sprouts, Tomatoes, Walnuts 285
Garlic Spinach with Peanuts 201
Pecan Pie 352
Pecan Pumpkin Pie 285
Pesto 396
Pignola Fruit Cake 209
Shrimp with Cashews 155
Spinach Walnut Pesto 381
Torta with Pine Nuts and Almonds 54
Whole Wheat Penne with Walnuts 378
Walnut-Pepper-Crusted Salmon 128
Walnut Pesto 326
Walnuts 367

O

Oils (Seasoned Dipping) 403
Olive and Pepper Cream Cheese 339
Olive, Fennel Salad 289
Olive Oil and Vinegar 384
Omelets (Chinese) 156, 342
Omelets (Frittatas) 341-2
One Hundred Vegetables 71
Orange and Berries in Lime 157
Orange Chiffon Cake 116
Orange Pumpkin Soup 215
Orange-Tangerine Sherbet 291
Oriental Chicken Salad 371
Orzo Salad 138
Osso Bucco 24

P

Paglia e Fieno (Straw and Hay) 353
Pancakes, Potato and Apple Cheddar 173
Pancakes, Pumpkin Spice 173
Panzanella 263
Parmesan Cheese Dressing 388

PASTA

Angel Hair/(Hot, Sweet Fennel) Sausage 293
Broccoli, Gnocchi and Salmon 376
Broccoli Linguine 296
Broccoli Rabe/Sausages, Farfalle 310
Broccoli Rabe, Wheat Penne, Cannellini 311
Chicken and Mushroom Lasagna 290
Crazy Spaghetti 354
Escarole and Maruzzelle 364
Farfalle/Artichokes in Red Pepper Sauce 320
Fettuccine Alfredo 334
Fettuccine Carbonara 361
Fettuccine w/Spinach Walnut Pesto 381
Gnocchi, Potato 349
Gnocchi, Potato Curry 350
Greek Pastitsio 337
Lasagna, Chicken and Mushrooms 290
Lasagna with Walnut Pesto 326
Lentil Soup with Pasta 224
Linguine, Broccoli 296
Linguine with Red Clam Sauce 329
Manicotti in Ragout 312
Maruzzelle,Shrimp,Broccoli/PepperSauce 358
Orzo Salad 138
Paglia e Fieno (Straw and Hay) 353
Pasta e Sarde 323
Pasta Primavera 369
Pastina 32
Penne Palermo 344
Penne with Salsa Puttanesca 250
Puttanesca Salsa with Pasta 300
Ravioli in Red Pepper Vodka Sauce 306
Spaghetti Aglio Olio 303
Spaghetti, Crazy 354
Spaghetti with Crabs 329
Spaghetti with Pomidoro Arrabbiata 317
Spinach Linguine/White Clam Sauce 340
Stuffed Shells 101
Summer Pasta Salad 127
Tortellini with Cream Sauce 332
Whole Wheat Penne with Walnuts 378
Ziti al Forno 372

Pasta, Angel Hair Fennel Sausage 293
Pasta e Sarde 323
Pasta Frolla (Pie Crust) 144
Pasta Primavera 369
Pasta Salad, Summer 127
Pastiera di Grano 144-5
Pastina 32
Pastitsio, Greek 337
Pea (Split) Soup 225
Peachy Melba, A 342
Peanut Butter, Chocolate Cupcakes 370

Pear and Ginger Cake   239
Pear Crunch   17
Pecan Crusted Pork Tenderloin   137
Pecan-Pepper Crusted Pork Tenderloin   28
Pecan Pie   352
Pecan Pie Crust   285
Pecan Pumpkin Pie   285
Penne Palermo   344
Penne with Salsa Puttanesca   250
Pepper and Provolone Salad with Croutons   6
Peppers and Egg with Shrimp Sauce   235
Peppers and Soy Bean Salad   212
Peppers Frittata   341-2
Peppers, Green (Stuffed) Frying   365
Peppers, How to Roast   148
(Peppers) Red Bells with Risotto   53
Pesto Sauce   396
Pesto Sauce, Walnut   326
Petit-Fours (Rainbow Cookies)   373
Pickles, Bread and Butter   183
Pickles, Chow-Chow   182
Pickles, Garlic Dill   181
Pickles, How to Process   180-3

PIES AND PASTRIES

   Berry Whipped Cream Pie   197
   Chocolate Mint/ Ice Cream Pie   213
   Fruit Tart   50
   Pasta Frolla (Pie Crust)   144
   Pastiera di Grano   144-5
   Pecan Pie   352
   Pecan Pie Crust   285
   Pecan Pumpkin Pie   285
   Petit Fours (Rainbow Cookies)   373
   Pizza   186-7
   Pizza Rustica   186
   Potato Pie   16
   Pumpkin Pecan Pie   285
   Shepherd's Pie   119
   Torta with Pine Nuts and Almonds   54

Pie Crust   144
Pie Crust Cookies   318
Pig Suckling, Roasted   225-6
Pignola Cookies   67
Pignola Fruit Cake   209
Pigs Feet/ Greens Soup   275
Pineapple in Rum, Compote   4
Pineapple with Grapes   294
Pine Cones in the Snow   346

Pine Nuts and Almonds Torta   54
Pizza Rustica   186
Pizzas, Three Easy Gourmet   186-7
Polenta   70
Polenta with Shrimp, Sausage   70
Polyphenol Delight, A   327
Pomidoro Arrabbiata   317

PORK

   Boneless Pork Stew   20
   Braciole   105
   Greens Soup with Pigs' Feet   275
   Minestra de Piede Porco (Soup/Pigs Feet)   275
   Pecan Crusted Pork Tenderloin   137
   Pecan-Pepper Crusted Pork Tenderloin   28
   Pig Suckling, Roasted   225-6
   Pork Chops with Fennel   53
   Pork Fillets/Apricots, Almonds, Proscuitto 124
   Pork Livers, Bay Leaves in Arezzio   196
   Pork, Shredded, w/ Shrimp   255
   Roulade of Pork with Apricots   3
   Sausages and Beans   57
   Sausages and Minestra   276
   Sausages, Fennel/ Angel Hair Pasta 293
   Sesame Ribs   247
   Shredded Pork with Shrimp   255

Pork Chops with Fennel   53
Pork Fillet /Apricots, Almonds, Prosciutto   124
Pork Liver and Bay Leaves in Arezzio   196
Pork Ribs, Sesame   247
Pork, Shredded with Shrimp   255
Pork Stew, Boneless   20
Pork Tenderloin, Pecan-Pepper Crusted   28
Pork with Apricots, Roulade   3
Portobello and Tomato, Grilled   302
Pot Roast, A Home-Style   6
Potato and Apple Cheddar Pancakes   173
Potato, Ceci, Curry Chowder   237
Potato Curry Gnocchi   350
Potato Frittata   341-2
Potato Gnocchi   349
Potato Pie   16
Potato Salad   115
Potato Salad, German   78
Potatoes and Mushrooms, Roasted   124
Potatoes, Red Bliss, Roasted   95

POULTRY (Also: See CHICKEN)

Cornish Game Hens, Roasted/Lime Juice 45
Turkey Barley Chowder Salad 316
Turkey with Stuffing 282 ff

Prosciutto and Ceci 2
Provolone, Pepper Salad with Croutons 6

PUDDINGS

Bread Pudding 79
Coffee Mousse 252
Italian Pudding 125
Lemon Mousse 165
Mocha Mousse 169
Strawberry Almond Cream 330
Strawberry and Banana 278
Strawberry-Banana Rice Pudding 356
Zabaglione with Strawberries 268

Pudding, Bread 79
Pumpkin Apple-Cinnamon Muffins 232
Pumpkin-Apple Pecan Bread 359
Pumpkin Pecan Pie 285
Pumpkin Soup 220
Pumpkin Soup, Orange 215
Pumpkin Spice Pancakes 173
Puttanesca Salsa with Pasta 300

R

Rabbit Stew (Coniglio Cacciatora) 11
Radicchio, Romaine in Parmesan 328
Radishes, Mesculin, Olives 319
Ragout Sauce 400
Rainbow Petit-Fours (Venetians) 373
Rainbow Sherbet /Raspberries, Mint 188
Ratatouille 106
Ravioli in Red Pepper Vodka Sauce 306
Raw Vegetables/ Lemon, Olive Oil 360
Red Clam Sauce 329
Red Pepper Sauce 402
Red Pepper Vodka Sauce 402
Red Snapper with Curry Salsa 238
Red Wine Vinegar, Olive Oil Dressing 384
Relish-Zucchini, Tomatoes and Corn 270

RICE

Arancine (Rice Balls) 67
Fragrant Rice 91
Lime Rice 165
Peppers, Stuffed with Risotto 53
Risotto Milanese 66
Strawberry-Banana Rice Pudding 356
Walnut Rice Pilaf 256
Wild Rice Stuffing with Cranberries 45

Rice Balls (Arancine) 67
Rice, Fragrant 91
Rice, Lime 165
Rice Pilaf, Walnuts 256
Rice, (Wild) Stuffing with Cranberries 45
Risotto Milanese 66
Roast Peppers, How to 148
Roast Seafood 82
Roasted Cornish Game Hens/Lime Juice 45
Roasted Suckling Pig 225-6
Rolls, Crescent 160
Romaine, Avocado and Grapes 195
Romaine (Baby), Cheddar, Blueberry Salad 343
Romaine, Cranberries and Oranges 322
Roulade of Pork with Apricots 3
Russian Dressing 386
Rustic Stew 42

S

Salad of Zucchini, Tomato and Corn 270

SALADS

Arugula, Potato and Tomato Salad 274
Arugula, Wild /Shrimp Vinaigrette 141
Arugula with Prosciutto and Figs 104
Avocado and Spinach Salad 185
Beet and Chicory Salad 380
Cannellini with Tuna 299
Caprese Salad 151
Carrot Salad 377
Carrots, Tomato and Stuffed Celery 339
Chicken Salad 371
Chicken Salad in Lime 192
Chicory, Dandelions and Grapes 333
Chicory, Oranges and Olives 254

Chinese Chicken Salad   159
Cicoria and Avocado   357
Dandelion Greens/Yellow Tomatoes   40
Escarole, Tomato and Feta   336
Fennel and Olives   289
Fennel, Cucumber, Egg Citrus Salad   147
German Potato Salad   78
Greek Salad   36
Italian Flag Salad   100
Lettuce (Iceberg) Wedges w/Capers   27
Lettuce, Tomato/ Spicy Salad Dressing   309
Mesclun, Radishes and Olives   319
Mesclun with Olives and Figs   176
Oriental Chicken Salad   371
Orzo Salad   138
Pasta Summer Salad   127
Peppers and Soy Bean Salad   212
Plum Tomato Sailboats   368
Potato Salad   115
Prosciutto and Ceci   2
Provolone and Peppers with Croutons   6
Radicchio, Romaine in Parmesan   328
Romaine, Avocado and Grapes   195
Romaine (Baby), Cheddar, Blueberries   343
Romaine, Cranberries and Oranges   322
Santa Fe Sardine Salad   375
Shrimp, Spinach, Red Onion, Pineapple   14
Southwest Salad   56
Soy Bean and Peppers Salad   212
Spicy Bean Salad   331
Spinach and Figs   292
Spinach, Arugula, Carrots, Mozzarella   109
Spinach, Carrots, Blueberries   19
Spinach, Carrots, Grapes   348
Spinach, Corn, Tomatoes, Apricots   208
Spinach, Roasted Potato, Corn   171
Spinach, Shrimp, Red Onion, Pineapple   14
Spring Salad   119
Three-Bean Salad with Feta   234
Tomato, Portobello, Grilled   302
Tomatoes, Stuffed   325
Tomatoes, Yellow/ Dandelion Greens   40
Tossed Salad with Ricotta Salata   93
Tuna and Lentil Salad   191
Tuna with Cannellini   299
Turkey-Barley Chowder Salad   316
Tuscan Greens   131
Vegetable Salad, Warm Key West   305
Vegetables (Raw) /Lemon, Olive Oil   360
Yellow Tomatoes /Dandelion Greens   40

Salmon, Honey Ginger Grilled   221
Salmon Mexicali   178
Salmon Walnut Pepper-Crusted   128
Salsa   132
Salsa, Curry   238
Salsa Puttanesca with Pasta   300
Salsa (Relish)-Zucchini, Tomato, Corn   270
Salt-(No) Salt Spice Mix   297
Saltimbocca, Veal   65
Santa Fe Minestrone   123
Sardine Salad, Santa Fe   375

SAUCES AND GRAVIES

Aioli   389
Apple Sauce   33
Barbeque Sauce   391
Béarnaise   391
Beef (Chopped) Tomato   397
Brown Gravy   396
Cheese Sauce   392
Chili Sauce   393
Chinese Barbeque Sauce   395
Cranberry Sauce   280
Curry Salsa   393
Curry Sauce   392
Ginger Sauce   163
Guacamole   167
Hawaiian Sweet and Sour Sauce   394
Hawaiian Tomato Sauce   403
Hollandaise Sauce   394
Marinade (Chicken)   246
Marinade (Ribs)   247
Marinade (Steak and Prawns)   251
Marinara Sauce   398-9
Meatball, Sausage Sauce   399
Mornay Sauce   390
Mushroom Gravy   395
Mushroom Tomato Sauce   397
Pesto   396
Pomidoro Arrabbiata   317
Puttanesca Salsa   300
Ragout   400
Red Clam Sauce   329
Red Pepper Sauce   402
Red Pepper-Vodka Sauce   402
Salsa   132
Salsa Puttanesca   300
Salsa (Relish)-Zucchini, Tomato, Corn   270
Salt (No) Salt Spice Mix   297
Sausage, Meatball Tomato Sauce   399

Seafood Cocktail Sauce   259
Seafood Tomato Sauce   401
Spinach Walnut Pesto   381
Walnut Pesto   326
White Clam Sauce   340

Sausage and Beans   57
Sausage and Black Bean Chili   89
Sausage and Eggplant Parmagiano   133
Sausage and Meatball Sauce   399
Sausage and Minestra   276
Sausage and Mushroom Stuffing   345
Sausage and Shrimp with Polenta   70
Sausage: Hot, Sweet Fennel with Pasta   293
Sausage, Mushrooms Parmesana   284
Sausages, Farfalle/Broccoli Rabe   310
Sautéed Spinach with Garlic and Oil   24
Scallops, Grilled and Broccoli Rabe   355
Scallops in Ginger Sauce   163
Scallops, Mediterranean   212
'Scarola Imbottire   196
'Scarola e Maruzzelle   364

SEAFOOD

Arugula (Wild)/ Shrimp Vinaigrette   141
Battered Seafood with Fruit   90
Broccoli Rabe and Grilled Scallops   354
Broccoli Rabe, Gnocchi, Salmon   376
Cioppino   177
Clams on the Barbeque   132
East-West Chowder   242
Eggs and Peppers with Shrimp Sauce   235
Fillet of Fish Piccata   216
Fillets/Crab, Shrimp and Apricots   243
Honey Ginger Salmon   221
Linguine with Red Clam Sauce   329
Maruzzelle, Shrimp,Broccoli/PepperSauce 358
Mussels in Beer   82
Salmon, Honey Ginger, Grilled   221
Salmon, Mexicali   178
Salmon, Walnut-Pepper Crusted   128
Scallops in Ginger Sauce   163
Scallops, Grilled, and Broccoli Rabe 355
Scallops, Mediterranean   212
Seafood and Escarole Soup   229
Seafood Cocktail   259
Seafood Genoese   152
Seafood Roast   82
Seafood Tomato Sauce   401
Shredded Pork with Shrimp   255

Shrimp and Sausage with Polenta   70
Shrimp, Marinated with Guacamole   167
Shrimp with Cashews   155
Spaghetti and Crabs   329
Spinach, Shrimp, Onion, Pineapple Salad   14
Surf and Turf Accompaniments, Grilled 251
Tomato Soup/Fennel and Shrimp   118
Tuna Steak, Grilled/ Olive Sauce   271

Seafood and Escarole Soup   229
Seafood Cocktail   259
Seafood Cocktail Sauce   259
Seafood Genovese   152
Seafood Roast   82
Seafood Tomato Sauce   401
Sea Shells, Shrimp, Broccoli/Pepper Sauce   358
Sesame Green Beans   172
Sesame Ribs   247
Shells, Stuffed   101
Shepherd's Pie   119
Sherbet, Rainbow/Raspberries, Mint   188
Sherbet, Tangerine-Orange   291
Shrimp and Sausage with Polenta   70
Shrimp, Marinated with Guacamole   167
Shrimp with Cashews   155

SOUPS

Black Bean and Sausage Chili   89
Borscht   204
Broth, Homemade Chicken   44
Broccoli, Cream of   64
Cheesy Vegetable Chowder   57
Chicken and Egg   48
Chicken Broth- Homemade   44
Chicken Soup (Stracciatella)   33
Chicken Vegetable   52
Chowder, East-West   242
Corn and Spinach Chowder   60
Cream of Broccoli   64
Escarole and Seafood Soup   229
Fish in Saffron   211
Fish Soup Provençale   199
Lentil Soup with Pasta   224
Minestra and Sausage   276
Minestra de Piede Porco   275
Orange Pumpkin   215
Pastina   32
Potato and Ceci Curry Chowder   237
Pumpkin   220
Santa Fe Minestrone   123

Sausage and Minestra   276
Seafood and Escarole Soup   229
Spinach and Bean   44
Split Pea   225
Stracciatella   33
Tomato Soup, Creamed   85
Tomato Soup with Fennel, Shrimp   118
Tuna Curry Chowder   81
Veal and Mushroom Soup   77
Vegetable Bean Soup, Greek   267
Vegetable Beef Noodle   113
Zucchini Soup, Tart and Spicy   69

Southwest Salad   56
Southwestern Fruitcake   62
Soybean and Pepper Salad   212
Spaghetti Aglio Olio   303
Spaghetti, Crazy   354
Spaghetti with Crabs   329
Spaghetti with Pomidoro Arrabbiata   317
Spicy Bean Salad   331
Spicy Salad Dressing   387
Spinach and Avocado Salad   185
Spinach and Bean Soup   44
Spinach and Figs Salad   292
Spinach, Arugula, Carrots, Mozzarella   109
Spinach, Arugula with Veal Schnitzel   78
Spinach, Carrot and Grapes Salad   348
Spinach, Carrots, Blueberries Salad   19
Spinach, Corn Chowder   60
Spinach, Corn, Tomato and Apricots   208
Spinach, Garlic with Peanuts   201
Spinach Linguine /White Clam Sauce   340
Spinach, Roasted Potato, Corn Salad   171
Spinach, Sautéed with Garlic and Oil   24
Spinach, Shrimp, Onion, Pineapple Salad   14
Spinach Walnut Pesto w/Fettuccine   381
Split Pea Soup   225
Spring Salad   119
Steak, T-Bone /Onions, Peppers, Grilled   260
Steamed Beets in Orange   230

STEWS

Black Bean and Sausage Chili   89
Beef Stew, Greek   37
Boneless Pork Stew   20
Capuzzelle di Agnelli (Sheep Heads)   142
Cioppino   177
Coniglio alla Cacciatora (Rabbit Stew) 11
Corn, Tomato and Mushroom   247

Country-Style Stew   41
Greek Beef Stew   37
Greek Lamb Stew   37
Grilled Vegetable Mélange   152
Lamb Stew   12
Lamb Stew, Greek   37
Minestra and Sausage   276
Minestra de Piede Porco   275
Pickled Vegetable Stew   263
Polenta with Shrimp and Sausage   70
Potato and Ceci Curry Chowder   237
Rabbit Stew, Hunter's Style   11
Ratatouille   106
Rustic Stew   42
Sausage and Minestra   276
Seafood Genoese   152
Seafood Roast   82
Shepherd's Pie   119
Sufrito   277
Tripa (Tripe) a la Creole   276
Veal Stew Paprika   208
Vegetable Stew Mélange, Grilled   152
Vegetable Stew, Pickled   263
Venison Stew   41

Stracciatella   33
Straw and Hay (Paglia e Fieno)   353
Strawberries and Banana Pudding   278
Strawberries, Cherries/Chocolate   161
Strawberries, Fresh Whole   98
Strawberry Almond Cream   330
Strawberry-Banana Rice Pudding   356
Strawberry Crostata   304
Strawberry Meringues   338
Struffoli (Honey Balls)   139
Stuffed Bell Peppers with Risotto   53
Stuffed Cabbage   86
Stuffed Green Frying Peppers   365
Stuffed Meatloaf   15
Stuffed Shells   101
Stuffed Tomatoes   325

STUFFING

Cornbread with Mushrooms   3
Cornbread with Sausage   282
Olive-Pepper Cream Cheese   339
Sausage and Mushroom   345
Wild Rice with Cranberries   45

Sufrito   277

Summer Pasta Salad   127
Sundae, Cantaloupe   359
Sundae, Coffee Kalhua   323
Surf and Turf, Accompaniments, Grilled   251
Sweet Potato, Mashed   220
Swordfish, Baked   168

T

Tandoori Lamb   239
Tangerine-Orange Sherbet   291
Taralli   74-5
Taralli and Honey Balls   72-4
Tart and Spicy Zucchini Soup   69
Tart, Fruit   50
Tenderloin, Beef in a Nut Crust   351
Three-Bean Salad with Feta   234
Three Muffins   231
Tomato Bruschetta   168
Tomato, Escarole, Feta   336
Tomato, How to Skin a   365
Tomato, Mozzarella, Olives (Caprese Salad) 151
Tomato, Plum, Sailboats   368
Tomato, Portobello, Grilled   302
Tomato Soup, Creamed   85
Tomato Soup with Fennel and Shrimp   118
Tomatoes, Plum and Baby Lima Beans   260
Tomatoes, Stuffed   325
Tomatoes, Yellow/Dandelion Greens   40
Torta with Pine Nuts and Almonds   54
Tortellini with Cream Sauce   332
Tossed Salad with Ricotta Salata   93
Tray of Melon Slices   227
Tripa (Tripe) a la Creole   276
Tropical Fruits/Lentils   217
Tuna and Lentil Salad   191
Tuna Curry Chowder   81
Tuna Steak with Olive Sauce, Grilled   271
Tuna with Cannellini Salad   299
Tunnel Cake, Marion's Version   218
Turkey-Barley Chowder Salad   316
Turkey with Stuffing   282 ff
Tuscan Greens Salad   131

V

Vanilla Bean Ice Cream/Liqueurs   102
Vanilla Ice Cream and Apple Crunch   193

VEAL

Braciole   105
Fricandels of Veal   297
Osso Bucco   24
Veal and Mushroom Soup   77
Veal Cutlet Parmagiano   102
Veal Saltimbocca   65
Veal Schnitzel with Arugula, Spinach   78
Veal Stew Paprika   208

Veal and Mushroom Soup   77
Veal Cutlet Parmagiano   102
Veal, Fricandels   297
Veal Saltimbocca   65
Veal Schnitzel with Arugula, Spinach   78
Veal Stew Paprika   208

VEGETABLES

Artichokes, Mushrooms, Sausages   345
Asparagus, Apple Slices, Grilled   221
Asparagus, Mushrooms, Almonds   143
Asparagus, Steamed   96, 138
Avocado, Stuffed   241
Bean (Three) Salad with Feta   234
Beets in Orange, Steamed   230
Bell Peppers Stuffed/Risotto   53
Bread 'n Butter Pickles   183
Broccoli, Ginger-Peachy   252
Broccoli Linguine   296
Broccoli Soup, Cream of   64
Broccoli, Steamed   149
Broccoli Rabe and Grilled Scallops   355
Broccoli Rabe, Gnocchi, Salmon   376
Broccoli Rabe/Sausage and Farfalle   310
Broccoli Rabe, Wheat Penne, Cannellini   311
Brussels Sprouts, Bacon, Pignola   46
Brussels Sprouts, Tomatoes, Walnuts 285
Cabbage, Stuffed   86
Cauliflower and Broccoli, Steamed   272
Chicken Vegetable Soup   52
Corn and Spinach Chowder   60
Corn, Tomato and Mushrooms   247
Chow-Chow   182
Eggplant and Sausage Parmagiano   133
Eggplant Croquettes Marinara   366
Eggplant Parmagiano (Baked) Pepper Sauce   29
Escarole, Stuffed ('Scarola Imbottire)   196
Fritto Misto   164
Garlic Dill Pickles   181

Garlic Spinach with Peanuts 201
German Potato Salad 78
Green Beans, Sesame 172
Grilled Vegetable Mélange 152
"How to Roast Peppers" 148
Lima Beans and Plum Tomatoes 260
Mushrooms and Roasted Potatoes 124
Mushrooms au Gratin 95
Mushrooms (Portobello), Tomatoes 302
Mushrooms Stuffed, a la Parmesana 284
Pasta Primavera 369
Peppers and Soy Bean Salad 212
Peppers, How to Roast 148
Peppers, Stuffed 365
Peppers, Stuffed with Risotto 53
Potato Gnocchi 349
Potato Pie 16
Potato (Red Bliss), Roasted 95
Potato Salad 115
Potatoes and Mushrooms, Roasted 124
Pumpkin Soup 220
Ratatouille 106
Sausage and Eggplant Parmagiano 133
Seafood and Escarole Soup 229
Sesame Green Beans 172
Spinach and Bean Soup 44
Spinach Sautéed in Garlic and Oil 24
Spinach Sautéed with Garlic/Peanuts 201
Stuffed Cabbage 86
Sweet Potato, Mashed 220
Veal and Mushroom Soup 77
Veal Schnitzel /Arugula and Spinach 78
Vegetable Accompaniments 49
Vegetable Bean Soup, Greek 267
Vegetable Beef Noodle Soup 113
Vegetable Chowder, Cheesy 57
Vegetable Croquettes 4
Vegetable Fritto Misto 164
Vegetable Mélange, Grilled 152
Vegetable Salad, Warm Key West 305
Vegetable Stew, Pickled 263
Vegetables Chinese, Fried 157
Vegetables, One Hundred 71
Vegetables, (Raw) /Lemon, Olive Oil 360
Zucchini Flowers, Stuffed 161
Zucchini Soup, Tart and Spicy 69
Zucchini, Tomatoes, Corn Relish 270

Vegetable (Chicken) Soup 52
Vegetable Chowder, Cheesy 57
Vegetable Croquettes 4
Vegetable Fritto Misto 164
Vegetable Mélange, Grilled 152
Vegetable Stew, Pickled 263
Vegetables, One Hundred 71
Vegetables (Raw)/ Lemon, Olive Oil 360
Vegetables (Warm) Key West, Salad 305
Venison Stew 41
Vinaigrette Dressing 389
Vinegar (Wine), Olive Oil Dressing 384

W

Walnut Cake with Orange Glaze 257
Walnut-Pepper Crusted Salmon 128
Walnut Pesto 326
Walnut Rice Pilaf 256
Walnuts 367
Watermelon Chill 235
Whipped Cream Berry Pie 197
White Clam Sauce 340
Whole Wheat Penne with Walnuts 378
Wild Rice Stuffing with Cranberries 45

Y

Yellow Tomatoes/ Dandelion Greens 40

Z

Zabaglione with Strawberries 268
Zeppole, Sunday Morning 248
Ziti al Forno 372
Zucchini Flowers, Stuffed 161
Zucchini Frittata 341-2
Zucchini Soup, Tart and Spicy 69
Zucchini, Tomatoes and Corn Relish 270

Vegetable Accompaniments 49
Vegetable Beef Noodle Soup 113

Kiss The Cook

(About The Author)

Marion Orlando Celenza's Italian heritage permeates her recipes and gardening. Even as a child, she experimented with recipes and planted a garden of vegetables, herbs and fruits. Over the ensuing years, she would grow and dry herbs and peppers, process homegrown pickles and tomatoes and harvest garden fresh garlic. Her garden has played host to beets, onions, zucchini, several eggplant varieties, Brussels sprouts, rapini, beans, corn and butternut squash. *(The latter as a result from a handful of seeds salvaged from the dinner menu.)*

In 2004 she published MENU LOG: A Collection Of Recipes As Coordinated Menus, original recipes, arranged in 52 dinner menus, and coordinated to marry appetizer to salad, to entrée, to dessert, in a seasonal ambiance. "It's easy to linger over these social dinners created for people who enjoy cooking (and eating) in the relaxed style one sees in Italy; indeed, the meal is the whole evening's entertainment...Caveat: Having pored over this excellent window into a tempting way of life (and of cooking), the urge to entertain may be overwhelming."Kirkus Discoveries, March 2005, vol. 1/issue 1.

In 2006 she published THE POETRY OF DOGS, a delightful and whimsical, yet insightful mix of original verse and colorful photography, centered around the intricate bonds between humans and dogs. Then, in 2008, a second menu cookbook was added: LUNCH IS IN THE BAG! A Celebration of the Midday Meal. "Lunch menus for the special weekend days or holidays on which readers actually have time to cook...A cookbook that provides reliable versions of old favorites"_____Kirkus Discoveries

As a child, she dreamed about careers as a stage actress, a classic essayist, a firefighter. Eventually, she taught English and Drama to secondary school students; worked 8 years, after high school and college, as a library clerk; was editor of the church monthly magazine for 25 years; published 4 books; and still tends the fires in the kitchen oven and outdoor grill. Not too distant from her childhood dreams.

Marion has spent all of her adult years on Long Island. Her husband, John, was the "local dentist". Their son and daughter-in-law are research geneticists (he's in plant genetics). They and a host of relatives and friends totally enjoy the bounty from Marion's kitchen (including the family's Labrador Retrievers).

Marion O. Celenza